Blessed Beyond Measure

Blessed Beyond Measure

More Stories from the Ozark Foothills
of Southern Illinois

Kestner Wallace

WOMBLE
MOUNTAIN
PRESS

Blessed Beyond Measure:
More Stories from the Ozark Foothills of Southern Illinois
Copyright © 2013 by Kestner Wallace

A Womble Mountain Press book

Library of Congress Control Number: 2013911567

ISBN 978-0-9770080-3-2

FIRST EDITION

Acknowledgement is made to the *Springhouse Magazine*, in which all of these short stories were previously published over the last six years.

For information, contact the following:
      Womble Mountain Press
      womblemtnpress@nc.rr.com
      919-622-2635

Publisher's Cataloging-in-Publication
(Provided by Quality Books, Inc.)

Wallace, Kestner.
   Wallace, Kestner.
      Blessed beyond measure : more stories from the Ozark
   foothills of southern Illinois / Kestner Wallace. –
   First edition.
     pages cm
     All of the short stories were previously published in
   Springhouse magazine.
     LCCN 2013911567
     ISBN 978-0-9770080-3-2

     1. Wallace, Kestner. 2. Saline County (Ill.)–Social
   life and customs. 3. Saline County (Ill.)–Biography.
   I. Title. II. Title: Springhouse.

   CT275.W25257A3 2013   977.3'04'092
                    QBI13-600112

Jacket and book design: Carol Majors/Publications Unltd
Illustrations: Janell E. Moore

In memory of my beloved wife, Evelyn

Preface

This book is a compilation of short stories written by my father, Kestner Wallace, since the publication of his first book, *A Dollar the Hard Way*, at the age of eighty-five. After the first book, I never dreamed there would be a second book, but my father clearly still has much more to say. As he kept turning out the short stories, it became clear to me that we had more than enough material for a second book. Therefore, plans for a ninety-third birthday surprise were hatched.

I want to thank several friends who helped with the various stages of the book: Robin Trout, who typed up many of the stories from Dad's longhand on lined notebook paper, provided initial input on each story during my editing process, and unfailingly supported my publishing efforts from start to finish; Miriam Baer and Felicia Kisselburg, who happily read every word of the manuscript and shared their helpful suggestions and comments; Rachel Bruder, who edited each story with an eagle eye and a passion surpassing my own; Janell Moore, who created the delightful illustrations for each story; Eileen Myers and Sharon Gladwell, my sister "grammar gurus," who provided advice on the thorniest grammar minutiae; and Carol Majors, of Publications Unltd — my "book shepherd" — who designed the cover and the layout of the book and guided me through the final stages to publication.

Undoubtedly, my father would like to acknowledge once again the ongoing support and encouragement of the long-time editor of *Springhouse Magazine*, Gary DeNeal, who has published these stories as Dad wrote them over the last six years. He would also want to thank all the people who have populated his life and his stories in his ninety-three years in Southern Illinois and beyond. His detailed memories of these people and his interactions with them never cease to amaze me.

I hope that you enjoy these stories as much as I have. Having been immersed in the details of this book, as well as the previous one, I feel that I know my father in a way that few daughters ever do. I will cherish all of these stories forever.

LeAnn Wallace
Raleigh, North Carolina
July 2013

Contents

Schools Then and Now

My dad was born in 1868 in Pope County, about eight miles north of Golconda in Southern Illinois. He attended the Rains School until his father — my grandfather, Jonathan Wallace — bought a large house on a number of acres of land that included part of Womble Mountain in Saline County.

After they moved, my father attended a large school in the woods north of Womble Mountain and south of Somerset, which at that time was a thriving community, with a post office and a large general store. This school was made of hewn white oak logs.

One teacher would attempt to teach from fifty to seventy-five students, ranging in age from six to twenty-one years. Older boys attended only in winter months, when they weren't needed for farm work.

Dad had a warm spot in his heart for that old log school. He had a good memory and seemed to take pleasure in answering my many questions concerning his early school days, as we worked together on our farm when I was about ten years old. When I asked Dad a question, he would stare into space for a moment and then smile as he relived the answer.

I asked, "Dad, what kind of teachers did you have back then?" After a moment, he smiled and replied, "They were strict, usually a different teacher each year—mostly good—some better than others. Some might open the day with prayer and might 'cuss' a little by the close of the day. However, they didn't tolerate fighting or bad language among the students."

"How many first graders might a teacher have? And how could he do justice by them, while teaching so many students in all the other grades?"

"There might be ten or so first graders. The teacher would give them their share of his time and then ask some of the older girls, who actually were young women attending school partly for the social aspect, to tutor the students. Also, it was surprising how much they learned by listening to the upper grades recite."

"Did the upper grades pay any attention to the first grade recite?"

"Yes, they loved the first graders and listened to them read."

"Do you recall any examples?"

"Yes, the beginning of the first grade reader was made up of words and pictures. For example, the question, 'Is it a cat?' with a picture of a cat and the word 'cat' above it, or 'Is it a dog?' with the picture of a dog and the word 'dog' above it. The same for a horse and a cow. It appeared to be rather effective.

"The reader also included a big bug and a big black ant. I need to inform you that men and boys often found these big black ants during their wood cutting. They, for some reason, without meaning to be vulgar, called them 'piss ants.' Girls and women just referred to them as 'big black ants.'

"One little boy appeared to be the loudest and sharpest

student in the class. As they read together, he shouted out, 'Is it a bug, or is it a piss ant?'"

Dad said the entire room, spellbound while listening to the darling first graders read, roared in laughter. In 1930, after the passing of fifty years, Dad still thought it was funny.

"Dad, do you remember any stories or poems in any of your readers while you were in the lower grades in school?"

Dad thought a moment while staring into space. Then he grinned and said, "Yes, a poem that goes as follows:

> *A woodpecker pecking on a church house door,*
> *He pecked and he pecked until his pecker got sore.*
> *And then he flew to an old oak tall*
> *And pecked a hole as round as a ball.*

"The older boys muffled their laughter. I didn't see anything funny about it back then. But I wanted to identify with the big boys, so I tried to 'bust a gut' laughing. My laughter drew the others' attention. I couldn't keep from wondering, 'Why in the world are they laughing at me?'"

We laughed together at Dad's story. I was proud that I understood what was funny about the poem.

I knew that Dad was one of fourteen children. I asked curiously, "Dad, how many in your family went to that log school at one time?"

"There were four of us—my sister Sarah, two years older than me, my brother George, two years younger, and Mandy, who was younger than George."

His situation was similar to my own. My sister Mabel, who was twelve and two years older than I, my brother Byrum, who was eight, and my brother Victor, who was six, were all in school with me at the same time. I had no problems with my brothers, but Mabel tended to be a big snitch. My friend Quay and I were as mean as striped snakes and were always up to some prank at school, but we usually didn't get caught. However, if Mabel happened to see us pull a stunt, she often took it upon herself to tell Mom when we got home. Even if I didn't get a whipping then, I had to endure Mom's disappointment and disapproval. That didn't reform me, though.

Thinking about being in trouble made me wonder if Dad had ever gotten a whipping at school. I didn't know whether he might be sensitive about the topic, so I approached it cautiously. "Dad, this could be an embarrassing question. You don't have to answer it. Did you ever get a whipping in school?"

Without any hesitation, Dad replied, "Son, I don't mind telling you. I got one when I was eleven or twelve years old."

Eagerly, I said, "Tell me all about it."

"I was sitting in my seat at school behaving as I should. From where I sat, well over in the room, I could see our lunch basket sitting in the cloak room. You see, Mom packed a lunch for all four of us in a fairly good-sized egg basket or picnic basket, with a curved carrying handle. She always included a good variety of food covered with an attractive cloth. I usually carried the basket to school. Since there was no shelf to place the lunch basket on, I set it on the floor along with the other lunches, which were in various types of pails or gallon molasses buckets.

"Every now and then I'd glance over at our lunch basket. Suddenly I was filled with anger when I looked over that way and saw a big, brown field mouse perched on the handle of our lunch basket. I hated mice, since they are so destructive and prolific.

"In my imagination, I wished I had a double-barreled

shotgun. I'd let him have it with both barrels and blow his brown butt over his appetite.

"Then I began to think more practically. I felt in my pockets to see if I had anything I could toss in there and frighten it away. I had a Barlow knife and a big spike nail I'd found on the way to school. I decided to use the nail.

"I waited until the teacher wasn't looking. I felt that the Code of the Hills would keep any of the students from telling on me. I stood up, drew back, hurled that nail at that mouse, and quickly sat down.

"It sounded like that nail bounced around all over the cloak room, hitting a number of buckets and making a terrible noise.

"I sat as still as that mouse had been sitting when I'd first spied it. I didn't look to my right or my left. The teacher looked around and stood silently, like a statue. Out of the corner of my eye, I saw two or more students point at me.

"I took courage in thinking that once I explained why I did what I'd done, all would be forgiven. It didn't work out that way. The teacher said nothing. He asked nothing. He pointed at me with his finger and motioned for me to come to the front of the room. He picked up a switch, gave me a fairly good switching, and motioned me back to my seat. I never disliked that teacher for whipping me. But I was disappointed that he didn't give me a chance to explain my action."

When Dad finished, I was much in sympathy with him. I passed an exaggerated sentence on the teacher: "He should have had his butt kicked!"

I never saw the old log school. Its replacement, which was called Sadler School, was a frame building built on stone pillars on sloping ground. This new building was about 36 feet by 40 feet, more or less. The school entrance, on the south side, was about a foot off the ground. The north side of the building was about three feet off the ground — a good place for the boys to play at recess on rainy days and wild hogs to take shelter on cold winter nights. The building had begun to look old by the time I started school in 1926.

My first grade teacher was Robert Blackman. He was young, kind-hearted, and the son of a preacher. He said he felt his own calling to become a preacher, and he later did so.

His students knew he loved them. One of Mr. Blackman's former students told me years later that one time, at the noon intermission, he had been wading in the creek, which was strictly against school rules. He had his pant legs rolled up to keep from getting wet. Mr. Blackman felt he should be punished and asked him to roll his pant legs down. When this fellow refused, Mr. Blackman first rolled them down and then switched him. This fellow said that Mr. Blackman's kindness so impressed him that he tried his dead-level best to obey and respect Mr. Blackman after that.

I looked forward to starting school and having Mr. Blackman as my teacher. I had a first-grade reader at home before the beginning of the school term. My sister, Mabel, who was a third grader and a good student, read the first five or six pages to me until I knew them by memory. The first page in that reader was a traditional nursery rhyme:

> *Jack and Jill went up the hill*
> *To fetch a pail of water.*
> *Jack fell down and broke his crown,*
> *And Jill came tumbling after.*

When it came my time to read on my first day of school, I reared back like a bantam rooster getting ready to crow and read my page. Mr. Blackman bragged on me. I felt as if I had the world by the tail.

The next three or four pages were short. I had Mabel read them to me until I could recite them in my sleep. I pretended reading them perfectly and enjoyed the praise. (I have always admired teachers who praised their students.)

After the first week, the stories got longer, filling a full page. Mabel got tired of reading to me. As a result, the following day when it came my turn to read, I fell on my face, so to speak. I didn't know one word from another. My pride turned to shame—a good example of pride going before a fall.

To save face, I became guilty of that commandment about "bearing false witness"—I lied. I complained of not being able to see the words—the words ran together. I had eye trouble big time. I asked Mom if I could stay home a few days until I could see better.

I didn't have Mom fooled. She pretended to believe me and allowed me to stay home, with the understanding that I read to her some each day. Mom had taught school before getting married. She liked teaching and soon had me reading on my own. I went back to school and was pleased to be an average reader in my class.

The help I got at home freed me up to listen to the upper grades recite. I learned by listening. I gazed at the pictures of George Washington and Abraham Lincoln. Even at six years of age, I knew that they were past presidents.

One morning Mr. Blackman spoke to the entire group of students. "Suppose we talk about Mr. Lincoln. First, I want to know what you know about him." I was surprised at all they knew about him. What one didn't know, another did.

One said, "He was born in Kentucky."

Another added, "In a log cabin when he was small."

A third said, "I hope to God it was when he was small. He became a big man."

Mr. Blackman asked, "Did he have a nickname?"

Several students answered, "Honest Abe."

Mr. Blackman replied, "Correct. He was my favorite president."

A.A. Moore, the Saline County superintendent of schools, was another admirer of Abraham Lincoln. Mr. Moore, who was short, very active, and about sixty years of age, visited Sadler School in 1926. He arrived during the noon intermission and enthusiastically played softball with the boys.

When school took up after the intermission, he talked to all the students in a friendly manner. He gave each of us a little celluloid card dated 1926, with a picture of Lincoln and these words: "I will study and get ready and one day my chance will come." I read those words many times. I still have that card around somewhere.

. . .

As I recall, things went well in 1927. But in 1928, money got scarce. For many, the Great Depression began in 1928, rather than when the banks failed in 1929.

Actually, rural farm folks didn't fare all that badly, compared with town and city folks. Most rural folks had a cow or two for milk and butter, chickens for meat and eggs, and a good garden. Wild blackberries were plentiful. Trees provided good crops of black walnuts and hickory nuts. Plenty of acorns made the squirrels fat for the frying pan. The Father above who fed the sparrows also fed the hard-working farm folks.

On the other hand, for the rural folks, money was almost nonexistent. It was hard for them to come up with a penny for a pound of meal to make cornbread. Flour to make biscuits was somewhat more expensive than cornmeal. Therefore, we ate cornbread three times a day. That was really better for us than eating food made of white flour. However, we found it easy to feel sorry for ourselves when we tried to sop our gravy with cornbread. We really knew times were hard when we had trouble coming up with three cents to mail a letter or a penny to send a postcard.

Mom owned a sewing machine. She traded cream and eggs at the Herod general store for cloth to make shirts and trousers for three sons and dresses for two daughters. I give Mom an A+ for her effort, but when we wore the clothes she made, we looked somewhat like orphans. However, at school, we looked as good as others, since they were poor, too.

Children from a really poor family attended Sadler School. They had a large, heavy-producing, three-legged milk goat. One evening, one of the boys, Phillip, came to our house and wanted to sell us that goat for ten dollars. Dad told him he wasn't interested in owning a goat.

While Phillip was talking to my brothers, Mom said to Dad, "Why don't you give him some money? They surely need money or they wouldn't part with their goat."

I'll never forget Dad's reply. He said, "When it comes to buying that goat, I wouldn't give them half as many dollars for it as it has legs. But since they may be in need, I'll give them two dollars. That will buy them some rice, sugar, and beans."

Mom seemed pleased. She asked Dad if it would be okay if she gave Phillip that ham bone that still had a mess of meat on it. Dad nodded.

A few days later, Mr. Guy DeNeal called after dark and said he was collecting money for this same family in need. I remember Dad gave him thirty-five cents.

Later in the winter, on a Friday morning, Phillip arrived at school just as school took up. He had a broke-down shotgun in the crook of his arm. He walked up to the teacher's desk, laid four shotgun shells on it, and said, "Mr. Williams, will you keep this shotgun and shells for me? If I may, I'd like to leave school a little early and shoot a couple of rabbits on the way home, so Mom can make us some stew for our dinner tomorrow. She has some potatoes and onions for the stew."

Mr. Williams replied, "No problem. Close the gun and set it over in the corner."

To the students, Mr. Williams warned, "Stay away from that gun—don't touch it."

Mr. Williams reached into his lunch sack on his desk and brought out a molasses cookie. As he handed it to Phillip, he said kindly, "Go back to the stove and eat this as you warm yourself before you go to your seat."

As Phillip reached for the cookie, with a little quiver in his voice, he said, "Thank you, Mr. Williams."

This entire family moved to Ypsilanti, Michigan, around 1935. When, at the age of seventeen, I accepted farm work near Ypsilanti in the summer of 1937, I had an opportunity to visit them. They were employed and had moved well into the middle class. They walked with their heads up and with smiles on their faces.

Years passed, and I saw many of my Sadler classmates grow older with me. But since 1937, I hadn't seen any member of Phillip's family.

However, in 2010, I answered a knock at the door and found myself gazing in the faces of a tall, well-dressed couple. Over their shoulders, I saw a new, expensive-looking car in the driveway.

The man asked, "Are you Kestner Wallace?"

I replied, "Yes, I am. Come in and tell me who you are."

"I'm Phillip, your old schoolmate at Sadler School."

In shock, I stuck out my hand and said, "It is so good

to see you again. I remember you well; however, you are taller than I remembered you to be."

Phillip laughed and said, "I've grown since you saw me last."

Then Phillip introduced me to his wife, Eva. I was impressed with Eva's attractive appearance and her pleasing personality. Phillip didn't give her a chance to talk very much. He commented, "My wife of many years died, and I felt life was over. The same was true with Eva. Her husband of forty-seven years was killed in an automobile accident. She, too, was in the valley of despair. By accident, Eva and I met and were immediately enchanted with each other. We later shared our beginning feelings for each other. We found them very much the same—a feeling of gentle kindness and sincere concern for each other.

"The thought of marriage crossed our minds early on, but we decided we would wait until we were sure our feelings for each other weren't old-age puppy love. It took only a month for us to decide for sure we wanted to spend the rest of our lives together." They told me they had a house in Florida.

Phillip said, "I've told you about us. Now you tell us about yourself."

All I told them was that my wife, Evelyn, and I had had a happy marriage of fifty-six years, and I didn't expect to get married again.

Eva spoke up and asked, "Why?"

I replied, "Cupid hasn't lined me up with a fair lady and shot us like he shot the two of you."

Eva smiled and said, "That is reason enough for me. I wish you well."

I tried to get them to let me take them down to the boat at Elizabethtown to eat catfish. They thanked me but said they really needed to be on their way.

Their visit was really too short; I had more questions on my mind that I didn't get to ask. I was also sorry that I didn't get to tell Phillip how much my mother and his mother had respected each other. I wished I had acknowledged the fact that his mother invited my mother and me to dinner on May 30, 1933. I've never forgotten the dressing—moist, flavorful and seasoned to perfection. The fact that to this day I remember the strawberry shortcake—made of homegrown berries—tells you it was good.

As I relive the days, months, and years from 1926 to the present, 2013, I have somewhat forgotten the unpleasantness of the Great Depression years and instead glorify the happiness strewn along the way. Those hard times helped to strengthen the fiber of my soul and body, enabling me to meet the challenges that followed.

I rejoice in the improvement that has taken place since the time of the log school to the present. In education, a slow upward trend has taken place. Some early schools were lacking in proper lighting and heating. Water was often carried in buckets from a nearby spring. The number of students per teacher was far too many. In too many cases, teachers were poorly trained to teach. However, a goodly number were gifted at teaching and did an excellent job. They are to be applauded.

While our present school system may not be perfect, my hat is off to it because of the giant steps forward in ways too numerous to mention. I will, however, name a few: better-qualified teachers, concerned superintendents and boards of education, a striving to care for pre-kindergarten children and those with special needs, increased use of technology in the classrooms, and concern for the need for art, music, and physical education. The list goes on and on.

Please join me in applauding the many who are working together to make our schools better, particularly the teachers. It will pay well in educational dividends to also praise the students for their cooperative effort. Were it not for them, there would be no schools.

I treasure all of my experiences there at Sadler School. They made me a better person. As I look back, very little of it would I change. That early chapter in my life laid the groundwork for all the educational experiences that followed.

For me, I don't feel the last chapter has yet been written. I hope it will be a good one.

* * *

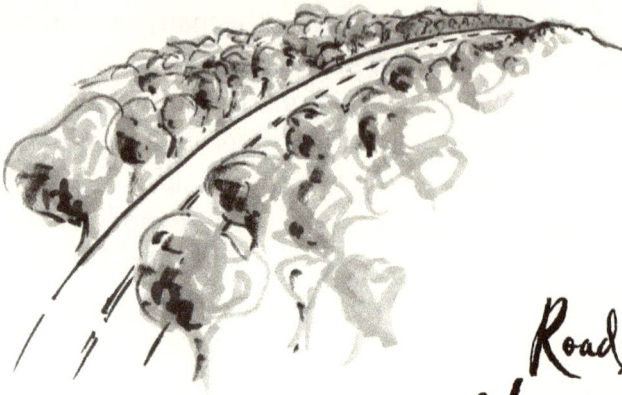

Roads of Yesteryear

On this first day of summer—at the age of eighty-nine—I am happy to sit in view of Womble Mountain and watch the sun brighten the eastern skies and slowly come into full view. Here I have spent my life, except for the short time I lived in Michigan just before I served in the Navy for three years during World War II. It is an ideal time to reminisce of bygone days.

I'm amazed at the changes that have taken place since I was seven years old—nearly eighty-three years ago. Sixty years ago, my present home on part of the original Wallace homestead was a cornfield with wild dewberry vines growing in abundance around the edge. Just a quarter-mile south was and is the place of my birth and my home for a number of years.

About one hundred yards east of that house was an old dirt road. Back then, this road was the main route between Harrisburg and Golconda in Southern Illinois. The road was either dusty or muddy, and always rough.

Our barn was within a few feet of this road. I had a slight fear of strangers who traveled by. Oftentimes, I hid in the barn and watched people pass—some on foot, some on horseback, others in wagons or buggies.

14

One day, while watching the road from the barn, I saw three covered wagons with people in each. The wagons were being pulled by small, pony-like horses, traveling at a snail's pace. Two men were on horseback, and a tall red-complected man was on foot. This man caused me to believe they were Indians, thus further leading me to wonder whether they were the scalping kind.

When this group was out of sight, with cold chills running up my back, I ran to the house and very excitedly reported to Mom that a wild band of mean-looking Indians had just passed. I told her I had stayed hidden in the barn to keep from being kidnapped.

Mom laughed and told me they weren't Indians but gypsies. She assured me I need not have any fear of Indians or gypsies. She somehow knew that this band of gypsies had been traveling north on the road from Golconda for days, as they traded goods and services along the way.

The next thing of interest I observed from the barn was a team and wagon. A man driving the team was sitting high on a spring seat. There was a tarpaulin over the cargo. The team of horses had to exert considerable effort to move the loaded wagon up the hill. I further noticed that the wagon had no tailgate. Hanging out so that it could fall off at any time was a white bag that appeared to be a hundred-pound bag of feed.

I told Dad what I'd seen. He didn't seem much surprised or concerned. He just commented that the guy probably was hauling a load of mash—ground corn residue left over from making whiskey—that he had bought or was given for hog feed.

I learned a few days later that the hanging bag of mash had fallen off the wagon at the top of the hill, where my Uncle Courty lived. At the time, he had an old sow and a number of pigs about weaning size. Uncle Courty took the entire bag of mash and dumped it out in a huge trough for the sow.

Later, I overheard Dad telling Mom about the result. Eating too much of the mash had made the old sow drunk. She wobbled when she walked and seemed to take pleasure in using her snout to toss the pigs, one after another, high into the air.

...

Around 1927 or 1928, that dirt road began to be referred to as the Old Road, because a new concrete road was being put in about one hundred yards west of our house. For quite a long while, we referred to it as the Hard Road or the New Road. When cars began to use the hard road, signs went up: "SPEED LIMIT 35 MPH."

The new hard road—now known as Highway 34 —was built from south to north from Golconda to Harrisburg. When the road had been completed past our house, and before traffic was turned loose on it, the older Wallace cousins and friends saw the potential of the nearest hill, then known as Trousdale Hill. They made three-wheeled carts, with cultivator wheels behind, a wheelbarrow wheel in front, and a steering wheel to guide the cart. They also took the tongue out of old buggies and rigged them with guide ropes. We pushed the buggies and carts to the top of the hill and coasted down more than a quarter of a mile at an exciting—and probably dangerous—speed.

Dad realized his three sons were really too young to operate a buggy or a three-wheeled cart, so he ordered us a "Flying Gold" rubber-tired wagon. It was about four feet long and thirty inches wide—just right for two boys. Dad was probably thinking more about our using the wagon to haul our fifteen or more bushels of potatoes from the garden to our fruit, vegetable, and storm cellar and to keep our wood boxes filled with wood for heating and cooking. However, in the meantime, we made good use of that wagon on the hill.

We were extremely happy that the new road passed very near our home instead of going on the east side of Womble Mountain and on through the Somerset community and Whitesville into Harrisburg. Once the new road was complete, however, there were a couple of downsides that cost us time, hard work, and money, which was hard to come by.

First, we were disappointed that the back of the house faced the new road in an unattractive manner. When I was eight or nine, I heard Dad and Mom talk of having the house turned around to face the new road. It seemed like an impossible task to me. The house sat about two feet off the ground on hand-hewn stone pillars, which had been drawn down from Womble Mountain on a sled behind a mule. The stones were set about four feet apart for the sills to rest on, around the circumference of the house. Others supported the center beam. The house was rather large with high ceilings and an unfinished attic. With its three porches, chimney, and fireplace, turning the house was not going to be a simple task.

Dad talked to a man about doing the job. The man told Dad that the chimney and fireplace would have to be taken down. The man said if Dad would have them taken down, he would turn the house around and set it on the same type of foundation for eighty-five dollars.

Dad got Jess Gibbs, a hard-working mason, to take the large stones apart and number them in order to put them back properly. Then the man who turned houses around took over.

The man and his three helpers knew what they were doing. They used jacks to raise the house about a foot above the stone foundation and blocked it with numerous wooden blocks. Long 8x8 wooden beams on rollers were drawn under the house with a rope pulled by a pair of big black mules. The house was lowered onto the beams. Then the turning process began, with the mules doing the pulling. The ground was hard and dry. The trained team master slowly and carefully maneuvered the house to its new position and set it down on the foundation pillar stones, which they had already reset for the house's new position. As Dad paid the man, he said, "That was the best eighty-five dollars I ever spent."

I was assigned the job of digging out and filling in with broken stone an area to be covered with concrete to form a base on which to rebuild the chimney. I don't know how much Mr. Gibbs got paid, but Dad was pleased with his rebuilding of the fireplace and chimney.

The other drawback to the new road was that it divided our hundred-acre farm into two parts—roughly forty acres on the east side and sixty acres on the west side. Our house was on the east side, and our fenced garden was on the west side. We pastured stock on land on both sides of the road, so the new road's positioning caused us to have to build almost a quarter of a mile of fence on each side of the road. However, Dad, with me as his helper, built the fences without complaining.

…

About that same time, while still quite young, I had a desire to do grownup chores. I fed the stock while Dad was milking our cow, a heavy producer. We had a cat that stayed at the barn and took care of the mice population. After Dad finished milking and took the milk to the house, I milked about a half pint of milk in a pan for the cat — thus proving to myself I could milk.

One evening, a few minutes before milking time, I took a six-quart pail and had the cow milked before Dad came to the barn. From a hiding place, I watched. He sat on his milking stool and looked surprised when he saw that the cow's udder was smaller than usual. He was further surprised to find the cow had no milk.

I jumped out from my hiding place, pointed to the pail I had placed where he would not easily notice it, and said, "Surprise — here is your bucket of milk!"

He was surprised. However, the joke turned out to be on me. From that time on, the job was mine. I milked with both hands, and it wasn't much of an added chore.

One evening, when I got up from the milking stool and turned around, I was amazed to see a medium-sized, older man with grayish hair and a two-weeks' growth of white beard. As he stood there like a statue, he didn't strike me as one to fear, but I was really surprised.

With a little grin, he said, "I'm sorry if I startled you."

I replied, "No problem. The cow was chewing so loudly on her corn, I didn't hear you come up."

He then asked, "Is your father around?"

"He is at the house. Do you need to talk to him?"

"Yes, I would like to ask for permission to sleep in your barn tonight. It is clear and will be cold tonight. I have a big piece of fresh head cheese and a piece of cornbread left from dinner, so I won't need anything to eat."

I said, "Come along with me. I'm ready to go to the house. Dad will likely give you permission. You won't be the first to spend a night in this barn."

We went into the living room. I handed the milk to Mom. She thanked me and said, "We were waiting supper on you."

I said, "Dad, this gentleman has a question to ask you or rather a request to make."

The man displayed a touch of culture when he stepped forward, extended his hand, and said, "I'm Arthur Anderson." He then made his request and added, "I have food for supper."

Dad said, "You are welcome to eat supper with us and sleep in the barn. We can fix you up with a pillow and some blankets and bed you down in sweet-smelling alfalfa hay."

The man replied gratefully, "Kind words like that help me to believe there is a God in Heaven."

Dad wasn't much to inquire into someone else's business. But with supper underway, he couldn't resist asking Arthur how long he had been roaming around and what had brought it about. For almost a minute, Arthur didn't respond. I didn't think he minded the question. It was easy to see he was in deep thought. Eating slowed to a standstill.

He said, "It is a sad story. It never should have happened. I thought at the time I handled the matter well, but since then I feel I could have done better."

Dad said, "You have caused me to want to hear your sad story. Suppose we enjoy the evening meal. Then we can make ourselves comfortable in the living room and hear your story." The man readily agreed to the plan.

Off of the living room, we had a large bedroom that was called "the other room." It had two beds, chairs, a table, and other items of interest to children. Dad said, "Mabel and Hazel, and you little boys—Byrum and Victor—go in the other room for a while, giving us more freedom to talk." He didn't need to worry about Mom, who sat in the kitchen writing letters.

I had the feeling that Dad wanted to hear Arthur's story in its entirety. Since Dad and I spent much time working together, I had grown-up status. He felt I could hear the story, even if it was material more suited for adults.

Arthur began, "What I'm about to tell you, I have never told before. I'm glad you sent the girls and the small boys out of the room. I'm going to tell you something that put a dagger in my heart and caused me to want to commit murder."

Arthur got Dad's attention from the jumpstart. He was pleased to have Dad in his spell. I had learned to hold a poker face before understanding the term. Arthur seemed concerned that he couldn't read me.

Arthur went on and on and on. I got the feeling that Arthur felt as if he were paying for his supper. He got Dad worked up to the point that he interrupted Arthur once to say, "I would have taken my .38 and shot the son of a b****!"

[While writing about Arthur, I considered cleaning up his story and saving it for posterity but decided it wasn't worth the effort. If you are disappointed, please forgive me.]

After Arthur finished his story, I lit a lantern, and Dad and I bedded Arthur down for the night. He ate breakfast with us the next morning, and we saw him no more.

. . .

With the new road in use, a chore I didn't mind was going the two-and-a-half mile trip to Rudement to get a few supplies. Sometimes I would walk. Other times, I'd get a ride in a wagon or a Model T Ford. Every trip was different.

About halfway to the store, on the left and close to the road, stood one of the few well-preserved log houses remaining in the area. It was made of huge, hand-hewn white oak logs, with a porch spanning the front.

At the south end of the porch was a well. From time to time as I passed the house, I wondered how deep the well was, if the water was hard or soft, and if it was cold. Usually, I saw an old man and old woman sitting on the porch. To me, they didn't appear happy or friendly.

One day as I walked along this stretch of road, I wasn't thirsty, but my "nose trouble" got the better of me. I left the road and approached the house some thirty yards away. As I reached the porch, this man stood tall and stiff as if he had swallowed a ramrod. I read the question on his mind. It was "What in the Sam Hill do you want?" I didn't give him a chance to ask it.

I said, "Good morning, sir. Could I get a drink of water? I can draw it myself."

His reply was short and snappy, "I'll draw it. You'd lose my can."

That didn't make any sense to me, but I followed him over to the well. From a nail on a log, he took down a pint-sized tin can with a wire bale on it. Then he picked up a long sassafras pole that had a nail that was slanted upward on one end of the pole. He hooked the can bail on the nail and lowered the pole into the well. After a sudden skillful swipe, he hoisted the pole out of the well and handed me a can of cold water. I had to prove to him I was thirsty, so I downed it all. I thanked him and was on my way. I always treasured that experience but was never again thirsty when I passed that log house.

This man's name was Elijah Gibbs. He was honest and hardworking. As the old saying goes, "He was as independent as a hog on ice."

I told my Uncle Lew Wallace, who operated the store at Rudement before my time, about the water drawing with a pole. He laughed and said that when he was the merchant at Rudement, he had filled a grocery list for Mr. Gibbs. "I listed each item and the price. I added a well rope and wrote 'No charge.' Mr. Gibbs flew angry and said, 'If I need a well rope, I'll buy it!'"

...

Mom had a hard time keeping her three sons from using idle words. (A fourth son was still in diapers at that time.) She chastised us for using expressions such as "hair fire" and "shoot fire," saying it would lead to cursing. We coined terms just to tease her. Some amused her and others did not. She was a good sport and was pleased we could entertain ourselves with clean tomfoolery.

One hot, summer day, we three brothers were taking a break sitting on the porch facing the new road. Mom asked, "Kestner, would you mind taking the little wagon, going to the garden, and getting sixteen big ears of corn—eight to eat off the cob for dinner and eight to cut off the cob for supper?"

I didn't mind at all, since I loved corn, whether on or off the cob. The garden, just beyond the road, had been fenced for many years to keep stray cows out. The wild blackberries and honeysuckle vines that grew around the fence made for much privacy.

On leaving the garden with the corn, I was surprised to see a truck with its back end piled high with watermelons. The driver had the truck's hood up and didn't see me. No, I wasn't tempted to steal one. But while I was trying to make up my mind whether to offer the driver sixteen ears of corn for a melon, he closed the hood and drove off.

My brothers had been watching from the porch. When I got to the house, Byrum quickly asked, "Why didn't you 'snipe' one of those melons?"

Victor said, "If I'd have been you, I'd have sniped two."

Mom was listening, and in her saddest, mournful voice, she said, "Boys, boys, boys, you know I don't want my boys sniping things."

Mom's picking up on our newly coined word turned our tickle box over. Our laughter exceeded the humor. I said with a grin, "Mom, you'll have to be careful about picking up on new words. It might lead to cussing."

Mom was a believer in the scripture, "Spare the rod and spoil the child." However, instead of using a rod, Mom used the swatting end of a fly swatter. Whenever I realized I had caused her unhappiness because of something I had said or done, I almost looked forward to her swatting me—to make her feel better.

Somehow Mom had the feeling the swatting was hurting. I always made out like I was dreading the upcoming swatting and feigned pain with the first swat. One time when I was about to get a swatting, my youngest brother, Gaylord, called out to Dad in an undertone, "Dad, you better get in here. Mom is about to use the fly swatter on Kestner. You don't want to miss out on the fun."

Realizing I had an audience, I began to pray. "Lord, have mercy on me. You know how I can't stand pain. You were with the Hebrew children in the fiery furnace and with Daniel in the lion's den. Please have mercy on me."

My clowning didn't strike Mom as being funny. She let me have it with that fly swatter. I feigned terrible pain with the first lick. I tried to imitate a scalded dog. I said, "Stop, Mommy, stop! I'll be good from now on." She stopped and said, "You better be."

[Author's note: Mom wasn't a dummy. She knew she wasn't hurting me. She didn't intend to hurt me. She just wanted to draw attention to the fact that she didn't approve of what I was saying and doing. Mom played her part well in our unrehearsed skit that brought laughter during the heart of the Depression when laughs were few and far between.]

···

On the top of the aforementioned Trousdale Hill, before I was old enough to remember, had lived a couple Mom admired by the name of Trousdale. They had sold their home and moved to Northern Illinois to work at a state hospital. After about fifteen years, they moved back and bought the farm between Trousdale Hill and Buzzard Roost Hill, less than a mile north of us.

Mom paid Mrs. Trousdale a visit and said heartily, "Welcome back, Mrs. Trousdale." (She pronounced it as we always had, with the first syllable rhyming with "cow.")

Mrs. Trousdale looked shocked and said a bit haughtily, "The name is 'Trousdale.'" The way she said the first syllable rhymed with "true."

Mom said, "Excuse me, I must be slipping."

A week later, Mom saw Mrs. Trousdale at the store and repeated her mistake. She was somewhat sharply reminded that the name sounded like "Trues-dale."

Mom declared to herself that she'd never again make that mistake. She said to herself, "Trues-dale, Trues-dale, Trues-dale," over and over until she was sure she had it down pat.

One morning Mom was planning on doing the week's wash. She said to me, "Kestner, wear these overalls today. I want to wash the trousers you wore yesterday." Her "trousers" came out sounding like "true-sers." Mom caught her mistake and laughed along with the rest of us.

Years ago, old-timers would have said concerning Mrs. Trousdale that she was "putting on the dog." That reminds me of the following story. It was told to me while on the island of Saipan, in World War II, by a soldier from Shawneetown, Illinois. His name was Woodrow Wooden, whom I've never seen since.

Woodrow said a couple, Mr. and Mrs. Kiser (rhyming with "miser"), a poor but proud, barely middle-class couple from Germany, came to the United States to enhance their standard of living. They brought their butler and hired hand, Mr. Brown, with them. Mr. Brown was keen-minded, hardworking, and nothing less than a member of the family. He worked faithfully with Mr. Kiser to move up in the world.

Mr. Kiser bought a run-down house and barn and a number of acres adjoining and partly in the city limits. With repairs, paint, and hard work, Mr. Kiser and Mr. Brown turned the house and acreage into a place of charm and beauty.

Mr. and Mrs. Kiser joined the largest church in town and took Mr. Brown with them. Mrs. Kiser soon found herself president of a "high-up" ladies' club. Mr. Kiser became a member of the county board.

One afternoon, Mrs. Kiser was entertaining her club ladies, and Mr. Kiser was attending a county board meeting. Mr. Brown rushed into the house in the middle of the ladies' meeting and asked loudly, "Where is Mr. Kiser?"

Mrs. Kiser, with an air of condescension and a brow slightly elevated, said, "I beg your pardon, sir, the name is 'Kizar.' Mr. Kizar is not here. Mr. Kizar is attending an important board meeting." The way she said it, "Kizar" rhymed with "bizarre."

Mr. Brown caught on quickly and replied, "Oh, yes, oh, yes, it is Mr. Kizar. When Mr. Kizar returns, please tell Mr. Kizar that Mr. KiBrown was in and has a load of Kinure on the Kiwagon and doesn't know where to Kidump it."

...

I'll return now to the early years of the new road. I recall three people—a man, a teenaged girl, and saddest of all, a mother of five young children—being killed, all struck by Model T Fords in separate accidents.

I remember two close calls that didn't result in death. One was a preacher from Rosiclare on his way to preach in or near Harrisburg. Mom and I had just stepped out on the porch as the car, a '29 Chevrolet, started going out of control. I later learned it was a result of getting two wheels off the road and overcorrecting. While the car was out of control, I said to Mom, "That car will turn over."

In her sad, mournful tone, Mom cried, "I don't want to see it turn over, I don't want to see it turn over, I don't want to see it turn over!"

With a commanding tone, I said, "Then turn your head."

Quickly, she replied, "Yes, but I want to see!"

The car did turn over. The preacher was not hurt and was taken by a friend to Harrisburg, to preach as scheduled.

The other rather serious accident was one that concerned a sharp trader who lived northwest of Rudement. My attention was drawn to him because he had a daughter about my age—twelve or thirteen years old. This gal in my opinion was a little beauty queen, with long brown hair, an easy smile, and eyes that sparkled. Neither she nor anyone else knew that she had caught my eye and caused my heart to beat a little faster when I saw her.

Her dad was well liked because of his friendly ability to relate to people. It was well known that he was fond of moonshine, but he was believed to be one who could handle his liquor well.

However, one Sunday afternoon, he must have gone heavy on the bottle. He passed our house going north about as fast as his Model T Ford would go. I don't remember the particulars after these many years. But about 150 yards past our driveway, he either struck a tree or a bridge abutment.

Hearing the loud bang, I hurried to the accident site. Several people were already there. The car was a messed-up wreck, with the top torn off. I went directly to the driver. In a vague sort of way, he seemed to recognize me. He put forth an effort to distance himself from being involved. As he stood there holding in both hands the steering wheel, which was still attached to part of the steering column, he said, "It looks like someone had an accident here and messed up his car."

He had an ugly cut on his forehead. Blood was running down his face and onto his white shirt. A man who knew him took him by the arm and said, "Come on with me to the doctor to get your head sewed up." About that time, Mom arrived. She quickly took off her Sunday apron and wrapped it tightly around his head. He must have gotten along all right, because I saw him around thereafter.

...

In the heart of the Great Depression, we sometimes peddled food on the road in front of our house on Sunday afternoons. The wild blackberries produced well back then. Mom would can at least one hundred quarts for winter use in pies and cobblers, and we sold a number of gallons for twenty cents a gallon. We also gathered and hulled black walnuts and sold them for a dollar a bushel.

Much work went into getting a bushel of walnuts ready to sell. We gathered them after the first frost. The outer hull was mostly green and full of brown sap that stained unprotected hands to a light chocolate brown. We could have bought gloves for fifteen cents a pair, but I never owned a pair back then. The walnut stain, after several weeks, would gradually wear off.

I had a white cloth hat that I didn't like too well. I boiled walnut hulls in water to make dye and changed the color of my hat. I liked the brown hat much better.

At that time, we had a flock of white Wyandotte chickens, including a number of roosters. One, the Cock of the Walk, intimidated the other roosters, particularly one that was nervous and afraid of his own shadow. All that Cock of the Walk had to do was to stretch out his neck and make a few fast steps toward this timid rooster, and he would almost dislocate his pulley bone getting away.

I decided to use some of my brown hat dye and make Cock of the Walk brown. As I carefully brushed on the dye, I soothed his nerves by telling him about the present, past, and future. When he was perfectly dry, I turned him loose.

The other roosters did not recognize him. They took after him, led by the timid rooster, with blood in their eyes. They chased him around the woodpile. The second time around, he was looking back and floundered over the little wagon. I'm sure he was saying to himself, "What on earth is this world a comin' to?"

Things turned out well for Cock of the Walk, however. The dye didn't change his crow, and he was soon acknowledged as Cock of the Walk again.

...

The changes and improvements in the nearly ninety-year span of my life have been interesting and delightful. I'm happy I experienced travel by horse- and mule-back, wagon, horse and buggy, Model T, Model A, and V-8 Fords, and now also in a snow-white Toyota. As the sun is setting, I sit at the end of the dining table, viewing from a bay picture window the hard road hill, now widened and black-topped, that more than eighty years ago we boys gleefully coasted down. Now, eighteen-wheelers laden with coal, sometimes six in a row, speed down that hill.

Along Route 34, you can still see the hollowed-out roadbed in some places where the old road ran. They're still a vivid reminder to me of the roads of yesteryear.

* * *

Johnson's Lot

I recall when I was seven or eight years old seeing a man shaking hands with my father and saying his name was Johnson. He said, "Mr. Wallace, I have been employed to do the dirt work on this new road that is coming through. You know all about that. The dirt work between Herod and Rudement will be done by a good many teams of mules that will pull slip scrapers, each handled by a man. I need about an acre-sized lot to keep my mules nights, Sundays, and other times when they are not needed.

"You have a plot such as I need just east of your barn and across the old road at the foot of Womble Mountain. I like that plot very much because of the shade trees, and a spring branch runs through it. Mr. Wallace, before I say more, would you be interested in leasing me an acre at a fair price?"

Dad said, "You have my attention, Mr. Johnson. Tell me what you will do."

"I'll set good solid posts and put a fence around the plot. When the dirt work is finished along here, you'll have a good hog lot or a good weaning pen for a calf or colt. Then, too, I'll cross your palm with a few dollars."

The next thing I knew, Dad and Mr. Johnson were shaking hands. I knew they had reached an agreement.

I observed with interest the fence building and the going and coming of the mules. I was also pleased with the friendliness the workmen showed me.

Time passed quickly, and the presence of Mr. Johnson, his men, and the mules were history. But for the next fifty years, that lot was "Johnson's Lot."

Little by little over the next few years, Johnson's Lot began to take on the appearance of a miniature park. A swing was hung from one of the trees, and a picnic table and a see-saw were added. There was plenty of space for washer and horseshoe pitching. Among the different kinds of trees were four walnut trees and one scaly-bark hickory nut tree. Naturally they brought in hordes of squirrels in the fall.

Most of our leisure activity in Johnson's Lot took place on Sunday afternoons. Oftentimes through the week, our free-range hens visited the lot in numbers. They had learned it was a good place to scratch for worms.

As a consequence, foxes from the nearby mountain learned it was a good place to get a chicken dinner. We had so many hens that we didn't get too excited if we lost one now and then. We may have been a little like Mr. and Mrs. John who, it is told, lived in alligator country in the South.

Mr. and Mrs. John were relaxing in the shade near their shanty by the bayou. They, like the old woman who lived in a shoe, had many children. An acquaintance strolled by and said, "Howdy, Mr. and Mrs. John." This man exchanged a few words with them and then said, "By the way, a few minutes ago, I saw an alligator taking off with one of your children."

Mrs. John replied, "You don't say. I told John this morning something is happening to some of these 'chilrens.'"

Dad's concern for the chickens involved me. Although I was only about nine years old, he suggested that I arm myself with a club and a slingshot and conceal myself near Johnson's Lot. He reminded me that the shepherd boy David killed a lion and a bear with a club and slew a giant with a slingshot. He said encouragingly, "I don't think you'll kill a fox with a slingshot, but you might scare the wax out of him."

Dad went on to say that a week or so back, on Sunday afternoon, his brother Lew, a preacher who was Lew's dinner guest, and he were sitting on the shady porch. Chickens were strolling in the wood yard just beyond the yard fence gate.

All of a sudden, a young gray fox rushed up and nabbed a full-grown hen. The hen managed to cover the fox's eyes with her wings. All three of the men rushed out. Dad said he picked up a club-like pole and whacked the fox across the back, and the preacher knocked it in the head with a stick of stove wood.

Dad's pep talk about David and the account of killing the chicken-catching fox fired me up to think maybe, just maybe, I might do the unexpected. Fully equipped with a club and my slingshot, I sat in a secluded spot near Johnson's Lot. I daydreamed and probably snoozed a little.

All of a sudden, I heard the nerve-racking squawk of a hen in distress. I sprang to my feet, picked up my slingshot that already had a steel ball bearing in the pocket of the sling, and grabbed my club as I took off.

I ran toward the continuous squawking. At first I saw nothing. On looking more closely, I saw a hen in a pool of water. She was mostly submerged, with her wings out flat on the water. Her head was up, so her squawking was unaffected.

I waded barefoot into the water to just above my knees. I thought perhaps the hen was entangled in some branches or brush. I grasped her by one of her wings and realized something alive had a hold of her. I slowly and gently gave an upward pull with my left hand as I held my balance with the club in my right hand.

An ugly sight came into view—the head of a logger-head turtle with a toe of the hen in its mouth. I gave that wicked-looking head a powerful whack with that club, and it turned loose of the hen's toe. She ran away unharmed. The turtle disappeared down the stream.

I related this incident to family members. They were amused, but it was my aunts, Mom's sisters, who almost succeeded in giving me a complex about the danger of turtles. With big eyes, they told me how lucky I was that the turtle's mate hadn't gotten me by the toe and caused so much pain that I'd faint, fall over, and drown. They didn't leave it at that. They went on to say they had always heard that if a turtle got hold of your toe, it wouldn't turn loose until it thundered.

When Mom saw I was troubled about the danger of turtles, she said, "Don't worry about the turtles. My sisters were just teasing you. Keep your eyes open the way you do about snakes. Give them their space and you need not worry about them." It wasn't until years later that I had another encounter with a turtle.

I made frequent trips to Johnson's Lot throughout the following weeks and very carefully looked for turtles. I saw none. However, I saw a number of little fish about as long as my little finger. I told my dad about them. He said they were "topwaters" or minnows that would never get any bigger and would disappear down the creek.

I began to wonder if I could catch them. I didn't have any hook or line and didn't know where to get any, so I took a straight pin and bent a small hook on the end of it. I tied a five-foot length of twine just below the head of the pin so it wouldn't slip off. I tied the other end of the string to a five-foot willow pole and put a tiny bit of worm on the pin hook. With an eye out for a turtle, I eased up to the brook, careful not to frighten the fish.

I had never before fished, but I'd been told give the pole a good hard jerk when a fish took the bait. Immediately a minnow took the bait and hung on. I manned that pole somewhat like I did my slingshot and threw that minnow halfway across Johnson's Lot. It came off the hook but made enough movement that I located it without much trouble.

I took that minnow to the house to show it off, but was disappointed to find no one there. Having nothing else better to do, I decided to cook the minnow. There wasn't much left when I cut off its head and gutted it. I put some lard in a big iron skillet and stoked up the smoldering fire with some corn cobs and wood chips. The minnow was soon a golden brown.

I took it up on a dinner plate. It looked small and lonely. I was at a loss as to what to do with the grease in the skillet. I recalled that Mom made gravy when she cooked any kind of meat, so I decided to make some gravy. I put a generous amount of flour in the grease, let it cook a little, then added some milk. Almost before I knew it, the gravy was as thick as mashed potatoes.

I ate the minnow in two small bites. Since I forgot to salt the gravy, it didn't suit my taste, so I gave it to the dog and then cleaned up my mess. It was many years before I fried fish again.

...

Using Johnson's Lot for a playground was grand for a few years. One Easter Sunday stands out. Different families customarily took food and went up on Womble Mountain on Easter Sundays. However, two Wallace families living nearby and Mom's brother's large family celebrated this particular Easter Sunday in Johnson's Lot. Most of the food was brought prepared—fried chicken, potato salad, banana pudding, and many other good things. We boys built a fire in a stone enclosure to roast hot dogs and marshmallows. Mom made lemonade with the cold spring water nearby.

After that Easter Sunday, Johnson's Lot declined as a play park and was used for a more practical purpose. Dad bought thirty head of sheep and kept them in the lot while he strung barbed wire over a rail fence enclosing the pasture that he planned to keep them in.

Next, Dad bought a beautiful, wild, gaited Western mare and kept her in Johnson's Lot for a while. She was halfway between a blond and a bay. She proved that she was gaited by beating a path around just inside the lot fence. She really put her different gaits on display. I told a friend who admired her that Dad had bought her for thirty-five dollars, and this man said, "If I owned her, I wouldn't take five hundred dollars for her."

Loving, gentle care turned this mare into the best all-around farm animal we ever had. She was the mother of my famous riding mule, Sampson.

In 1938, I started driving a 1920 Model T Ford that had been on blocks for ten years. I was beginning to be a "big shot." I could either ride Sampson or drive an eighteen-year-old Model T Ford. I drove the Model T around Womble Mountain and visited a neighbor, Mr. Irvin.

Mr. Irvin hit me up to buy a young Hampshire sow from him. She was grazing in full view—lean, tall, and long-legged. Mr. Irvin said they were tired of having her around in the way. He said, "I'll sell her to you for five dollars."

I said, "Mr. Irvin, if you and your hired hand will help me put her in the floorboard of the back seat of my car, I'll take her." With the hired hand standing by, Mr. Irvin took an ear of corn and coaxed her into the car. Her tail hung out over one side and her snout over the other. I got her to Johnson's Lot without mishap. Good fresh spring water and all the corn she could eat added a hundred pounds, mostly fat, to her weight, making 350 pounds of hams, shoulders, side meat, and sausage—all very tasty when cured and smoked.

...

After I was married, a lonely World War I vet named Lonnie became my fishing buddy. He fished all the time. I fished with him now and then. Sometimes we did really well; other times we did poorly. He taught me we could enjoy a fishing trip whether or not we caught any fish.

I told Lonnie about Johnson's Lot and the turtle that almost did away with the hen. He took great interest in that story and asked if I'd ever eaten turtle meat. I told him I hadn't. He assured me that it was good to eat. He said that a turtle has seven different kinds of meat in it.

Lonnie said, "There may still be an eating-size turtle in Johnson's Lot. I'll check it out one of these days. If I get a good-sized one, I'll dress it, and you and Evelyn can enjoy eating turtle meat."

Several days later, Lonnie showed up all smiles. He said, "Kestner, I have you a mess of turtle meat all dressed and ready for the skillet." I'll spare you the step-by-step details of his catching and dressing the turtle on the tailgate of his Dodge pickup, which he had driven into

Johnson's Lot. Briefly, he removed the turtle's head, laid it on its back, cut some pieces with his hatchet, and then cut some tough skin around the top of the shell with his knife. Then Lonnie said that he rolled out about three pounds of clean white meat that he washed and rewashed with spring water.

Evelyn fried the turtle the same way she fried chicken. I can assure you it was good. I thought to myself, "One of these days I'll try my luck at dressing one for the skillet."

It was another few years before that chance came. From time to time as I fished, I caught a number of small turtles. Some would turn loose of the hook. Others I was able to remove from the hook and release without mistreating them.

One day after a big rain, I was fishing at the spillway at Lake Glendale. My catch was fair—it could have been better. I caught a big fish I was having trouble landing. A fellow fisherman grabbed my net, landed the fish, and exclaimed, "A bream! They are really good to eat if you know how to cook them."

"Do you know how to cook them?" I asked.

He replied, "I sure do."

I said, "It is your fish."

I decided to go from the spillway across the highway and fish in a creek, which may have been Sugar Creek. I was able to drive close to it. The creek appeared fishy—wide and deep. However, fishing was no better than at the spillway—only a blue gill now and then.

Suddenly I realized that either my line was hung on something, or I had hooked a big fish. Movement on the line told me the line wasn't hung. After what seemed like a long time, I realized I had a turtle on the line. Little by little I drew that turtle near the bank. I took the five-gallon bucket I was sitting on and got the turtle headed into it.

It overfilled the bucket, with its hind part sticking out the top. The turtle twisted and squirmed and fought like a tiger and let it be known that it was an unhappy camper.

I managed to get the two 5-gallon buckets to the car—one with fish and the other with the turtle. I put the bucket of fish in the trunk of the car. I was afraid to put the turtle in the trunk, for fear it would mess up my signal taillight wiring. So I put the bucket in the floorboard of the car on the passenger's side. I drove with my left hand and held that turtle down with my right.

I asked myself, "Is the meat I'll get out of this turtle worth the trouble?" I really had no idea what I was about to get myself into.

It was dark when I got home, which was not unusual. Evelyn, happy I was back safely, met me in the garage with a bundle of papers, a bread pan, a knife, and a pair of catfish skinners, and then hurried back inside, not wishing to see the poor little fish.

I put the fish on the papers and removed the turtle's head, which dropped among the fish with its mouth open, probably silently cussing me. I laid the turtle on its back, so it could "kick the bucket" while I skinned the fish.

I always skinned blue gill the same way I skinned catfish and then fried them whole. That was faster for me than scaling or filleting them, and it caused less waste.

I soon had the fish cleaned and gave them their first wash out at the nearby hydrant. Evelyn took them to the kitchen sink for a final wash before icing them down.

I somewhat dreaded getting that turtle ready for the skillet. I needed a clean place to work, so I turned a five-gallon bucket on its side and started raking the fish heads and other waste into the bucket with my right hand. Suddenly I felt pain like I'd never felt before. I looked down and saw the head of that turtle clamped down on my trigger finger between the first and second joint. For the first time in my life, I realized what real pain was. I saw stars. Remembering my aunts' warning, I fervently wished it would thunder. I thought I was tough, but actually I felt faint. I grasped that head with my left hand and pulled and twisted. That only added to the pain.

Those pliers-like fish skinners saved the day. One side of the handle was much like a screwdriver. With that handle in my left hand, I was able to pry the turtle's mouth open enough to remove my finger, which was still intact. The realization that my finger would be all right helped relieve the pain.

The terrible fear that I might lose part of my finger had taken all the desire for turtle meat out of me, even after I saw my finger had survived the ordeal. I dumped that turtle in the bucket along with the fish cleanings. I put them in the trunk of the car and headed for Johnson's Lot. There, I wouldn't have to bury the fish cleanings. Varmints would come off the mountain and consume them.

I wasn't sure what to do with the turtle. I decided that by the light of the silvery moon, I'd take it to the edge of the woods and leave it. On the way, being somewhat of a religious person, I decided I should say a little something on behalf of this turtle and all turtles. I had attended many funerals and was amazed at the ability of men of the cloth to put the deceased over in the Glory Land.

I placed the turtle on the ground, and as I did so, I felt a sharp pain in my finger, as well as a dull pain that lingered.

With renewed disgust, I said, "May your soul rest in pieces."

[Author's note: Now for all you animal lovers out there, let me say that I have reformed in my old age. My dear, late wife, Evelyn, had a gentle influence on me over the years. I stopped hunting many years ago and have no wish to harm any animal (although I still love to fish when my bones tell me they'll bite). Even as I write, there is a squirrel on one of the tomato plants in my garden near the carport, and it's helping itself to a juicy tomato. I have decided that there are plenty for both of us, so it can just enjoy its snack.]

Squirrels in Johnson's Lot were not so fortunate. Their plentiful numbers afforded us many a tasty squirrel dinner. But that was a long time ago. Things have changed a lot since then, in so many ways it is mind-boggling for me, as I turn ninety.

I recently visited the area that was Johnson's Lot. It is on land now owned by my son, Ray. I found it somewhat sad to find that it no longer has any appearance of a park or a lot. It has reverted to nature. It is full of stove-pipe saplings and larger trees. The creek still flows, now under overhanging briers and bushes.

Here and there are signs of the past: a few rotting fence posts and barbed wire running through a tree more than a foot in diameter. Anyone not knowing could hardly believe that in times past, this lot was a place of usefulness and beauty. As she does with all of us, Nature has again reclaimed a place once filled with frolicking children and roaming livestock as her own.

* * *

Trading Days

Trading and buying and selling were in my blood from way back. Even before my first sale, I enjoyed hearing my dad strike a bargain whenever he was angling to buy anything—whether a mule or some feed or provisions.

I had my own first taste of bargaining and selling around 1926, at the age of six. I wanted a dog so badly I could taste it. Dad said bluntly, "Son, a dog is more trouble than it is worth."

I responded quickly, "If you will get me one, I promise I'll take care of it."

Thoughtfully, Dad said, "Well, Mel Reynolds told me he has a young terrier sort of a dog that he wants to give away because 'all he wants to do is dig in the yard for mice and moles, and so far he hasn't dug out his first one.'"

"Dad, get it for me," I pleaded. "I'll name him Jack, and as he digs holes, I'll fill them up."

Dad got Jack for me. Mel Reynolds wasn't lying about him being a digger. He dug one hole after another. By the end of the second day, I had had my fill of filling up holes.

Aaron Lambert happened by and said to me, "I bet that dog would make a good squirrel dog. What would you take for him?"

Dad was standing nearby. Remembering some of Dad's trading sessions, I stood up tall and asked, "Mr. Lambert, what will you give me for him?"

Mr. Lambert replied, "For that dog, I'll give you a brand new one-dollar bill with George Washington's picture on it."

Dad gave me a nod of approval. I said, "Mr. Lambert, you have bought a dog named Jack."

I soon had another lesson in buying and selling, although I had to endure some severe disapproval first. On May 30 that same year, our family visited Grandpa and Grandma Millikan, who lived six miles north of Golconda. Mom had a number of younger sisters there. The Millikans owned a Model T Ford. In the afternoon, the sisters suggested taking Mom and me to the cemetery where Aunt Nora was buried. She had died in 1918 of influenza.

We were gathered around Aunt Nora's grave. Aunt Hattie, who, as the most pleasant of the group, couldn't talk without smiling, took on the saddest look I had ever seen on a person. With a mournful voice and her face dripping with tears, Aunt Hattie said, "I sure would like to see Nora again."

I was scampering around the cemetery, much like Jack would have if he had been there. Even though I could sell a dog, at that age I had few other refined social skills. I could hardly stand still. Without one thought about how it sounded, I eagerly said in response to Aunt Hattie's sad statement, "Let's scratch her up then!"

No one said a word. All eyes turned on me. Had I heard of the "unpardonable sin," I would have known that I had committed it. I didn't say anything on the way back to Grandpa's.

Since I was the oldest grandson, Grandpa and Grandma and my aunts loved to spoil me. They asked Mom and Dad if I could spend the following week with them. Mom and Dad agreed.

Realizing I was still feeling glum and guilty from the previous day's incident in the cemetery, Grandma and Aunt Eva decided that they would take me to Golconda in that Model T Ford to cheer me up. Before we left, they gathered together some eggs, butter, and buttermilk they said they were going to trade with in town. After they had sold their goods, we went into a store that had on display bolt after bolt of cloth of all colors and designs. They asked me to pick out some cloth for them to make me a shirt. It took me about two seconds to pick out some red cloth, which they bought with the money they had just earned from the sale of their goods. So at the end of my week's visit, I went home with a new red shirt, which I wore proudly until I outgrew it. Even if I had not already learned it, the lesson was clear: selling and trading could reap some wonderful benefits.

Throughout my youth and early adulthood, and then in the Navy during World War II, I continued to refine my selling skills while selling or trading one thing or another. However, after I returned home from the Navy, my focus turned to older cars, which I regularly bought, fixed up a bit, and sold for a profit.

My brother-in-law Stan was a school principal in the Fairview Heights area. His hobby and pastime also was buying and repairing used cars to sell. Once in a while he would buy an extra good "old clunker" worth the money and let me have it at his cost. He brought me one such car. It looked good and ran well, among other good qualities. But once in a while, it wouldn't start. Stan told me that all one had to do to get it to start was to take a broomstick, which was carried in the backseat, and punch a certain part under the hood—a procedure I learned would work.

I put this car in front of my house out near the road—my "showcase"—with a "For Sale" sign on it. A young man around eighteen years old stopped by with his mother to look at the car. The young man gave me the impression he was a "know-it-all." He knew how to start the car, raise the hood, and listen closely for engine imperfections. He checked for defects in the transmission.

I had a little trouble getting his attention to tell him about the use of the broomstick. He paid no attention. He said, "You can't tell me anything about cars. I'm a mechanic."

As I signed the car over to the "mechanic's" mother, she said, "His dad runs a garage in Golconda." I felt somewhat relieved.

Since then, to people who know the story, when I've heard all about something that I want to know, I say, "You can't tell me anything about that. I'm a mechanic."

Along about that time, I got in trouble buying a car in which another man, Louis Gibbs, was interested. First, I'll tell you about Louis Gibbs. He was the son of Elijah Gibbs, who had drawn water with a pole instead of a rope when I had met him years earlier. At that time, Elijah was already a fairly old, cantankerous man. The personalities of Elijah and Louis were a good illustration of "like father, like son," as you will see.

Louis had worked out a retirement in Northern Illinois and then moved back to Southern Illinois. He lived in a one-room cabin near his father's homeplace, where Louis's sister, Sarah, and her husband, Lonnie Hyden, lived. Louis's cabin was about a mile from our place. He raised a big garden, seemed happy, and lived well.

I hadn't really formed an opinion of Louis, but that changed one day when I went to see him for just a neighborly call. He was sitting under a large black oak tree, with a .22 rifle across his knees. Louis was friendly enough. Neither of us made mention of the rifle. I didn't think it was any of my business—I just thought perhaps he planned to shoot a young rabbit to fry for dinner.

It wasn't long until he lifted the rifle and shot. He called out, "Seventy-one," and then explained that he had shot seventy-one birds out of a scrawny cherry tree. The cherries didn't appear fit to eat. The birds were all kinds, including songbirds. I don't have to tell you how that made me feel.

Not long after that, Louis paid me a visit. He drove up in his good-running 1930 Chevy. From the moment he stepped out of his car, I could tell he was hot under the collar about something.

I greeted him, in what I hoped was a soothing voice, "Good morning, Mr. Gibbs. Is anything wrong?"

He stated the obvious. "I'm angry."

Remembering his apparent willingness to shoot whatever angered him, I said quickly, "Not at me, I hope."

He replied, "Maybe yes and maybe no. I'm mostly mad at my brother-in-law, Lonnie Hyden. He sold you a car that he knew I wanted to trade him out of."

Somewhat relieved, I asked, "Mr. Gibbs, did you make Lonnie an offer?"

He snapped, "No, but I made it plain that I was interested, and to get his attention, I told him I might give him my car and a hundred dollars for his car."

I inquired cautiously, "And what did Lonnie say to that?"

With disgust in his voice, Mr. Gibbs said, "He didn't say anything—he just walked away. The next thing I knew, he had sold it to you. I would like to know if you knew I was interested in that car."

I assured him, "No, Mr. Gibbs, I had no idea you wanted that car. Lonnie came down and asked if I'd be interested in buying his car—he said he had a Studebaker spotted that he and Sarah liked very much. He said, 'Kestner, make me an offer.'

"I said, 'Lonnie, tell me how much you want for your car.' He told me. I paid him, and he went happily on his way."

Relenting a bit, Mr. Gibbs said, "Kestner, I have no grounds to be mad at you, but I plan to stay mad at Lonnie. I may have given him more cash for his car than you did."

Seeing an opportunity, I said, "I'm sorry you didn't get the car, Mr. Gibbs. But cheer up—you can still buy or trade for it."

He brightened considerably. "Kestner, do you mean that?"

I replied, "Yes, I do. Your saying you *might* give me your car and a hundred dollars doesn't excite me. But if you say, 'I *will* give you my car and *fifty* dollars,' you have bought the car of your dreams."

Mr. Gibbs grabbed my hand and shook it vigorously as he said, "I'll give you fifty dollars and my car." That clinched the deal. But it still didn't change my opinion of him.

I don't know how many older cars I bought for less than $300, tuned with new points, sparkplugs, and wires, and sold for a few more dollars than I had invested. That hobby supplemented my beginning teacher's pay of $150 per month for eight months per year.

Why I came by one particular car, I'll never know. A young man around twenty years of age drove up in a blue

1932 Chevy. He said, "My dad told me to bring this car out here and give it to you."

Puzzled, I asked, "Give it to me? For how much?"

He said, "Free—for nothing."

In amazement, I said, "I look for bargains, but I don't expect to have things given to me. Who is your dad?"

He told me his dad's name and added, "He works at a bank in Harrisburg where you get your check cashed each month. My mom is dead. My dad is sweet on a woman whose daughter is a student of yours. I know she speaks highly of you. So maybe that's a clue. But it might make more sense to say, 'Dad got a new car and gave me his old one, and this one was in the way.'" [Would you say this boy was a free talker?]

Over the years, as I traded old cars, my mom would warn me to always be fair, honest, and truthful with people I dealt with. That I tried to do.

Each Saturday morning, I took Mom to Harrisburg to do her shopping. Oftentimes, I'd be driving a different clunker I'd bought or traded for. Mom took an interest in what I was driving. The car I was driving one Saturday morning was a small Buick I'd bought the evening before. It looked good on the driver's side, where a pole light had illuminated it. However, on the passenger's side, there was some sideswipe damage that I didn't see until the next morning.

Mom got into the car smiling and commented, "I see you have a different car."

I replied, "Yes, I bought it yesterday."

Mom waited patiently for further comment. After a little while, I said, "I bought it after dark."

Mom laughed and said, "You may have to sell it after dark."

That car turned out to be one of my better buys. I took

my time and taught myself how to do body work on it. It wasn't a first-class job, but it did make it look better. I used what I learned on future cars, if needed.

One of my more unusual deals involved a car I bought from a man named Von Linnen, who lived near Somerset in Saline County. It was a small- to medium-sized car that was underwater in a pond when I bought it. Von Linnen had left it in neutral where the ground sloped toward the pond. The car rolled into the pond and was completely submerged for a day or two. Von Linnen thought the car was ruined and planned to leave it in the pond. I had seen the car before and knew it was pretty good-looking. I asked him what he would take for it.

Von Linnen said, "Make me an offer."

I replied, "I'll give you fifty dollars for it in the pond, or I'll give you a hundred dollars for it if you will take your tractor and pull it out for me."

He quickly closed the deal by saying, "I'll let you have it for a hundred dollars, and I'll pull it up onto higher ground."

I watched Von Linnen and his son hook up the car to the tractor, pull the car out, and park it in the hot August sun. I paid for the car and told Von Linnen I'd be after it in a couple of days.

Two days later, a neighbor took me over to Von Linnen's house in his pickup truck with a chain to pull the car home. No one was home at the Von Linnen's.

The neighbor backed the pickup to the car and had the chain hooked to the rear bumper of the pickup. He was about to hook onto the car as I got behind the wheel of the car. I was somewhat surprised when I saw the dome light was burning because the door was open. I got the surprise of my life when the horn worked and was further amazed when the car started when I touched the starter switch. I drove that car home. If you don't believe this account, I understand. I wouldn't have believed it either if I hadn't witnessed it.

When I got home, I decided to drain the oil and water from the crankcase and put in new oil. After completing those tasks, I sat in one of the three chairs under the spreading maple tree and pondered what needed to be done next.

I was hardly settled in my chair when an older six-cylinder Chevy came limping up my driveway. It was smoking, which caused me to believe it was a heavy oil user. It had an unnatural quiver as if it wasn't firing on one cylinder and was missing on another, which could have been the result of a number of things. The most likely diagnosis was that the car was a candidate for an overhaul.

Two fellows in their mid-fifties piled out. One had a cigar he was chewing and puffing on. The other had a big chew of tobacco in his jaw.

One of them asked, "Mind if we join you?"

Although curious, I replied, "Please do."

Then the other said, "I'm Joe, and this is Tom."

We shook hands, sat down, and took a long look at each other. My first impression of them was that they were slaphappy and fun-loving guys who had had enough to drink to make them want to do anything wild and exciting.

Tom led off by saying, "We know you, and we don't really know you. We want to know you better. As a man who will buy and trade for anything, you are a man after our own hearts."

Joe chimed in with a grin. "We bought this car this morning to trade to you, so you can fix it up and make yourself a pretty penny."

Pointing at my newly purchased pond car, Tom said, "We like that car and will trade for it without asking any questions."

I replied, "Ask anything you wish about that car. I'll answer truthfully anything that you ask."

Tom said, "You don't ask any questions about our car, and we won't ask any questions about yours."

With an inward smile, I replied, "That's okay with me." All the while knowing that I wouldn't be buying their poor excuse for a car, I continued, "However, I'd like to know whether you both can drive."

They both said that they could. Joe asked, "Why do you want to know?"

I answered, "Your car may need a complete overhaul. I do only tune-ups and minor repairs."

They looked disappointed, but it didn't slow them down. Tom said, without skipping a beat, "If you don't want to trade for our car, perhaps we can buy yours. You may not know it, but you have a name for pricing your cars so poor people can buy them."

Joe didn't like Tom's suggestion that they were poor, so he quickly added, "We are not lacking in that old 'green stuff.' We could pay cash for two cars like that one."

Smiling, I said, "I understand you, gentlemen. You, same as I, like to feel when you spend a dollar, that you are getting your money's worth. Tell me what you will give me for this car that has captured your eye."

They looked at each other. Tom said, "Joe, shoot him a price."

Joe looked at me and asked, "What dollar amount did you have in mind?"

I asked, "How does five hundred dollars sound?"

They both jumped as if they had been shot. However, I felt their reaction would have been the same if I'd quoted a price much lower. Shaking his head, Tom said, "We are too far apart to do business. We thought you sold cars for no more than three hundred dollars. That is the amount we are willing to pay."

I explained calmly, "When I have a three-hundred-dollar car, I sell it for three hundred dollars. When I have a better car, I ask more."

Joe took on a bargaining tone. "Most traders will come down some when their arm is twisted. I'm twisting your arm. What do you say to that?"

In response, I said, "If a buyer is really interested, he'll raise his offer some. What do you say to that?"

Tiring of our dickering, Tom said, "We are getting nowhere fast. Quote us your rock-bottom price."

I replied, "If you will come up from three hundred dollars to four hundred, I'll come down from five hundred to four hundred. If we were playing checkers, I'd say 'It's your move.'"

Joe looked at Tom and asked, "What do you say, Tom?"

Tom, with a mixture of relief and disgust, said, "Joe, give the man four hundred dollars, and let's take that pile of junk back to the junkyard and thank the owner for the loan of it."

They both quickly returned to the jolly mood they were in when they arrived. One of them said, "It's been a pleasure doing business with you."

The other quickly agreed. "Same here. I haven't had so much fun since the old sow ate my little brother."

They both laughed uproariously. I smiled when I recalled what my dad would have said about that remark. He would have said, "My grandfather fell out of the cradle laughing at that one." What I really laughed about was that I had relieved these two shysters of some of their "green stuff."

Trading was a pleasant pastime for me for many years. I think most times I made a good return on my trading, although I'm sure I got skinned a few times. But that's all in the game. As time went by, however, cars became more sophisticated with their computerized mechanics, and it was also harder to find the bargains I once had found rather easily. I declared myself retired from trading over twenty years ago and now content myself with recalling the glories of my trading days.

* * *

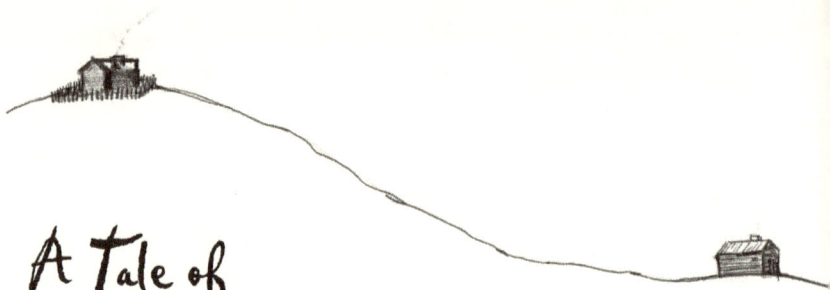

A Tale of Two Houses

My grandfather, Jonathan Wallace, was a man of many talents. He was a Civil War veteran, a blacksmith, and a justice of the peace. As a justice of the peace, I have been told he heard cases of various kinds of theft, attempted murder, and rape. On the lighter side, he married couples now and then. He was also a farmer, and he ran a thrashing machine powered by a steam-powered engine. (In modern times, the thrashing machine was replaced by the combine.)

Grandpa had a total of fourteen children—five boys and nine girls. One son, George, and twin daughters, Cindy and Bendy, all died under twenty years of age and are buried in the Wallace Family Cemetery near the foot of Womble Mountain.

Around 1880, Grandpa moved his family from their home six or seven miles north of Golconda, Illinois, to a section of land he bought that included a part of the west side of Womble Mountain in Southern Saline County, just north of the Pope County line. For those who might not know, a section of land equals 640 acres.

On this land was a house with an extra-large living room and an equally large kitchen, with a fireplace in each, using the same chimney. A 32-foot by 12-foot side room was on the west side of the two rooms. Doors from the kitchen and living rooms went into the side room, with outside doors to match, making for good ventilation.

Grandpa set about to improve the property. Off from the kitchen, he built a large guest bedroom, later called the "organ room," and an L-shaped porch extending east and south. At the end of the south porch was a deep well that furnished plenty of good cold water.

A picket fence enclosed the grounds around the house. In the back, inside the fence, Grandpa built a large smokehouse used for salt curing and smoking pork: hams, shoulders, and side meat. The hams and shoulders, after being salt cured and smoked, were stored in oak barrels. The family kept a winter's supply of flour and meal in barrels, also.

[Speaking of barrels, it is told that a somewhat religious neighbor, who strongly believed in prayer to help him get his winter's supply of food, prayed: "Lord, please send me a barrel of flour, a barrel of meal, a barrel of hams, a barrel of salt, and a barrel of pepper." With sudden awareness, he exclaimed, "Hell, Lord, that is too much pepper!"]

Also inside the fence was a large, underground multi-purpose cellar. Grandpa built bins for storing potatoes, apples, and turnips, as well as shelves to store fruit the family had canned. The space was also used as a storm cellar. The family was afraid of tornadoes and used the cellar as their safe haven whenever storms threatened.

There were two chicken houses, one on the north side of the house and one on the south. Geese were kept in the south one. Some of the fine, down-like feathers were plucked each early summer to make feather beds and pillows.

Grandpa acquired eighty acres of good bottom land north of Rudement—it was referred to as the Rudement

Bottoms. He gave that eighty acres to my dad, William Francis Wallace. He divided the original 640 acres among the other three living sons. His thinking was that the daughters would marry and have homes. That almost worked out well, as you will later see.

Grandpa died in 1893. Grandma, Jane Wallace, died in 1913, seven years before I was born. My dad, being the oldest of the sons, took over as the head of the family. His position as family leader wasn't questioned. All the family members contributed according to their ability and received according to their need.

Dad was happy with his large yield of corn in the Rudement Bottoms. He fattened hogs for home use and put a number of hogs on the market. He bragged of selling clover seed for sixteen dollars a bushel during World War I, which was quite a handsome sum in those days. The daughters did the housework and helped their brothers with outside work—caring for the orchard and vineyard and planting garden crops.

Dad's brother Lew built a small general store east of the house, just beyond the yard fence closest to the old road. Interesting customers passing through the area were sometimes invited to spend the night with the Wallaces. One man who had worked on the Panama Canal had some tall tales to tell. On finding the family interested, off and on throughout the evening and the next morning, he would bring up the subject again by saying "Another little thing about the canal. . . ." That became a family saying—"another little thing about the canal." I heard it mentioned by one of the few remaining second-generation family members only a short time ago, over a hundred years later.

Two marriages resulted from one overnight guest. A Mr. Reinhart from Southeast Missouri fell in love with

Aunt Sarah. Months later, they married. Aunt Rosie, the youngest of Grandpa's daughters, was visiting her sister Sarah and met and married a Mr. Affolder, thus producing cousins for the second generation of Wallaces — but that is another story.

The youngest member of the family, Uncle Courty (shortened from "Courtland"), got a nickname that stayed with him for many years. The family tale is as follows:

A man of Polish birth passed the store often in a horse-drawn buggy. When he wanted the horse to move on faster, where we would have said "Giddy-up," what he said to the horse in Polish sounded like "Coo duke." Uncle Courty, then about ten years of age, ran along beside the buggy and sang out, "Coo duke, coo duke, coo duke." This man, for fun or jest, leaped out of the buggy with his buggy whip drawn and exclaimed, "I'll coo duke you!" He took a few leaps toward Uncle Courty, who was by then hitting the high places getting away. For many years, his friends addressed him by saying, "How are you doing today, Coo Duke?"

There is no end to the jokes the fun-loving Wallaces played on their welcome guests. For example, it is told that one evening before bedtime, with an overnight guest present, Aunt Florence asked my dad, "Willie, do you still have that old .45 pistol that is easy on the trigger — all you have to do is touch the trigger and it goes off?" Dad replied, "Yes, Florence, I still have it. I sleep with it under my pillow every night."

Everyone went to bed a short time later. The guest was in the guest room. All was quiet for a minute. Then came the most nerve-racking, ungodly scream the family had ever heard. A voice wailed out, "Willie, bring a light in here." Dad and Aunt Sarah rushed in, with a lamp turned down low.

Dad asked, with seeming great concern, "What on earth is wrong? Did you have a bad dream?"

The terrified guest blurted out, "Bad dream, hell. I haven't been asleep yet. I think that damn .45 you were talking about has gotten in *my* bed somehow and slipped down to where it could blow my butt off!"

Dad said calmingly, "Just hold still, and I'll reach in easy-like and get it."

It wasn't a .45. It was a monkey wrench put in the bed to fool him. Dad managed to slip it out of the bed without the guest seeing it, and the guest was never told the real story.

...

Both Aunt Florence and Uncle Lew, who was tall, slender, and mild-mannered like Abraham Lincoln, never married. They lived their entire lives at the homeplace. They didn't lack for opportunity; neither were they antisocial. The single life appeared to be right for them.

Life went on for them in perfect harmony. Aunt Florence took pride in acting as a matchmaker. Uncle Lew was a justice of the peace and prayed for and practiced justice and peace for all.

Uncle Courty built on a hundred-acre tract of land 300 yards south of the homeplace. Dad sold his eighty acres in the Rudement Bottoms and bought the house and farm from Uncle Courty. Uncle Courty then bought land from Uncle Lew and built a house about 300 yards east of the homeplace.

Dad and Mom had four boys and two girls. Uncle Courty and Aunt Nellie had five boys and one girl. So with twelve nieces and nephews nearby, Uncle Lew and Aunt Florence had no need of children of their own. As many jokes as they liked to play on others, they played no jokes on us. We were treated as kings and queens, which led us to visit frequently. The homeplace continued to be a hub for all the Wallaces — all of Aunt Florence and Uncle Lew's brothers and sisters, the twelve of us cousins, and other nieces and nephews that they saw less often but thought no less of.

Uncle Courty's boys, being older than Dad's boys, left the area to find work. In November of 1940, I had to do the same.

Uncle Lew and Dad were in poor health when I left. I wondered if I would see them again alive. The following May, Dad died. I came home from Michigan for the funeral. Uncle Lew died a short time later. I didn't ask for time off from my defense job to come home again so soon.

Aunt Florence was crushed at the death of her brother Lew. She had fallen and broken her hip but was getting around on crutches at the time of his death.

Mom wrote a sad letter to me in Michigan. She said that Uncle Lew had failed to make a will to give to Aunt Florence the homeplace and the twenty-seven acres he owned. He had never doubted that the homeplace would continue to be hers for the rest of her life. Mom told me that some of the heirs thought Aunt Florence should go to a nursing home and the place be sold, with the proceeds distributed to the heirs. A process was underway. Mom wanted to know if we could do anything.

I wrote to Mom to suggest that she go to the lawyer in charge of handling the case to tell him the sad story and explain that Uncle Lew never dreamed of Aunt Florence not being allowed to live out her life there. I urged her to point out that Aunt Florence was a semi-invalid because of a broken hip, but that she was still able to live alone with Mom's free assistance as a loyal sister-in-law.

The elderly attorney, whose heart was on the right side, saw Mom's point of view. Somehow the advertising of the sale was meager. I turned in a sealed bid and bought the place for a song. The heirs were left scratching their heads, and Aunt Florence was one happy woman.

About five years later, when I returned home from the Navy in 1946 after World War II, Aunt Florence thanked me generously for buying the place and wanted to know how much rent she should pay me. I told her just enough to pay the taxes and light bill—about $7.50 per month. The light bill ran $3.00 per month. She said she would be willing to pay me more, but I said that would be plenty. She gratefully accepted my terms.

Aunt Florence called me "Son" from the time I was a small child. She never stopped. One time she asked, "Son, whose place is it to cut the weeds just inside and outside the yard fence?"

It came as a surprise to her when I said, "Oh, it is my place."

Then she asked, "Son, who do you plan to get to do it, since you are too busy?"

I replied, "Jack."

Since she didn't know any Jack, she asked, "Jack who, Son?"

I replied, "Jack Frost."

She laughed and forgot the weeds for the time being. I really got Aunt Florence's mind off the weeds by telling her that I planned to tear down the old smokehouse, the two chicken houses, and the store house, all of which were in poor repair, and use the material to build a solid deck on her house's rafters and then put a new roof on the house.

Aunt Florence, not even trying to disguise her eagerness, quickly said, "Son, the roof isn't too bad. It only leaks when it rains. When are you going to start?" With a twinkle in her eye, she said, "I guess you'll get Jack to help you."

I replied, "Aunt Florence, I'll do most of the work myself, with the help of Gaylord." (Gaylord is my youngest brother, ten years younger than I am.)

The four structures came down rather easily. On the homeplace, we removed the old brittle shingles, along with the lathe, down to the rafters. We then replaced them with a solid decking.

Gaylord and I worked well together putting on the new green shingles. The pitch of the roof was gentle, so there was no fear of slipping. I showed Gaylord how the shingles went on. We then fell into an easy rhythm—he put the shingles in place, and I nailed them.

Next I put new life in the old weatherboarding on the sides of the house by first painting it with one quart of white paint to three quarts of linseed oil. Then I painted the entire house white. My payoff was the thrill of seeing how pleased Aunt Florence was when she first saw the house afterwards. When Aunt Florence viewed the finished job after the green shutters went on, she was never happier in her life.

Thereafter, Gaylord and I were doing some touch-up painting below the roof where the porch rafters connected with the house. Aunt Florence was sitting on her porch observing. At each rafter, wasps had built small nests that housed four or five wasps. Gaylord was so afraid of the wasps buzzing around that I was somewhat displeased with the amount of work I was getting out of him. Impatiently and repeatedly, I advised him to just keep slapping the paint on, to dab the nest with a brush wet with paint, and to swat the wasps flying around with the brush. Gaylord did more flailing around than painting. Finally, exasperated at all the delays, I exclaimed,

"Gaylord, if you don't bother them, they won't bother you!"

Aunt Florence felt I was being too hard on poor, little, six-foot-tall Gaylord. She sat there with a disapproving look on her face.

Gaylord reluctantly went back to work. Little did I know that a wasp soon lit on my collar. It crawled all around my collar, to the amusement of Gaylord and Aunt Florence, neither of whom said a word. Eventually, it crawled down inside my collar. When my shirt touched the wasp, it began to sting me. I came off my stepladder like a madman. The wasp stung me repeatedly while I did an Indian dance all around the yard, and it didn't stop until I took my shirt off.

Of course Aunt Florence and Gaylord enjoyed the scene immensely. I never saw two people laugh harder in my life. I didn't crack a smile. Somehow we managed to finish the job without further ado.

...

By this time, Aunt Florence thought I could wave a magic wand and put up a house. She asked, "Son, do you think you could build a two-room house where the old store building stood and rent it to my schoolmate, Minnie Seets? She would be a lot of company to me."

Reluctant to commit to such a project, I said, "No, you could move her in with you. This house is big enough for two."

She hastily replied, "Son, I don't want anyone in the house with me."

Along about that time, in 1947 or so, Lonnie Hull, an honest and hard-working man, bought and set up an old used sawmill about two miles south of the Saline-Pope County line. He hired Gaylord, then seventeen, to work for him. Poor lumber sales and trouble with his mill made it difficult for Lonnie to pay his work hands. Lonnie owed

Gaylord several dollars and asked if he could pay him in lumber.

Gaylord asked me if I needed any lumber. I told him to ask Lonnie how much cash he would ask, in addition to what he owed Gaylord, to deliver enough lumber to frame up and box in a 14-by-28-foot two-room house. I gave him a material list as follows: 2x8s for sills, 2x4s for studding and rafters, 2x6s for ceiling joists, and enough wide boards to deck and box it in.

Lonnie quoted a fair price, and Gaylord and I accepted it. The lumber was delivered and stacked near where the old store had stood. Aunt Florence was thrilled. She thought I was planning to build a house for her friend, Minnie. I told her the lumber was to trade or resell. At that time, I wasn't really sure what I'd do with the lumber. I didn't want to get her hopes up.

Aunt Florence sat on her porch and watched my every move whenever I came by the homeplace to do a little work. One day, I was doing a little cleaning near where the lumber was stacked. She called out from the porch, "Son, are you going to cut down my rose bush?"

I wasn't in the mood to explain my every move, so I simply answered, "No."

Aunt Florence had been hard-of-hearing for some time. Not understanding my first response, she asked again.

Again, I answered, "No."

The third time she asked, instead of going to the porch and telling her I was just cleaning up a little, I acted like a juvenile and shook my head long and hard. Her answer was fitting: "Son, you don't need to shake the hair off your head!"

A few days later, I was going home from Harrisburg and picked up a Mr. Langford, who was hitchhiking. He looked to be about seventy-five years old and was blind in his left eye. However, he seemed to have plenty of get-up-and-go. He said he lived alone and had recently moved into a big, old two-story house not far from Rudement and wasn't very well satisfied. He said he needed only two rooms. To him, the big house was spooky.

I told Mr. Langford if he was a carpenter, we could work together and build him a two-room house. I said I would give him six months' free rent for his labor and then charge him only fifteen dollars a month thereafter.

Without hesitation, he said, "I'm a carpenter. I'll take you up on that offer. Where do you live? When do we start?"

It was agreed that I would pick him up along with his tools the following morning. After that, he said he'd have no trouble hitchhiking to my place.

Mr. Langford and I worked well together. I suggested, since he was more experienced, that he take the lead. That pleased him well.

One day he told me about the time he was working for a stingy, cantankerous man, for whom he was putting in an oak threshold. He was using slim finish nails on wood he said was "as hard as hammered hell." As the man was looking on, Mr. Langford said he bent about every other nail and had to use another. He told me the man complained, "Mr. Langford, those nails cost five cents a pound."

Mr. Langford said, "I took off my nail apron and said, 'Mister, you can get someone else to drive your nails.'" That was all the warning I needed about his touchy side.

Near the end of one trying day, Mr. Langford set a window. On one side of the window, he had failed to cut off the extension used in fitting the window. As a result, the window was cockeyed. I observed, as he viewed the window, that he was tired and angry—ready to throw up his hands and quit. He asked, with disgust in his voice, "How does that look to you?"

I lied, "Just fine. That is an okay job."

He looked shocked and said, "What?" He thought a few seconds and said, "I'll see you in the morning."

As soon as he was out of sight, I took the window out and reset it correctly. The next morning, Mr. Langford took a long look at the window and commented, "That window looks better than it did last night."

I said, "That is because you have the sweat and sawdust out of your eyes this morning."

He gave me a little grin that said, "You're not fooling me."

When the house was complete, Mr. Langford said, "Kestner, I have enjoyed working with you, but since I have a new lady friend in town, I want to live close to her. If we can agree on a cash settlement for my labor, I would be much obliged to you."

I asked, "What would you suggest?"

He replied, "How about six months' rent at fifteen dollars per month—ninety dollars?" I gave him a hundred-dollar bill, and we parted friends.

In a short time, Minnie Seets, who was in her eighties, moved in the little two-room house, just as Aunt Florence had planned all along. Minnie and Aunt Florence were happy to be close neighbors. However, in about two years, Mrs. Seets' health worsened, and her family moved her to Harrisburg to be nearer to them and the doctor.

John Hancock, who was just out of the Army and newly married, rented the little house. He worked long hours at a rock quarry in Hardin County. John's wife, Lucille, was lonesome. Aunt Florence took her under her wing, and they spent many happy hours together.

It was years later, after John became a well-known and respected minister, that he told me he had spent the happiest days of his life in that little house, and that he had taken his grandson to show him where he and his grandmother had started their happy life together.

Over more than a forty-year span, many singles and a few couples lived in the little house. I don't even remember them all. However, another couple in particular stands out.

John Henry Gibbs and his second wife, Fern, lived there a long time. John liked the ring of "John Henry," so that was what we called him. In fact, the little house became known within the family as "the John Henry house."

John Henry and Fern were uneducated, and both had been brought up in hard times. John and his first wife had lived somewhere in Southeast Missouri. John spoke of chopping cotton, which involved small pay and hard work. He also hewed crossties with a broadax.

John Henry told me that he and his first wife and young son needed a place to live near where he had a tie-making job. Nearby, there happened to be an old rundown house where no one lived. He said they moved into it and fixed it up some and lived there for two or three years.

John Henry said one day a big-shot–looking man drove up in a bright shiny car, jumped out, and bellowed, "What in the hell do you think you are doing 'squatting' on this land?"

Continuing with his story, John Henry said, "That went all over me—made me mad as hell. I got right up close to that so-and-so, shook my finger in his face, and said, 'I'm just going to say this once. I'm not doing any damn squatting on this place. We have an outhouse out back.'"

John Henry said that his first wife, as well as his second baby, died in Missouri during childbirth. He and his nine-year-old son went on the best they could. His son became big enough to pick cotton with him. Late one fall, when the cotton-picking season ended, John Henry heard of a tie-making job in Union County, Illinois. He took his son, their cotton sacks, and his broadax and got a job making crossties. He said they didn't have enough money to rent a house—they just cut some poles, opened up their seven-foot cotton-picking sacks, and made a tent to live in until he drew his first pay. They then rented a house and got by pretty well.

I don't know the particulars of how John Henry and Fern met and decided to get married. He got acquainted with her in Anna, Illinois. She was cross-eyed and had a speech problem. Aside from that, when one got to know her, she appeared to be a rather likeable person. After they moved into the little house, I observed that Fern liked to cook, keep house, and help John Henry make a garden. She took pride in helping Aunt Florence.

I respected John Henry and Fern, and they held me in high regard. They also liked my mother. Mom did little things for them, feeling she was fulfilling the scripture that says, "Inasmuch as ye have done it unto one of the least of these my brethren, ye have done it unto me." Mom took Fern to a little nearby church at Mountain Grove, where Fern made a profession of faith. That made a noticeable change in her life and had a good effect on John Henry, as well.

John Henry was slow to warm up to people. Uncle Courty, who lived 200 yards east of John Henry, told me this incident. The road to Uncle Courty's mailbox ran within thirty feet of John Henry's porch, where John Henry sat a great deal. Day after day, Uncle Courty said, he passed Mr. Gibbs and spoke or nodded to him but got no response. One day he decided to try harder to be a little friendlier. He had a pair of binoculars hung about his neck. He had been looking at birds and one thing and another. In front of John Henry's house, a plane went over. Trying to be friendly, Uncle Courty remarked, "Mr. Gibbs, when I look at that plane through these glasses, it looks much bigger and closer."

Uncle Courty said that John Henry replied tartly, "I don't believe a damn word of it."

John Henry was talented in many ways. One time, he developed a cough that hung on a long time. He said he could cure it if he had some whiskey, rock candy, and scotch emulsion. But no one would get the whiskey for him. I told him I was a Sunday school superintendent and didn't want anyone to see me in a place that sold whiskey. However, it wasn't long until I was in Sikeston, Missouri, and I got him a pint of whiskey. At a drug store in Harrisburg, I got him the rock candy and the scotch emulsion. John Henry then made his cough syrup and cured his cough.

...

My wife, Evelyn, and I, along with our two children, LeAnn and Ray, lived a short distance up the highway, in a house I had built on the upper part of the land I had gotten with Uncle Lew's estate. LeAnn and Ray had a shortcut path they used often to visit Aunt Florence. I drove down frequently to check on her and take her food that Evelyn willingly prepared. (Aunt Florence fixed some of her own food, but a great deal of it was taken to her by my mother or me.) When I'd take food to her, Aunt Florence would tell me to tell Evelyn, "This is just like living in a hotel." She was referring to the times she and Uncle Lew would go down to Dudley, Missouri, in a horse and buggy and spend the night along the way in Cairo, Illinois.

Aunt Florence took a spell of feeling she was too much

of a burden on Mom, Evelyn, and me. She would say, "Son, I want you to take me over to the nursing home in Eldorado and see if I like it."

Trying to discourage this line of thinking, I said, "Aunt Florence, I know you won't like it. There is no use to go and look." She would not let it go, however. Finally I took her. She used one crutch and held on to my shoulder as we walked down the hall of the nursing home. She looked in the first open door and frowned. She did the same at the second. At the third, she said, "Son, there are old, sick people here. Get me out of here as quickly as you can." She never mentioned a nursing home again. She seemed happy and content to live one day at a time at the homeplace.

One hot afternoon, when Aunt Florence was past ninety years old, LeAnn, Ray, and I went down to Aunt Florence's house to do some porch repair. Aunt Florence saw the need and was pleased. She said, "Son, I'll go in and lie down, so I won't get in the way."

I said, "You won't be in the way."

She replied, "Son, it is a little warm out here for me."

LeAnn, Ray, and I went about doing what needed to be done. Rather often we drew a fresh bucket of cold water. Each time, we took Aunt Florence a drink in a little tin cup she liked to drink from. A little half-grown, gold-colored kitten would dart in with us. Aunt Florence would take a few swallows and say with feeling, "Good water!" I took the kitten back out each time.

When I went in a short time later, I was surprised to see that kitten sitting on Aunt Florence's chest. The kitten had its motor running, and Aunt Florence was stroking it tenderly and saying, "Pretty cat, pretty cat, pretty cat." She thanked me for checking on her, and I took the cat out again.

In no more than ten minutes, Ray said, "I'll check on Aunt Florence." He was back immediately and said, "I think Aunt Florence is dead."

LeAnn and I hurried in and viewed her as she lay there with her eyes closed and a little smile on her face. I surmised she had dozed off to sleep and simply stopped breathing. I was both sad and happy—sad that she was gone, but happy she didn't really die alone. She had the kids, her cat, and me with her at the end or at very near the end.

The funeral was well attended by relatives, neighbors, and friends. Aunt Florence, the last of Grandpa's family of fourteen children, was gone. Her only home, the one she loved well, lived on for only a short time thereafter. A tornado blew in from the west and damaged it beyond repair.

I called the insurance company. A friendly adjuster came to assess the damage. I told him he could see the worst of the damage from the back side—the west side. I asked him to follow me, since there might be a mean old snake back there—one that I would likely see before he would.

He was stepping on my heels. I looked back. He was as pale as death. In a weak voice, he said, "Let's go back to the car. I have seen enough." Without saying a word, he took out a checkbook and wrote me a check for $2,500, the full amount of the policy. Feeling it was manna from Heaven, I thanked him.

The state offered me $1,500 for some fill dirt north of the homeplace. I agreed to accept the offer if they would bulldoze the old house off a ways and burn it. They agreed.

The John Henry house outlived its usefulness. There ceased to be a demand for two rooms and an outhouse. A man recently took it down for the lumber.

Although the two houses are no longer there, I pass where they were every time I go to the Wallace Family Cemetery. There in the cemetery, as I make my way to a chair by Evelyn's grave, I walk by the final resting places of those who have gone before: Grandpa and Grandma, Mom and Dad, Aunt Florence, Uncle Courty and Aunt Nellie, Aunt Sarah, Uncle Lew, and several more. I don't believe in ghosts, but all these family members are with me still — through the stories passed down and in my many wonderful memories of the old homeplace and all those who once lived there and nearby. I feel rich to have such a sense of family heritage. I'm happy to share many of the stories in this "Tale of Two Houses."

* * *

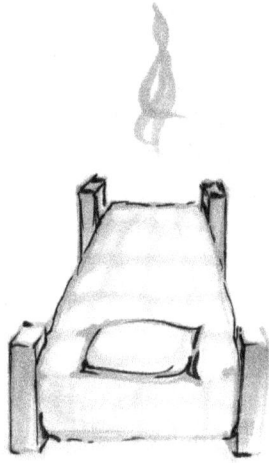

My Uncles' Spirits

In every family tree, there are some characters that are—let's say—more inclined to believe in the existence of a spirit world. Just within my own knowledge, I know of two in my extended family, namely, my Uncle Doc and my Uncle Courty. I will tell you more about their experiences in just a moment. But first, let me tell you a bit about my Uncle Doc.

My grandfather, Jonathan Wallace, a Civil War veteran, had a brother, Harrison Wallace. I just barely knew him as Harrison because my dad always called him Uncle Doc. Uncle Doc probably never went to school to become a doctor. However, he spent many hours studying about medicine and being a doctor and started practicing following the Civil War. I have no knowledge of his serving in the Civil War. He may have been too young.

At some point growing up, I realized that Harrison Wallace was my great uncle. I learned what I could about him from my dad, since Uncle Doc died many years before I was born. Dad knew more about his Uncle Doc than any of his other older family members.

72

Uncle Doc and his family had lived less than a mile from the Jonathan Wallace homeplace near Womble Mountain, where Dad continued to live with his brother Lew and sister Florence after their parents died and until Dad married much later in life. When Uncle Doc's wife died, he lived with his daughter, Kate, until she married Joe Gibbons. Then for the rest of his life, Uncle Doc lived alone.

Dad told me he would ride his horse down to Uncle Doc's after supper and visit with him until bedtime. Those visits kept Uncle Doc from getting too lonely and gave Dad a chance to hear more of Uncle Doc's stories.

Uncle Doc enjoyed telling Dad about sick people he had gone to see on horseback or by horse and buggy. One evening, Uncle Doc told my dad that he had been called to see a middle-aged man who had a chronic ailment he couldn't explain. The man said he felt depressed more or less all the time—he was happy at times but was mostly sad and draggy.

Uncle Doc examined the man carefully and couldn't find anything wrong. He asked, "Have you had this ailment in the past?"

The man answered, "Yes, a few years back."

Uncle Doc quickly replied, "Well, you have it again." He went on to say, "Don't lose heart. I have a cure for it."

The man replied, "I knew you could help me if anyone could."

Uncle Doc opened his black leather medicine satchel and took out a bottle of good-sized pink sugar pills. He counted out fifteen, put them in a small bottle, and told the man to take a pill and a large glass of water morning, noon, and night for five days. Uncle Doc said, "I'll stop by in a week, and if you are not much better, you will owe me nothing. If you are much better, you can pay me one dollar." In a week, Uncle Doc collected his dollar.

...

My dad told me that Uncle Doc had mood changes. At times he was as brave as a lion—not afraid of man or beast. Other times he was afraid of his own shadow. Sometimes he would go to bed with his house unlocked. Other times he couldn't make the house secure enough.

One cold winter night, after making several house calls, he had a bright fire burning in the fireplace, with a big back log and two smaller logs in front. His bed was in the middle of the room. Without bothering to lock the door, Uncle Doc went to bed. He hadn't been in bed very long when he heard a loud knock on the door.

He yelled out, "Come in." In walked a tall, rough-looking man, with long, unkempt hair and a short white beard. He appeared to be wearing layers of clothes, but shivered from the cold. Just inside the door, this man dropped a burlap tow sack that probably contained all of his earthly possessions.

He asked, "Mister, may I warm up a bit by your fire? I have just walked from Thacker's Gap. I've been looking for a barn to sleep in tonight. After I've warmed a bit, I'll go on. I'll surely run across a barn before I go too far."

Uncle Doc said, "Draw that cane bottom chair close to the fire and warm yourself up."

After a while the man asked, "Mister, would you give me permission to sleep here on the floor in front of that fire?"

Uncle Doc told my dad he wanted to tell him to get the hell out and go on down the road, but he said, "Make yourself at home there on the floor."

Uncle Doc's heart began to soften a bit. He pitched him a pillow from his bed and handed him an army blanket from a chair beside his bed.

The man said earnestly, "Kind sir, you don't know how much I appreciate this act of kindness."

Both of them settled down and tried to go to sleep. Uncle Doc pretended to be asleep, but he kept an eye on the man, who was restless.

Finally the man asked, "Are you asleep?"

Uncle Doc answered, somewhat gruffly, "Not yet."

The man said, "I can't sleep either. It is hard to go to sleep on an empty stomach."

Uncle Doc quickly replied, "Well, sleep on your back then."

He had no more than said that before he was ashamed of himself. After a moment, he said, "Mister, I think I can do something about your being hungry. I have half a skillet of cornbread there in the side room. I can set it in close to the fire to warm along with a chunk of ham meat and pour you a big glass of milk. Do you think that will hold you until morning? We can have ham and eggs for breakfast."

The man broke down and cried like a baby.

...

As Uncle Doc got older, he became more afraid. He began to lock and bar his door for fear someone would come in, rob him, and do him harm.

Dad said Uncle Doc claimed that, after he had gone to bed, it wasn't uncommon for the spirits of some of those he had treated prior to their deaths to appear and warm themselves before the fireplace. One nearly scared him to death when it asked him, "Are you ready to die? Are you ready to meet your Lord?" Uncle Doc said the spirit disappeared, and he eventually drifted off to sleep.

I vaguely recall Dad's telling me of Uncle Doc's removing a man's appendix sometime after the above scary experience. In the middle of the operation, Uncle Doc began to lose his nerve. He became fearful of all the things that could go wrong. He prayed that the Lord would take over and steady his nerves. He said, "Lord, if you will help this operation turn out right, I'll confess my sins and become a Christian before I sleep tonight." The operation went well, and Uncle Doc kept his promise.

Uncle Doc spent hours reading his doctor books and was thought to be a pretty good country doctor. He also kept seeing people—or rather, their spirits—after he went to bed and before he went to sleep. Some of his nieces and nephews believed the mysterious things really happened. Others thought he may have dozed and merely had dreams that seemed real to him.

Uncle Doc told my dad of an unnerving experience he had had one night. He said a man had stood before his fireplace after he had gone to bed. The man looked very much like his brother, Jonathan Wallace. However, he appeared just a little taller and older, and his beard was much longer. Otherwise, he was his brother made over.

This spirit said, "Brother Harrison, I came to say goodbye." Then he suddenly disappeared. What made this experience different from the others was that only a day or two later, in 1893, Jonathan Wallace died.

I don't really know when Uncle Doc died. However, I like to think that, with his advance warnings from the spirit world, he was ready to meet his maker.

...

My great aunt Sally Wallace, who was the sister of Jonathan and Doc Wallace, never married. She made her home with Doc's daughter, Kate, and Kate's husband, Joe

Gibbons. Until I was twelve years old, I mistakenly thought she was Joe Gibbons' mother. When I learned she was my great aunt, I began to have a warm feeling toward her. She knew me as her great nephew, Willie Wallace's son, and was always kind toward me. I, as well as everyone else who knew her, called her Aunt Sally.

Joe Gibbons and Kate had two daughters, Sadie and Nellie. Sadie married Aaron Lambert and moved out of the house. Nellie didn't marry until later in life. She, Joe, Kate, and Aunt Sally lived happily together until Aunt Sally died in 1934. They all four worked in perfect harmony without complaint. Joe farmed with a little team of mules. They kept a cow for milk and butter; fattened hogs for ham, bacon, and lard; and raised chickens for fryers and eggs, as well as to have some to take to market. Each year they grew a big garden. They stored Irish and sweet potatoes for winter; canned sweet corn, green beans, and tomatoes; and dried apples and peaches for pies. You get the idea—they worked all the time. In their spare time, the women also grew flowers and made quilts.

Aunt Sally was almost a hundred years old when she died. She, along with Joe, Kate, and Nellie, had lived south of Womble Mountain. The Wallace homeplace was about a mile and a half from there on the west side of the mountain.

I was there at the homeplace when Dad, Uncle Lew, Aunt Florence, and Uncle Court were trying to decide whether or not to inform their sister Sarah, who lived on the north end of Eagle Creek, that Aunt Sally had died. Aunt Sarah was up in years herself and not well. Once they decided to let her know, all eyes turned on me. I was not yet fourteen.

Dad said, "Son, you can ride your mule, Sampson, over to Eagle Creek to let Aunt Sarah know of Aunt Sally's death and that there will be a graveside funeral tomorrow at eleven o'clock." He further suggested a shortcut, which would take me from Blue Springs Church east to the top of Eagle Mountain, then north following the mountain ridge to Horseshoe, then right on a little-used road in the back way to Sherman and Sarah's house.

Sampson seemed to know we were on an important mission. When the going was rough, he proceeded slowly and carefully. When conditions were better, he would strike out on his own in a slow, lazy gallop I call a cat lope. Aunt Sarah was grateful to get the word and said that she and Uncle Sherman would be there at eleven o'clock. My return trip went well.

I wanted to be a part of laying Aunt Sally to rest, so I went to the gravesite to help with the grave digging. Five or six skilled grave diggers showed up. They were careful to make the sides of the grave smooth, the corners square, and the depth six feet. I slipped into the grave and threw out a few shovelfuls of dirt.

About 10:45 a.m., people began to come to the gravesite on foot or horseback, by horse and buggy, and in wagons. Aaron Lambert drove the wagon that carried the casket and Aunt Sally. The casket was placed on two sawhorses. The preacher talked for about ten minutes as people stood around. Then it was suggested that people line up for a final viewing. That was a solemn occasion. Showing the most sorrow were Joe Gibbons, Kate, and Nellie.

I was the last one to view Aunt Sally. I put concentration in my gaze. I wanted to remember her as long as I lived. I allowed her wrinkled face, the mole on her forehead, and her cracked lips to burn a picture in my mind.

The night following the funeral, I went to bed and relived the happenings of the day. It dawned on me to recall Aunt Sally. Without much effort, I was viewing her as clearly as I had seen her in the casket. I was neither elated nor frightened. I felt it was the magic of recall.

A few years later, I was visiting with dad's younger brother, Uncle Courty, who was ten years younger than Dad. He had five sons older than I. They were all married and gone from home. Uncle Courty was somewhat lonely and was glad for me to visit with him. There wasn't anything we didn't talk about. Our conversations ranged from the sublime to the ridiculous.

One evening we got on the subject of witchcraft. Uncle Courty said he was trying to get so he could call people up from the grave. He said he was having borderline success—he wasn't there yet but was making slight progress.

I didn't want Uncle Courty to outdo me, so I told him of my ability to bring up Aunt Sally. Then we got into an argument concerning the color of the eyes of an attractive lady we both knew. He was sure she had blue eyes. I was just as sure she had brown eyes. It had been some time since either of us had seen her, but I knew she was still living.

I suggested to Uncle Courty that I'd call up Aunt Sally that night to get my magic working, and then I'd call up the lady so we would know the color of her eyes. Uncle Courty promised to call up someone or something, and we'd talk about it the following evening.

I was successful. After bringing Aunt Sally in view in my mind, I switched my concentration to the other lady. In my vision, she peeked out from behind a tree as plain as day. Uncle Courty was correct. She had blue eyes.

Pleased with my success, I admitted to Uncle Courty that he was right about the blue eyes. I explained how I knew. Uncle Courty was far from being jubilant over winning the argument. He wasted no time in declaring that he was done with witchcraft.

I asked, "Uncle Courty, what's wrong? I thought you had something interesting underway."

Uncle Courty replied, "When your mother learned that I was dabbling with witchcraft, she told me that according to the Bible, witchcraft is wrong. What I witnessed last night made a believer out of me."

"You seem all shook up, Uncle Courty. What happened?"

Uncle Courty explained, "I tried harder than usual last night to call up someone or something from the grave. I began to feel weak and lightheaded. On the footboard of my bed appeared two imps like devils. I felt like I was dying. I pulled the cover over my head. I pledged to forsake witchcraft and got to feeling better. When I uncovered my head, the imps were gone."

I said, "Uncle Courty, I plan to quit witchcraft before I start."

He quipped, "Good idea. We will have our hands full dealing with the living, without dabbling with the dead."

Now, sometimes, I wonder about the spirits Uncle Doc saw before his fireplace, and the little devils Uncle Courty saw on the footboard of his bed. My great uncle and my uncle seemed to have had some ability to tap into a world usually unseen. I'll never know whether I had inherited some of that ability, because I never tried to develop it. Aunt Sally died seventy-seven years ago. Uncle Courty died fifty-six years ago. I've not tried to call them back, nor will I ever. And I'm content to leave it at that.

* * *

Miss Gibbs and Kitty Cat

In 1928, when I was around eight years old, we had a lady, Miss Gibbs, who washed and did housework for us now and then. She was actually "Mrs." Gibbs, but back then I didn't know the difference between "Miss" and "Mrs.," and most others didn't care. Therefore, she was known as Miss Gibbs or Becky Gibbs. Years later when she became old, she was addressed as Aunt Becky.

Miss Gibbs took great pleasure in showing interest in me and teasing me. I enjoyed the attention and the hubbub between us and almost went overboard in teasing her back. I recall her saying one time in response, with a big smile, "I ought to break your neck." Another time, she said, "You ought to have your neck stretched"—a statement commonly said back then about Charlie Birger, the notorious Southern Illinois bootlegger and gangster who was hanged in 1928 for involvement in a murder.

Miss Gibbs dug ginseng from time to time. Her husband, Sam Gibbs, hunted and dug ginseng full time for miles around. I was astonished when Miss Gibbs told me that ginseng root sold for fifteen dollars per pound. I dug a few pounds of Mayapple root for five cents per pound, and so did Miss Gibbs. Except for a lucky day now and then, it might take Miss Gibbs a week to find a pound of ginseng. For those who looked for ginseng years ago, it became a passion that grew on them. [I later learned that China was the biggest market for ginseng; the Chinese people valued it highly for medicinal purposes.]

Becky and Sam were unable to read or write, but they had what was referred to back then as good "horse sense." It's too bad more people don't have it today. They were poor but got by reasonably well. They had a number of children, who were never required to go to school. Three sons were still at home at that time. They weren't very work brittle (that is, they were a bit lazy) and were happy to do other things while their mother worked a large garden that supplied a big portion of their food, did the housework, and dug different sellable roots.

However, the sons did cut the firewood for cooking and heating. They trapped fur-bearing animals and kept the family supplied with squirrels. Coon pelts brought a good price, and they ate the meat. When they had an opportunity, the boys worked for sixty cents a day and their dinner. Those occasional jobs more than kept the menfolk in the family in chewing and smoking tobacco.

The Wallaces lived on the west side of Womble Mountain. The Gibbs family lived on the east side, across the mountain from us. A well-beaten path circling on the south side of the high part of the mountain connected the two houses. Miss Gibbs called often to get a gallon of buttermilk, which Mom freely gave her.

Miss Gibbs was working for us the day following a township election. I remember her asking Dad, "Did you vote yesterday?"

Dad answered, "Yes, I did. Did you?"

She answered, "Me and Sam and Johnny went. Sammy

isn't old enough to vote." She paused and then asked, "What did you get for your vote?"

Surprised, Dad answered, "I didn't get anything."

With her eyebrows raised, Miss Gibbs said, "Don't tell me that."

Dad said earnestly, "I swear on the Bible that I didn't get anything."

She replied, "I believe you."

Curious, Dad then asked, "What did you and Sam and Johnny get for your votes?"

She explained, "We went to the voting house, sat on a bench off to one side, and watched what was going on. Once in a while, someone would ask if we had voted yet. We told them we were still thinking things over.

"After a while, a man came up and said, 'My name is the first name on the ballot. If all three of you will put an "X" in the box beside that name, I'll drop three dollars on the floor and walk away. Wait a little bit and pick it up.'

"I made sure Sam and Johnny understood how to vote. We walked up and told the people running the election we were ready to vote. We voted the way I promised we would vote. We learned later what the man's name was."

Dad said to Miss Gibbs, "I was interested in the outcome of the election. It might surprise you to know the man you voted for was elected by three votes."

Miss Gibbs smiled and said, "I'm glad. He seemed like a good man."

That day, as Miss Gibbs ate dinner with us, we heard a mouse behind the corner cabinet, which had room enough behind it for us to store empty meal and flour sacks.

Dad said, "That's the first mouse I have heard in a while. We need a cat to sleep under the house at the base of the fireplace and catch the mice before they find a way into the house."

Miss Gibbs replied, "You are in luck. We have a kitten a little more than half grown—I'll give it to you. I'll have to slip it out when Johnny is not looking. I'm sick and tired of the way he 'makes over' the cat. This kitty cat is a really good mouser. She doesn't eat them. She just catches them for the fun of it. She will sit around outside and look for mice."

Pleased, Dad said, "The next time you come over for buttermilk, bring the kitten, and I'll give you a mess of sweet potatoes."

Within a few days, Miss Gibbs was over with a not-too-attractive black cat with yellow and brown spots on it. Miss Gibbs said, "Before I left the house, I said to Johnny, 'It may turn colder. I better take a light coat.' I threw the coat over my arm, hid the kitten in the coat, and sneaked out without Johnny paying any attention."

We were glad to get the kitten and promptly named her Kitty Cat. The kitten seemed healthy, friendly, and happy with the attention she got at her new home, but we were surprised she wouldn't eat. However, she followed me to the barn at milking time and happily lapped milk from a little pan.

When we next saw Miss Gibbs, we told her about our having trouble getting Kitty Cat to eat anything except milk. She laughed and said, "Johnny had her spoiled. He chewed her meat for her and put it in her mouth."

Later, Mom explained to me that some mothers chewed meat for their babies before they had any teeth, when they felt the baby needed the extra nourishment. We never did any chewing for Kitty Cat; she soon learned it was "take it or leave it." However, she still expected her serving of milk at milking time twice a day.

One evening I had other things on my mind and didn't give Kitty Cat her milk first off. I was sitting on a stool and milking away with both hands. I had the pail about half full. Before I knew what was happening, I was kicked off that stool and was covered with milk. Kitty Cat had her claws hung in the hide of the cow's leg. I hadn't yet learned to cuss, so I yelled, "Shoot, shoot, shoot fire!" I saw there was still a little milk left in the pail. I poured it in Kitty Cat's pan, rubbed the cow a little to soothe her, reseated myself, and finished milking. Thereafter, I always served Kitty Cat first.

About a year later, we became aware that Kitty Cat was expecting kittens. We stacked some baled hay in such a way that she would have a good home for the kittens. She proved to be a good mother and spent the necessary time with her kittens.

Living a quarter mile south of us was the Partain family. A son, Lacy, who was my age, visited with us from time to time. We were playing in the barn. Lacy spied Kitty Cat and her babies. He threw up both hands in excitement and said, "Here is our cat, with kittens! I am going to take her home."

I don't know why I did not set him straight that the cat was ours. I just let him go ahead and think Kitty Cat was his.

He found a tow sack, put the kittens in it, and started off for home. Kitty Cat followed along. I knew enough about cats to know she would be back. I was curious to see how it would work out. I figured Lacy had seen Kitty Cat down at his house a number of times when she was working on their barn mice and honestly thought she was their cat.

The next morning, when I went to milk, Kitty Cat was waiting there by her milk pan. I gave her a pan of milk. She lapped it up quickly and went to her cozy home in the hay bales. I took a look, and there were all five of her kittens. The kittens were too small to have walked back home, so Kitty Cat had made five trips and carried them back one at a time.

The next time I saw Lacy, I asked casually, "How are your cat and kittens?"

In a downcast manner, he replied, "You know, they up and disappeared."

I responded, "A coyote must have eaten them. They like cats."

Around that time, I found a baby rabbit that had gotten separated from its family. I put it in with the kittens when Kitty Cat wasn't around. When Kitty Cat returned, baby rabbit nursed along with the kittens. It wasn't many days until I had to put baby rabbit back with the kittens each time I came to the barn. One day baby rabbit was nowhere to be seen. What happened to baby rabbit? Your guess is as good as mine.

...

Miss Gibbs loved flowers. She bragged of having morning glories on both sides of her porch — one side pink and the other side white. She also bragged about having a beautiful bed of four o'clocks. These flowers indeed would open up around four o'clock each afternoon.

As for me, I was interested only in growing something to eat. But my sister Mabel, two years older than I, begged me to go with her to visit Miss Gibbs and see her flowers. So we took off around the mountain.

Miss Gibbs greeted us in a friendly manner and said she would set some cane bottom chairs on the shady north-facing porch. It was a hot day.

The house was made of logs. The small porch on the north side was about six inches off the ground. There were the morning glories climbing or running on the strings from stakes driven in the ground to 2x4s that were attached to the posts supporting the porch. The morning glories made the porch look homey. The four o'clocks were just beginning to open.

Miss Gibbs' son, Sammy, who was about sixteen years old and the youngest of the family, came out and sat on a block of wood used for a seat. He appeared tall, slender, and not too strong. I had a feeling he was more able-bodied than Miss Gibbs gave him credit for. He wasn't required to get a bucket of water from the spring or to bring in a stick of wood for the cook stove. His brothers didn't shoot the squirrels around the house, but left them for Sammy to "shoot" with a broomstick.

Sitting there on the block of wood, Sammy looked nervous. He had something in his hand that he passed back and forth from one hand to the other.

After a while, Sammy stood up and whined, "Ma, I don't want this dollar fifteen cents."

He threw the money out in the yard. Miss Gibbs sprang to her feet, ran out into the yard, picked up the money, and put it in her apron pocket. Then for the rest of the time Mabel and I were there, every little bit Sammy pleaded, "Ma, give me my dollar fifteen cents. I want my dollar fifteen cents." She didn't pay any attention to him.

[Now as I think back, poor little Sammy wasn't much different from a lot of people today, who in various ways strive to be noticed. Sammy's antics reminded me of a time when I was about fourteen. I was riding my mule, Sampson, down to the south end of Sodom in Pope County to look at a good milk cow we had heard was for sale. As I traveled down the road, I could see from a distance a number of people sitting on the porch of a house that was near the road.

I had Sampson moving along in a slow, lazy cat lope, when I let out a squall like a panther and warmed his hind end with a little switch I was carrying. Sampson took off like the devil was after him. We streaked by the house, with all the people gaping at us in surprise—just as I'd hoped. Sampson wouldn't have run faster if his tail had been on fire. I had taught Sampson to walk slowly, walk fast, pace, trot, and gallop. I'm glad I hadn't taught him to talk. He would have asked me, "What in the Sam Hill was all that about?" or "What is wrong with you?"]

As Mabel and I were leaving Miss Gibbs' house, she gave us a warm invitation to come back and made me a big promise to take me ginseng hunting with her some time. That never happened. Why would she create competition?

. . .

One day when Miss Gibbs was over helping Mom with different chores, she asked if Mom had any hens setting.

Mom replied, "I have one hen setting on fifteen eggs from White Wyandotte hens and another hen setting on fifteen eggs from Rhode Island Red hens."

Miss Gibbs said, "I'd like to talk you out of a baby Rhode Island Red rooster for a pet for Sammy."

Mom and I knew Miss Gibbs was asking Mom to give her a baby chick, which I knew Mom would do. When the eggs hatched, one baby Rhode Island Red rooster stood out. It was strong and had a comb larger than the other baby roosters.

A few days later, when Miss Gibbs showed up for buttermilk, Mom made her happy by giving her the little red rooster chick for Sammy. Miss Gibbs put it in her apron pocket, took her buttermilk, and headed off for home, without staying around to talk.

When Miss Gibbs was next over, she said, "Nothing else could have pleased Sammy more. He named the rooster

Chick Chick." Then she wanted to know about Kitty Cat. We told her that Kitty Cat lived mostly at the barn and got warm milk twice a day.

I'll never forget how amused Miss Gibbs was when Mom told her the following incident:

"I was getting supper after dark. Dad [referring to my dad] was sitting by the window watching me. Kitty Cat was sitting on the windowsill just outside the window. Dad looked at the cat with a frown. He feared that it was just one step from being a house cat, which he detested.

"A downdraft caused the stove to smoke. I raised the window to let the smoke out. Having the window open caused Kitty Cat to appear to almost be in the kitchen. That got under Dad's skin.

"After two or three minutes, I pulled the window down without Dad's noticing. Dad, with sudden disgust toward Kitty Cat, and thinking the window was still up, doubled up his fist and yelled 'Scat!' while giving a mighty thrust toward Kitty Cat. Dad shattered that window all to pieces. He was unhurt but was really embarrassed."

After that incident, Kitty Cat didn't park in the window any more. That goes along with the saying by Mark Twain: "The cat that sits down on a hot stove-lid . . . will never sit down on a cold one."

One day, Dad teased Miss Gibbs by asking, "Becky, have you cussed Sam out lately?"

She quickly retorted, "No, have you knocked any windows out lately?"

Kitty Cat learned that if she would show up at the back door around eight o'clock in the evening, she would find a serving of leftovers. About that time one evening, it was coming up a storm—lightning and thunder—as fierce as I had ever seen. I wondered if Kitty Cat had ventured out to get her nightly snack, so I opened the back door. There was Kitty Cat licking the platter clean. Just then, I heard a clap of thunder and simultaneously saw a fireball of lightning just above the wild cherry tree in our backyard. I remember it as well as if it were yesterday. That cat let out a squall as if she had received an electric shock and streaked out of there. She cleared the gate of the backyard fence, which was about five feet high. Somehow it struck me as funny; still today, when that scene passes through my mind, I smile.

...

Miss Gibbs kept us amused from time to time by telling us how Sammy was caring for Chick Chick. Sammy set a block of wood even with their dinner table so that Chick Chick could stand on it and eat crumbled cornbread, beans, and homemade hominy off a tin plate. Sammy cut the beans and hominy into small pieces. Chick Chick spent the night on another block of wood near where Sammy slept.

Sammy could not read, write, or sing, but he could crow like a rooster. Miss Gibbs told us that when Chick Chick was about the age to start crowing, Sammy would crow as soon as he woke up. One morning Sammy overslept, and the family was surprised to hear Chick Chick crow instead.

One afternoon, I had Sampson saddled to take a scouting-around, goof-off ride. Miss Gibbs came running up out of breath and said, "Sammy has his head hung between two logs at our house. He is scared to death and about to go nuts."

I took Miss Gibbs by the arm and said, "Let me help you onto my mule." Before she knew what was happening, she was on Sampson, I was on behind her, and Sampson was cat loping toward her house.

On our arrival, I saw Sammy standing on the porch with his head in a small opening about thirty inches above the porch floor. I already knew there was a small opening beside the door to let fresh air in and smoke out, with a false block to close it up and make it unnoticeable.

I said, "Sammy, don't worry—your ma and I will have you out in no time. Your head went in to that opening sideways, so it will have to come out sideways." I got hold of one leg, and Miss Gibbs latched on to the other. We gently lifted him up and turned him sideways, and his head slipped out.

Miss Gibbs asked, "Son, what got into you that caused you to get your head hung that way?"

"Ma, I decided to go around the bend away from the house to that mulberry tree and watch the squirrels come and go as they ate the mulberries. I locked the house before I left so no one would get in and steal my dollar fifteen cents. I hid the key and forgot where I hid it. I took that chunk of wood out and tried to get in that way and got my darn head stuck. I heard a fellow say once: 'Anywhere I can get my head through, I can go.' He was a low-down lyin' son of a monkey."

I said soothingly, "Sammy, you are out, and that is all that matters. Let me rub your neck, so you won't get a crick in it."

Trying to cover up his embarrassment, he replied ungratefully, "Never mind. I can rub my own neck. Anyway, I just about had my head out when you showed up."

Miss Gibbs said, "Kestner, you know how he is. Pay him no mind. Next spring I will bring your family a big mess of mushrooms."

I replied, "That will be big pay for what I did."

...

About a year later, as Miss Gibbs was eating dinner with us, she announced, "This will be my last day to work for you. The place where we have lived rent-free for many years has sold; we will have to move. We have a better place to live a ways south of Herod. It is too far for me to walk back to work for you."

Mom said, "Miss Gibbs, we will miss having you for a neighbor. But, from time to time, we will see you at the Herod store."

Miss Gibbs took a small chunk of meat from the table and said, "I want to give this to Kitty Cat and say goodbye to her."

For several years after her family moved to Pope County, I never saw Miss Gibbs, since I was away from Southern Illinois. However, Mom kept me informed to the extent of her knowledge. She told me that Sammy was struck by a car and killed. He had walked from behind a parked car into the path of an oncoming car. Miss Gibbs' husband, Sam, who was older than Miss Gibbs, died of natural causes. Mom told me that she did all she could to comfort Miss Gibbs at the time of both deaths.

I was told that Miss Gibbs's brown hair had turned to an attractive gray, and that she was well respected at the spacious general store at Herod, where people gathered around the old potbellied stove in the winter months to visit.

Everett Partin, a tall, big-hearted, jovial man in his sixties, had brought a sturdy rocking chair that had belonged to his mother and placed it by the potbellied stove. On a flat place on the top of the chair back, he printed "Aunt Becky." It became known that when Miss Gibbs came to the store, the chair was to be vacated and made available for her.

Everett teased Aunt Becky about first one thing and another. She would become angry, or pretend to be angry. Their carrying on was entertainment for those present.

Recently back home after World War II, I decided to go down to the store on Thursday, which was cream day—the day the merchant bought cream—so I could see how many people I knew. I hoped I'd see Aunt Becky.

I parked at the back of the store and went in the back way. I knew and shook hands with the store owner. He put his arm around my shoulder and said warmly, "Welcome back."

I had taken a few steps from this friendly merchant when I stopped suddenly, like a bird dog on point. My feeling must have been similar to that of Rhett Butler, as portrayed by Clark Gable in "Gone with the Wind."

In the movie, Rhett Butler and Scarlett O'Hara were fleeing Atlanta, Georgia, at night in a stolen horse and buggy as the city was being burned during the Civil War. The fire raged, and it appeared that all hell had broken loose. The horse was nearly beyond control. Clark controlled it enough to say to Scarlet, "Look—this is the last of the 'Old South.'"

I said to myself as I gazed around the store, "Look, Kestner, this is the last of the general store of the past." Since the last time I had stepped foot in this store, I had been in modern stores in Chicago, San Francisco, and Honolulu, and then traveled halfway around the world, so I realized I was observing a scene that would soon be no more.

I could view the entire store from my vantage point. Off to one side was a room where cream was being tested for butter fat and eggs were being candled for quality. To my left were all kinds of hardware, kegs of nails, bolts, harnesses, blocks of salt, sacks of feed, work shoes and boots for men, and bolts of cloth for dressmaking for women.

On my right, before reaching the old potbellied stove, was a counter about four feet from the west wall. On this counter were a number of brown paper sacks of varying sizes and a set of scales. Lining the wall behind the counter were shelves laden with all sorts of canned goods, including lard in three- and seven-pound buckets.

On the floor next to the counter were large sacks of beans, sugar, rice, potatoes, and peanuts to be sold by the pound. Flour was sold in twenty-four-pound sacks, and meal and sugar were available in ten-pound sacks. The center of the store was filled with all sorts of other things and stuff. What I've written doesn't do justice to the vanished "general store," but it will give you some idea.

I moved a little closer to the group gathered around the potbellied stove, where Aunt Becky was sitting in her rocking chair. Everett Partin was standing about six feet from her. The first part of the ongoing dialogue I heard was Everett's asking, "Aunt Becky, how is Johnny getting along with his Poland China cow?"

Aunt Becky replied, "Everett, you old dimwit—you don't know nothin'. There ain't such a thing as a 'Poland China' cow. There is a 'Poland China' hog. You don't know the difference between a cow and a hog."

Everett replied, "Aunt Becky, you misunderstood what I meant. I meant that Johnny had to drive his cow up at milking time with a 'pole' and milk her in a 'china' teacup."

Aunt Becky, in a huff, almost came out of her chair. I froze in my tracks. She shouted, "Teacup, my foot—Johnny milks a big bucket of milk morning and night, and I sell a dollar's worth of cream each Thursday."

I moved closer and stood motionless, not wanting to miss what was being said. Next Everett asked, "Aunt Becky, do you think you and Johnny will get home in that

Model T Ford he bought for fifteen dollars? It doesn't even have a top."

She gave a quick, angry reply: "Let me tell you something, Mr. Everett Partin. I have confidence in that car. I wouldn't be afraid to take off to Harrisburg in it."

Everett said, "Now, now, Aunt Becky. I'm just concerned that you might get wet if a rain were to come up before you get home."

Somewhat more civilly, Aunt Becky replied, "I won't get any wetter than the many times I've walked home in the rain."

I moved a little closer. Aunt Becky saw me. She got to her feet surprisingly fast and took two or three steps toward me. Her silver hair almost formed a halo around her wrinkled face. The tears in her eyes caused them to sparkle. My eyes filled to overflowing, as the past flashed through my mind. Next we embraced in a big hug.

I motioned for Aunt Becky to sit down. Someone set a cane-bottomed chair beside Aunt Becky for me.

After Aunt Becky asked me a few questions, I asked, "Aunt Becky, how are you getting along?"

She replied, "I was never happier in my life. I attended a revival here at Herod Springs Church and got the life-changing 'old time religion.' Now I love everybody. Everett is a good man. We carry on just for fun. I love him like a brother."

Aunt Becky went on to say, "I don't do any more washing for people. Johnny's cow furnishes us plenty of milk. I have a dozen hens for eggs to eat or sell. We make a garden. That's not all—every two weeks, we get a government relief order that lets us buy what we need at the store."

I replied, "Aunt Becky, I'm happy for you. You have seen more than your share of hard times."

I rose to leave, and Aunt Becky got up, too, to give me another hug. As we said our farewells, the last words I ever heard Aunt Becky say were these: "Bring your mother down to see me. She is the most wonderful person I ever knew."

As I think back about Aunt Becky and her life, I firmly believe that if there were a "Hall of Fame" for outstanding people in the Womble Mountain-Rudement-Herod area, Aunt Becky would be one of its esteemed honorees.

* * *

Fellowship Withdrawn

C hurch attendance has made a positive impression on my life. Three churches in particular had an impact: Rudement Social Brethren Church, Herod Springs Missionary Baptist Church (my father's choice), and the First Church of God in Harrisburg (my mother's preference).

One Sunday, when I was six or seven years old, Mom and three of us children were returning from attending church at Rudement. Mom was driving a big black mare hitched to a closed-in buggy. As we reached home, Dad rode up from the opposite direction on his bay riding mare, on his way back from attending church at Herod Springs.

While Mom was preparing Sunday dinner, Dad told her the church had "withdrawn the right hand of fellowship" from three members of the church—two men and a woman—for running whiskey stills. Dad explained that all three had been previously warned and admonished to stop making whiskey and "bootlegging," a term used for selling liquor illegally. However, they had continued despite the warnings, and the church members had felt the need to act.

After his expulsion from the church, one of the two men gradually got away from making whiskey. He was a good worker and made a living for his large family by working at various jobs, among which were molasses-making and stone and brick masonry. My dad had played a big part in expelling this man from the church. But there didn't appear to be any hard feelings in the late twenties when Dad hired him to do some masonry work for us.

This man ate dinner with us each day while he was working for us. I recall his saying one day at the dinner table, "Times are hard, and money is scarce." He went on to say that he had been trying to sell some molasses. He had an old touring car that he had converted into a pick-up. He had loaded it with molasses and gone as far as Vienna in Southern Illinois but had been unable to sell even a gallon.

He said that on the way home he was stopped by a policeman for not having license plates on his vehicle. He said to the policeman, "I hope I can pay my fine with molasses. I have about forty gallons I've been trying to sell for forty cents per gallon. I haven't sold a gallon. I have fifteen cents in my pocket and barely enough gas in my car to get back to Thackers Gap (Herod)."

He said the policeman replied, "For God's sake, go on home."

I was never close to this man but kept a roundabout interest in him and his well-being. He had three sons whom I knew about and three good-looking daughters. His youngest daughter, about my age of thirteen at the time, was present at an outdoor gathering. She knew she was attractive, and she was about as feisty as she was good-looking. She suggested that the boys who were about her age line up, and she would see which one was the best looking. I snapped to and helped to get others to do likewise.

My cousin, Dallas Millikan, didn't line up. He was alert, sensible, and rather solemn. This gal glared at him and shouted, "I said, 'Line up!'"

His reply was one I'll never forget—I wish I had been the one who said it. He said, "I don't have to line up just because you said line up."

That remark caused the line-up to fall out. The girl was put out for about half a minute. I wondered who she would have chosen.

...

The other whiskey-making man kept on making whiskey. Years later he took pleasure in telling about his making and selling days. My brother-in-law, Wallace Baldwin, admired his ability to tell a good story. He took a tape recorder and got a thirty-minute recording. I never heard the recording, but Wallace laughingly told me some of what he recorded. It went as follows:

"I ain't got no idee how many times I was 'rested and toted in to Harrisburg, fined ten dollars, locked up in jail overnight, and sent home the next mornin'. The next day, I was back at it."

Wallace asked, "Why did you stop making?"

"The Feds got word how pig-headed I was and snuck in on me one night while I was wolfin' down my supper at the table. They found the goods on me. I knowed I was a gone goslin', but I didn't let on. I turned on my good side. I asked them to have a bite to eat with me. They told me they already et. Then I asked, 'How about a drink of good whiskey?' I told them that a good snort would put a smile on their sad faces. That seemed to rub them the wrong way. Nary one of them Feds smiled, and one of them snapped, 'We are here to take you to town.' I looked as surprised as all get-out and asked, 'Why for are you goin' to do a thing like that? I ain't stole nothin' or shooted nobody.'

"They didn't give me a chance to wipe the gravy off my chin, but jerked me up and slapped the cuffs on me. I screamed like I had been shot. I told them they hurt my back that was broken when I fell out of a tree that I went up after a possum.

"They marched me out to the car. I turned cheerful-like. I commented that the dry weather was going to play the Devil with the corn crop, might cause the price of corn whiskey to go up. Still these peckerwoods didn't say nothin'. I started in to commence to feel this trip might turn out to be a little tougher than the others. Instead of ten dollars and a night in jail, it might be a good cussin', a twenty-dollar fine, and two nights in the slammer.

"I knowed I was spinnin' my wheels, but I said, 'Gentlemen, after I have paid my fine, if you'll take me home, I'll see you are put up in a good clean bed, and my darlin' wife will feed you a mouth-smackin' good breakfast of ham and eggs, biscuits, and gravy.'

"They didn't say nothin'—just looked at each other and shook their heads like their best coon dog had been whacked by a big, old rusty rattlesnake and had no chance to live. Their only remark was 'You won't be going home soon.'

"They was right about that. I got a year in the pen and a hundred-dollar fine. I told the ramrods that were railroadin' me that they could send me over the road, but I knowed already I wouldn't be satisfied.

"I didn't get salvation in the pen, but I learned my lesson. I decided to go home, live off welfare, garden, coon hunt, and make a few dollars tradin'. So, Wallace, my friend, that is what I did. By the way, good buddy, thank you for the sawbuck."

...

The woman who was removed from church fellowship stopped making whiskey when she met a stately looking gentleman who was in charge of the Civilian Conservation Corps camp at Herod. They married and lived happily for a few years. He was a World War I veteran with a heart condition, which brought on his sudden, untimely death. She grieved his death but was fortunate to draw a widow's pension.

...

When I was quite young, I occasionally attended Herod Springs Church with my dad. Out in front of the podium were regular pews, where most of the congregation sat. But there were also three long pews on either side of the podium, facing the right and left sides of the speaker. Older women in hats and their Sunday best sat on the left side, and several men sat on the right, which was known as the Amen corner. I remember that five of the seven or eight men who usually sat in the Amen corner had big mustaches—at least two were big handlebars.

Back then, the pastor preached at least an hour and a half to two hours on the first Saturday and Sunday of each month beginning at 11:00 a.m. He had a full month to prepare two messages and came and spoke life into the service. He fired up the men, and they shouted, "A-men." The women smiled and nodded their heads.

Of all these memories that took place more than eighty years ago, one that stands out in particular was that of Arthur Wilson, a man of medium build, who was referred to as Brother Arth by the minister. He always sat about midway on the right side of the church. He was the great-grandfather of Deloris Stuby, a present-day member of Rudement Church. When called on to dismiss the church service with a word of prayer, he always raised his right hand in an Indian-salute fashion as he said a short, inspiring prayer. That unusual stance made a lasting impression on my young mind.

...

Attendance at Herod Springs reached an all-time low in the late 1930s. Along about that time, Roy Thurmond moved into the area from St. Louis and ran a fluorspar mine. His wife and four daughters operated the Fairy Cliff Café in Herod. Roy also had a son in the Navy and a young son at home.

The entire Thurmond family joined the Herod Springs Church one Sunday night. Mr. Thurmond stood before the church along with his family. With his voice breaking with emotion, he said, "You see my entire family except a son who is on the high seas tonight. We love the Lord and would like to become members of this church." They were received with open arms and extended the right hand of fellowship.

Herod Springs had stopped having church on Sunday nights because of poor attendance. The Thurmond sisters and a few others got the blessing of the church to have Young People's Meeting on Sunday nights. More girls started to show up, and then young men began attending in numbers.

These young men were among the rural best but not too church-minded. They sat in the back and laughed, joked, made wisecracks, and had a good time. To me, they were the "good old boys" whose behavior would soon spell doom to the Young People's Meeting. I was no better or worse than these boys, but I had a greater respect for the "House of the Lord."

One Sunday night, at one of the services, I was sitting in a pew near the middle of the church. At or near the end of the service, which was going poorly because of the rudeness of the boys, I asked if I could say a few words. Some previous experiences had given me a little confidence in my ability to speak. I was a member of a debating club in high school and a "pretend preacher" at a "play church" — in a log structure built by my cousins, my brothers, and me with the blessings of my uncle (who later turned the structure into a hog house).

I stood to speak with my back to the wall, so my view could take in the entire church. For perhaps a minute I eyed everyone present and said nothing. The church became as quiet as death.

I began, "I have great admiration for the Thurmond sisters and their friends for pulling the Young Peoples' Meeting together." Then, looking directly at the boys, I said, "These girls are serious and sincere and are putting their heart and soul into trying to help the good pastor make the church a shining light in the community. You need to behave as you have been taught and in the way you know you should. If you don't, their efforts will fail. If you shape up, you will have a good place to meet and socialize."

What I said had a sobering effect on the boys. The spokesperson of the girls said, "We need to elect a young people's leader."

Another responded, "I nominate Kestner. All in favor say 'Aye.'"

Everyone said "Aye," even the boys in the back. I was shocked. However, I offered to give it a try.

I served only a few times before going to Michigan in

1940 to get work. About the third meeting after I took over as leader, I put forth a special effort to include the "good old boys" in a discussion. One fellow, who was looked up to by the others, responded to the question I set forth. He talked at length.

After the meeting, he remarked, "This was the best meeting we have had so far." He became my replacement after I left.

At the next to-the-last meeting in which I was in charge, a man, his wife, and his sixteen-year-old daughter showed up. The man had a voice that commanded attention. The wife was keen eyed and pleasant. The daughter's looks cried out for one to take a second glance. She had blue eyes and strawberry-blonde hair. She didn't appear to know she was good-looking. All three were back the following Sunday night.

That night, I told the group I was leaving for Michigan the following day to look for work. I assured them they were off to a good start and wished them well.

I asked the strawberry blond if I could take her home. She knew I was driving an eighteen-year-old Model T Ford. She replied, "I'm with my parents. Suppose you ask my daddy." Like a big, brave soldier, I marched over to him and asked if he would grant me the pleasure of taking his daughter home. I felt a little weak in the knees as I waited for his answer.

In his deep bass voice, he came out with his byword, "Doggone, I don't see why not." He went on to say, "When you get her home, you come on in — the wife and I will go in the kitchen for milk and cookies and give you a chance to talk."

That is what we did. We felt at ease in each other's presence. I told her when I got an address in Michigan, I would write her a letter. She promised to answer by return mail. She did. In her second letter, she wrote several pages on narrow writing paper. In a statement near the end, she wrote, "I could write to you all night." I answered and waited for a letter that never came.

Mom, without knowing that I had taken the girl home or that we were corresponding, in her zeal to keep me abreast of current events, wrote that so-and-so's daughter got married last week. Was I crushed? No, not crushed. Surprised? Yes. Fortunately, my feelings for her had not yet exceeded those of friendship. To keep myself from feeling too downcast, I relied on my old standby quote from Job: "The Lord gave and the Lord hath taken away."

...

In Michigan, I got room and board with a lady who ran a boarding house. She set a good table and packed a tasty lunch. However, she soon took a job in a defense plant and didn't wish to keep boarders any longer. I then rented a one-room efficiency. It worked out well for a while but was far from ideal.

I learned that the Herod woman who was expelled from church, and who later married and then lost her veteran husband, had moved to Michigan and was keeping boarders on Cass Street—not far from where I worked. I went to see her. We were glad to see each other and greeted one another as friends from home. She had an extra bedroom and was happy to take me under her wing.

My dad was dead by this time. She told me she didn't hold it against him for his part in throwing her out of the church at Herod Springs. She said he was the only one of those who had taken part in removing her from "church fellowship" who didn't come to her to buy some whiskey. She raised her eyebrows slightly and added, "For medical purposes."

This woman was all one could wish for in a landlady. Her place was clean. She was kind and a good cook. She had survived many hard times and appeared surprisingly young for whatever age she was. My own hard times made me feel older than my early twenties. She and I had many friendly, confidential talks concerning bygone days, which resulted in a deeper bond of friendship. I came to believe that if my dad had known her as I did, he would have had no part in expelling her from the church.

...

After spending time in the Navy in World War II, I returned to Southern Illinois in 1946. I made Mom happy by taking her to the First Church of God on Charleston Street in Harrisburg. Mom must have told the church folks about my teaching a Sunday school class in Michigan before going to the Navy, because they wasted no time in making me Sunday school superintendent. That delayed my return to the church of my childhood—Rudement Social Brethren.

In 1950, Evelyn, the love of my life, and I were married. She was adored by the Church of God folks. However, when we felt the time was right, we started going to church at Rudement, near our home. I taught the men's Sunday school class for the next thirty years. Evelyn was chosen as secretary of the women's class and continued in that role until her death in 2006. Even today, the church folks' concern and respect for me touches a tender spot in my heart. If I miss any of the three services per week, they will call and ask about my well-being.

I never joined any church, although I was considered a member of the Church of God by a profession of faith and attendance. But like a rabbit chased by a hound dog, I made the round and came back to where I started.

* * *

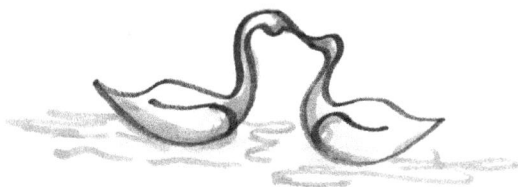

Goosey Goosey Gander

As a child and later as a young married man, we had horses, mules, cattle, hogs, sheep, goats, chickens, and ducks—not all at the same time. When I was about six years old, we had three geese. One was a gander. Why these three? I don't know. Perhaps Grandma, Mom's mother, gave Mom three goose eggs, and she put them under a hen and hatched three goslings—one male and two females.

I remember them only as full-grown geese. Dad thought of them as a botheration and a nuisance, with an enormous appetite.

Dad added a special, expensive ingredient to our laying hens' feed to increase egg production. At feeding time, my job was to give shelled corn to the geese and keep them separate from the hens while they ate. When the geese learned that the hens' feed was something special, it was more than I could do to keep the geese out of the hens' feed.

One day the geese were helping themselves to the hens' feed. Dad shooed the two geese away, but the gander refused to be shooed. In defiance, he stuck his head high in the air and let out a loud honk. By his action, he said, "I shall not be moved."

That got Dad's hackles up. While I held my breath in fear of what was about to happen, Dad expressed his disgust by whacking that gander on the head with his walking stick.

If that goose had time to think, he probably thought the world was coming to an end. He fell over dead. I felt it was my fault for allowing the gander to get to the chicken feed, and I feared Dad's reaction. Dad, however, became remorseful that he had killed the gander I'd thought of as my pet. He had whacked the gander on impulse without really intending to do it harm.

That event occurred when times were hard and nothing went to waste. Mom's sister, Aunt Eva, was visiting us. When she and Mom learned what had happened, they suggested the gander be dressed and brought in for cooking.

In a short time, that gander was in the kitchen for Mom and Aunt Eva to turn into a delicious supper of baked goose and dressing. How that bird met its fate never crossed our minds at mealtime. It graced our table much the same as would a turkey or a big ham at Thanksgiving or Christmas. I haven't eaten goose since, but I remember it pleasantly and still look forward to another serving of goose—tame or wild.

...

My next experience with geese was at my Grandfather Millikan's home north of Golconda in Pope County. My grandfather, grandmother, and aunts lived on a 240-acre farm on top of Rambo Hill, east of War Bluff. My aunts, younger than my mother, had brought me down to visit for two or three days. I felt quite special riding in their Model T Ford.

The Millikans had a large flock of geese. When that Model T came within hearing distance of Grandpa's house, the ganders began to sound off. To me, in a roundabout sort of way, it was exciting and musical.

Being the first of a number of grandsons, I was fussed over and given a lot of attention. Everyone made sure that I was a part of all the chores around the farm.

Aunt Nellie took me with her to gather the eggs — a good-sized basket full. I was excited when I found an egg at least three times larger than a chicken egg — a goose egg. In my excitement, I exclaimed, "I want to eat this egg for my breakfast!"

Sure enough, the next morning it was on my plate. I didn't let on, but I was somewhat disappointed in it. It was tougher and lacked the flavor of a chicken egg. However, I never regretted the experience.

The day after I arrived was the beginning of summer, which was the time to pluck the down feathers from the breasts of the geese to make pillows and feather beds. Any surplus feathers would sell for a dollar a pound. I was a willing helper. The feathers came off easily and made the geese cooler. The feathers would have shed little by little on their own.

A great many geese — no ganders — were in a stall of the barn. Aunt Nellie and Aunt Mamie were seated in the hallway of the barn outside the stall. I was assigned the job of catching the geese and bringing them to my aunts to pluck. That was a challenge. But I managed it well — so well that they rewarded me with abundant praise. Even at that age, that was the best reward I could get.

...

As an adult, I was out of the livestock business for several years. I got married in 1950 to my wonderful wife, Evelyn. Our daughter, LeAnn, was born in 1955, and our son, Ray, seventeen months later. They inherited my love for animals, and I hadn't lost mine. That gave me a good excuse to provide them with different farm animals: a pony, horses, cows, goats, pigs, chickens, rabbits, and a pair of ducks.

At an early age, LeAnn wanted to be a carpenter, a cowboy, and a doctor. So I traded a .22 pistol, four laying hens, and ten dollars for a beautiful, black, two-year-old stallion quarter horse. He was headstrong and unbroken to ride. LeAnn's turning him into a well-behaved marvel is a story for another time.

However, the need to house that horse caused LeAnn and me to do some building, which we both enjoyed doing. I got a quantity of used lumber at a bargain price. First, LeAnn wanted us to build her a playhouse, 10 feet x 24 feet. She called it her clubhouse. We added a lean-to to the clubhouse for hay and grain for her horse, and a lean-to to the lean-to for other stuff. Then south of those three structures, we built two stables out of concrete blocks. LeAnn mixed the mortar, and I laid the block. That time together was one of the happiest times of our lives.

I gave Bob Butterworth one hundred dollars to bring his bulldozer down and dam up a ravine not far from the stables, which we called the barn. This pond soon filled with water. Little white crawdads took to the pond on their own, giving me a good supply for fish bait.

One spring day a year or two later, I was standing inside one of the stables facing south toward the pond. I heard the honking of wild geese south of me. When they came into view, I saw it was a small flock—only about twenty—in a "V" shape.

Just behind the lead goose was a goose that was dropping below formation. It appeared to be struggling to stay in the air. The flight of the geese appeared to be slow, perhaps in consideration of this goose. All of a sudden, the ailing goose gave up just above the pond and hit the water with a splash. The lead goose made a U-turn and led the flock to a soft landing in the pond with the injured goose.

The goose that had splashed down into the water appeared to be rather alert. However, one wing drooped, which caused me to think someone must have winged it, perhaps with a .22 rifle.

I have heard stories that lead me to believe that some wild geese mate for life. That caused me to wonder whether the lead goose and the injured goose were mates.

Somehow I had a feeling that the geese may have been in flight a long time and would perhaps spend the night on the pond and leave sometime on the following day. I went out of the building on the north side in order not to cause the geese to leave the pond until they had rested.

I told Evelyn some wild geese were on the pond. She, with real concern in her voice, replied, "I hope you don't plan to shoot them."

I quickly reassured her, "No, baby doll, you have made a pussycat out of me. I won't hurt them."

With a relieved smile, she said, "Good — they want to live, too."

I put the geese out of my mind and spent the evening after supper as usual. But when I went to bed, I couldn't go to sleep. My mind was on wild geese. I thought of a time several years earlier, while I was teaching in a one-room school. A boy who was a son of a hunting and fishing buddy came up to my desk, where the pencil sharpener was located, and sharpened his pencil. He lingered. I inquired, "Do you want to tell me something or ask me something?"

He replied, "I wanted to tell you that Dad went goose hunting today."

I answered, "Don't forget to tell me tomorrow how well he did."

The next day, the boy was back to sharpen his pencil. I asked him, "How did your dad do goose hunting yesterday?"

With eyes shining and a big smile, he replied, "He got two gooses." I could tell he looked a little embarrassed, thinking that didn't sound right. I didn't let on. I told him his father did well.

He did much better than I did the following Saturday. Deciding to go goose hunting myself, I went somewhere along the bank of the Ohio River, where I was told wild geese were flocking. I had an old, long-barreled Winchester 97—the kind that you cock to pump a shell into the barrel.

I slipped along the shore out of shooting range of the water's edge. I saw geese on the water near the shore. A lone gander was on the shore about twenty feet from the water's edge. I was sure he was a "lookout" for the others to alert them of any danger.

I knew there was no way to get within shooting range of that gander without its taking off. However, on the shore within shooting range of that gander was a log as big around as a barrel. I decided to lie flat on my stomach and stay out of view of that gander while scooting myself and my gun to that log. It took a long time. I wondered at times if the goose was worth the effort.

When I got to the log, I knew I'd have to slowly and quietly shift a shell into the barrel of the gun. I did it so slowly that there was no alarming sound. My gun was cocked. All I had to do was spring up and shoot. I jumped up, took aim, and pulled the trigger. The gun snapped. I had failed to snug the gun chamber tightly enough for the firing pen to strike the shell. I was too surprised to pump the gun and try to fire again. The gander flew away along with the geese in the water near the shore. To say I was disappointed would have been an understatement.

I walked down the shore and came upon a duck. I up and shot it. I felt pretty good until I met a couple of hunters.

One commented, "I see you have shot a damned old coot." Shaking his head, he said to the other, "They aren't fit to eat." Disappointed and disgusted, I left the coot on the bank of the Ohio and went home.

Evelyn asked, "How did you do?"

I answered, "I didn't do any good."

She tried to look sad for my sake. But I could tell she was inwardly happy.

After reliving those stories, I fortunately couldn't recall any more duck or goose stories. So I went on to sleep.

I waited until mid-morning the next day to go to the viewing stable to check on the geese. I was hoping the injured goose would be gone with the rest. However, that was not the case. They were all still there. But much unrest was visible. The former lead gander was hovering close to the injured one. Another gander appeared to be encouraging the others to think about getting underway. This gander was springing out of the water about four feet and getting the others to do likewise. Then all of a sudden, it took to the air, and the others followed.

The former lead gander stayed by the injured goose until the others were in the air, then he, too, took off. He circled her one time and then was soon in formation with the others. I hoped that he told her, "I shall return."

Evelyn, being the soft-hearted person she was, immediately decided to care for the goose. She referred to the goose as "my goose." She called out "Here, Goosey Goose" to let her know whenever she had food for her. However, Evelyn didn't try to tame her or pet her for fear she wouldn't be willing to leave with her friend if he returned for her.

Goosey Goose spent the summer in and near the pond. She grazed around for plant food and insects and spent the night in the middle of the pond for safety.

The summer turned to fall. We realized that Goosey Goose had made a full recovery. She got so she wanted to stand on the levee end of the pond and exercise her wings. She would sometimes fly out in the meadow for a short time and return to the pond. I felt sure she would leave with her mate, or sooner or later, she would join some other flock flying south for the winter.

One Saturday afternoon, between Thanksgiving and Christmas, I saw a small flock of geese light on the pond around three o'clock. I didn't want to take a chance of frightening them away, so I waited until morning to check on them.

In the morning, Evelyn and I quietly entered the barn from the north side. We stood where we would be unnoticed, at the south entrance facing the pond. There sat Goosey Goose and a gander, as close together as they could get. I felt sure it was her former mate. The whole flock was as "idle as a painted ship upon a painted ocean."

Suddenly, a gander sprang out of the water and let out what must have been a wake-up call. Movement began to take place. Other geese honked and exercised their wings. However, Goosey Goose and her mate remained motionless, as if they didn't wish to break the charm of their present bliss.

The lead gander cleared the water, and the other geese followed. Just as Evelyn and I began to feel the lovebirds were choosing to remain behind, they rose from the water and fell in line behind the others. With tears in her eyes, in a voice just above a whisper, Evelyn said, "Bye-bye,

Goosey Goose." She and I stood in each other's embrace. We didn't need to say a word. We were able to read each other's thoughts: "Like Goosey Goose and her mate, we are together for the long haul."

*   *   *

Sampson's Memoirs

Before telling my story, let me introduce myself. I am a mule named Sampson. You may have heard of me before. Kestner Wallace, who owned me for several years, wrote at least six stories about me that were published years ago in the *Springhouse* magazine and later in his book, *A Dollar the Hard Way*. Now that's all right as far as it goes, but in all that time, who is doing all the telling? Kestner. And who haven't you heard from? Little ol' me. I feel like in all fairness I should be allowed a chance to tell my side of the story—and maybe even some things Kestner wouldn't tell you. So here goes. . . .

I actually have had the name Sampson throughout my life except for the first year. That year my twin half-brothers and I were collectively called Hard Tails.

My first owner, Willie Wallace, who was Kestner's father, had two mares—a black mare and a bay mare. In April of 1930, the black mare brought twin horse mules. They were black with white noses. On the same day, the bay mare brought a brownish-bay mule, which happened to be me. Mr. Wallace was overjoyed and boasted to neighbors that he got three $100 mules out of two mares on the same day.

Mr. Wallace hadn't raised mules before, but he was proud of us. He decided to make us look like mules from the first day. So he took a sharp pair of shears and trimmed our manes and the hair of our tails, skin close, from the root of our tails down about four inches. That made us look like mules. At least that is what everyone said who looked at us.

Mr. Wallace's three sons were lined up, watching this hair cutting. It must have been one of Mr. Wallace's better days at barbering, because when he finished, our haircuts looked better than his sons' haircuts. That may have been because his shears were sharper than his barbering scissors.

When the shearing was complete, the three sons, beginning with Kestner, rubbed the sheared part of each of our tails. Kestner commented, "What hard tails they have!" That's when the three of us were immediately named Hard Tails.

If you will forgive me for bragging on myself, I'll let you in on a little secret. I had those twin mules beat by a country mile for looks. But do you think anyone paid any attention to me when the Wallaces invited people out to see the Hard Tails? No, they didn't. That was my first bitter disappointment in life. People "oohed" and "aaahed" and had fits and blind spells about how "precious," "darling," and "cute" the twins were. They paid no attention to me. That got under my hard-tail skin. If you think a mule doesn't have feelings, you have another think coming. I consider myself fortunate that my personality wasn't warped beyond repair.

Aggressive behavior, beyond that of mule play, had already set in. I would bite one of the twins on the sheared part of his tail and pretend that the other twin did it. They soon caught on to that trick, and both of them tried to kick me when I got close to them.

Then I tried to take out my frustrations on my mother. When I started to get my dinner, I very slowly, with increasing intensity, began to bite down on mother bay mare's teat. Very slowly and unconcerned like, she turned her head around, and with her teeth, she caught me by the root of my tail. I saw stars and decided my tail wasn't very hard after all. I didn't try that again.

Mr. Wallace's decision to give each of his sons a mule was a turning point in my life. He gave me to Kestner, which turned out to be in my best interest. I received social enrichment and personality improvement. He renamed me Sampson. I liked that name. The name "Hard Tail" was beneath my dignity. The twins were given to Byrum and Victor, who were both younger and quite a bit smaller than Kestner. Byrum named his mule Barney, and Victor called his mule Pete.

Byrum and Victor didn't take an interest in the twins that Kestner took in me. They saw that Barney and Pete had feed and water and their noses rubbed, but they soon became afraid of their mules. Barney let his feelings be known at the ripe old age of one day old, when he kicked a rude, curious visitor in the stomach with both feet. That was his way of saying he didn't like to be "goosed."

Kestner broke me to halter-lead and to pull a little sled when I was three months old. He had less trouble breaking me to work than my mother did weaning me. When he'd use my mother's back to take a big bag of shelled corn to the mill to be ground into meal, he would put a small bag with about five pounds in it across my back. He was guarding against the day I might have bucked him off had he not worked with me while I was young.

One day when the twins were three years old, a mule buyer came and told Mr. Wallace that he was looking for a small team of mules for a farmer who lived on a forty-acre hill farm in Kentucky. As Mr. Wallace showed the man the twins, he pointed out that they were well matched and as tough as pine knots. However, he went on to say that they were as green as gourds and wouldn't ride.

That statement, "As green as a gourd," set me back about three ax handles. I wasn't sure if Mr. Wallace was losing his marbles or if I was colorblind. It further confused me when the mule buyer said that the mules being green would not make a dime's worth of difference to him. He went on to say that Billy Jim Jones would rather buy a team of mules green and break them to suit himself. You can imagine that I felt like a jackass when I realized that a green team of mules were mules that hadn't been handled or "broke" to work or ride.

They agreed upon a price of $200. I had mixed emotions when the twins were loaded up and hauled away. I missed them, but with them out of the way, all the extra attention I got helped me to put thoughts of them out of my mind.

When Byrum and Victor got home from school and learned that Barney and Pete had been sold, they wanted to know if they would be getting the money. Mr. Wallace told them that the money would have to be divided among the three of them. He explained that he had furnished all the corn and hay Barney and Pete had eaten. He handed Victor and Byrum two dollars each and asked them if they were satisfied.

Byrum grinned as he said, "I'm satisfied that that's all we'll get."

Victor's comment was, "Now that I'm out of the mule business, I plan to stay out."

As Kestner and I bummed around, I learned that almost everyone liked to play pranks on each other. His cousins, whom he referred to as Uncle Courty's boys, were the world's worst. I won't be able to include some of the things they did because it would cause me to blush. When something causes a mule to blush, it isn't anything to write home about. Now don't get me wrong. What they did wasn't sinful, but for the lack of a better term, I would say it was a little on the hellish side. However, a multitude of the things weren't really too bad.

One fall evening, Kestner rode me to a country church a ways off the highway. His cousin had arrived just ahead of us. He was holding his horse and talking to four or five fellows. He offered to take me around back and hitch me along with his horse. He said that his horse would be happier with another animal for company.

This cousin hitched his horse, but instead of also tying me to a tree, he caught three or four lightning bugs and spread the illuminating part of their back ends on my front teeth. That made me appear to have a mouth of gold. Then he led me back around and told Kestner he had better tie me up himself, because he didn't want to be responsible in case I got loose. Then he began to make a little fun of Kestner for being so fussy about me. He said that it would not surprise him if my front teeth were crowned with gold.

I didn't pay much attention. You know, talk is cheap. I had free rein, but I stayed close without turning my back on the group. I started smelling around on the ground. When I detected something that smelled bad, I raised my head and stretched out my neck as far as I could, like a wild goose in flight. I stuck up my upper lip and stood that way for the longest time. I had seen the twins act that way many times. But I had no idea it was so funny. That hillbilly group laughed like crazy. Kestner's face turned as red as a gobbler's snout. I was confused and felt downright silly. We vowed to ourselves that we would soon get even.

One evening Kestner and I saw one of Uncle Courty's boys pass the house going to Joe Tucker's to get a bucket of buttermilk. We knew it would be dark when he would be coming back the half mile up the road. So Kestner fastened a sheet around me and made it still more secure by putting a saddle over it.

When it was dark enough that one couldn't tell a horse from a cow at a distance of thirty feet, we were waiting about thirty feet across the fence. We were hidden among some bushes about a quarter of a mile south of our house.

This fine young man was wearing a pair of four-buckle overshoes with no shoes under them, as protection from snakes. They were loose on his feet and terribly noisy. Since this was the scariest part of the trip, this "dear" cousin whistled—off-tune, of course—continuously. The whistling got so horrible that he decided to sing. The song he chose was "I Shall Not Be Moved."

When he got about ten feet past us, Kestner got on my back; we moved along holding our distance of about ten feet behind him. He soon heard the sound of my feet and looked back over his shoulder. The first thing he did was quicken his pace. The second thing he did was lose the tune of "I Shall Not Be Moved." But he didn't stop singing. That was his way of saying, "I'm not afraid of death, hell, or the grave."

We moved in close to the fence and only about five feet behind. This was more than our dearly beloved could stand. Still singing, he broke into a dead run.

What happened next not only scared the gizzard out of the buttermilk-toting cousin, it also almost frightened Kestner's pants off (and my sheet, too). Kestner gave me an urgent request for full speed ahead. In my zeal to comply, I sprang forth. Just as we got even with this "I Shall Not Be Moved" cousin, I jumped a rabbit from its hiding place. As it darted away, it startled me so badly that I ran sideways over a six-foot bush. Kestner let out a shriek that didn't sound like man or beast. The dear "cuz" not only stopped singing but also moved in ways I thought impossible for the human body.

As we headed for the barn, I could tell that Kestner was shaking with muffled laughter. Well, you know a mule can't laugh, so I did the next best thing. I closed both eyes and snorted as loudly as I could.

We learned the following day through informed sources that what started out as a full gallon of buttermilk ended up being less than a quart. What a loss! My heart bled. But not much. When anyone remotely suggested that we might have had anything to do with the deal, we just acted dumb. That came naturally.

Seeing Uncle Courty's boys and Kestner play jokes on one another made me want to get in on the fun. One day Kestner led me to the watering hole in the spring branch at the edge of the barn lot. I was in the habit of wading knee deep into the water where it was cool near the water gate. Kestner would stand on the bank and give me all the rein he could by leaning on a sassafras staff.

On this particular day, I pretended that I couldn't get enough water. I kept my lips in the water for the longest time and only swallowed once in a while. When Kestner tried to get me to go, I would start drinking again and then stand there with my lips in the water and refuse to be reined out of the water.

Kestner dropped the rein. I thought I had put one over on him. Before I knew what was happening, he let me have it across the lower part of my hindquarters with the staff on which he had been leaning. I almost ran through the water gate. I didn't try that again.

I was in a bad mood as Kestner saddled me for a ride. I was disappointed at his inability to see the humor in a perfectly innocent joke. So for the first hundred yards after we started, I cat-loped in the normal way. When he tried to change my direction to a right angle, I pretended to be obedient and turned my head around until my nose touched his leg, but I continued going in the same direction until I crashed into a sycamore tree.

That crash put some sense in my head. I decided that pranking stuff was for Kestner, Uncle Courty's boys, and the birds. I became satisfied to be in on some of Kestner's pranks, but I didn't really pull off any by myself.

However, the only way I know how to get even with Kestner for busting me at the watering hole is to tell about his first poor, pitiful crack at taking a girl home. The evening church service was over, and a number of people of different ages were walking south on a dirt road east of Womble Mountain. The crowd got a head start on Kestner and me. When we caught up, it appeared that all the people were paired off, with one exception. At the back of the spread-out group, a young gal was walking along with a married couple. Kestner didn't know her. But she looked good to him by the light of a harvest moon. Her hair was shoulder length. She wasn't too big or too little — she was filled out in the right places and certainly looked better than a hundred-dollar mule.

Kestner was as nervous as a cat about to pounce on a rat. He didn't know whether to get off and walk with her or show her how much dirt I could kick up as we tore off down the road. The gal solved that problem by suggesting that he get off and walk with her, or that she get on and ride with him.

Kestner got off. While she fiddled around with her shoe, the other couple walked on. There Kestner stood like a knot on a log, trying to look macho, but shaking in his boots while racking his brain trying to think what to talk about. Again he lucked out. She grabbed him by the arm, and they took off. Kestner didn't need to talk. She talked enough for both of them. I tagged along behind on a lead rein. I hoped he would make a good impression, because I liked the gal. With my interest in people and psychology and with 20/20 vision, I didn't miss a thing.

The first thing to catch my roving eyes was the sway that this gal took on from her waist down. I had to look away now and then to keep from being hypnotized. Even then I kind of got in the swing of her artistic movements and was surprised when I noticed my back half swaying from east to west. This carefree song sprang from my heart:

> *This is east, and this is west,*
> *The Ohio River is at its crest*
> *And will it be a noble quest*
> *When I jump o'er the cuckoo's nest?*

It wasn't long until those swaying hips began to brush Kestner's hips ever so lightly. I held my breath because I wasn't sure whether that was going to turn him on or off or cause his blood pressure to run away with itself. I didn't have to worry long. The bumps against him became more pronounced. Kestner swayed over to his right with his hips and caught her as she swayed to the left. He almost knocked her off her feet.

Kestner's inability to get on the same playful wavelength with her, along with his rudeness, embarrassed me so much that I could have fallen down and stuck all four feet in the air and died — dead. Even as a dumb, unschooled donkey, I knew this little gal was putting on a little innocent hanky-panky playacting to see if he had the pulse of a man or a boy.

However, Kestner's awkwardness didn't seem to ruffle the feathers on that little beauty queen of a wampus cat. She just laughed and said, "Big boy, I'm going to give you just thirty minutes to settle down and walk right."

Kestner gulped before asking, "What will happen then?"

Grinning, she declared, "I'll probably haul off, draw back, wind up, and knock your can over Womble Mountain." But the musical laughter that burst forth from her, and the way she put her arm around him and pulled herself close to him, made what she said sound like a big joke.

Kestner began to talk more as we walked along. It would be more correct to say that he gave repeated, detailed excuses why they couldn't walk more slowly and enjoy the moonlight. When she suggested that they sit on the nice, soft grass and rest for a while, the excuse was still the same—he had to get home, so he could get up early in the morning and plow corn. I would have been in for resting now and plowing that corn sometime later. But we kept walking.

As we neared the house where this gal was visiting, Kestner began to get nervous again. By putting three and seven together, I later figured out what was bothering him. He wanted to do things up like a regular Romeo, but he wasn't sure of himself. He didn't know whether or not to kiss her on the first date.

They turned off the dirt road and walked up and stopped in front of the house where she was a guest. I could tell from the look in the gal's eyes that the potential for a kissing scene was higher than hickory cane corn in August. I began to hurt all over because I knew in my bones that Kestner would make a fool of himself. I just didn't want to see him do that. So I sat on my haunches and put my ears so far back they touched my neck. That cut off my hearing. I closed my eyes, so I couldn't see anything; I just sat there and almost died wondering what was taking place.

When I could wait no longer, I put my ears forward. The first thing I heard was a loud "whoo-ee!" I managed to keep my eyes closed a few more seconds. When I opened my eyes, I saw Kestner stagger back about three steps and stand there in the moonlight, much like a goose in a hailstorm. He didn't know if the earth was round or square. In my heart of hearts, I knew his mind wasn't on plowing corn.

He took two steps forward and one step back. It didn't take me long to figure out what he was thinking: "Shall I go or shall I stay a little longer?" Then, if my mind-reading was correct, he, quite disgusted with himself, thought: "After all my talking of getting home and plowing corn, there isn't much else I can do except say 'Good night' and leave."

It was easy to tell by the rigid way that Kestner sat in the saddle that all was not well with him. Since I had been on my good behavior, I knew he couldn't be sore at me. Nevertheless, I was the victim of three hot flashes of anger. Each time, he would warm my leather with a hickory switch he had fastened to the saddle, I would tear up the road for a short distance, then he would make me walk until the next hot flash struck. Finally, I saw Kestner throw the switch away. When he stopped under an apple tree and began to feed me apples quartered with his knife, I knew all was well again.

After seeing what Kestner went through that night, had he offered to change places with me, I would have replied,

"I'd rather be a mule." He never saw that gal again after that night. If I were a betting mule, I would bet four ears of corn and a bundle of hay that "going out and hanging herself" never crossed the gal's mind.

Now, my dear spellbound readers, there is much more that I intended to write. But inasmuch as my backend is numb from sitting on this stump, and I'm about to get writer's cramp, I'll say so long for now.

Your friend,
Sampson

*   *   *

God Bless the Mountain People

In the 1920s, cottage prayer meetings were common in the area around Womble Mountain in the southeastern part of Saline County. Hardly anyone is now alive who attended those meetings. One of my younger brothers, Byrum, is at least one. He and I were probably around eight and ten years old at the time.

These prayer meetings were held at different homes once a week. Church services were held only once a month at Herod Springs Church. For the religiously inclined people around the mountain, that wasn't enough church to keep their souls blessed.

[You readers can rest at ease. There will be no sermonizing, passing the hat, or altar-calling—just a reminiscing of how things were for a short time many years ago.]

These meetings were held on a high level of respectability and were attended by old and young—actually, mostly women and young people. The social aspect of these meetings was far-reaching. People learned from each other what was going on far and near. The budding of a few romances took place at these meetings.

On the evening of the meeting, after an extended period of visiting and socializing, the meeting was started by the one who had volunteered or been appointed to lead. Someone gifted in speaking was called on to offer a prayer. The prayer set the tone and a more serious atmosphere. People were then given an opportunity to recite Bible verses they had learned the past week.

Singing was an important part of each service. Thinking back on those times, I'm amazed that the people could sing so well without accompaniment. They made their own music. Young people would sing duets and quartets. That part of the service verged on being a talent show.

The real part of the service seemed to begin when someone would lead the entire group in two or three songs. Once when the song leader asked if anyone had a selection, Byrum suggested, "She'll Be Coming 'round the Mountain." The song leader said she liked that song very much, but it wasn't a church song. Byrum in no way felt put down.

Someone suggested, "Bringing in the Sheaves." It was sung with much vim and vigor. Then Byrum asked, "Why don't we sing 'Bringing in the He's'?" People laughed, and he did, too, without knowing why.

At one of these meetings, three young men showed up from the community known as Eagle Creek, which was across the mountain range that ran north and south just east of Womble Mountain. They didn't mind being referred to as Eagle Creekers. They were fine young men, as I later determined most Eagle Creek people to be.

These young men weren't drunk, but they had had a drink or two. They added to the quality of the group singing. In fact, they showed talent. However, they got carried away with the singing of "When We All Get to Heaven." Their enthusiasm caused them to spring to their feet and jump up and down like jumping jacks as they tried to raise the rafters. I found their behavior very amusing and wondered why all our meetings couldn't be that lively.

Aunt Alice Lambert (no relation to us), who was in charge of the service, had a kind, serious look on her face. In no way did she try to shame the young men for becoming carried away. She commented that she, too, felt like shouting when thinking of getting together in Heaven. Directing her attention on one of the young men, she commented, "Your mother is a wonderful Christian woman. I love her. I hope you will make her heart glad by singing praises to God." Aunt Alice's comments had a sobering effect on the boys.

...

Speaking of "When We All Get to Heaven" reminds me of something that happened about six years later that sort of shocked as well as amused me. Please pardon the digression.

My dad had the ability to sing. (Unfortunately, none of it rubbed off on me.) Among his favorite songs were the following: "Uncloudy Day" (perhaps since he was deathly afraid of storms), "Where We'll Never Grow Old," and "When We All Get to Heaven."

Already fifty when I was born, my dad was old when his sons were young. The four of us were wild enough at times to send him on to the Glory Land. Since I was the eldest of the boys, Dad at some point had appointed me as bouncer and expected me to exert whatever authority necessary to maintain order.

One time I came into the living room where Dad was sitting. Wishing to get him to join in, I was trying to sing "When We All Get to Heaven." However, he was in a low, nervous mood. His mood affected me. My three brothers—Byrum, Victor, and Gaylord—who were two, four, and ten years younger than I was, were carrying on rather wildly in the adjoining room. Dad gave me an order to go in and give the boys a good thrashing and make them quieten down.

I walked in and found Byrum and Victor in a nose-to-nose, rooster-fighting posture and six-year-old Gaylord on the sideline enjoying the show. I walked up and roughly shoved the boys apart as I tongue-lashed them. I back-handed them a time or two on the shoulder for good measure.

Thinking I had taken care of my job, I turned to leave while still having the song "When We All Get to Heaven" in my mind. I sounded off on the chorus with "When we all get to Heaven . . ." and turned to see what effect my carrying on had had. Out of the corner of my eye, I saw little Gaylord, in obvious sympathy with his brothers, nod toward me and in an undertone say, "*If* we all get there."

...

Now, back to the cottage meetings. One time, a very kindly older man, who traveled around in a closed-in horse-drawn wagon while selling various goods, was an overnight guest where prayer meeting was held one week. He was intrigued by our part of the country and the people. I don't know where he was from. He commented that he had a religious background, and if we liked, he would sing us a song, "Amazing Grace."

The thing that amazed me was the way he musically hung on and drew out each word in the song. He closed his eyes as he sang and almost appeared to be having an out-of-body experience. He concluded by saying, "After tonight we'll probably never meet again. For now, let me say, 'God bless you mountain people.'"

I would like to hear "Amazing Grace" sung again that way. However, I equally enjoy the song every time I hear it, as it is so wonderfully sung on many different occasions.

The last cottage prayer meeting I recall attending was at our home. It was the only one my dad ever attended. He invited a well-known Social Brethren minister, Sherman Rector, the grandfather of the late Sherman Rector of the Rudement community. Reverend Rector lived a quarter mile west, across the field from us. A well-beaten path joined the two houses.

Dad was a Missionary Baptist. He believed "once in grace, always in grace" and in closed communion. However, the two men had great respect for each other and addressed each other as Brother Sherman and Brother Willie.

Mom was to lead prayer meeting that evening, but she invited Reverend Rector to take charge instead. He gladly accepted. His talk, following the usual singing and prayer, was a full-blown sermon. I was nervous throughout for fear I wouldn't get to show off in reciting the 100th Psalm. Mom saw to it that I was called on, and Reverend Rector complimented me. That put the icing on the cake for the evening.

Dad appeared to be blessed by Reverend Rector's message. The next morning as he hitched the black mare to the buggy to go to the store at Rudement, he spoke more kindly to the dog, the horse, and me.

(Now I don't want to give you the wrong impression about my dad. He was an honest, truthful, hard-working, God-fearing man, respected by all who knew him. When I take into consideration his age, undiagnosed and untreated ailments, the Great Depression, and a houseful of six noisy kids, he was a saint of sorts.)

On the way to the store, we met Reverend Rector. Walking with a basket on his arm, he was returning from the store. He said that he had traded some eggs for some coffee and sugar and a few little things his family needed.

Dad complimented him on his sermon of the evening before and handed him a dollar. Reverend Rector seemed surprised and said, "Brother Willie, you don't need to do that." However, he took the money without too much arm twisting and seemed very pleased to get it. After exchanging a few remarks, they shook hands and continued on their separate ways.

Having Dad and Reverend Rector at the same meeting was outstanding in itself. I will always be thankful that this last cottage meeting at our house was the one that topped them all.

...

In case you are wondering whether Gaylord forgave me for my rough treatment of his buddies, he did. As he began to get sleepy that night, he climbed into my lap and asked, "Kestner, will you sing me a song?"

I asked, "What do you want me to sing?"

He replied, "I don't care — 'Darling Nellie Gray' or that song you made up last night."

"What song was that?"

"It was 'Bye Oh Sugar-Coated Skunk Cat.'"

...

When roads got better and cars came into use, cottage prayer meetings faded away with the horse and buggy. With easier accessibility, people instead started attending churches at Herod Springs, Rudement, Spring Valley, Blue Springs, Big Saline, and Sulphur Springs.

How the years since then have flown — gone, never to return, but not forgotten. When I compare then and now, the difference is remarkable. Back then, we didn't have indoor plumbing, electricity, electrical appliances, telephones, or central heat and air conditioning. Never having had them, we didn't miss them. We lived close to nature, worked hard, and were happy in so doing.

You all know about today. You can take it from me — it is better in many ways. However, people aren't any happier than they were years ago, leaving me to believe that happiness is a state of mind. I am certain that expressing our thankfulness in cottage prayer meetings made its contribution.

* * *

A Doggone Good Lesson

When I look back more than seventy-five years ago, in the mid-1930s, I realize that despite my having a number of admirable qualities, I was, underneath the surface, rather self-centered. Oh, I cared about my family—no doubt about that—but I was always looking out for number one. I hang my head in shame to admit that now. However, in just a three-day period, when I was around fourteen years old, something happened that created a rather drastic change in my personality.

As I awoke one sunny morning in mid-September, before school started its fall session (school started later back then), I really had no idea what the day would bring. I had thought only as far as breakfast. However, my dad, who was in his early sixties, gave me my marching orders soon after breakfast.

He said, "Kestner, you and Byrum hitch Lil and Maud to the wagon for me."

Surprised, I asked, "Why?"

He answered firmly, "I'm going to R.S. Hart's slope mines near Mitchellsville to get a load of coal. I can get a load for a dollar if I load it myself. That will keep you boys from having to cut so much wood."

Being free to express my opinion, I immediately objected, "Dad, with your heart condition and Lil's being unnerved so easily by passing cars and trucks, it won't be safe."

Dad was unmoved. He replied, "I'll take my chances. I'm sure some fellows at the mine will pitch in and help me load."

The real reason for my objecting to Dad's going after the load of coal was that I wanted him to send me instead. I thought it would be an exciting trip. But Dad was firm in his resolve to go himself.

I saw there was no point in arguing further. Just before he left, Dad informed us that he had just filed our crosscut saw. He told my brother Byrum, who was then nearly twelve, and me to go up on Womble Mountain and cut at least one wagonload of heating wood that day. Byrum and I never had second thoughts of doing otherwise.

I took a close look at Dad's filing job on the saw. He must not have been wearing his glasses, because he had missed filing some of the saw teeth, and others he had filed too much, leaving them ragged and uneven. Nevertheless, we took the saw, along with the ax, wedge, and maul (a heavy hammer), and took off to the woods.

The saw cut worse than before Dad had sharpened it. Byrum commented, "I watched him sharpen the saw. He wrapped a tow sack around the saw and held it under his left arm to file it. He should have let me hold it for him."

We had half a load cut when we went in to dinner around noon. In the afternoon, we rounded out what we thought was a load.

Dad returned a while before sundown. He was unnerved and exhausted from the trip. We had to help him off the wagon and into the house. He said that the wagon had very nearly turned over in the ditch when the team had spooked as an old, loud truck went by. At Mom's urging, he ate a light supper and went to bed early. The night's sleep almost brought him back to normal.

The next morning, Byrum and I took two large blocks of wood about thirty inches long and set them up on end. Then we sawed a groove in each of them about four inches deep and erected the blocks about three feet apart. Into these grooves we placed our crosscut saw—teeth up—to hold the saw firmly in place. I sat on a shorter block of wood and started filing. I chalked the long saw teeth to file them down and make them even with the others. It was close, tedious work, but I had a feeling all was going well.

Byrum was some distance from me, doing some needed repair on a homemade wheelbarrow. He was a wonderful, mischievous brother. While two years younger than I and several pounds lighter, he was very nearly as strong as I was and just as sharp in the head. I always pretended to be smarter, however.

Byrum was closer to the driveway when a man pulled up in a nice car with a Missouri license plate. I thought to myself, "It's someone wanting directions. I'll just stick to my filing and let Byrum talk to him."

Sure enough, the stately man in his sixties asked Bryum, "Young man, can you tell me where the road is that turns off this road and goes to Eagle Creek?"

I was sure Byrum knew, so I decided to let him have the experience of giving directions. I kept my eyes on the saw and my ears on the conversation.

I was a little embarrassed as well as amused at Byrum's reply: "That depends on why you want to know. If you are a revenue man, I don't have any idea where it is. But if you are interested in some good molasses or some good smoked hams, I might be able to recollect where that road is."

That answer and comment amused this man. His belly-shaking laugh relieved my feelings a bit. Nodding at me, the man asked Byrum, "Is this your brother filing the saw?"

Byrum replied, "Yes, he is my brother. He knows everybody on Eagle Creek. In fact, he went over to Eagle Creek last week to get a blacksmith, Ezra Seets, to shoe his mule."

The man commented, "That's interesting. I didn't know people shod mules."

Byrum said, somewhat proudly, "Sampson is an unusual mule. My brother plans to race him in about two weeks over on the county line road between Saline County and Gallatin County. A man has a fifty-dollar bet on Sampson. He is giving my brother five dollars for racing the mule, win or lose, and half of the fifty if he wins. Other men are betting, too."

The man said, "That must be a fine mule." After a pause, he continued, "Young man, it was good talking with you. By the way, what is your name?"

Byrum answered, "I'm Byrum Wallace. I was carrying on a little just for fun. Around here we have to create our own fun."

The man said, "No problem, Byrum. In fact, I liked it. If I had a boy, I'd want him to be just like you. My boys all turned out to be girls." He added quickly, "But I love them to death." Looking thoughtful, he then said, "I think I'll have a little talk with your brother."

I stood as the man came over to me. He stuck out his hand and said, "I'm Jacob Crabtree. I'm a retired railroad executive. I live out in the country outside of Poplar Bluff, Missouri." He continued, with a twinkle in his eye: "I don't hunt, fish, or play golf. I bet you can't guess what my hobby is."

With my tongue in my cheek, I responded, "Well, maybe you like to chase women."

Appearing amused, Mr. Crabtree said, "Instead of women, I like to take a good coon dog and chase coons and tree them. My hobby dates back to my childhood, when we hunted coons to eat and to sell the pelts to buy food. I don't eat them now, but instead give them to an elderly man who has worked for me for years. He barbecues them and shares them with his family." He continued, with a faraway look in his eye, "You may wonder what I get out of a coon hunt. Well . . . I get to pray, meditate, and live in the past while the dog hunts."

I extended my hand and said, "Mr. Crabtree, it is a pleasure to meet you." I told him I was Kestner Wallace and hoped that I could be of some help to him. I let him know that I had heard every word of his and Byrum's conversation.

Mr. Crabtree replied, "I'm sure you can help me find the man I'm looking for on Eagle Creek. His last name is Milligan."

When he supplied me with the first name, I said, "Mr. Crabtree, I know the man. I bought a cow from him about six months ago. He told me the cow would produce a gallon of milk, morning and evening. That is exactly what she does, too."

Mr. Crabtree's eyes lit up, and he said, "Wonderful, you will be able to tell me where to turn off this road to go to Eagle Creek and where to find Milligan's place."

Happy to be of help, I said, "Yes, I can tell you. You continue on down Route 34 for two miles. Just before you get to a large country general store, a road turns a sharp left. That is the Eagle Creek Road. It runs north. About four miles up this road, people begin to proudly call themselves 'Eagle Creekers.'"

Mr. Crabtree asked, "Do many people on Eagle Creek coon hunt?"

I replied, "To be truthful, Mr. Crabtree, I don't know. I have an uncle by marriage who lives on Eagle Creek. He has a couple of foxhounds. He says it is music to his ears to hear their baying bark when they are after a fox. He doesn't try to kill the foxes, though."

Thoughtfully, Mr. Crabtree said, "It occurs to me that I should hire you to go with me to Mr. Milligan's and take a look at his coon dog. I learned about his dog a couple of months ago and have been corresponding with Mr. Milligan about it. He told me he wouldn't take a hundred dollars for his dog and added it wasn't for sale. I asked him if he would take two hundred dollars for it. His answer was, 'I wouldn't turn down two hundred dollars.' So, now, Kestner, what would you charge to go with me to look at the dog?"

Excited about having an outing after all, I said, "Mr. Crabtree, I wouldn't charge you anything. It would be a pleasure to ride over there with you. That would give me a chance to tell Mr. Milligan how pleased we are with the cow."

I informed Dad and Mom of my offer to go with Mr. Crabtree to look at a dog, and we took off. We stopped at the general store at Herod and got a pound of wieners to win over the dog.

In less than an hour, we were sitting on Mr. Milligan's front porch. After Mr. Crabtree and Mr. Milligan had made their introductions, I took the opportunity to assure Mr. Milligan that the cow—Daisy Bell—was our prized possession and was doing well.

We then met the black coon dog—Midnight. It seemed as though he couldn't get close enough to his master's leg. He was alert, bright-eyed, and healthy, and neither overly friendly nor standoffish.

Mr. Crabtree commented to Mr. Milligan, "I hope that I can get him to like me as well as he likes you."

Mr. Milligan replied, "He won't take up all of a sudden and walk off with a stranger, but neither is he antisocial. He can easily be won over with food. He has a good appetite."

Mr. Milligan paused, and then continued, "I want to tell you of Midnight's big fault, at least in my eyes—I can't have him in the trunk of my car. When the lid goes down, he goes crazy. And he's not content to ride in the back of the car, either. He wants to ride in front with me. That isn't the worst of it. He can't get close enough to me. He wants to get in my lap and help with the driving."

Mr. Crabtree responded with a knowing look, "Mr. Milligan, I think you don't want to back out of selling the dog to me, but you might want to discourage me from buying him."

Shaking his head, Mr. Milligan said, "No, no, Mr. Crabtree, I'm a straight shooter. I just want to be fair with you. I'm willing to sell him to you, since you want a seasoned coon dog. I have a pup that Midnight sired. He will make me another coon dog."

Without further talk or opportunities for second thoughts, Mr. Crabtree handed Mr. Milligan two $100 bills, as he said, "I'm now the owner of another coon dog. Thank you, Mr. Milligan."

Mr. Milligan said earnestly, "I have a gut feeling you'll give Midnight a good home, or I'd be heartsick about letting you have him."

Mr. Crabtree assured him, "You can bet your last dollar I'll do that."

With that, Mr. Crabtree held out his hand toward me and said, "The wieners."

Mr. Crabtree opened up the sack, which immediately got Midnight's attention. They did smell good. Mr. Crabtree took one out of the sack and held it out to Midnight. Midnight's mouth watered as he looked up at his former master. Mr. Milligan gave him a nod, and he went over to Mr. Crabtree, gently took the wiener out of his hand, and then went back over to sit beside Mr. Milligan, where he made short work of downing it.

The whole process was repeated a time or two. Each time, Mr. Crabtree patted Midnight on the head. Then he broke a wiener in two and handed half of it to me. Both Mr. Crabtree and I fed Midnight the pieces of wiener and patted him on the head.

Then Mr. Crabtree announced, "We need to be on our way, Mr. Milligan. It was nice meeting you. Thank you very much for Midnight. I'll write and let you know how he is doing. I'm certain that my wife will love him."

Mr. Milligan walked with us to the car. I got in the back seat. He motioned for Midnight to get in with me. He did, and Mr. Crabtree drove off. I held Midnight's attention by pinching off bits of the remaining two wieners. When the wieners were gone, I pacified Midnight by patting him on the head and talking puppy-dog talk to him.

As Mr. Crabtree drove along, he said to me, "Kestner, I'll give you five dollars to ride over to my home near Poplar Bluff and keep Midnight company. You can spend the night with my wife and me. I have business in Sikeston tomorrow. I can bring you back that far and you can hitch-hike on home. What do you say to that offer? Would you feel comfortable hitchhiking that far?"

I replied eagerly, "I've hitchhiked a lot before, so I'll be glad to take you up on your offer. But I better ask my parents if it will be okay."

Mr. Crabtree stopped by our house, so I could seek their blessings for the trip. With permission granted, we were on our way. All went well. We found a number of topics to discuss as we traveled along, with me in the backseat with Midnight.

Midafternoon found us at a barbecue restaurant in Cairo, Illinois. Mr. Crabtree suggested I put the collar and leash on Midnight and take him for a walk. He said in the meantime, he would go into the restaurant to get each of us an extra-big barbecue and a milkshake to go, as well as some raw hamburger for Midnight.

We ate our barbecues and sipped our milkshakes while we sat on the hood of the car. Midnight ate his hamburger off a paper plate on the ground. He seemed happy with his new friends. When we finished, Mr. Crabtree said, "That should hold us until we get home. My wife will have a good supper for us when we get there."

We crossed the Mississippi River on the old two-lane bridge. At the high point of the bridge, Midnight stood up and peered out. He acted nervous, but I was able to soothe him by petting him and speaking softly to him.

Midnight eventually went to sleep. Mr. Crabtree and I talked less so as not to disturb him. When we did talk, we did so in a low tone.

By and by, Mr. Crabtree asked, "Kestner, do you have a girlfriend?" I told him I didn't. He seemed surprised and asked, "Why?"

I told him that girls who got my attention had little regard for a young man wearing a poor-fitting homemade shirt, sporting a wild haircut by a non-barber, and using a vocabulary too well blessed with double negatives and poor English.

Mr. Crabtree interrupted, "I have a far better opinion of you than you have of yourself. I'd say that your grammar and speaking ability are above average."

"Thank you, Mr. Crabtree. I know my speaking ability has improved in the past six months, since I've been tutored by an English major, and I've forced myself to read into the night and work on self-improvement. However, all that didn't give me time to think much about girlfriends."

"That's wonderful you're working to improve yourself, Kestner—I predict you will make something of yourself. The reason I brought up the subject of girlfriends was to perhaps give you a little advice in choosing a lifetime mate when the time comes. Making a good choice is better than having corn in the corncrib and money in the bank. It is a choice of a lifetime. My wife is one of the world's best. She is an angel. The good Lord chose her for me in answer to my mother's prayers. She prayed I would get a good wife—one that would love me and overlook my faults and make a man out of a wayward young man. That has been a work in progress. I don't think my wife will ever give up on me. She is an excellent teacher, and I try to be a good student.

"My dad was a good, God-fearing man. I once asked him: 'Dad, how can a man know if a woman loves him?' His answer, I will never forget. He said, 'You can see it in her eyes—they will sparkle. You can hear it in her voice—it will be musical. You can feel it in her touch—it will be magical. She will cause you to want to adore her and make her happy.'"

I listened intently and mentally took notes for the time, if it ever came, when I would be choosing a mate. However, I knew that wouldn't be anytime soon. At that time, I couldn't really imagine loving someone that much.

Mr. Crabtree and I talked continuously all the way to his lovely country home. His wife was sitting on a porch swing, waiting for his return. She appeared somewhat younger than her husband. By the time the car rolled to a stop, she was standing by the door on Mr. Crabtree's side of the car. When he got out, she placed a little kiss on his cheek and said, with her eyes sparkling, "I'm so glad you are back. I missed you."

In turn, Mr. Crabtree said, "I'm really glad to be back." He took her in his arms and gave her a big, warm hug. I marveled at the love that was so casually displayed before my eyes.

Releasing his wife from the hug, he said to her, "I have three introductions to make." He nodded at me and said to his wife, "This is Kestner Wallace; I'll tell you about him later. And this is my new coon dog, Midnight." Then, looking at me, he said, "Kestner, this is my wonderful wife."

Mrs. Crabtree smiled and said, "Hi, Kestner—I'm happy to meet you." To Midnight, she cooed, "Welcome, Midnight—good boy—you're a good puppy dog." As she stroked his head, Midnight wagged his tail in return.

Mrs. Crabtree said to Mr. Crabtree, "Honey, while you put Midnight in the pen and give him food and water, I'll put supper on the table."

As we seated ourselves for supper at an attractively set table for three, Mrs. Crabtree said, "I'll never know how I knew to prepare a complete meal for three."

Mr. Crabtree replied, "I'm not surprised. You always listen to a small voice within."

We did more eating than talking. Mrs. Crabtree made me feel very welcome, with her friendly smile and consideration of my feelings. I complimented her on a delicious meal and then asked if I could be excused to go and check on Midnight. My main reason was to give Mr. Crabtree a chance to tell his wife all about the days' happenings and me a chance to think about how I was going to spend my five dollars.

Midnight was stretched out asleep. I didn't disturb him but instead made myself comfortable in a lawn chair.

I watched the sun go down and listened to the katydids and other night sounds while I did my thinking about my future expenditures. I have to admit that I was thinking mostly of things for myself. All the possible scenarios were running through my mind until Mr. Crabtree came out and joined me. We talked until our eyes became heavy with sleep. He told me his wife had laid out a pair of his pajamas for me to sleep in, after a shower. I never slept better in my life.

At an early breakfast, I extended my sincere thanks to Mrs. Crabtree for her good food and kindness. She thanked me for my willingness to be of help to her husband and his dog. She handed me a little sack and said, "Here is a big peanut butter and jelly sandwich for you on the road." I thanked her once again. We said our good mornings and goodbyes to Midnight and were on our way. The miles sped by as we chatted away.

As we neared Sikeston, Missouri, Mr. Crabtree said, "I have the 'five' I promised you here in my shirt pocket. I'm doubly pleased with your service, so I want to double your pay."

In response, I told him happily, "When you paid me, I had planned to smile and say, 'Thank you for the five,' but now I want to smile and say, 'Thank you, thank you, thank you!' I would bet a nickel your wife put you up to doing that."

Surprised, Mr. Crabtree asked, "How did you know?"

"Your wife is an angel," I replied. I was touched by her easy generosity.

On reaching Sikeston, Mr. Crabtree let me out on a good-sized road with quite a bit of traffic, and we said our goodbyes.

It turned out that I had a long wait for a ride toward Cairo. I wasn't hungry, but to have something to do, I ate and enjoyed my sandwich. I folded the sack and put it in my pocket.

A rough, but friendly gentleman in a pickup truck finally gave me a ride. I was glad to get off my feet.

I said, with a smile, "Good morning, sir. Please tell me you are going to Cairo."

He laughed and said, "Hardly — just about halfway between Charleston and Cairo. I own a cotton field there. This morning, I had four pickers there who planned to leave when they each got their sacks full. They'll probably be gone by now. I have a caged-in wagon with about a ton of cotton in it. My pickers' hundred-pound sacks of cotton will be outside the cage for me to put in and lock up."

That gave me an idea. I said, "I'll gladly throw them in the cage for you if you'll allow me to pick this little sack full of cotton, so I can tell my grandkids one day that I picked cotton when I was a boy."

The man smiled and said, "It is a deal. . . . You know, you would probably make a good member of our liar's club. We meet once a month and tell white lies, black lies, and damn lies. In what group would you place your lie?"

"I guess it could be called 'a cotton-pickin' lie.'"

This guy was still amused when we reached the cotton cage wagon. I put the sacks in the wagon for him. He locked the cage, thanked me, and drove off.

I opened my paper lunch sack and then found an unpicked cotton row. The palms of my hands and the undersides of my fingers were tough and calloused, but the backs of my hands and fingers were tender. So I felt discomfort each time I put my clumsy hands into the rough cotton plant to get a bunch of cotton. By the time I got my little sack full, I had had all the cotton-picking experience I wanted. I went to the wagon, stuffed my less-than-one-pound sack of cotton through the bars, and headed back to the road.

As I neared the road, a car headed toward Cairo made a sudden stop. I thought happily, "I'm being offered a ride." I was sure wrong about that. The car door flew open and a woman carelessly and swiftly thrust a puppy dog out before the car sped away. That hardhearted act of cruelty almost made me sick to my stomach. The male beagle pup looked to be about six weeks old, healthy, and slick as a ribbon, with ears that were just right — long and attractive.

The puppy felt forsaken immediately. He went to the center of the road, sat down, and made a mournful sound much like that of an older dog howling at the moon. He got up, took three or four steps in each of the four directions, and then sat and howled again.

I hurried to the puppy. He saw me coming and ran to meet me while vigorously wagging his tail. I took him up in my arms and felt kindness toward him instantly. He responded by trying to lick my face. That was my first experience of "love at first sight." He had captured my heart. I thought, "Mine, all mine." My mind immediately started racing, thinking of how I would train the pup, and how we would hunt rabbits together. I could imagine him being my best friend for a long time to come. I decided to name him Lucky.

Holding the puppy in my arms, I started off down the road. I talked sweet puppy-dog talk to him, and he responded by reaching up to lick me and wiggling with delight, as only a beagle can. At that point in my life, I had never had a dog of my very own, so I felt a special bond with Lucky.

Not too long thereafter, a pickup truck with stock racks enclosing a white-faced yearling bull calf stopped. In the cab of the pickup were a rather young man, his wife, and a frail six- or seven-year-old boy.

The woman explained, "Our son, Billy, wanted us to stop so he could take a good look at your puppy. We are looking for a pup for Billy. Would your pup happen to be for sale?"

I said firmly, "No, he isn't for sale. I haven't had him long, but I don't want to part with him. We seem to belong to each other."

The woman asked eagerly, "Where did you get him? Are there more like him?"

Shaking my head, I gave her the bad news: "About fifteen minutes ago, a car stopped here and abandoned this pup. I found him, and he is mine."

The man chimed in, "How far do you live from here?" When I told him it was about ninety miles, the man asked, "Don't you fear you'll have trouble hitching a ride with a pup?"

I responded quickly. "No, people will feel sorry for me for not knowing better than hitchhiking with a dog, and they'll give me a ride."

The man asked me where I lived. When I told him my home was near Harrisburg, Illinois, he said, "We are headed to Carmi, Illinois, going through Harrisburg. If you don't mind crowding up a bit, we'll take you home."

I insisted, "I don't want to crowd you."

The woman spoke up, "We'll make room." She sat in the middle of the truck cab with the pup in her lap. Billy stood and held the dash until I got in and pulled him onto my lap. I saw there was room for him to sit between me and his mother when he wanted to change off.

We got underway. After a bit, I noticed that the woman was weeping softly and silently, while stroking the pup. Billy was touched when he saw his mother. He alternately patted the pup and his mother's hand, trying to comfort her. I had to look out the truck window on my side while I tried to deal with the big knot in my throat.

I had some serious thinking to do. I really wanted that pup. But I also couldn't help but remember the generosity of Mr. Crabtree and his angel-like wife, and the kindness that others had shown me, including these folks for giving me a ride. Even though I didn't know what was wrong with Billy, his mother's sadness and concern touched me.

After we had traveled about sixty miles, I made my decision. Before I could change my mind, I asked, "Billy, would you like to have this pup?"

Billy looked at me with big eyes and asked, "What?" His mother pleaded, "Please don't tease him. He gets upset easily."

I replied, "I'm not teasing. If Billy wants this pup, he can have him. He needs him worse than I do." Billy exclaimed with delight, "I want him!" Before covering the pup with kisses, he reached up and hugged my neck.

My heart melted, and I found that I was happy in my soul. I said to myself, somewhat in wonder, "It really is better to give than to receive."

Billy's dad offered, "I'll pay you the going price for a young beagle."

I replied, "I won't accept anything for him. The ride home is pay enough. The only way I can feel good about parting with this pup is to let Billy have him, because I know he really wants him." Looking at Billy's face, I had no doubt about that.

On our parting at Harrisburg, we exchanged thanks and big hugs. I got home in time for a delicious country supper. At the supper table, Dad questioned me all about my trip. After hearing some of the details, he got around to asking, "Did Mr. Crabtree pay you the five dollars he promised you?"

I declared, "Yes, he sure did."

Naturally, Dad then asked, "What do you plan to do with it?"

I stated proudly, "I plan to give it to you."

Without too much conviction, Dad responded, "You don't have to do that; I am sure you earned it."

To that, I explained, "Dad, I want you to have it. I haven't forgotten that you gave me Sampson. When I win that mule race in two weeks, I'll make a twenty-five dollar payment on top of that."

Dad replied with emotion, "Thank you, son. I'll spend it so the money will benefit us all. Thank God you are home safely."

In my heart, I was equally thankful. During those three days, I had learned a lesson of a lifetime. (Now I won't say that I totally learned it in those three days. I obviously kept the other five for myself. But it was the first step in a lifetime of learning, and I'm glad that I took that first step at age fourteen. It's a lesson that continues to this day.)

* * *

That Mule Won't Ride

One Friday afternoon in the spring, during my freshman year in high school, my elderly father told me, when I returned home from school, that he had hitched the black mare to the buggy and gone a few miles south of Thacker's Gap on the Harrisburg-Golconda dirt road to Hartsville, where he had bought a mule. With disgust in my voice, I asked, "Dad, why didn't you wait until tomorrow, so I could have gone along and passed judgment on the mule?"

I saw a warning signal on Dad's face, but I continued anyway, "You know I'll be the one working that mule after school and on Saturdays and sometimes on Sundays."

Dad didn't swear unless he became angry. I saw I was getting under his skin by questioning his judgment. At such times, rather than really swearing, he would say "sir" in a short, snappy, negative sort of way. He really meant, "By damn."

He said to me sharply, "Let me tell you, *sir*, I bought and sold mules more than fifty years before you were born."

Trying to smooth over my criticism, I said, "I'm sure you did a good job trading, Dad. I'm a little surprised that we need another mule."

Somewhat soothed, Dad said, "I can explain that, son. Both mares are expecting colts soon, so we won't be working them. Since Old Doc got struck and killed by lightning, we don't have an animal to team with Old Pete. If we plan to race Sampson at the fair this year, we need to shield him from hard work. So that's why I bought the mule today from my friend, George Smith."

I replied, "That's beginning to make sense." I certainly wanted to save Sampson, my gaited mule, for riding and not have him pulling plows, wagons, and cultivators. I thought that perhaps we did need another mule, although I still was not happy that Dad had bought him without me. Preparing to go take a look at the new acquisition, I asked, "Where is the mule now?"

Dad stated, "I didn't bring him home with me. I plan for you to catch a ride in the morning and go down to George's and lead him back."

I exclaimed, "Lead him back! Since when have I not been able to ride a mule?"

Dad said firmly, "I know, son, you are a mule rider, but George said this mule won't ride. He made me promise I wouldn't let anyone try to ride him. Walk that mule home, sir."

Midmorning on Saturday, with a check for a hundred dollars in my pocket, I was at George Smith's home in Hartsville. A small mule was hitched out front when I arrived.

I asked with surprise, "Mr. Smith, is this the mule you sold to my father?"

He answered, "Yes, son. He is small, but powerful, and is as tough as a pine knot. Your dad saw him pulling a wagonload of corn with another mule. What do you think of him?"

I said, not very politely, "I think he is a seventy-five dollar mule."

Mr. Smith assured me, "You will like him better when you have had him for a while."

With some effort, I got control of myself. I replied with a tight smile. "We'll work him this summer and trade him this fall for a yearling mule, and by and by, we'll have a hundred-dollar mule."

Mr. Smith looked relieved and replied, "You're a smart boy. You've got a good head on your shoulders."

"Thank you, Mr. Smith. I'm glad it's not a turnip." We laughed together.

Mr. Smith asked, "Did your dad tell you the mule won't ride?"

"Yes, Mr. Smith. He told me that in no uncertain terms."

I handed Mr. Smith the check. He looked at the check and then looked at me. I wondered if he was questioning whether my dad's check was good. I was both relieved and disgusted when he complained, "Do you know that it will cost me ten cents to cash this check?"

I replied, "I sure do. I paid a dime to cash a dollar check sometime back." Then I added, "You know that ninety-nine dollars and ninety cents is a good price for that little mule."

With our business settled, Mr. Smith and I shook hands, and I took off with the mule following like a puppy dog. When I was out of Mr. Smith's sight, I stopped and put the bridle rein over the mule's head. I called him a good mule as I petted him on the neck and wobbled the long ear next to me. I placed my hands on the mule's back and noticed that he had swiftly drawn his ears back as far as they would go. (For those of you who don't know mules, this was a sign he was about as unhappy as he could be with this turn of events.)

I went through the rubbing process again. I said to myself, "It is now or never."

I put my hands on the mule's back and began to spring up and down. Without wanting to sound vulgar, I can tell you all hell broke loose. That mule took on the appearance of being a demon possessed. He squealed more nerve-wrackingly than a jenny (a female jackass). He put his nose to the ground and stuck his hind legs high into the air. The split-second his hind legs hit the ground, he reared up on them and turned completely around while pawing the air. He carried on for a few seconds that seemed like a very long time. I said to myself, "This mule won't ride!"

When he finally calmed down enough for me to get close to him again, I rubbed his neck and wiggled his ears. We then proceeded on down the road.

We hadn't gone far until we met three girls, perhaps high school age, walking abreast down the middle of the road. They were all gaily dressed in skirts that flared out at the bottom. The girl in the middle looked a little older and was pleasingly plump.

Their forward movement was really an attention-getter. They had a rhythm that would lead one to think they were performing to music. They would take three steps forward, then a half step back. The gal in the middle would grab her skirt by the sides and lift it a bit above her knees. That seemed to be the cue for the other two girls to twirl around with their skirts flaring.

I was afraid their behavior would spook the mule, so I held a short leash on him and parked him to one side until they could pass by. One line of a song I'd heard years before came to mind: "Big-legged woman, please put your dress tail down!"

They walked up normal-like and stopped even with the mule and me. We grinned and nodded to each other. None of us uttered a word. The mule looked on.

The big girl approached the mule, placed her hands on his back, and sprang up and down a little. That set the mule off, and he repeated another full course of the previous behavior, a little worse this time.

I stood there like a goose in a hailstorm. The girls laughed so hard they could hardly stand up and then went merrily on their way. I muttered to myself, "Silly girls." The mule didn't say anything.

I stood for a couple of minutes rubbing the mule's neck as he got his ears in a friendly position again. Then we moved on homeward.

That encounter with the girls didn't improve my mood any. I walked down the road, kicking at stones, while I stormed inwardly at my dad for buying an overpriced mule and sending me after him. I was still grumbling to myself when we met a red-haired, freckle-faced boy, in patched overalls, wobbling along on an old oversized bicycle. He appeared to be about ten years old. When he was within ten feet of me, he stopped and supported the bicycle by leaning against it. Since he appeared to want to say something or ask something, I stopped beside him.

With a pleasant look, this boy asked, "Why ain't you riding that mule? Why?"

I calmly replied, "That mule won't ride."

He tried to look shocked and said, "I'll be a son-of-a-gun."

I began to suspect that this little mule was somewhat famous around these parts, and that the boy knew more about the mule than he was letting on. So I asked, "Would you like to ride him?"

With a slight shiver, he shot back, "Good Lord, no!" He shoved off on his bike and never looked back.

The mule and I headed home once more. As we were walking, a big, black horsefly started buzzing around the mule's and my ears. The mule kept his short tail going from side to side and in circles, probably thinking, "I'll keep him off my back end."

Knowing the horsefly would light, I stopped. Immediately, the fly lit on the mule's shoulder. I slapped it dead. Again we moved on. It wasn't long until another fly started buzzing around. That mule stopped dead still and looked at me as if to ask, "What are you going to do about it?"

I popped the second fly with the palm of my hand. It fell to the ground as the mule looked on. I thought, "You mean little dickens—I just might learn to like you—someday."

With his latest problem resolved, the mule, on his own, moved forward. I walked beside him so that I could observe his ears, which were a very accurate barometer of what was going on inside his head. Suddenly, his ears went forward, as if to help him hear better. I listened closely and heard what I thought must have been a flock of guineas.

I had heard that guineas could serve as watchdogs. They must have heard the mule and me coming and sounded off with their distinctive, piercing call. When I got closer, I saw "Coy Horner" on the mailbox and a man standing in the yard between the house and the road.

I greeted him, "Good morning, Mr. Horner."

He replied, with a big smile, "Good morning, Mr. Mule Buyer." Then with a belly laugh, he asked, "Is that the George Smith mule? Did you really buy him?"

I saw that he was a joker, so I responded, "I sure didn't *steal* him. If I were a mule stealer, I would have stolen a larger mule. My dad bought him from George Smith."

He asked with a grin, "Did George tell your dad that the mule won't ride?"

"Yes, he told my dad, and Dad told me, too, but I had to find out for myself. Mr. Horner, that mule won't ride." I knew he knew, and we laughed together.

Then I said, "I stopped to see if I could buy a setting of fifteen guinea eggs. A neighbor woman, who Mom calls Grandma Neighbors, told her that the yolks of guinea eggs are richer than chicken eggs and make custard pies that are out of this world. Mom has wanted some guineas ever since."

Looking agreeable, Mr. Horner replied, "I'm pretty sure the Old Lady could let you have fifteen guinea eggs for fifteen cents. I'll go in and see."

He was soon back. I handed him fifteen cents as he handed me the eggs in a paper sack. With a big smile, he said, "Good luck with your mule and your guineas."

As we walked along, I thought of the custard pies that Mom would make. Mom certainly thought a lot of Grandma Neighbors. She told Mom that when she made vegetable soup, she always put a sweet potato in it. Mom immediately had to check that out. I couldn't tell it helped or hurt the soup.

I walked that mule on home without further excitement. At the end of our long walk, that mule appeared as good as new. I, however, was dragging my tracks out with the seat of my pants.

Coming out to meet us, Dad asked, "How do you like the mule?"

Rather tartly, I replied, "I like him fine, *sir*."

The look Dad gave me said, "Don't get smart with me."

I watered the mule, put him in a stall, and gave him four ears of corn and a bundle of hay. He ate with a good appetite.

Monday morning found me back at school, bodily, but my mind was far away at times—on George Smith, that bucking mule, those attention-getting girls, the red-haired boy, and the jovial Coy Horner.

I admired my math teacher. She taught well and was

careful not to embarrass her pupils. She seemed especially kind to me. She brought me back to reality by asking me if I'd mind going to the chalkboard and demonstrating how to square a circle. She was sure I knew how.

As I went to the chalkboard, I wished George Smith were years younger. I'd square off with him and jerk a knot in his tail. Again I returned to reality, then squared the circle and received the approval of the teacher.

Another morning class was English. My teacher was a good teacher. I had her English classes for three years in high school. The second and third year, I had a greater appreciation for her. That first year, however, I didn't like her any better than I liked that mule I had brought home on Saturday. Unlike the math teacher, she liked to embarrass a student, especially a student from the country.

On that Monday morning, she asked the class to tell what they had done over the weekend—almost like "show and tell" in the lower grades. Her idea was to listen for spoken mistakes in English and then make a big deal out of them. She had two girls and one boy who were A+ students. They talked at length. She held them in high regard and had broad smiles for them.

I knew that the less I said, the less she would have to criticize. So when I was called on, I stated, "I went down in Pope County and led home a mule my father had bought." I thought to myself, "Old Lady, what is wrong with that?" She uttered not a word, but the looks exchanged with the anointed three said, "He is country through and through."

My first afternoon class was World History, taught by Coach McCool. The girl who sat next to me was Sammie Stump. She and I usually came to class after the noon break, about ten minutes before the class began. We talked about various things. We were just a couple of dumb freshmen with no idea what we would do in life. (Little did we know that later we would spend thirty years together at Independence School, with her as a teacher and me as principal.)

Sammie asked me how I had spent the weekend. Without giving any details, I told her about my dad buying the mule and my walking him home from Pope County.

Sammie asked, "What did you name the mule?"

I replied, with a shrug, "So far, I have just called him 'Mule.' What would you call a small mule?"

Without having to think, she quickly said, "You should call him Sammie."

After mulling over that suggestion, I said, "I'll call him Sam for short."

The name stuck. Sometimes, in a disciplining tone, I called him Sambo. Much later, he became Old Sam.

At the time of Sam's arrival, we had separate stalls with a hay manger and a grain box for each animal. Sam wouldn't touch his hay until he got his grain. While he waited, he pawed, whinnied, bellyached, and brayed. My brothers and I found this funny, so we always fed him last—shame on us.

Dad left the feeding up to my two brothers and me. He would check now and then to see if we were feeding properly. One day he came to the barn and asked, "What in tarnation is wrong with Sam?"

I explained, "He is singing for his corn. We feed him last, so he can entertain us." At the look on his face, I quickly added, "It's never more than a three- or four-minute wait."

Dad made his disapproval abundantly clear. He commanded, "Listen to me, sir. That is a good, hard-working mule. After this, feed him first." And that is what we did. I liked Sam by then and actually took pleasure in feeding him first. I was a little ashamed of myself for having to be told to feed him first, when his gut was growling for grain.

Always looking for new entertainment, I wondered, for some strange reason, if Sam was "goosey." To find out, I got a long cane pole and touched him at the base of the tail. He bucked, kicked, snorted, and put on a pretty good show. Naturally, I had to do that several times just for the fun of it. Eventually, I felt ashamed of myself and stopped a few days later, before I could get caught.

I got to wondering how the other mule would react to a similar touch with the cane pole. When I tried it, I got no worthwhile reaction. The mule looked around at me, and if I read him correctly, he asked, "What is your problem?" Since he was no fun, that was the first and last time I tried that stunt with him.

Years later, when I became a teacher, I tried to use what I learned from the reaction of the two mules. I had a pupil we'll call Jack. Around eleven or twelve years old, Jack was a good student, likeable, and well behaved. However, a number of boys his age and a little older teased him about a certain little girl, who was actually good-looking. But Jack was, in no way, interested in any girl, good-looking or not. He made that clear by his fierce reaction. These mischievous boys increased their teasing, since they enjoyed Jack's almost out-of-control response. In fact, he threatened them with a ball bat if they didn't stop.

I felt it was time for me to deal with the problem. When I got an opportunity, I took Jack to one side and explained to him that if he would show no reaction to the boys' teasing, it would no longer be funny, and they would stop.

I continued, "For example, when I was a kid, we had a little mule that would kick, buck-jump, snort, and carry on when goosed with a stick or a cane pole. Since it was funny back then, we hardly knew when to stop. We had another mule that paid no attention to the same treatment. I didn't find it funny and didn't try it a second time. So, Jack, don't pay any attention to the teasing, and I guarantee it will stop."

My corny example wasn't very effective with Jack. He whined out, with self-pity in his voice, "Yes, Mr. Wallace, but I'm not even goosey!" I wasn't even sure what to say after that comment, which was just as well, since it took all I had in me to maintain a straight face.

...

I suppose you are wondering how the guinea egg deal turned out. We put those eggs under a hen that was staying on the nest—she would have been called a brood hen or a setting hen. Every egg hatched. The hen made a good mother to the guineas. She stayed with them in a flock when they were grown. I wonder why she wasn't driven to distraction by their shrieking clatter.

Later, one of my brothers-in-law offered to bring me eight or ten duck eggs to put under a hen and see how they would turn out. The result was interesting. It takes twenty-eight days for a duck egg to hatch—a week longer than chicken and guinea eggs. When the baby ducks were two or three days old, the mother hen took them for a stroll in search of a variety of food. She took them near the pond. The baby ducks thought that it was heaven, as one after the next slid off into the pond and began swimming around with delight. The old hen thought it was the end of time and almost went off her rocker while running around and clucking at them from the shore, in her fear that they would all be drowned.

Speaking of duck reminds me of another school incident. I came from a long line of teachers on my mother's side—five aunts, three uncles, two sisters, two brothers-in-law, and my mother. Therefore, when I returned home from the Navy in 1946 and was invited to teach Rudement's one-room school, I couldn't turn it down.

I had a good opinion of my ability to do a good job because of my experience of dealing with people in and out of the service, which included some teaching. However, Mom was as nervous about my teaching as the old hen was about her ducklings. She realized that I had a certain amount of "war nerves" and that I hadn't seen the inside of a one-room school in ten years.

Mom was hired to teach Spring Valley School, the next school over from Rudement. Her school started on August 20. Rudement School was to begin the day after Labor Day. She invited—rather, she insisted that I visit her school a day or at least half a day, so I could be refreshed on how to teach in a one-room school.

I promised to comply with her wishes, but I stayed so busy doing things that needed to be done that it was near closing time when I got over to her school on Friday. It was a hot afternoon. As I entered the open double doors, I could see that the students had already put away their books to go home.

I sat in an empty seat in the back of the room. Mom instructed, "Now, I want the seventh grade to take out your geography books." A look of astonishment came over the children, since Mom had just told them to put away their books.

With much insisting, she got the seventh graders to take out their geography books. She started out by saying, "Today's lesson is about lumbering in the Great Northwest about a decade ago." Then she proceeded to explain that a decade is ten years. It sounded as if she was on a roll.

A heavyset boy, who was evidently the class clown, put up his hand. Mom ignored him at first. But when he halfway stood up and kept waving his hand, she gave him a nod of recognition. He whined out, "Mrs. Wallace, if a duck egg is ten years, how long is a goose egg?" He grinned, obviously pleased with his play on words.

A giggle of amusement swept across the room. I acted as though I was quite interested in a book I'd picked up, and I didn't let on.

Deciding she had reached the point of diminishing returns, Mom said, "Now put away your books. It is time to go home."

I furnished Mom's transportation to and from school. On the drive home, I commented, "You sure have a fine group of students," and made no mention of the goose egg remark.

About twenty years later, in Mom's presence, at a sort-of family reunion, I told that story, to the amusement of the group. Mom laughed heartily along with the others. I barely heard her say to the person next to her, "He is just lying about that." She had forgotten, or maybe suppressed, the whole incident.

...

Sam became a permanent fixture on the Wallace farm. Over time, I imagine he felt assured that no one would again attempt to ride him. If he could have sung a variation of that old, snappy jukebox song, he would have sung out: "You can ride Dick, Tom, and Jack, but you can't put that monkey on my back!"

One day I went to the barn and led Sam into the sunlight at the south end of the hallway. I had learned that he liked to be curried with a steel curry comb and brushed with a soft brush. He seemed to know it was an act of kindness. If he could have talked, I'm sure he would have said, "Thank you." While I brushed him, I thought about what a good farm animal he had made for us.

I happened to recall the commandment that says: "Honor thy father and thy mother." I gave myself a C-concerning my part-time honoring of my father. I promised myself that I'd do better.

About that time, Dad walked up, leaning heavily on his walking stick, and with a grin asked, "Are you getting ready to ride him?"

I replied, "No, I'm thanking him for being such a good work mule." Thinking this would be a good time to start working on my vow to myself, I continued, "Dad, I have something to say to you that I should have said a long time ago. You are to be congratulated for buying such a good mule."

I'll never forget how Dad glowed with pleasure. He smiled and simply said, "Thank you."

Many times when I was with Sam over the years, I was asked, "Do you ride that mule?" My answer was always the same: "That mule won't ride."

* * *

People Are Different

My daughter, LeAnn, is always exclaiming about my "incredible memory" of things that happened in the past. I suppose that is true—I can remember events and conversations of long ago as if they were happening right now. As I sit here and think about some of the events that stand out most vividly in my mind, I can see that many of them involved people who struck me as being different from me. Sometimes those interactions made me want to be more like the person, and sometimes they helped me see what I did not want to become.

Poet Maya Angelou is famous for a quote that I can imagine myself saying: "I've learned that people will forget what you said, people will forget what you did, but people will never forget how you made them feel." I have found that people who are different can sometimes create the strongest feelings. I will give you a few examples.

Floyd Haney, a neighbor boy who was my age, lived across Womble Mountain from us. Everyone called him Buddy. He was a big laugher who was happiest when he was clowning around.

Buddy was a good worker. When work was available, he would work for a dollar a day. With some of his earnings, he managed to buy a beat-up old car when he was around sixteen.

One Saturday evening after Buddy had collected five dollars for that week's work, he asked me if I would like to go to town with him and "live it up." Now, up to that point in my life, I would say that I had had little experience with "living it up." Since I was the eldest son in a family with an elderly, ailing father, the weight of planning for our family's welfare had fallen on me early. Although I liked having a good time, I always was conscious of cost and usually settled on the conservative, common-sense side of the scale.

In response to Buddy's offer, I told him that I would love to go with him, but that I had worked only four days that week. For that work, I had made $4.00 and already spent $3.80 of it for two shoats (small hogs) to grow into winter's meat. The two dimes I had left wouldn't go very far in "living it up."

Waving aside my concerns, Buddy replied, "I just put seven gallons of gas in my car for a dollar. We can go to the skating rink and watch the gals and boys skate, drink some pop, and then go to the late show for ten cents each."

With Buddy's enthusiastic encouragement, my conservative side decided to take a night off. I replied eagerly, "Buddy, I'll drink a tall glass of cold, fresh-churned buttermilk before we go, so I'll not need any pop. I will pay for the show. That would be a good night out for me."

As we took off for Harrisburg, I felt like a bird out of a cage. We drove around some before heading to the skating rink. Once there, we were content, at first, with just sitting and watching the pretty girls skating round and round. However, it wasn't long before Buddy started flirting with a girl who, unfortunately, turned out be another guy's girlfriend. I managed to get Buddy away from the rink when I saw he was about to get into real trouble with that guy. Laughing at our narrow escape, we drove over to the movie theater. I paid my twenty cents for two tickets. The movie was a Wild West cowboy show that really entertained us.

After the show, I said, "Buddy, we have had a good time—let's get out of town before we really get into trouble."

However, Buddy was not quite ready to call it an evening. He drove around a little and pulled into a small joint. He suggested, "Let's check it out." We went in and were surprised there was a cover charge of twenty-five cents each. With a big smile, Buddy paid it for both of us. He threw out his chest and called so everyone could hear, "Two beers please and make them 'root.'" I saw Buddy spend his last dollar for a sandwich and a drink for a girl he'd never seen before.

On the way home, Buddy said, "We have had a good time, haven't we?"

I thought of all of the adventures we had packed into one night and of Buddy's easy generosity. I truthfully replied, "Buddy, I will never forget tonight."

...

I started high school a year later than most students because of the need for me to help out on the farm. The first two years I hitchhiked the twelve miles each way.

I was fortunate to get to work twenty-four hours per month on an NYA (National Youth Administration) program under the supervision of the head custodian, Ray Goben. The NYA began in 1935 under President Franklin D. Roosevelt's leadership. NYA's Student Aid Program provided grants to students in high school and college in exchange for work. I was paid twenty-five cents per hour, for a total of six dollars per month.

One day after school, I went into the room of a history teacher, Mr. H. B. Bauman, to sweep and clean his room. He impressed me as being solemn and unfriendly. He had just finished hanging a large picture on the wall behind his desk.

He asked me, "Do you think I have this picture hanging straight?"

I had worked as a carpenter's helper and was good with a level and at eyeballing. I took a close look at the picture and replied, "The bottom of the picture needs to be pushed a tiny bit to the left."

From the look on his face, I quickly realized that Mr. Bauman wasn't really asking for my advice. He simply wanted me to compliment him on his hanging.

After that, early of mornings, I would meet Mr. Bauman in the hall, and he would not speak. That didn't really bother me. I thought perhaps he had other things on his mind. However, I was soon to have much more interaction with Mr. Bauman.

When school was out that spring, I went to Michigan to seek summer work. The best I could find was a farm job working for Fred and Sarah Parsons, who were brother and sister, both unmarried, and sixty-five and sixty-seven years of age, respectively. They were college graduates and hard workers.

I hired in at wheat harvest time in 1937, the last year before farmers began combining their wheat. The thrashing was done by farmer helping farmer. The thrasher went from farm to farm.

The workers would eat the noonday meal at the farm where the thrashing was being done. The women tried to outdo each other with their cooking. That made for a good feast for the workers. Mr. Parsons sent me around to the different farms to be in charge of the team and wagon, with another hired hand along to help.

From other farmers, I learned their opinion of the man I worked for. They told me that Mr. Parsons and his sister were penny-pinching people who were worth millions. However, I could hardly believe them because of the good meals they served me three times a day. Although many years have passed since I dined at Sarah and Fred's table, I can still picture in my mind the bountiful spreads — two kinds of meat, many different vegetables, a big glass of milk at my plate and a small pitcher of milk for a refill, and often, apple pie with cheese. Sometimes Sarah served half a cantaloupe, its center filled with ice cream. In my mind that certainly brought into question the comment that the Parsons were as "tight as the bark on a tree."

One evening after supper, Mr. Parsons said to me, "There is a carnival tonight over at Ann Arbor. Among other things, livestock and the latest farm equipment will be on display. I plan to go over, and if you wish, you can go along. We can go our separate ways and meet at the truck at a certain time and come back." That sounded good to me, so I went along.

I recall it was not yet dark, a full moon was in view, and there was a cool, pleasant breeze. I was strolling along between attractions on my right and left, when whom do you suppose I met?

It was none other than Mr. and Mrs. Bauman. Looking straight ahead, I walked past them. I'd supposed that being away from Harrisburg would not have increased their fondness of me.

After I had passed them, Mr. Bauman called, "Hey you! Are you from Harrisburg? Is your name Kestner?"

Mr. Bauman seemed as glad to see me as if I were his long-lost brother.

He had a number of questions concerning what I was doing up there and if I would be back in school in Harrisburg that fall. I told him I had agreed to work for a farmer for two months and would be back in Harrisburg in time to take up a field of hay before returning to school.

Mr. Bauman told me that he and his wife had been in summer school in Ann Arbor. I never learned what degrees they were working on.

Mr. Bauman wanted to know what subjects I planned to take the following year. I told him, "English, agriculture, geometry, and U.S. history."

He asked, "Do you like history?"

I told him that history did not come easy for me because I had trouble concentrating. I informed him that I had brought a U.S. history book to Michigan with me to read in my spare time, so I could make a passing grade in it.

Mr. Bauman asked, "How is that working out, your history reading?"

I told him that it wasn't: "The fellow I work for and his sister want me to play cards with them until it is too late to read."

A big smile crossed Mr. Bauman's face. He said, "I will be teaching U.S. history this fall. If you will take history from me, I think I can help you with your concentration and make history interesting."

I thought to myself that that sounded like a buddy-buddy good deal. I replied, "Mr. Bauman, I will take history from you."

After the two months, Mr. Parsons paid me for my work and invited me to come back the next summer. He put me on the Greyhound bus for Harrisburg. I was happy to be back home. That was the longest I had ever been away.

My younger brothers — Byrum and Victor — and I put up our winter's hay in the barn. I was all set to start school after Labor Day.

On the first day of school, I seated myself in the back row of Mr. Bauman's room, along with a classroom full of students. Mr. Bauman slipped his glasses down on the end of his nose and looked at me over them. He showed me no recognition. He commented, "Tomorrow, I will seat you in alphabetical order. After we get underway, I will give a weekly test and seat you according to your grade — the better the grade, the nearer the front of the room you sit." I thought to myself, "I'll likely sit in the back where I like to sit." That turned out to be pretty much true.

Mr. Bauman informed the class that later in the month, he would give us an IQ test for his own use only, so he would know if we were performing up to our full potential. I had never had an IQ test before, so I somewhat looked forward to the new experience.

The day came for that test. It was a multiple-choice test. The answers were to be recorded on an answer sheet by blackening in the correct choice, which was a new type of test to me. We had thirty minutes to complete the test.

Somehow, it was confusing to me how I was to read the different possible answers and record the correct one on the answer sheet. I became nervous and upset. The thirty minutes were about over when I finally caught on how to record my choice of answers. To my distress, Mr. Bauman announced, "Five more minutes."

I was barely underway. So, I used the Eeny-meeny-miny-moe method to mark the rest of my sheet and was among the first to turn in my answer sheet.

The next day, Mr. Bauman reported, "I have your IQs recorded. A few were remarkably high; most were average. A few were a little below average. One — no comment."

As he made that last statement, he looked briefly at me over his glasses. My card playing with the Parsons came into play, as I held a pleasant poker face, pretending to be too dumb to know what he was saying. I read his thoughts: "That IQ test must be pretty accurate."

To myself, I thought: "I am in a pretty good position. I can concentrate enough to make a passing grade, and he will think I am performing up to my potential."

That same year, I took English from Miss Pemberton, a good teacher with a kind, understanding personality. Students loved Miss Pemberton. I was particularly grateful to have her for a teacher, given my experiences with Mr. Bauman.

That year, Miss Pemberton had the members of her class make monthly book reports. The end of the month came suddenly. I only had a day or two before having to go to her room and report on a book.

A good friend showed me a book he had just reported on to another teacher. He told me about it and suggested I take the book and report on it. I took the book and read a paragraph here and there. Then I went to Miss Pemberton's room to report on it.

Miss Pemberton was an elderly lady who could read me better than I could read a book. She asked me, "Did you read this book?"

I answered, "Yes, Ma'am." She said, "Tell me about it." I was pleased with my short report.

Then, she asked, "What is the moral of the story?" That question did me in. My reply told her I had not read the book. The look on her face told me that she knew I was lying and that she was disappointed in me. However, she was too kind to say so. As it turned out, she reported the story to me, which made me want to read it. She marked down in her grade book that I had given a book report.

About a week later, I went in to Miss Pemberton's room and told her I was in to apologize for lying to her about reading the book I had tried to report on. I said, "I could tell you knew I was lying about reading the book and were too kind to tell me. Your reporting on the book to me made me want to read it. So, I did. I am not lying this time."

Miss Pemberton said, "It took courage on your part to come to me and admit the truth. Now, I am going to ask a favor of you. You know we have a variety show coming up. An assembly will be called in about a week. The entire student body will be on the bleachers. Teachers and students will give a plug from the gym floor for the various activities. I am in charge of playing up the magic show. In my place, I would like for you to make a few statements that I will write out for you to memorize. Will you do that for me?"

I was pleased with the opportunity to redeem myself. I eagerly replied, "Yes, I will be honored to do that for you. Thank you for asking me."

A few days later, the student body assembled on the bleachers. Six or eight of us who were promoting the activities of the show were standing in a group, in the center of the gym and off to one side. In a prearranged order, each of us was to come to the center of the gym and give our presentation.

When my turn came, I walked out as if I owned the place, held up an object, and said, "Now you see it." I put it in my pocket and said, "Now you don't." That brought a laugh. Then I said, "See the great magician Newton perform his works of magic. The magic show is the highlight of the evening—don't miss it!"

Following the assembly, I went to my history class and took my seat in the back row. Mr. Bauman slipped his glasses down on the end of his nose so he could see over them, gave me an astounded look, and asked, "Kestner, was that you down on the gym floor? You could have knocked me over with a feather."

Both he and I had been surprised—he at seeing me calmly making an announcement to the entire student body, and I at his admitting it. I hoped I had elevated myself in his opinion.

Mr. Bauman was curious about the family backgrounds and nationalities of his students. He polled the class members and did some jotting down of notes. When he was about two-thirds down his list, he commented, "I am surprised we don't have any Indian blood in a class this size."

I thought to myself, if he wants a part-Indian in his class, I'll oblige him. When he called my name, I said, "On my father's side, I'm Scottish, Irish, and English." I paused, forcing him to ask, "What about your mother's side?"

I replied, "My great-grandmother was an Indian of the War Bluff gang in Pope County—no particular tribe. Some time ago, I inquired of an old man I thought might know about that particular group of Indians. All I learned from him was, 'They were as mean as hell.'"

Mr. Bauman didn't say anything for a few seconds. Then he said, "From your nose and your high cheekbones, I can tell you are part Indian."

After Mr. Bauman finished with his nationality inventory, he gave a little speech about the Native American Indian. He said they were badly afflicted with venereal diseases and had a weakness for whiskey. My poker face didn't give away how I felt about that statement.

[Seventy-five years have passed. I've never regretted taking history from Mr. Bauman. May the "powers that be" not hold me accountable for being critical of him. He was a good teacher and admired by his students. I know my experiences with him and with Miss Pemberton helped mold the teacher I was later to become.]

The school year came to an end. The last day of May 1938, I traveled all night with Floyd Johnson, who hauled passengers from Harrisburg to Pontiac, Michigan, for five dollars. I arrived at the Parsons' in time to start my two months' work on the first of June. My pay was the same as before — forty dollars per month. I had napped during the night and felt able to work.

Mr. and Miss Parsons were happy to see me and requested I call them Fred and Sarah. Fred told me I would have time to milk the cow while Sarah prepared breakfast. So, a long day began.

At breakfast, I answered a number of questions from Fred and Sarah. They seemed concerned. Fred asked, "Do you have any money?"

I answered, "I have a five-dollar bill and some change."

Fred offered, "If you need money, I can advance you a few dollars." I was touched by his concern but declined.

After breakfast, my first job was to mow an overgrown lawn — with a push mower. It took all day and took the pep out of me.

The next day, Fred had me paint his garage, which didn't need painting too badly, to see if I knew how to paint before he turned me loose on the house. The house didn't need paint either, but Fred wanted to take advantage of cheap labor. He wanted me to stay busy when he wasn't around to supervise. I expected to stay busy. Fred must have stayed awake at night thinking up little things for me to do to round out a full day.

Each day's work typically ended at 6:00 p.m. One day, it rained from 4:30 to 5:00 p.m. I felt sure we would call it a day. That was what we did at home. Fred, however, thought otherwise.

He said, "It is an hour until quitting time." He had an old Fordson tractor that he hadn't started for years. He asked me to crank on it until 6:00 p.m. He said that would keep the motor from freezing up. There was enough compression on the cylinders to make it hard to crank. It was hard work at the close of the day. I would crank for a minute and rest a minute. I welcomed 6:00 p.m. and supper.

At supper, with a big smile, Sarah said, "Kes, Fred and I are going to a really good show tonight. If you want to spend thirty-five cents of your money, we will take you along."

I replied, "Thank you for your offer, but cranking on that tractor tired me out, so I will stay here and rest."

Sarah and Fred were well within their rights in asking me to pay my own way to the show. However, it caused me to think of that "penny-pinching" comment of a year ago and to remind myself that people are different. I was comparing the wealthy Parsons with Buddy, who had so freely taken me for a night on the town when he had only a few dollars to his name.

I noticed that Sarah almost appeared bossy with Fred. She said it was her concern for his health. I agreed with her that he worked too much for his age. In addition to his large acreage of hay, wheat, and corn, Fred had ten acres in an apple orchard. He and I worked together a great deal in spraying the trees and thinning the apples, so the ones left would get larger.

Another ten-acre apple orchard adjoined his orchard. The only time Fred indicated that he was a man of means, he said to me: "I could buy those ten acres of orchard for ten thousand dollars. If I were ten years younger, I would buy it in a minute." Each year, Fred would sell his apple crop to a company that would come in and harvest the best and leave hundreds of bushels of apples for him to make into sweet apple cider.

One day at dinner, Sarah told me that the church she attended was having a picnic at a park that evening, and that she and Fred were attending. She said, "I hope you will go with us. I talk a great deal on the phone and have told a number of ladies what a nice, young man from Down South we have working for us. They are anxious to see you. I have washed your Sunday shirt, pressed your dress trousers, and shined your dress shoes. Will you go?"

I replied, "I will be glad to go."

Fred and I came in early from work to clean up and get ready to attend the picnic. I was surprised when Sarah said, "Kes, I have something set out here for you to eat. You are a big eater, and I don't want any of my lady friends to think we don't feed you." She sat me down to a full meal, and I ate it.

At the picnic, I must have made Sarah happy because I took only very small servings of food. I also followed Fred's example in displaying good eating manners.

The two months went by quickly, and it was time for me to leave the Parsons. They invited me to come back the following summer, but I turned them down, saying I planned to take up the carpentry trade.

Fred gave me another example that "people are different." He couldn't resist the temptation of being tightfisted with me. When he went to pay me, he said, "I owe you eighty dollars minus one day. We didn't work the Fourth of July."

I wanted to leave feeling we were the best of friends. So I smiled and took what he offered me as if he were doing me a favor for paying me less than eighty dollars. My poker face kept my true feelings hidden.

The next ten years were busy years. I helped two carpenters build two houses, worked in a defense plant, spent time in the Navy during World War II, worked some in two different spar mines, and started a teaching career in a one-room school.

My sister Hazel was six years younger than I and also a teacher. In the summer of 1948, we decided to go to Michigan to see our brother Victor. We attended an evening religious camp meeting in Anderson, Indiana, spent the night in Anderson, and went on to Pontiac, Michigan, the following morning. When we were two miles from Ypsilanti, Michigan, I saw a road named Ellsworth Road. I knew then we were within a half mile of the Parsons' farm. I couldn't resist the urge to check on Fred and Sarah.

With mixed emotions and memories of the past, I pulled in close to the house. It was still a remarkable house, but it lacked the grandeur of ten years before. I wondered if the paint was the same I'd put on it.

Hazel and I stood at the door. I knocked, and Sarah opened the door. She looked remarkably well. She recognized me immediately and exclaimed, "Kes!" as she reached to embrace me. I introduced her to Hazel. Sarah graciously invited us in. She looked somewhat embarrassed when she nodded at Fred and said, "He is not too well." At a glance, one could tell that Fred was "out of it." He sat in an easy chair, weak in mind and body.

I got the feeling that Sarah didn't wish to discuss Fred's condition, so we talked about other things. Sarah insisted we stay for dinner, but we told her that our brother was expecting us in Pontiac a little before noon.

We said what to me was a sad farewell. My heart went out to them. They loved life and hard work and had much in their favor. However, I saw that Fred had limited time left to enjoy his and Sarah's earthly possessions. I never saw or heard of Sarah or Fred after that day.

Our arrival at Victor's was near perfect. Dinner was ready to be taken to the table. Victor and I had seen very little of each other since World War II, so we had much to talk about. He helped me locate a new-looking 1940 Dodge car, a big improvement over the one I was driving. I bought a used tow bar and pulled the Dodge home. The better-looking car boosted my morale and helped my social life.

I had the happy privilege of being a classroom teacher in one-room schools for eleven years and then the principal at Independence School for the next thirty. During that time, I strived to put to use the lessons learned from all the "different" people in my life. I remembered well my feelings when I interacted with teachers such as Miss Pemberton and Mr. Bauman, and I think I was kinder for it during my forty-one years in the school system. Likewise, the time I spent with Buddy and the Parsons made me a more generous person than my otherwise conservative nature might have allowed.

Sometimes I think we believe that people should be more like ourselves. However, I have found people to be more different than alike, and I have learned much more from them on this earthly sojourn than from ones more nearly like me. Probably the Good Lord planned it that way.

On this fourth day of July, 2012, as I fast approach my ninety-second birthday, I am happy to be a pilgrim on that highway that leads to a habitation not made with hands, brighter than a city built on a hill. In addition to my sweet wife, Evelyn, and blood kin, I hope to see Miss Pemberton, Mr. Bauman, Fred and Sarah, and Buddy Haney, who (if he makes it there before me) will slap me on the back with a big horse laugh and say, "I'm surprised you made it!"

* * *

The Good Old Days

Do you want to know about the "good old days"? If so, I'm the one who can tell you a small part of what they were like. Those good old days were actually a mixture of the good and the not so good. Whether they were good or bad was really a state of mind. Our family maintained a good state of mind; therefore, we never fully realized that we were living in a period of history that would forever be referred to as the Great Depression.

Many people believe the Great Depression began in 1929. In our family, it came sooner than 1929. We were a family of seven—our parents and five children under the age of ten, with another child yet to be born. At that time, my father was in his sixties and had a heart problem, so we had no breadwinner in the family. He did as much as his health allowed and then expected of his three sons work that normally would have been beyond our years. However, we three saw the problem and faced it bravely, believing that if we had food, shelter, and clothing, then we were well off. It was the beginning of making men out of us.

Our thrift and hard work on a worn-out farm made us as well off as other families around us. We were miles below the poverty line as it is measured today, but we didn't realize it. Consequently, we didn't feel sorry for ourselves.

We planted fifteen acres in corn and harvested around 150 bushels—about the amount farmers today produce on one acre. When the ears were almost mature and the stalks were somewhat green, we cut the stalks by hand with corn knives and put them in shocks to further mature. The mature shocks were called "fodder"—they served as feed for cattle and horse stock. As the fodder was brought to the barn, the ears were removed and put into the corn crib to be fed to our milk cows, chickens, and two or three hogs that we were fattening for market. Some choice ears were shelled and taken to a gristmill to be ground into cornmeal. The gristmill took a share, and we got the rest.

We planted large gardens to raise vegetables to round out our meals. We ate some of the produce fresh and canned the rest for the winter. We planted cane to make molasses, which we used to make popcorn balls, molasses candy, and molasses cakes. We also raised broomcorn, to make homemade brooms.

Farming was a grind from start to finish. Then, as now, too much rain, too little rain, late frost in the spring, early frost in the fall—any could spell disaster and greatly affect the size of the harvest.

We often ate oats or rice as an unsweetened cereal for breakfast, because we couldn't afford the five cents per pound for sugar. For a dollar, we could buy one hundred pounds of cornmeal but only seventy-two pounds of Big M flour. Therefore, we ate cornbread three times a day. I'm not complaining—we couldn't have eaten anything better. However, we had white milk gravy every morning for breakfast. The problem was that it was hard to sop gravy with cornbread—it was just too crumbly. But we managed.

Despite being able to provide ourselves with plenty to eat, we were miserably lacking in money to pay for the things we were unable to produce. Hard times were accepted as a fact of life, since the scarcity of money was so common among country people in the late twenties and early thirties. No times in the decades before or after were people friendlier or more willing to give, share, and barter. Some would trade milk for eggs, or apples for turnips, or honey for sweet potatoes. The list goes on and on.

...

Storing food for the winter was only one of our ongoing concerns. Another was ensuring we had enough coal and wood to keep us warm during the winter.

On a cold Saturday in January 1936, an Alberta Clipper came down from Canada, preceded by rain that froze on fences and trees and on the ground, making getting around difficult. While it looked beautiful outside, it spelled trouble for us. With all the other work my brother Byrum and I had had to tend to the previous summer, we had failed to cut enough wood for the winter heating.

Dad, who was getting along in years and very much under the weather because of his heart condition, still called the shots. However, he depended on Byrum and me, thirteen and fifteen respectively, to do the work he would have done if he were able.

After breakfast, Dad said to Byrum and me: "That knotty chunk of wood and some hickory sticks burning in the fireplace are the last of our firewood. That bucket of coal is the last of our coal to burn in the heating stove. It is cold and will get colder. What do you boys propose we do?"

"We have no other choice than to go up on the side of the mountain and cut some firewood," I replied boldly, trying to convince both him and myself.

He countered, "There is sleet on the ground and on everything. You won't be able to stand up, much less cut wood."

With the bravado of youth, I stated, "You may be right, but we'll have to give it a try."

Dad, with a mixture of reluctance, concern, and hopefulness, finally gave us his consent: "You can't be too careful. Each of you take one of those sturdy, sharpened-off sassafras beanpoles to use for walking sticks."

"We already have sharpened-off, club-like sticks we used when we did the milking and cut the ice at the pond for the stock to drink," Bryum informed him.

Byrum took his stick in one hand and an axe in the other. I put a two-man crosscut saw over my shoulder and my stick in my right hand, and we took off for the side of Womble Mountain. We stumbled, slipped, and slid, but managed not to fall.

We trudged on uphill until we came to a grove of tall hickory trees, each about the size of a stovepipe, eight-inches in diameter. We chose four close together to cut.

With our clubs and the axe, we beat out areas in which to stand while we cut down the trees. Ice completely coated the trunks and limbs of the trees. For fear it would dull our saw, we chipped the ice away where we planned to cut.

We soon downed all four of the trees. I told Byrum that, while he trimmed two of them, I'd saddle our mare, Lil, who had cleated shoes on her front feet, and make a round to the wood yard and back to the downed trees. Then while he made a second round on the mare, further breaking a runway, I could trim the other two trees. Byrum agreed to my plan. Those two rounds made the passage somewhat better.

Next we put the harness on Lil and a little mule, Sam — not Sampson, my riding mule. (I didn't want Sampson to bust his "you know what" on the icy ground.)

With her cleated shoes, Lil did a fairly good job of standing. Sam, however, fell short of appearing graceful. If mules have guardian angels, they would have been amused at the valiant effort Sam put forth to stay on his feet.

With a log chain, we hitched Lil and Sam to one of the logs. Sam was impatient to do what he was supposed to do. He stood and pawed the ground with his front feet and pranced around with his hind feet until he had a clear footing.

We had a neighbor who did some sharecropping with a pair of mules on a piece of our land. He yelled commands so loudly at his mules that he could be heard for almost a quarter of a mile.

I got far better results with our team by speaking softly. I shook the lines slightly to get Lil's and Sam's attention. Then, I said, "Giddy-up." They took the slack out of the traces and eased forward. The log, however, was stuck to the ground. I feared the team would be unable to move it. My command for them to do their best was "Hip." So I called out "Hip!" Sam pressed forward as far as he could, rising up on his hind legs in the process. As he slowly came down, and with Lil doing her part, the log moved out and down the slope and on to the wood yard.

Byrum followed along with the saw and axe. We unhooked from the log and tied the team to the yard fence. Turning back to the log, we sawed off a half dozen blocks about a foot long. We then took them inside the house and placed them on the hearth of the fireplace to dry.

Mom asked if we were ready for dinner. We assured her we were and quickly gathered around the table. The morning's activity had given us a hearty appetite. Mom couldn't have fixed anything that would have tasted better. She had a huge pan of golden brown cornbread, a bowl of freshly churned butter, and a large glass of milk at each plate, along with a pitcher of milk for refills.

Best of all, a plentiful amount of Great Northern soup beans, with a goodly supply of side pork cooked in chunks, steamed in a pot on the stove. After Dad returned thanks, to which we all echoed a hearty "Amen," we each took a large bowl of beans and ate to our hearts' content.

Just as we were finishing our dinner, we heard a knock at the door. Mom answered the knock. The man had a loud, clear voice. We could hear him say, "I slipped off the road out here in front of your house and can't get back on the road. I wonder if I could get a little pull with your team that is hitched out front."

Mom said, "I'm sure my sons can help you — they are just finishing their dinner. Will you have a bowl of beans and cornbread with them while they finish? We have plenty."

The man answered, "I wasn't hungry for breakfast, but I'm hungry now. Beans and cornbread sound good." Mom fixed him up with a full meal of what we had.

Byrum finished his meal and took a look at the 1926 Model T Ford that was off the road. He said: "Mister, we won't have to hook onto your car with our team. My brother and I can put a coal bucket of ashes in front of your back wheels and give you a little push, and you'll be on your way."

The man replied, "You do that, and I'll pay you well."

Mom was quick to say, "You will owe them nothing. They will just be doing a neighborly act."

The man replied gratefully, "I'm overcome with your kindness."

As we went to his car with the ashes, I said, "When you get going on the road, don't stop to thank us. Just keep going and good luck."

"In that case, I thank you in advance."

After we spread the ashes, the man pulled back on the road without any trouble. We were pleased that we had gotten him underway.

Those other logs came down to the wood lot without much trouble. Sam proved he wasn't a dumb donkey. He managed to do his pulling in the path made by the previous log. Each trip was better than the one before.

Before we "called it a day," we again sawed off a number of hickory blocks and placed them on the hearth to dry. A block of wood in the stove made the house warm and cozy.

As the shadows of night began to appear, we led Sam and Lil to the barn. They were at liberty to get a drink at the pond and come to their stalls for their grain and hay.

I asked Byrum, "Do you want to milk, or do you want to talk to Lil and Sam and make them feel good by telling them what fine animals they are?"

With a grin, Byrum quickly replied, "I'll milk the cow. You're better at mule talk and horsing around than I am."

As Lil and Sam ate their grain and munched on their hay, I took a large horse brush and rubbed them down as I told them what fine animals they were. They seemed to know I was their friend.

By the time Byrum and I got to the house with the milk, it was almost dark, and supper was ready to be served. Supper was good. It consisted of fried potatoes, home-canned green beans seasoned with pork, cornbread, butter, and milk.

When supper was over, I remained at the table as I often did, while Mom washed the dishes. I feel bad now that I didn't help her. But back then, men did very little housework.

I can still see her clear the table, wash the oilcloth table covering, and draw the small coal oil lamp near the end of the table where I was sitting. She placed my *Old World Background* history book before me. She shook her head in sympathy for me as she saw me sigh deeply as I looked at the book.

I turned to the chapter that my history class was to be tested on the coming Monday. Mom said she wished she could take the test for me.

Mom was only twenty-three years older than I was. She had a strong desire to have more knowledge and a stronger desire for me to do well in high school. I would have had a better chance of doing well in high school if my dad hadn't kept me out of school about half the time all throughout grade school to help him on the farm.

While I was gazing bleakly at my history book, Mom put on her coat and a man's hat. She put her feet in a pair of leather boots with some barbed wire wrapped around the toe end of her boots. As she lit a lantern, I asked, "What on earth are you planning to do?"

She replied, "I am going to the spring to get a bucket of water. The water bucket is empty."

I got up from the table and said firmly, "Mom, I will not have you going to the spring. I'll go get a bucket of water."

She protested, "I can get it. I'm sure you're tired from all your work today." When I insisted, she gave in and said, "Well, if you go, take this lantern."

I replied, "My eyes will soon adjust to the darkness. I'd need a third hand if I took the lantern — one for my walking stick, one for the bucket, and one for the lantern."

I took off to the spring, some 300 yards or more away. The spring was called the "tent spring." I recall, when I was much younger, asking my dad why it was called the tent spring. He told me that many years ago, Indians lived in tents around the spring, which distinguished it from other springs around. I remember I couldn't keep from wondering how the Indians kept from freezing while living in tents in the winter.

I took my time, dipped up the water, and carefully made it back to the house without slipping. There at the kitchen table, Mom was hovering over my history book. I placed the water bucket on its table, set the gourd dipper beside the bucket, and sat down with Mom.

Mom had read five or six pages. With a great deal of enthusiasm, she told me what she had read. I became interested enough that I read another five or six pages.

The next thing I knew, Mom was shaking me and saying: "Wake up and go to bed. We can work on this tomorrow." That is what I did.

After I went to bed, Mom read the entire chapter and went over it with me on Sunday afternoon. She suggested I read the chapter, which I did. I was happy with the B+ that I made on the test.

...

Sometimes, things would happen that made us realize how well off we were, compared to others struggling to get by. I'll tell you about two incidents in particular.

One summer day after dinner, we were sitting in the shade of the porch facing the road before going back to work. A man who appeared to be about sixty years old approached. He had black hair streaked with gray and was wearing a blue shirt and well-worn dress trousers. He appeared to be pleasant and educated. He addressed

Dad by saying: "Good day, sir. I have fallen on hard times. I haven't eaten today, and I'm hungry and thirsty. I would appreciate as little as a crust of bread and a cup of water."

Dad said, "We have just eaten. There is plenty left for you to have a full meal." Mom was standing in the door and heard all that was said.

Appreciatively, the man replied, "Whatever you can spare. . . . I'd be happy to eat it here on the porch."

Dad said, "Mom, fix this man something to eat." I don't remember what he was served, but I know it was good and plentiful. We asked him no questions, and he made no comment as to what had brought him to the sad condition he was in. He thanked us in a kindly manner and was on his way. As scarce as money was back then, I would have given two cents for his story. I'd give much more for it now.

Only a few days later, as Dad and we children were again sitting on the porch while waiting for Mom to call us to dinner, a young, tall, slender, and very nervous black man walked up and said, "I'm hungry. Could I have something to eat?"

Dad told him that dinner was almost ready and that he would be welcome to eat with us. That seemed to make him more nervous. He wasn't expecting to be invited in. With a little insisting from Dad, he entered the house while looking to his right and left as if he were walking into a booby trap.

Dad sat at one end of the table, and this fellow sat at the other. He never drew himself up to the table, but sat a ways back and had to lean forward to reach his food.

Mom saw that he was slow about helping himself to the dishes of food on the table, so she served the children on either side of him and put food on his plate likewise. He watched closely and imitated what we did as we ate.

We had learned from our previous mistake of not

asking questions, so Byrum and I asked him a few. Dad didn't seem to mind.

We first asked, "Where are you from?"

He answered softly, "Chattanooga, Tennessee."

The fellow seemed willing to answer our questions, but he never made direct eye contact as he did. Our next questions followed in rapid succession:

"Where are you going?"

"Harrisburg, Illinois."

"Why are you going to Harrisburg?"

"I have a sister living there."

"Have you had many rides on your trip?"

"I walked every step of the way."

"Did you ask anyone for a ride?"

"Yes, one time. I walked up to a fellow who had just fixed a flat tire and was about to move on. I asked him for a ride. He told me that he was just going to the next house. I watched him and I watched him, and he went on up the highway." He paused, glanced down, and continued even more softly, "I never asked anyone else for a ride."

When I thought about how many miles I had hitch-hiked, even at my young age, and how relatively easy it had been to catch those rides, it made me sad to hear his story. But with our relative isolation in the country, I didn't really fully understand at that time about the many faces of prejudice.

...

A great deal of what I'm writing about our family also applied to many who lived south of Rudement to Herod, and around Womble Mountain to Somerset. Since we compared ourselves to each other, it wasn't until I first started attending high school in Harrisburg that I began to have a better awareness of our true financial situation.

In high school, I was happy to have the opportunity to take part in the National Youth Administration (NYA) program. I was able to work twenty-four hours per month under the supervision of the head custodian, Ray Goben. I swept and cleaned after school and on some Saturdays to put in the twenty-four hours, for a grand total of six dollars per month. I was pleased to have the chance to make the six dollars, even though some students and teachers looked down their noses at me.

One incident at school showed me that both the poor and the better off were feeling the effects of these good old days. I was amused at a young high school kid who appeared to be well off, since he wore a three-piece suit and a tie to school. One day after school, in a full hallway of students, the three-piece-suit kid sidled up to me while looking straight ahead and asked, "You work here, don't you?"

I answered, "Yes, I work an hour each day after school."

This kid didn't seem to want to be seen associating with me, being of a lower class. Glancing around to make sure he wasn't attracting attention, he said softly, "I lost some money under my locker. Would you mind reaching under there and getting it for me?"

Curious as to how he would react, I replied, "No, I'll be glad to get it for you. Tell me the number of your locker."

He told me. I had a new tablet in my hand. I dropped it down on the floor in front of his locker, placed my knee on the tablet, and slipped my arm around under the locker but felt nothing. I observed this young man walking back and forth, watching me in an unconcerned sort of way. I reported to him that I didn't feel anything, but I'd be back up there the next day, Saturday, and I'd take a long-handled brush and try to get his money for him. He replied, "If you will, I'll do something for you sometime."

I kept my word. I really tried to find his money for him. I figured it was folding money—perhaps a five or a ten. On Monday, he spotted me and asked me if I had found his money. With sincere sorrow in my voice, I said, "I'm sorry I didn't find it." Then, curious, I asked, "By the way, how much did you lose?" He reluctantly admitted, "A nickel." I was really surprised he would make that big a deal over a nickel. Does that give you a little different insight into the good old days of long ago?

...

With times being so hard, more people turned to their churches for spiritual guidance and fellowship. Sunday school and church attendance was much better back then. The minister was paid with gifts of produce.

Once, I recall the Rudement Social Brethren Sunday school superintendent, Guy DeNeal, announcing to the church that if each of them would put a penny in the Sunday school offering each Sunday, it would be enough to pay for the Sunday school literature he ordered every three months.

For three Sundays in a row, Mom and three of us children went by horse and buggy to Sunday school with our pennies. Back home, Mom commented on the penny plan. In an uncritical manner, she stated that a certain very prominent man had said, "I laid out my penny for Sunday school and forgot to pick it up." Then the same man forgot his penny again the next Sunday. He said, "I'm so embarrassed that next Sunday I'll up and put in a dime." I think he really had forgotten his pennies, but what strikes me most about that story is that he thought a dime was a big penance for his failure to bring them.

My dad was a member of the Herod Springs Baptist church. As a child, I went with him once in a while. When I was older, if Dad was unable to go to church, I went alone sometimes. It seemed the penny plan was used in that Sunday school also. One Sunday, I proudly decided to put a dime in the offering. The young people's class was rather large. The eyes of the class followed the offering plate as it moved along. I held my dime in a vise grip between my thumb and forefinger while I waited for the plate to reach me. When it did, to make sure others saw my generous contribution, I held my hand a "wee" bit higher than I needed to and tried to release the dime. To my chagrin, it stuck to my finger. I shook my finger. That dime really hung on. I had to take my other hand and rake the dime off, amid snickers from the class. I flushed with embarrassment over the whole deal.

...

Although those good old days were hard, were it not for them, I'm sure I would be less thankful for the better times I have seen since then. From 1940 to the present time, I haven't failed to have a monthly paycheck, for which I'm thankful many times over.

Living through that time made me feel as if no obstacle could come up that I couldn't overcome. A certain work ethic and industriousness was instilled in that generation, as girls became women and boys became men, even if a bit sooner than usual. Seeing, even during those times, that we could secure food, clothing, and shelter made me feel confident that I would always have the necessities of life. I would never want to part with the memories of those good old days.

* * *

One Measly Week

I was a sophomore in Harrisburg High School in the late winter of 1937. In my grade-school years, I had missed as many school days as I had attended. Dad didn't like working alone, so I had helped with all phases of farm work. As a consequence, I was poorly prepared for high school. Once there, I resolved that I would miss no more school days.

On this particular Friday morning, my resolve was being tested. I was feeling poorly and should have stayed home. However, I went to school thinking that if I could make it through the day, I would have the weekend to snap out of what ailed me.

By midmorning, I was beginning to break out in a red rash on my stomach. I had a bad, mealy taste in my mouth and an unpleasant sensation in my eyes each time I blinked.

No one had to tell me what was wrong. I knew by what I had read and been told that I had the old-fashioned German measles, which were different from the three-day measles. For some strange reason, I had failed to get the measles the previous winter when my brothers and sisters had them.

I went to the office to report to Principal Harry Taylor that I was sick and needed to go home. When I reached the office, Mr. Taylor was standing just outside the office door. He stared at me like a bird dog on point. I trudged up with my head down. He growled out at me, "What is your problem?" I felt within myself he was thinking I'd been kicked out of class and had been sent to him.

I answered, "I'm sick and need to go home."

Mr. Taylor softened up somewhat and asked, "What do you think is wrong with you?"

I replied, "I have the measles."

He then asked, "What makes you think you have the measles?"

"I feel like I have a fever, and I have a red rash on my stomach."

Mr. Taylor ordered, "Show me." I opened my shirt and exposed my stomach. Mr. Taylor drew in a quick breath and exclaimed, "Good God Almighty! You get out of here and don't come back all next week."

Then his voice softened as he asked, "Would you like for me take you home?"

I answered, "No, thank you. I'll manage."

Every day, I hitchhiked the twelve miles to and from school. So I walked over to Route 34 to catch a ride. The first vehicle to come along was a pickup truck with three people in the cab. I stuck up my thumb. When the truck stopped, I climbed into the truck bed. As we drove the twelve miles to my home, the breeze felt good on my fevered face.

When I went into the house, Mom and Dad were surprised to see me since I'd made no mention of feeling bad that morning. In answer to their question why I was home, I replied, "I'm getting the measles."

Dad had inherited his Uncle Doc's medicine books and felt he was well on his way to having the knowledge of a doctor. With confidence in his voice, Dad stated, "I'll have to make a point of seeing that the measles are well broken out."

I replied quickly, "You won't have to worry about that. They are already broken out."

I showed him my stomach. As he was taking a brief look, we all heard a tap on the door. Dad didn't seem as surprised as Mr. Taylor at my rash, but I soon realized that he was somewhat distracted by our neighbor, Amos Bixler, who was walking into our house the way he always did when he had had a drink or two. Alcohol was his weakness.

Amos was a self-made vet and was considered to be very good. His success in treating animals—from cats to horses—and his sincere love for them made him much in demand.

Amos wasted no time in expressing his genuine concern for my measly condition. He, too, emphasized the importance of getting the measles well broken out.

Then Amos asked, "Would you like to know how people 'broke out' measles years and years ago?"

Knowing he would probably tell me anyway, I went ahead and said, "Yes, tell me."

Amos explained, with a little grin, "They would gather sheep droppings and make a tea to be drunk hot. That was a sure shot way to break them out."

I exclaimed, "Amos, I'd rather die of the measles than to drink that kind of tea! In my opinion, if you would give that type of tea to a sick mule, he would 'break out' of the horse lot and would be last seen going over the hill."

Amos laughed and said, "I don't really recommend that remedy. My first choice is 60-proof whiskey."

Dad cleared his throat—his way of letting us know it was his time to talk. Mom had been standing by. Dad addressed her the way we children did. He said, "Mom, will you go to the right-hand, bottom corner of the wardrobe and get me that pint bottle of tonic?"

I saw that statement got Amos's attention immediately. I observed him lick his lips slightly. He said, "Mr. Wallace, I'd recommend the tonic you mentioned over the tea I mentioned."

Mom soon returned with a dishtowel wrapped around a bottle, with only the cork showing. She handed the bottle to Dad. He observed that it was still full. He removed the cork and then said to me, "Take a good snort out of this bottle, and it will break out your measles."

I protested, "Dad, my measles are already broken out. Didn't you see?" I was prepared to be obstinate, since I knew Mom didn't want me to taste Dad's tonic.

Dad replied, "This is just to be doubly sure—do like this." Dad put the bottle to his lips and tipped the bottle. I heard it gurgle once. Before he swallowed, he breathed in. Either the fumes got to him, or he choked on some of the tonic. During the sudden coughing spell that followed, he blew the tonic across the room with a powerful whoosh—much like the sound a mother deer makes to warn her young of danger. Mom patted Dad on the back as he recovered from the incident and his embarrassment.

When Dad could speak again, he turned to me and said, "When I sent you to Eagle Creek to get this tonic, I asked you to call for 60 proof. I'd bet the farm that this is 100 proof."

I could have explained that Mr. Tonic Maker was out of 60 proof when I went, but I said nothing. Amos spoke up and declared, "I can tell you for sure what proof it is and who made it."

Dad knew that was Amos's way of asking for a dram. He said, "Mom, see if you can find a dram glass and let Amos determine what proof this tonic is."

Mom produced the dram glass. Dad filled it to the brim and handed it to Amos. He smelled it and took a sip. Then he emptied the dram glass and wiped his mouth with the back of his hand. He said with authority, "Mr. Wallace, that is 90 proof—it's known as Nick's Best."

Amos got up from the straight-backed chair as he said, "I better get back home before the Old Lady comes looking for me." He shook hands with Dad and me.

I don't wish to imply that Amos was drunk, but it was his turn to be embarrassed. As he backed up, bowing, he got his feet tangled in a throw rug and fell backwards over the chair he'd been sitting on. We didn't laugh until we were sure he was okay. Amos laughed with us.

I breathed a sigh of relief as Amos left. Even though he could hold my attention with his tall tales, at that time I was interested only in peace and quiet.

I was sitting in Mom's chair, which had a back that slanted slightly backwards. I had made the chair for her out of oak sawmill one-by-threes and had sanded it smooth with a flat sandstone rock. The back was covered with a colorful, homemade rug-type covering. Mom had stuffed straw in a flour sack—the kind women made dresses and aprons out of—to use in the seat. It was comfortable, but I longed to get to bed and start the process of the measles running its course.

Mom asked if she could fix me some food. I shook my head no. Then she asked, "Something to drink?"

I answered, "Yes, a glass of buttermilk."

Mom or one of us children churned every other day, using 3 one-gallon crocks of sweet curds of milk with a thick layer of cream on top. The churning was done in a four-gallon churn. The process yielded a good-sized bowl of butter and some buttermilk that was out of this world—sweet, mild, and delicious—much tastier than the kind sold in stores today. [My reason for mentioning the buttermilk was because I didn't want you to feel sorry for me when I tell you that my only food on Saturday was buttermilk.]

I found it unpleasant to blink my eyes, so I sat in the big, rough chair with my eyes closed. I'm sure I appeared worse than I was as I sipped my buttermilk.

When I finished the milk, Mom asked if she could get me anything else. At that moment, I felt more feverish. I replied urgently, "No, thank you. I really need to go to bed."

I asked Mom if she would fix my bed and lead me to it, because I wanted to keep my eyes closed. That didn't turn out to be such a good idea. Honestly, my eyes weren't all that bad. Mom walked me to the bed and turned me around so I could sit on the side of the bed and proceed to lie down. However, I failed to back in to the bed as close as I should. My knees buckled, and I crashed backwards into the bed with such a force that it caused the slats to fall out of the bed. I landed most ungracefully on the floor, along with the mattress and bed covering.

Mom let out a scream that would have raised the hair on a cat's back. I feared a slat had fallen on her foot and may have broken it. However, that wasn't the case. Her concern was for me.

I forgot it hurt for me to blink my eyes. I walked back to the chair. Dad, knowing what to do, took over, and the bed was soon usable again.

I returned to the bed under my own power, with both eyes open. Mom followed me to the bed. There was no heat in the room—just the heat from the living room stove. The room was pleasantly cool, which suited me very much.

Mom tucked the cover up around my neck, which gave me a cozy feeling. Then she placed her hand on my forehead. I thought it was to see if my temperature had changed. When her hand remained on my forehead for an extended length of time, I realized she was silently praying for me.

Mom had a number of people request that she pray for them, with good results. I persuaded myself to relax, which caused me to feel better. Knowing that Mom was praying for all to be well, I very dreamingly said in my mind, "Amen, Lord, bring it to pass." Then I was out as though I had been given ether and slept all night.

I wasn't aware of having a fever on Saturday. It no longer hurt to blink my eyes. However, I had an appetite only for buttermilk that day.

On Monday, I began to eat lightly but felt weak in the legs. On Tuesday, I had improved enough that I wanted to see my dog, King. King was a black, curly-haired mutt of the highest order. There must have been some royalty in his family tree because he was one of a kind. He was an outside, one-person dog. He was reluctant to take orders from anyone except me. He loved me and liked to be near me.

In healthier times, I amused the family by showing him off. One time, without King seeing me, I chewed three pieces of Double Bubble gum—enough to make one big ball of gum. Then I got myself a stick of regular gum and chewed away on it as King sat by my side. As he watched me closely, King appeared to wonder, "Where is mine?" I gave him his big wad of bubble gum and called the family outside to watch King and me chew away on our gum, with our heads close together.

Although dogs were not ordinarily allowed in our house, Mom told me she would invite King in to my bed to see me. I heard her at the door asking him to come in, without any result. From the bed, I called, "King, come."

King came slipping and sliding at top speed to my bed. He seemed surprised that I was in bed. He sat on his haunches and put his head on the bed so I could pet him. I felt better just having him near.

After that Tuesday, I improved each day. By Saturday, I felt able to go to the high school and work on the NYA (National Youth Administration) program to make up for the hours I had missed that week. I could work at the school twenty-four hours per month for the sum of six dollars. It was okay with the custodian, Ray Goben, for me to bring my brother Byrum with me to help me put in the needed hours. That day, Mr. Goben gave me a job where I could sit and clean chalk erasers with a vacuum-type electric cleaner.

On the way home, I realized I wasn't yet out of the woods, so to speak. Byrum and I got a ride to the top of Pearson Hill, about five miles out of Harrisburg. Since it was cold, we decided to walk on down the hill. About halfway down the hill, both of my legs began to ache just below the knees. Byrum and I both laughed when I said, "If this ache was in just one leg, I would be doing some tall limping." Fortunately, very soon we got another ride that took us home.

On Monday, my experience with the measles was history. I was back in school, making up the schoolwork I had missed.

I was blessed indeed by being able to attend high school for four years, go to college for my bachelor's and master's degrees, teach eleven years in one-room schools, and serve as principal of Independence School for thirty years without missing a day or being tardy, the only exception being those six days with the measles.

* * *

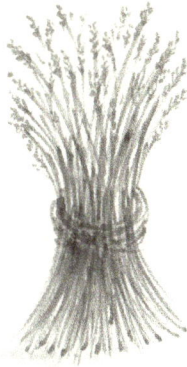

Twenty-Four Hours of Work, Work, Work

When I was fourteen years old and in the eighth grade at a one-room school, I went with some older cousins on an all-night coon hunt. It was a grand experience. The cousins got the coon pelts, and I got a big, fat, young coon for Mom to roast as only she could do.

With no time to sleep, I went to school the next day. It was a miserable day. I could barely keep my eyes open. All that kept me from nodding off was the fear of the teacher and a big hickory switch in the corner.

I should have remembered that incident when Mr. Guy DeNeal, a former school teacher, neighbor, and friend, came to our home on a Friday evening about five years later. He asked if I would be available for work the following day. He said, "I have forty acres of wheat that needs to be harvested. The crop is thick and ripe for harvest. I fear a little wind and rain would break it down and make it hard to cut and bind."

Mr. Guy asked me if I knew how to set up wheat after it was cut with a binder. I told him I'd worked for a farmer

203

in Michigan who had harvested eighty acres of wheat in 1937 and 1938. Another fellow and I had set it up for him. In 1939, farmers in Michigan began combining their wheat. However, I didn't go back to Michigan in the summer of 1939.

The setting up of wheat was a process as follows: The binder pulled by horses or a tractor cuts and drops the wheat in bundles. The person setting up the wheat starts out by taking two bundles, one in each hand, and jamming them against the ground with their tops together. They stand alone. Then, two by two, other bundles are placed around the first two while keeping the heads of wheat close together, thus forming a shock. The shocks are kept small so that a single bundle, after it is bent over a man's arm, can make a cap for the standing bundles. This bundle sheds the rain and protects the wheat until it is thrashed.

Mr. Guy said that he would like to hire me to work along with Verdon Lambert and Thomas Hogg, who was a teacher, and that he paid $1.25 a day — a long day. Trying to entice me, he added, "Lula will fix you a good dinner." I knew his wife, Lula, was a great cook.

However, I replied, "Mr. Guy, I like setting up wheat, and I am good at it, but I'm afraid I won't be able to help you because I work every Saturday night from 6:00 p.m. to 6:00 a.m. at the Dixie Diner in Harrisburg. I fear that working all day for you and then working all night at the Dixie Diner would be a little too much."

Mr. Guy knew what he wanted and didn't easily take no for an answer. He tried to make me feel good and said, "Oh, you're probably in charge up there at the diner and can take it easy during the night, and then you'd have all day Sunday to rest."

I quickly dashed his hopes. "Yes, I'm in charge — of

the dishwashing. That usually keeps me pretty busy."
Seeing his face fall, my resolve softened, and I continued,
"However, Mr. Guy, the only time a friend can help a friend
is when he needs help, so I'll help you Saturday. But I'll
have to leave the field in time to clean up, go to the diner
and eat, and be ready to wash dishes at 6:00 p.m."

With a big smile, Mr. Guy said, "I'll see you early tomorrow morning. Verdon and Thomas will be there."

I replied, with more enthusiasm than I felt, "I'll see
you there."

Bright and early the next morning, we all gathered at
Mr. Guy's field. The three of us worked a slow, steady pace
close together. We talked a lot and never stopped to rest.
We placed the shocks in neat rows for easy loading into
wagons to take to the thrashing machine.

The morning passed quickly. Lula's good dinner was
the highlight of the day. We made the food and the iced
tea disappear. The delicious apple pie hit the spot.

When we returned to our work, the sky was somewhat
overcast, with a slight breeze that made for pleasant working. By the end of the afternoon, Mr. Guy was well pleased
with the amount of wheat we had set up, but a good half
of the field remained to be done. We promised to come
back Monday and finish the job. Mr. Guy was elated.

I rushed home, took a quick shower, groomed myself,
and dressed in the clothes Mom had laid out for me.
My sister Hazel had shined my shoes.

I took off for Harrisburg, about twelve miles away. With
a souped-up three-to-one ring-and-pinion gear in the rear
of my Model T Ford, I may have hit fifty miles per hour
on the way to town—about twenty miles per hour faster
than I usually drove. I arrived at the diner by 5:30 p.m.

The Dixie Diner was a railroad dining car, which
was located on the east side of what is now known

as Commercial Street. It was not far from the Martin Gas Station and across the street from the Cook Gas Station—both now long gone. The dining car had built-on extensions on the northeast and south sides, making it possible to serve a goodly number of people.

As I was entering the kitchen door, I could hear the diner's jukebox loudly playing "You Are My Sunshine." The first thing to catch my eye was a high, piled-up stack of dirty dishes. However, with my mind intent on my supper, I passed up the dishes and first spoke to the manager, Scottie Younger. He was a relative of Cole Younger, who had been a bank robber along with the notorious Jesse James.

Scottie had taken a liking to me. When he hired me, he told me that he had had my mother as a teacher at Sadler School, when she first started teaching, at the age of eighteen. He said that at the time, he was nineteen, and other boys and girls in the school were his age, also. He said that he told them if they didn't behave, he would break them up into little pieces.

Scottie was good to me. When I left work after my shift each morning, Scottie insisted I take home leftover food, which was a welcome supplement to my $1.25 pay.

After speaking to Scottie, I proceeded to dish myself up a big, free supper. Since I was going to be wolfing it down, I ate in the kitchen. I tried to rest on the double while eating.

At 6:00 p.m., I turned from a farmer to a dishwasher. I tackled the piled-up mess of dirty dishes with plenty of hot water and dishwashing soap. By and by, I got the dishes washed, rinsed, drained, dried, and placed ready for use. Then I gathered dirty dishes from the tables after customers left and kept up with the dishwashing the rest of the shift.

The diner was always busy on Saturday nights until after midnight. The five-cent chili hot dogs brought in the old and the young. The hot dogs weren't large, but the tasty, mild chili made them delicious. Other sandwiches and complete meals were served also. The time I worked there may have been the heyday of the diner.

To learn the business, I pitched in when I was caught up with the dishwashing and made hot dogs, barbecues, and other sandwiches. At that time a novice at cooking, I soon learned that from a ham, I could make hot or cold ham sandwiches and a ham and egg breakfast. From a pork shoulder, I made hot or cold pork sandwiches, as well as barbecues.

By 3:00 a.m. on this particular shift, I was definitely feeling the effects of lack of sleep. Luckily, at that time, we had no customers. Scottie said, "Kestner, I'll strip the cash register of all but a few dollars and go home for a couple of hours. No more customers than will come in, you can take care of them."

I was looking forward to some rest, but it was not to be. Scottie had been gone only two or three minutes when in came a man who appeared to be in his late sixties. He was not quite six feet tall and probably weighed around 200 pounds, with salt and pepper hair and a two-day's growth of white beard. He appeared to be pleasant, although something seemed a bit off about him. I wondered if he had been drinking. However, he walked perfectly straight to a table a ways back from the entrance.

Even back then, I was well aware of the fact that we were not supposed to judge one another. However, as a hobby, whether right or wrong, I allowed myself to psychoanalyze some people upon meeting them, so I could later see how well I did. My first impression in this case was that this man was an all-around good fellow, but at the same time, I wondered whether he might be half a bubble off level.

Shrugging off my weariness as much as possible, I walked briskly to the man's table and said jauntily, "Good morning, sir. Are you out late or up early? Not that it makes any difference. Welcome to the Dixie Diner. I'm somewhat new here. Have you been here before?"

The man replied, "Yes, young man, I've been here several times. The name is Shadrach. People call me Shad."

I was sleepy enough to be just a little slaphappy. I stuck out my hand and said, "I'm Kestner. People call me Kes the Mess. Would you like a menu or do you know what you want?"

As Shad shook my hand, he replied, "I know what I want—three of your chili hot dogs and a cup of coffee."

"Three on one coming up. The coffee was made around midnight, so it will be free."

"The coffee will be okay. I'm not fussy."

"Here is the Saturday *Daily Register*. It will take me a couple of minutes to heat up the chili for the hot dogs."

"Thank you. I'll see if I'm in the obituary." He flashed me a little grin.

When I returned with Shad's hot dogs and coffee, he was gazing at the newspaper on the table but appeared to be lost in thought. He had a silver-toned pocket watch in his hand. He was mindlessly flipping open the cover and snapping it closed, without ever looking at the time. At the same time, his right leg was constantly jiggling up and down.

Maybe it was the lack of sleep, but without thinking, I offered, "Shad, you appear to be a bit sad or worried. If you want to talk after you eat your hot dogs, I'll listen—your choice. I'm not trying to pry—just willing to help. I'm young, but I have a good many miles on me."

Looking surprised, Shad responded, "Kes, I'll give your offer some thought."

I watched Shad eat. He had pocketed his watch for the time being, but his leg never stopped jiggling. It was obvious to me that his mind wasn't on his hot dogs. When he finished eating, he motioned for me to come to him. I noticed that he again had his pocket watch in his hand. I could hear the rhythmic snap as I approached his table.

He said, "Kes, I do need to talk." He paused, while opening and closing his watch a few times. During one of the brief moments that the cover was open, I caught a glimpse of a photograph of a lovely woman. Finally, Shad managed to say, "I fear I've been rolled to the tune of five hundred dollars, but I'm afraid to look in my billfold to know for sure. I have change in my pocket to pay for my hot dogs and coffee, but I fear that five one-hundred-dollar bills are missing from my billfold." Snap, snap, snap went the watch as his leg jiggled faster.

I thought to myself that I surely would have looked in my billfold by now if I had thought $500 of mine was missing. I also was amazed at the amount of money he was carrying. But out loud, I merely said, "Shad, I was sleepy, but your story has made me wide awake. I sure hope your bills are still in your billfold. What makes you think they are missing?"

"Kes, first let me explain a little about myself. I am a farmer, and I also have a sideline of buying mules for a mule dealer who sells them to cotton farmers in the South. I buy only the best of the best and get a hundred-dollar bill for each one of them. I had just completed a good sale, so I had the price of five mules in my pocket.

"I love mules and sometime refer to women I admire as being 'as lovely as a hundred-dollar mule.'" Seeing my reaction, he continued, "Yes, it's crude, I know. My wife has been dead for several years now. She was a real beauty." To prove what he was saying, he popped open his pocket watch again and let me take a good look. When I nodded my agreement, he continued, "Anyway, enough time has passed that I have begun to notice women again to see if they look as good as a hundred-dollar mule.

"Today, I met this beautiful lady at the five-and-dime store. She was a lovely doll. She had black hair, brown eyes, and a quick, easy smile. It seemed natural for her to reach out and touch me. Without thinking twice, I said to her, 'I would like to have your phone number.' She replied, 'For a handsome man like you, I'll give you my phone number and my address. You are welcome to call or drop in any time. I live alone at this address.'"

After hearing only this much of his story, and seeing the look in his eyes as he thought about this woman, I had to revise my initial opinion of Shad. I now thought that he was not half a bubble off level in general, but probably only where women were concerned. Even at my young age, I knew how thoughts about a woman could cloud one's good judgment.

Shad continued, "I called on this lady tonight and enjoyed some cake and ice cream. At some point in the evening, she asked me if I liked guns. She said she had a new Smith and Wesson that a friend had given her for protection. She said she didn't want it and would sell it to me at a bargain.

"I asked her, 'What do you want for it?'

"She replied, 'For anyone else, I would ask twenty-five or thirty dollars, but for you, I will let you have it for fifteen dollars.'

"I said, 'I'd like to see it.'

"As she went into another room to get it, I realized again how well-built she was. Let's say she looked like she had a flake of alfalfa hay on her right hip and a flake of red clover on the left." He paused and then said with a goofy grin, "When she began to rotate the crops, I almost fainted." He snapped his watch case a few times, while his leg gave an extra-big jiggle.

I laughed appropriately at his attempt at humor and expectantly waited for him to continue his story.

Shad said, "She came back from the other room carrying a box. I could see that the gun was new in the box. I held it in my hand and remarked, 'This gun is worth more than fifteen dollars.'

"She replied, 'I'm willing to give you a good buy.'

"I said, 'In that case, I will take it.'

"I reached into my pocket for my billfold. I pulled it out, opened it, and then said, 'Let me get my eyes on, so I will give you the correct amount.'

"Then this gal said, 'I'll be your eyes for you.' As she took some money, she said, 'Ten and five make fifteen dollars.'

"She put the money in her shirt pocket and quickly asked, 'Would you like some more cake and ice cream—just a little bit more?'

"I consented to another small serving, and she served me the cake and ice cream. But as I left her house, I had an uneasy feeling."

Privately, I thought how foolish he had been to open his billfold and let her take the money. But I said sympathetically, "Shad, I'm concerned, too. Suppose you take a look in your billfold. I hope and pray no money is missing."

Shad pocketed his watch, took out his billfold, held it in both hands, and looked up as if in prayer. Then, he slowly opened it. He didn't have to tell me what he saw there—I read it on his face. His five one-hundred-dollar bills were missing.

Now that I was involved, I felt that I should help in some way. I said to Shad, "My heart goes out to you. If I can help you, I will. When my boss Scottie returns, I'm sure he'll know what to do."

To my surprise, Scottie came back to the diner sooner than expected. Shad gave him a thumbnail sketch of what he had told me.

If Scottie shared my feelings about Shad's foolishness, he didn't let it show. He immediately asked, "Do you have this gal's phone number?" Shad produced the number.

Scottie went to the phone and called the woman. He got a prompt answer. Scottie must have had some of Cole Younger's grit, because he said gruffly and authoritatively, "I'm the night manager at the Dixie Diner. A good customer of mine was relieved of five one-hundred-dollar bills at your house tonight. He is heartbroken, and I'm as mad as hell. I can be there in five minutes and pick it up for him, and that will be the end of it. Or, we can turn the matter over to the police. I will pull up out front and toot the horn, and you bring the money out to me. What do you say?"

The woman must have replied that she would turn over the money, because Scottie hung up, looking satisfied. Shad got in the car with Scottie and directed him where to go. I heard later that Scottie didn't have to toot his horn at the house. This gal was standing in the doorway with the money in her hand. She took the few steps to the car and handed the money to Scottie. He checked it out, said "Thank you ma'am," and drove back to the diner.

Shad was overjoyed and so was I. I was thankful that all had ended well, and that I had had some excitement to get me through the night. I also resolved to keep a close watch over my billfold, a habit that I continue to this day.

At six o'clock that Sunday morning, I wobbled out to my Model T Ford with $1.25, some mashed potatoes, green beans, cole slaw, wieners, and other things. I was worn out, but happy—happy that I had survived my shift, and happy that I was leaving with a goodly supply of leftovers.

At home, I turned the food over to Mom. She seemed pleased to get it and commented, "I will add some eggs, onion, and other things to those potatoes and make some potato cakes. They will go well with cole slaw and green beans."

I hurried off to bed, but as strange as it sounds, I didn't go to sleep immediately. I first had to relive the happenings of the past twenty-four hours of work, work, work.

* * *

Life's Other Side

My dad had four brothers and nine sisters. The youngest of the sisters was Rosie. She visited one of her older sisters, Sarah, who lived near Dudley, Missouri. While there, Rosie met and later married a Spanish-American War veteran by the name of Affolder. He died when I was very young. I never saw him. Dad thought highly of him and called him Mr. Affolder, since he was a county judge, with an office in Dexter, Missouri.

Mr. Affolder and Aunt Rosie had three sons—Rudolph (Rudy), Eugene (Gene), and Ralph (who was nicknamed Hoot because of his hoot owl–like eyes)—and one daughter, Marie, who had eye problems and wore wraparound sunglasses. I never saw her without them.

When I first saw Aunt Rosie, I was impressed with her appearance. She was tall, large-boned, freckled-faced, and stately looking. The three sons were well-liked by most of those who knew them. Their main hobby was playing practical jokes on people. Some of their jokes showed a mean streak in them. Their mother, however, thought they could do no wrong. She was much amused at the pranks she knew about. I'll not go into the jokes my cousins played, since I'm writing a short story, not a book.

Marie was only a little like her mother and brothers. She attended church, and it had a noticeable effect on her personality and outlook on life. She was critical of her mother for expressing amusement at what she termed "dumb stunts" the brothers pulled. She also chastised her brothers, which added to their amusement.

In 1934, at the age of fourteen, I hitchhiked my first trip to Dudley to visit Aunt Rosie and family. At that time, her oldest son, Rudy, was married and running a sawmill nearby. Her second son, Gene, was on a hobo trip—riding boxcars for the thrill of it—to Oregon to visit relatives on his father's side of the family.

I asked about my cousin, Hoot (the youngest member of the family at around nineteen). Aunt Rosie said that Hoot and a neighbor had taken a truckload of watermelons to Chicago to sell.

I learned quickly where the three boys had gotten their devilishness by a trick Aunt Rosie played on me while I was visiting. With a big smile, she said, "I think we can have some fun with a neighbor girl, Bessie."

I said, "Tell me about Bessie."

Marie entered into the spirit of what Aunt Rosie and the boys thought would be fun. They told me that Bessie was twenty-nine years old and lived nearby on the adjoining farm. She was a member of a proud, well-respected family. To the embarrassment of her family, Bessie wasn't too bright—to put it in present day slang, she wasn't playing with a full deck, or her elevator didn't go all the way up. I think you get the picture.

Aunt Rosie and Marie agreed that Bessie was "man crazy," but wasn't having any luck getting one. They said Bessie was a good worker, could cook, and had a cow. They went on to say she would be over the next afternoon, and we'd have some fun. I thought to myself: "I don't want to see Bessie. I'll take an afternoon walk in the wood lot."

The next morning, I was out where an old barn was

being torn down to build a new one. I stepped on a nail that went deep into my foot. Marie and Aunt Rosie washed my foot clean and had me soak it in coal oil. Then they got some peach tree leaves, bruised them with a hammer, made a poultice, and bound it to my foot with a strip of cloth. That turned out to be a remarkable cure. However, for a day or two, I had pain in my foot, and it especially hurt to bear weight on it.

There was a cot in the living room that served as a good place for me to recline. That was where I was lying when Bessie came in. She was about five feet, five inches tall, with a stocky build, and with poorly cared for blondish-brown hair and wild-looking gray eyes. She plodded in as though she had flat feet. When she saw me, she stopped and exclaimed, "Miss Affolder, this ain't one of your boys! But he has big eyes like Hoot." I thought to myself, "I have a good reason to have big eyes."

Aunt Rosie replied, "No, Bessie, that's my brother's boy." Then she introduced us. She said, "Kestner, this is our neighbor, Bessie."

Bessie rushed over and grabbed my hand and shook it like a pup would shake a sock. She said, "You'll never know how glad I am to make your acquaintance." Marie placed a rocking chair for Bessie in the middle of the room, some distance from me.

After a little chat with Bessie, Marie said, "Bessie, Kestner is down here looking for a wife. He doesn't want just any wife. He wants one that can cook."

The rocking chair that Bessie was sitting in was a light one. She began to make it walk by lifting first one rocker and then the other and moving toward me. I thought of holding my breath and trying to faint, but I held steady. With a big smile, Bessie said, "I shore know how to cook. I can cook cornbread, beans, and taters."

Marie spoke up, "Bessie, there is something else Kestner is looking for."

Bessie asked, "What is that, Marie?"

Marie replied, "He wants someone with a Jersey cow."

That was when Bessie was almost overcome with joy. She cried, "Praise the Lord—I have a Jersey cow!" Simultaneously, she walked that rocker ever closer to my bed.

Aunt Rosie saw the panic on my face and thought it was time to put the brakes on that affair. She said, "Bessie, we wouldn't be treating you right if we didn't tell you that Kestner has 'mad spells' at times—almost like a dog with a fit."

Bessie began to make that chair rock in reverse. Aunt Rosie went on. "Kestner never hurts anybody, or he hasn't yet. If he is standing, he falls down and rolls around." At that point, I rolled off the cot and started to kick a little.

Bessie said, "Miss Affolder, I spect I'd better go now."

Aunt Rosie said, "Bessie, you don't need to hurry off, but if you have to go, come back and see us soon." Was I ever glad to see her go!

Bessie had a friend, Monroe, whom she sometimes thought of as a boyfriend. He was friendly and likeable but not too smart, either. He dropped in that same day to say "hello" to Marie and Aunt Rosie, on his way home from wherever he had been. He was on cloud nine.

He said, "Marie, I bought me a one-horse wagon. I plan to haul wood into Dudley and sell it and make me some money and buy me some stuff."

Marie asked quizzically, "Monroe, do you have a horse?"

He answered, "No."

Then Marie asked, "Monroe, why on earth did you buy a wagon if you don't have a horse?"

Monroe answered, "For the simple reason a wagon don't eat."

Marie, with forced mock surprise in her voice, asked, "Monroe, do you mean to tell me a wagon doesn't eat?"

In amazement, Monroe exclaimed, "My God, Marie! I thought you had better sense than that!"

In a couple of days, my foot was okay. I helped Rudy for two days at the sawmill while one of his work hands had to be off.

In the meantime, Gene returned from his trip to Oregon. He was tan, tall, and handsome. He came in riding a used motorcycle with a sidecar, which he had bought at Fisk, the next town over. He told Aunt Rosie he had forged her name to get it. He said he hadn't paid much for it and would pay her back. She laughed and said, "That's all right, son. Just make sure you pay me back."

Gene told his mother he had been by to see his girl-friend. She was glad to see him and made him promise he would attend the tent revival that was going on in Dudley. Marie and Aunt Rosie liked this girlfriend and said she was the pianist for the revival.

Gene had much to tell about his trip to and from Oregon but said he was more than happy to be back. He told me he was glad to see me and looked forward to showing me a little of "life's other side." At that comment, Aunt Rosie smiled and Marie frowned.

The following morning at the breakfast table, Marie said, "Gene, I want you to introduce Kestner to Mary Ann at the revival tonight." Then she said to me, "She is the sweetest little Christian girl one could ever hope to meet." Gene, with an amused look on his face, said he would.

That day, Gene took me to Skagg's beer joint, which was tame of day and wild at night. Charlie Skaggs, a long-time friend of Gene's, owned and operated it. Gene ordered two Cokes. Charlie seemed surprised and said, "What— no beer?"

Gene replied, "By the way, Charlie, this is my cousin from Illinois. We are going to the revival tonight and will be courting some upright girls afterwards, so we don't want the smell of booze on us."

"Well, well, well, Gene, when you start preaching, I'll attend and say, 'A-men.'"

That night, we were taking our seats under the tent as Gene's girlfriend was taking her seat at the piano. She sent him a smile, long distance. In reply, he touched a finger to his forehead.

I was busy looking around to see if I could spot Mary Ann. I saw no one who matched the picture I had in mind of her. However, I saw a pretty good-looking girl who kept eyeing Gene and me. I took her to be someone sweet on Gene. I glanced at Gene and saw him give her a sly wink. She flashed a big smile. Gene nudged me with his elbow and whispered, "That is Mary Ann." I thought to myself, "Mary Ann has Marie fooled."

Gene's girlfriend breathed life into the song service with her playing. I didn't hear anything the preacher said for wondering about Mary Ann. Had she learned more about "life's other side" than Marie had any idea?

At the close of the service, Mary Ann came to Gene and me, and Gene introduced us. He told her that Marie had suggested that I walk her home. Mary Ann smiled and said, "Gene, you know me. I'm game if he is."

Gene said to me, "I'll pick you up in front of her house in a short time."

Mary Ann and I started strolling off toward her house. I wondered if I should take her hand. I didn't wonder long. She put her arm around me and pulled herself close. I thought to myself, "Mary Ann has been around the block."

When we got to her yard gate, which was close to the street, I wondered in what manner I should conduct myself in bringing the short walk to a conclusion with dignity and good taste. Should I show a little affection—maybe place a little kiss on her forehead? Or, maybe a handshake would be fine.

Suddenly, with my hardly knowing what was taking place, we were in each other's arms, with our heads close together. I thought that would be a good ending—just say "Good night" and that would be the end. However, there was no end to the surprises. It happened like a flash of lightning. She nailed me with a kiss that I didn't know existed. Just then, Gene rolled up and stopped. I bid Mary Ann good night and crawled into the side car.

As we were leaving Dudley with our hair blowing back, Gene yelled out, "Did you kiss her?"

I tried to look macho and yelled back at him, "I sure did!"

Gene looked pleased and said, "Atta boy!"

The next morning at the breakfast table, I was sitting across from Aunt Rosie. Marie was on my right, with Gene across the table from her. All was quiet for a while. Then Marie asked, "Kestner, did you meet Mary Ann?"

I tried to look happy and replied, "I sure did."

I looked over at Gene and hoped he would back me favorably. I caught a glimpse of glee and merriment on his face. He was about to plunge into laughter. Aunt Rosie was quick to catch on. Both of them burst into hilarious laughter.

Marie broke in and asked sternly, "Gene, who did Kestner walk home?"

When he stopped laughing, Gene answered, "Daphne Taft." He and Aunt Rosie started laughing all over again.

Marie reacted with disgust and exclaimed, "Gene, Gene, Gene—you are no longer my brother!"

Gene asked with a taunt in his voice, "Who are you going to replace me with—Monroe?" Marie didn't comment further but just sat there looking like a thundercloud.

Now I don't want to leave you with the impression that the women of Southeast Missouri are fast and unladylike. None better can be found anywhere. My late wife, Evelyn—the best of the best—was from that area.

I have great respect for all women. However, among the many, there are some that I adore with great admiration because of an inward beauty that I do not see in all. You have seen some, too. I'll tell you of one.

We met many years ago. I've never forgotten her, even though her name now escapes me. I'll call her Ruth. In the Bible, Ruth showed great affection to her mother-in-law. This Ruth was equally loving, kind, and loyal to my cousin, Marie.

When I returned from the service, in 1946, I went to Dudley to see Marie. I hadn't seen her since I was fourteen years old. However, we had corresponded some. She was the same Marie, personality-wise—kind, friendly, and alert of mind—and she was happy I had come to see her. She had moved from the farm to a nice home in Dudley. Aunt Rosie had died, and Marie's brothers were working in Michigan. Sadly, by this time, Marie had lost her eyesight.

Ruth was the sister to Marie that she'd never had. Ruth was a single woman, between fifty and sixty years of age. She lived near Marie and devotedly cared for her. Marie did what she could for herself and paid Ruth a fair wage. However, Ruth was always going the extra mile to serve Marie well.

The times I visited Marie, Ruth treated me as family—always glad to see me. Like Marie, she had an intellectual mind and a sense of humor.

I couldn't keep from wondering why Ruth had never married. I felt our friendship was strong enough that I could ask her. I pointed out all the good qualities I had observed in her and told her I was amazed that she had remained single. Then I asked, "Would you mind telling me why?"

She didn't seem annoyed that I had asked her something that wasn't any of my business. She smiled and set my mind at ease. She replied, "Kestner, it wasn't something I planned. I was the youngest of five children who had the most wonderful parents people could have.

"As my brothers and sisters came of age, they married and left home. Dad and Mom had grown older, and I felt the need to stay home to care for them. When Dad and Mom died, the men I would have married when I was younger were married. It just didn't appear to be in the cards for me to marry."

"Thank you, Ruth, for answering my question. I didn't want to be nosy, but I couldn't help wondering."

Ruth commented further, showing her kindness and sense of humor. "I have older men who make overtures in my direction. For example, old Frank Potter came by the other night, as he does pretty often. He was dressed to impress me. He wore a yellow shirt that hadn't been ironed. He was in overalls with a red necktie hanging over the bib of his overalls. His remarks were also to impress me. As he entered, he said, 'Whoo-ee, the weather sure is . . . am a-changin'. This mornin' the wind blewed and blewed. This afternoon it snewed and snewed, and now I think it is going to turn cold and frez.'" With a little smile, Ruth added, "Bless his heart."

The number of Ruths is not a few. But too often they are, as Thomas Gray wrote, like the flower that blooms in the desert—"born to blush unseen, and waste its sweetness on the desert air."

For several months, I didn't see Marie. One day in 1948, the Wallace clan got word from Gene in Michigan that Marie had died, that Rudy and Hoot were already in Dudley, and that he was leaving for Dudley immediately.

My Aunt Nellie Wallace, her daughter, and two of her sons told me they were planning to attend the funeral and asked me to go with them. We left early, ate breakfast in Cairo, Illinois, and were in Dudley by 9:00 a.m. Ruth and the three brothers met us and greeted us warmly. We went in the house, where Marie was lying in state. Ruth filled us in on Marie's last days.

Rudy, Gene, and Hoot told me they needed to take care of some business in Dexter and asked me to go with them. A cloud of gloom hovered over each of them. Before leaving Dudley, Rudy said, "I need some 'hold-up tonic'—we can get it at Charlie's."

Gene went into the bar and came back with something in a brown paper sack. He and Rudy almost used sleight of hand passing and nipping the tonic. Hoot spoke up and asked, "What about the back seat? Kestner and I need some hold-up tonic, too." The tonic was passed back. Hoot partook generously. I declined, saying, "I'm holding up all right."

We got back to the house about half past eleven. At noon, Marie's casket was brought from the house and placed in the hearse. Ruth rode with the driver of the hearse. The three brothers and I were in a car immediately behind the hearse, followed by the car from Illinois.

At the church, the brothers indicated they wanted me to walk in behind the casket with Ruth and then sit with her. I was pleased to do so.

When the standing-room-only group began to sing "In the Sweet By and By," Ruth began to quiver and weep softly. My tears flowed freely. The brothers looked at us and buried their faces in their handkerchiefs. I didn't feel as if the tears that swept the church were bitter tears but, rather, were tears of love and friendship.

Following the burial, a number of friends and relatives went to the home for food and visitation. Gene stood up and indicated he wanted to speak on behalf of the brothers. He said they wanted Ruth to take anything she wanted, sell the rest, and keep the money as a thanks for her love, service, and friendship to Marie. He further said that the brothers had authorized that the house be sold and the proceeds divided four ways, with Ruth getting a quarter share. At this announcement, the group showed their love for Ruth by cheering.

Even though my cousins at times had been as mean as snakes, I admired them for their generosity and kindness to Ruth. I like to think their devotion to Marie and the long association with Ruth caused them to realize the better side of life.

* * *

The Transformations of Andy and Tige

Some people you meet you like immediately. Others, it takes a lifetime before you can feel that connection. A childhood neighbor, whom I'll call "Andy," fell in this latter category.

Andy and I went through grade school together. He was just months older than I and somewhat smaller. He was a good reader and excelled in spelling and adding matches, but he was a big snitch. He didn't know how to keep a secret. Therefore, he wasn't in the "In" group, of which I was the captain. This fact grieved Andy deeply.

One time, Andy had a talk with me concerning the matter. He asked, "Why am I not included in your group?"

I replied, "The answer is simple. You don't know how to keep your mouth shut. If we do something for fun, you snitch on us. In other words, you blow your guts."

Andy countered, "I know I've been that way, but I'll change. Trust me. I swear on a Bible, and I cross my heart and hope to die."

I said, "Okay, Andy. I'll check you over the next three days and let you know if you are in or out."

After the first recess the next day, Kenneth Howton reported to the teacher that he had lost his pocketknife on the playground. He said it had a bright yellow handle and would have been easily seen. He said he had looked where they were playing ball and thought someone must have seen it and picked it up.

The teacher, showing kindness and consideration, asked, "Have any of you seen Kenneth's lost knife?"

I saw Andy watching me like a hawk. I thought to myself that this was my chance to check him out. I knew nothing of the lost knife and was fond of Kenneth. He was in the "In" group.

I gave Andy a big wink and placed my hand on the bib pocket of my overalls. Andy almost went nuts. He waved his hand and yelled out, "Teacher, teacher. I know who has that knife!"

The teacher asked, "Who, Andy?"

Andy answered, "Kestner Wallace. He has it in the pocket in the bib of his overalls."

I kept my hands away from the bib of my overalls and invited the teacher to check. Of course, she found no knife. Andy had egg on his face. He had failed the test, and he knew he would never be allowed in the "In" group. Kenneth later found his knife where he had slid into third base that morning.

Back in those days, it seemed that hunting for possums, coons, and foxes was much in style. We hunted whenever we could. Since Andy lived nearby, sometimes he would hunt with us. Andy owned a good rabbit dog and a new .22 rifle, with which he became a crack shot. He could hit a rabbit running. I had an old worn-out rifle that threw the bullets sideways, and I couldn't hit a rabbit *sitting* more than twenty feet away.

Although we played and fished together, as well as

hunted, I didn't really consider Andy a good friend. In addition to being a snitch, he seemed to have no sense of fairness. For example, even though he shot many rabbits on our land, he never offered to share them.

Hunters depended on their dogs, whether hunting rabbits, foxes, coons, squirrels, or possums. Some foxhounds had sense enough to chase rabbits in the daytime and foxes at night. Most hunters wouldn't allow their hounds to run rabbits anytime for fear it would spoil them as foxhounds.

Some dogs would tree squirrels in daytime and coons at night. These dogs were valuable, and their owners thought very highly of them.

On the lower end of the totem pole for hunting dogs was the possum dog. Possum dogs were not as valuable as coon dogs or all-around hunting dogs. However, they were good watchdogs and good pets.

We had one such dog. His mother was a high-grade mutt, and his daddy was a German shepherd. We named him Tige. He was black, short, and heavyset, with extra-large paws. He had strength and endurance, but he lacked the speed to make a coon dog. I hoped by my working with him, he would become a squirrel and possum dog.

Once, when Tige was beyond the pup stage, my two brothers—Byrum and Victor—and I took Tige with us to our land on the side of Womble Mountain, where we were cutting a winter's supply of wood for heating and cooking. We took a rifle with us in case Tige treed a squirrel. If he did, we would shoot it and thereby honor his effort.

We were encouraged by Tige's running around with his nose to the ground—a good sign he was hunting. Tige had a strong, musical bark. After quite a long time, he let out a rapid string of loud and clear barks, which sounded a good distance from us.

Hunters try to encourage their dogs by going to them when they tree or bay something. While my brothers went ahead with the woodcutting, I took the rifle and went to see what the barking was all about. I ran all the way to Tige.

When I got to him, I was out of breath. Tige was on a room-sized rock that sloped down on one side to about four feet, but appeared to be flat on top. While Tige continued to bark, I stood for about a minute to get my breath. I had no idea why he was barking, but I surmised he had cornered a snake or a possum. I laid the rifle on the rock and climbed up on it.

When I saw nothing, I thought poor Tige had lost his marbles. But on looking more closely, I saw that he was using his huge paws to control the movement of a big, black ant.

You can imagine my letdown feeling. I had referred to Tige as being "my dog," but when I got back to my brothers, I said, "*Your* dog was barking at a big, black ant." They laughed. However, we didn't give up on Tige. I was always thinking of new ways to train him.

The fall after Andy failed the snitching test at school, a revival meeting was in progress at Blue Springs Church, a church that has been gone for many years. A road went to the church south and east of Womble Mountain, but there was also a footpath and bridle path that cut through the woods to it.

One night during the revival, my two brothers, my cousin Donald, Andy, and I took the one-and-a-half mile cut-through and attended the church service. Donald was the oldest of the group. His dog followed us to church. We hardly knew the dog was along; he may have taken a nap outside during the service.

I can recall very little about the preaching, but I still remember the trip home. It was a moonlit night. Donald had a carbide light that showed us the way through the heavily wooded areas. About halfway home, Donald's dog treed some distance from us. Donald said, "We'll have to go and see what he has treed. He'd be disappointed if we don't."

We made our way to the dog. Upon reaching him, we saw that he had a possum up a small tree no more than eight feet tall.

Donald said, "The fur season is not in yet, and since this possum is only half grown, we'll shake it out and pet the dog to make him feel good. When he is not looking, we'll turn the possum loose."

I said, "Donald, let me take it home with me and use him to train our dog, Tige."

Donald said, "He's your possum."

Andy spoke up, "Donald, I'll give you a quarter for that possum. My mother loves to eat possum."

Donald said, "Kestner, I can't turn down a quarter. I'm going to let Andy have him."

The possum sulled up as if it were dead, and Andy proudly carried it home by the tail. Before we parted ways, I asked Andy if I could bring Tige down the following evening and drag the possum around without Tige seeing it. My plan was to then put the possum up a bush and let Tige tree it. Andy thought that would be fun and agreed.

The next evening, when I got to his house with Tige, Andy said, "Kestner, you are too late. We skinned that possum this morning and ate it for dinner. Mom baked it with candied sweet potatoes, and it was really good."

Hiding my disappointment, I managed to say, "That's okay, Andy. I'm glad you enjoyed it."

I was glad that was over and done with. However, it was not quite over. I found out that Andy had told Donald that he would have to look to me for the quarter for the possum. Andy said that I had come down after he had put the possum under a tub and gone in the house, and then I stole the possum away. I assured Donald that I had done no such thing. He didn't seem excited about the matter, but he may have wondered which of us was lying.

At the age of fourteen, Andy graduated from the eighth grade. His mother signed him up to join the CCC (Civilian Conservation Corps) camp at Herod, as though he were sixteen years old. Andy got room and board, clothes, and five dollars a month, and his mother got twenty-five dollars a month. Andy's mother kept him happy by letting him drive her car when he came home occasionally.

The first time Andy came home from camp, he drove the car to our driveway and stopped. He didn't get out. He wanted me to see him in his army-type uniform. I obliged him by taking a good, nosy look. Since it was about dusk, he struck a match and held it down as if he were looking for something. My opinion was that he wanted me to see his highly polished, brown shoes.

I could have made Andy happy by going on about how good he looked in his uniform. But I didn't. Instead I asked, "Andy, are you ready to admit you lied about that possum?"

Andy flew angry. He was almost off his rocker in nothing flat. He screamed out, "Are you calling me a liar?"

He acted as if he were reaching for something under the car seat as he said, "I've a damn good notion to make you a necktie out of this crank under the seat."

I knew him too well to be frightened—he had always been more talk than action. I said, "If you come out of there with a car crank, you better put some salt and pepper on it, because I'll make you eat it." He fired up the car and spun the wheels taking off.

Our paths went in different directions thereafter. For years, Andy and I never saw each other. I was away from Southern Illinois for a few years. Mom tried hard to keep me abreast of happenings around Rudement, Herod, and Mountain Grove. Once, she mentioned briefly that there had been a revival at Mountain Grove Church and that Andy had been converted.

After that, Andy felt he was called to preach. I learned from time to time that he was "walking the straight and narrow way" and preached here and there when called on. I heard that he did a good job, preaching with enthusiasm.

After being away from home for some time, I visited with Mom for an extended weekend. Mom asked if I would take her to a minister's meeting on Sunday. She explained that ministers from a number of churches both far and near would attend and would preach for five to ten minutes. Such meetings were held yearly and were well attended.

When Mom and I arrived, the church was full. The ministers, about a dozen, were seated in an area usually reserved for the choir—to the right of the podium. To my surprise, Andy was sitting among them, "shining like a star when only one was shining in the sky."

These ministers energized each other. Enthusiasm ran high. Each minister, when introduced, came on strong. "Amen" and "Praise the Lord" were heard frequently from the appreciative audience.

When Andy was called on, he didn't wait until he got to the podium to start talking. He sprang to his feet and began preaching in a high-pitched voice that seemed to turn the group on. I can't recall much of what he said, but his conclusion went as follows: "I love God with all my heart, soul, mind, and strength. I hate the Devil with every fiber in my body. I plan to chew on him as long as

I have a tooth in my head and then gum on him until I die." Numerous calls of "Amen!" resounded from the audience, along with hearty applause.

Years passed. Mom had a friend who gave her a running account of Andy's ups and downs. Mom informed me that Andy had given up preaching and had started drinking, gambling, and carousing. She went on to say that he had been in a car accident and was on crutches, and that he might be on them for the rest of his life. Mom said that she wished I'd go visit Andy and help him get back on the "straight and narrow way."

I figured that it would do Mom more good for me to visit Andy than it would do him. So I went. Andy, on crutches, met me at the door, with a big smile on his face. We sat and talked and laughed about old times. We had plenty to talk about.

Finally, I asked Andy about his accident. He went into detail, explaining what had happened. He said he hoped he wouldn't be on crutches the rest of his life.

Andy told me a lady from his insurance company was coming the next day to offer him a cash settlement. He said, "I hope you can come by the following day, so I can tell you how I made out." I promised to check back with him.

Andy's dad had been in a bad mining accident and was on crutches the last few years of his life. His legs helped balance him; otherwise, they were useless. As I left, Andy walked with me to the door in a manner identical to the way his dad had walked on crutches.

The next evening, I called on Andy. He greeted me with a big smile and without his crutches. I was astonished. I said, "What—no crutches?"

He said, "Come in and have a seat, and I'll tell you all about it."

He told me the insurance gal had come to the house and asked, "Are you ready to get down to business and settle this claim for once and for all?"

Andy said, "I told her, 'Let me get my handkerchief out, because I know I'll break down and shed some tears in the process.'"

Andy continued, "She told me to try to hold up, and that she would be as fair with me as she knew how. When I asked her how much she was willing to pay me, she said that they had talked my case over at the office and decided to offer me twenty-five hundred dollars. She asked me how that sounded to me, and I told her, 'It sounds good, but not good enough. I had at least three thousand in mind.' I allowed my voice to quiver a little as I stated the amount and put my handkerchief to my eyes.

"With an expression of relief, she said, 'You sign this release, and I'll write you a check for three thousand dollars.' And that is what we did."

What Andy said he did after he put the check in his billfold made me want to kick his butt until his nose bled. Andy told me he asked the woman if she would do him a favor. When she readily agreed and asked what he had in mind, he said, "I borrowed these crutches from the pharmacy. Would you mind dropping them off for me as you go back to your office? I'm not going to need them anymore." As Andy described the look on the insurance woman's face, it took some effort on my part for me to laugh along with him.

Several years passed. Once again Mom had a request of me. She told me that Andy's late wife's aunt had called her and requested that she pray for Andy. The aunt said Andy was dying of cancer and feared he would go to hell. Mom's request was that I go and visit with him and help him get his feet reestablished on "solid rock."

As usual, I did some good-natured arguing with Mom. I said, "Mom, I don't want Andy to go to hell, but maybe his feeling a little 'hell-fire heat' would be good for him."

Mom gave me that look she had given me years before when she had found my hand in the cookie jar before dinner. "The look" still worked on me. I quickly said, "Okay, Mom, I'll go see Andy. Maybe I can be of some encouragement to him."

I called at Andy's upstairs apartment. He met me at the door. He looked bad—really bad—and weak, but his voice was strong.

He greeted me with these words, "Come in, Kestner. I'm dying with cancer, and that's not all. I'm going to hell."

Shaking my head, I said, "Andy, you are not going anywhere. You are a sick man with a bad case of the blues."

Andy cut me off and began to tell me all the bad things he had done. Believe me, he enumerated several before I could calm him down.

I said, "Andy, confession is said to be good for the soul. But you are confessing to the wrong person. I couldn't care less what you have done or haven't done. You need to make your confession to God. The Bible says that if you confess your sins unto God, 'He is faithful and just to forgive your sins and cleanse you from all unrighteousness.' Before you sleep tonight, confess to God, by faith accept His mercy, and He will give you a free pass to the Glory Land." Having delivered that sage advice, I said, "Andy, I must be going. I'll call back in a few days."

Andy said, "Not so fast. You are not leaving until we have prayed together."

I was pleased enough to comply with his wishes. I prayed some but did more listening than praying. Andy got carried away. He got louder and louder. I thought to myself, "The Lord isn't deaf." You can't imagine how loud he got.

Someone from the apartment below must have used a broomstick to bump against the wooden ceiling and with curse words yelled, "Knock off that loud disturbance up there!"

The rest of Andy's prayer sounded sincere and effective in a more conversational tone. When he said, "A-men," he got to his feet. He rejoiced and said, "My sins are gone."

As I took my leave, Andy walked with me to the door of his apartment. There, we stopped and faced each other. I realized as never before that we were the same height. We looked straight into each other's eyes, as we grasped each other's hand in an expression of warmth and friendship and without any immediate desire to let go.

In lightning speed, my mind swept over the years of our childhood, and I remembered many more pleasant experiences than otherwise. I had a feeling he was doing likewise. Had our combined thoughts been captured with pen and ink, they would have made a long, long short story. We were too emotionally full to speak, so we embraced with tears in our eyes and never saw each other after that night.

...

Now, my good dog lovers, you may be wondering if Tige ever became a hunting dog. The truth is, I got too busy with my freshman schoolwork to think of hunting. However, late one cold Friday night, after other family members had gone to bed, I was finishing reading a book to be reported on in English class on Monday.

I decided to go out for some fresh air before retiring. I armed myself with Dad's crude walking stick and a flashlight.

Tige was overjoyed to see me. He made three wild circles and picked up on a trail that took off toward the woodlot. I thought to myself that he was on the track of a wild varmint. Since it went in a straight line, I thought it must be a coon or a bobcat.

In a short time, Tige bayed—he was standing guard over something on the ground, barking fast and excitedly. I was relieved it wasn't a bobcat. It was a possum on the verge of having a nervous breakdown, as was Tige. They were carrying on and baring their teeth at each other.

I tapped the possum on the head with my stick. It played dead, and I finished the job. I decided to give the carcass to Andy's mother, and I sold the pelt for seventy-five cents. Tige had made a possum dog after all.

* * *

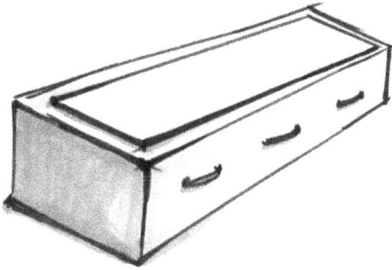

Recalling the Passing

Over the ninety-plus years of my most-interesting life, I have seen many changes. However, the sorrow that one feels at losing a loved one remains the same from one generation to the next.

I know some funeral homes were in existence in Southern Illinois in the early 1900s, but at that time, funerals were generally held in the home or in churches. In fact, back then, some funeral homes were not set up to hold funeral services.

Although I was around eight years old before I attended my first funeral, I can remember hearing about funerals from the time I was six or seven years old. We had a neighbor, Mina Bixler, who had been married for a number of years but had no children. She wasn't educated or very religious, but she liked to go to funerals to see the people who attended and observe their reactions.

Mom had small children and a poor way of getting around, so she was pleased to have Mina drop in and tell her in detail about any funerals she had attended. One time, while sitting inconspicuously in the next room, I had my ears sticking up like donkey ears and heard every word Mina said. The best I can remember, this is the story she told Mom:

237

"The funeral was to be at eleven o'clock. I got there early so I could see everyone come into the church. The church was full well before eleven. Just a little before the time to start, the hearse pulled up out front. Through the double doors of the church, I could see that Reverend Sherman Rector was riding with the undertaker, Claude Gibbons. Six men were waiting to carry the coffin when it was removed from the hearse.

"Reverend Rector moved along in front of the coffin with his face about a mile long. That told me it was going to be a *sad* funeral. I have heard him lots of times; that is the only kind he preaches. The first part of the sermon wasn't too sad. He got the person over in the Glory Land. Then the rest of his sermon was a tear-jerker."

Mom must have heard about all she wanted to hear, so she cut in with a few questions: "Did Reverend Rector preach very long?"

"It seemed a long time to me. Those old homemade benches got to feeling pretty hard before he wound down."

"How did the family and the congregation react to the sad part of the sermon?"

"Handkerchiefs out all over the church—people wiping their eyes and blowing their noses. I didn't want to look like an oddball, so I did the same."

Mom then asked her final question: "Did the folks file around and view the deceased?"

Mina replied excitedly: "All the people not related marched around and returned to their seats. Then the family of about fifteen people went up to the coffin. Then if you will excuse me for saying so, 'All hell broke loose.' I ain't never heard such crying and taking on in my life. The ones who were less broken up were holding up the ones who were boohooing the loudest and unable to stand alone. After a while, the mourners sat down, and

Reverend Rector said, 'The final benediction will be said at the gravesite. For you who are not going to the burial, may God's richest blessing rest upon you.'"

While funerals will never pass out of fashion, I feel there has been a noticeable change in the public display of sorrow at funerals—from the way Mina described long ago, to a much more controlled sobbing. I much prefer the latter.

. . .

My grandmother on my mother's side was a fine woman. She was thought by many to have had the gift of healing, and she prayed for many with good results.

Around September 1, 1936, Grandpa and Grandma's fiftieth wedding anniversary was celebrated at their home. One of their sons and five daughters, all teachers, were present along with a few neighbors. My mother, one of her sisters, and a brother had six or more children each, which made for a fun time. It was a lovely day—with food abounding, children playing, and the older folks visiting and having a good time.

To highlight the occasion, Grandpa and Grandma renewed their marriage vows. With the pair and Reverend Hill standing on the high front porch and everyone else standing on the ground to watch, Reverend Hill asked, "Do you, George Millikan, take this woman, Saluda Jones, to be your lawfully wedded wife?" Grandpa answered, "Yes."

Then he asked Grandma, "Do you, Saluda Jones, take this man to be your lawfully wedded husband?"

Grandma answered, "Yes, yes, yes, a thousand times, yes." As Grandma uttered those words, her face shone like the face of an angel. At that moment, my love for her matched the love she had for Grandpa. It never changed.

The last year or so of Grandma's life, she and Grandpa lived alone. They were able to care for their chickens and stock themselves.

One morning, Grandma went with Grandpa to the barn to do the morning chores. They came back to the house, and Grandma said, "George, let us pray." Grandpa later told his children that their mother prayed for each of them and their grandchildren. Then, he said that she reclined on a daybed in the living room and suddenly died. Grandpa was devastated. Grandma had had no previous sickness, so there was no warning whatsoever.

Grandma died in January during the Great Flood of 1937. Fortunately, Grandpa's home was on a hill, and no floodwater was near.

The daughters were teaching in Pope County schools and boarding away from home. Their son Reuben was teaching in Hardin County. All made it home without too much difficulty when they learned of their mother's death.

Their son Ottis, who lived in the Cottonwood community, had to contend with high water. He walked the road and hitchhiked when possible, and walked the railroad tracks when the water was over the road. With difficulty as well as good luck, he made it home in record time.

The family's next problem, due to the high water, was to get a coffin from the funeral home in Golconda. They hitched the large team of bay horses to the farm wagon and drove as near to Golconda as they could get. They tied up the team, borrowed a rowboat from a farmer, and rowed in to Golconda, where they bought a coffin, and returned home.

Neighbor women prepared Grandma for burial and placed her in the coffin. The funeral was set for the following day, since no embalming was done. The night before the funeral, a light rain froze on the trees.

The day of the funeral, which was performed by Reverend Hill at Grandma and Grandpa's home, the sun shone brightly. However, the temperature was cold enough that the sleet remained on the trees and the roads. Conditions on the roads were too hazardous for cars, so we had to rely on wagons and buggies drawn by shod horses.

Again the bay team was hitched to the wagon that would carry Grandma and some family members to the cemetery following the funeral. Since Grandpa understood his team, he wanted to drive the wagon. At his feet were a bale of straw and two short pieces from a 2x4. Grandpa took off, and the caravan of wagons and buggies followed. They were headed for the Millikan Cemetery, just north of the Dutton Chapel Church. It was a sad occasion, but the winter scene was picturesque, with the sleet sparkling on the trees and fences along the way.

At the cemetery, the grave was already dug. Grandpa requested that the strong, black check-lines be removed from the harness and laid on the ground about four feet apart. At his direction, the bale of straw was broken and half of it scattered in the grave. The two short 2x4s were placed about a foot in from the head and foot of where the coffin would be placed.

Grandpa then directed that the coffin be placed on the check-lines. Two men on each side of the coffin picked up the coffin with the check-lines and lined it up with the grave; then they carefully lowered the coffin into the grave. Two men on one side released the lines. The opposite two drew them out and put them back on the harness.

Grandpa put the other half of the straw on top of the coffin. I had to admire him for the way he expressed his love and concern the only way he knew how. The straw deadened the sound of the soil falling on top of the coffin.

Three years later, in 1940, Grandpa died of what was termed "natural causes." I attended Grandpa's funeral, which was conducted by Reverend Hill, again at Grandma and Grandpa's home. I wondered what the reverend would say. I knew Grandpa was honest, truthful, and hardworking. He was well liked by his neighbors and friends. Among the positions he had held in his lifetime were school director of Little Grand Pier School and road commissioner of a dirt road from Golconda to Herod. Part of his commissioner pay was from a dollar poll tax from each family per year.

I can't reconstruct Reverend Hill's sermon, but I do know I was pleased with what he said. His message was plain and soothing—not at all laden with sadness. His text came from Acts 11:24 in the Bible, which makes the following statement about Barnabus: "He was a good man." At least four times in Reverend Hill's remarks, he very masterfully repeated his text as it concerned Grandpa: "He was a good man."

Grandpa was taken in a hearse, followed by a number of cars, to the Millikan Cemetery. There he was laid to rest beside his beloved wife, Saluda.

...

I have attended a number of funerals over a span of more than eighty years. Almost without exception, I have admired the ways ministers have conducted themselves with love, dignity, and respect. These funerals have varied in length from very long to very short. Most have been in between.

My dad told me of a funeral he attended many years before I was born. The hearse was horse drawn. The minister at the funeral went on and on and on. The undertaker finally whispered in the minister's ear, "I'd like to get back to town before dark."

In the shortest sermon I ever heard, the minister said: "I'm sure the beloved deceased would like me to tell you that he loved his Lord and all of you and hopes to see you in Heaven."

The minister then read the 23rd Psalm and prayed a short prayer.

Years ago, out of concern for the family, most ministers would say a multitude of good things about the deceased. It is told that at the funeral of a man named John, his widow and young son were sitting in the front pew. The preacher was making one glorifying statement after another about John. Finally, looking confused, John's widow whispered to her son, "Son, slip up there and see if that is sure enough your pa."

. . .

Over the years, I have been amused by several gravestone epitaphs. One story that has made the rounds is about a man and his son who were reading remarks on tombstones. One tombstone read as follows: "Here lies a lawyer and an honest man." The boy asked, "Pa, why did they bury two men in one grave?"

I remember reading about the following epitaph in a cemetery in England:

> *Remember man, as you walk by,*
> *As you are now, so once was I.*
> *As I am now, so shall you be.*
> *Remember this and follow me.*

Someone felt a need to add a comment beneath the epitaph:

> *To follow you I'll not consent*
> *Until I know which way you went.*

I heard about another epitaph that made me smile. The dearly departed's dates of birth and death spanned from 1918 to 2006. Underneath the dates, it simply read, "See, I told you I was sick."

The following epitaph I believe to be true. It was told to me by a girlfriend from Kentucky. It goes as follows: "Some have one. Some have none. But I'm the father of 21."

My comment: "I hope the Lord had mercy on him."

...

I believe that the relationship between my father and me was closer than the relationships he had with his other five children, perhaps because I was the oldest son. From the time I was six years old, he and I worked together and bonded. In his younger days, Dad had been a big, strong man. However, the last year of his life, he walked slowly and with difficulty and was largely housebound.

Dad always had a good singing voice. He had even taken voice lessons when he was younger and had the ability to lead singing at church. Dad had two favorite songs: "Uncloudy Day" and "Where We'll Never Grow Old." I always loved to hear him sing. He would often move his right hand like a song director as he sang.

In the last year of his life, on different occasions, I'd enter the living room where he would be sitting, appearing sad and depressed. With a great deal of effort, I'd try to sing part of one of his favorite songs. Dad would return to reality and say, "This is the way that song goes." I'd sit in amazement at the clear, gentle melody he produced.

On the evening of November 29, 1940, I went into Dad's bedroom to tell him goodbye because I was leaving for Michigan before daylight the following morning. I felt compelled to go and seek work to remove a small mortgage on the farm. I would have given anything if we could have

sung "Where We'll Never Grow Old" or "Uncloudy Day."
As I left his bedside, I was correct in feeling that I'd never
see him alive again. I went to sleep that night with tears
in my eyes.

I worked and did well in Michigan, but my heart was
back home. Mom and I exchanged letters often. I can't say
I was homesick or felt sorry for myself—I just felt I was
doing what had to be done.

On an early May morning in 1941, I got a telegram from
home telling me that Dad had had a stroke and wasn't
expected to live. I arranged to catch a ride with a man
who hauled passengers between Pontiac and Harrisburg,
Illinois. We left Pontiac that night, and I got home around
nine o'clock the following morning. I was met with the sad
news that Dad had died an hour earlier.

I was standing over Dad's lifeless form when two strong
men from Turner Funeral Home in Harrisburg came to pick
him up. I was speechless, with tears in my eyes. However, I
managed to say, "Please handle him carefully."

It was decided that the visitation and funeral would be
held at home for the convenience of older family members,
neighbors, and friends. The men from the funeral home
placed Dad's coffin in the southwest corner of the living
room. A large number of people gathered for visitation.
Many left around midnight. But, in keeping with the cus-
tom of the day, several "sat up" all night. The men talked
about all things under the sun. Laughing was limited, but
there was no limit on the coffee, pie, and cake consumed.

Since the funeral was set for 2:00 p.m. the next day, a
meal was served at noon. Much food had been brought in
by friends and neighbors. A goodly number had gathered
to eat. The gravediggers from the nearby family cemetery
were invited, too. Upon arriving, they reported they were
down only about four feet and had struck solid rock.

A small man, Ed Hayes, said with a loud voice, "Don't any of you worry. I have dynamite, fuses, and caps. We can set off two or three light shots, and the grave will be ready by the time it is needed." Soon we heard two or three blasts and knew the grave digging was moving forward.

Family, neighbors, and friends gathered for the funeral. Extra chairs and a portable podium were furnished by the funeral home.

Reverend Hill stood behind the podium. Reverend Rector, who was a friend and close neighbor of the family, was seated so he could view everyone, me in particular. I realized he was wondering how I was taking the loss of my father. I'm sure he regretted that he wasn't called on to preach the funeral. However, Reverend Hill did call on Reverend Rector to pray, which I thought was considerate. His prayer reminded me of how Mina described his sad funeral sermons. I made up my mind I wouldn't shed a tear.

Reverend Hill, as always, did a good job with his sermon—it was solemn, sincere, and not a tearjerker. When the sermon was over, all except family members made a final viewing and went outside to wait.

My two brothers, Byrum and Victor, walked up to the casket with Mom, followed by my two sisters, Mabel and Hazel, with our youngest brother, Gaylord, age ten. Tears of sadness were in all of their eyes.

Mom held a handkerchief in her left hand and brushed the tears from her eyes. With her right hand, she held Dad's hand for a few seconds.

I was last in line, with Reverend Rector holding my arm. He seemed surprised that I wasn't all broken up. He addressed me as "Brother Wallace." In a sad and quivering voice he said: "You'll never hear your father's footsteps again or hear his voice as he says grace at the table." He just about reached his goal of making me weep.

You'll never guess how I avoided crying. It was mean of me. I'm almost ashamed to tell you. Although I ordinarily didn't use this kind of language, in my mind, I said, "Hell, no, I'll not hear his voice or his footsteps. He is dead."

The look on Reverend Rector's face told me that he was thinking to himself, "He is a hard nut to crack."

At the cemetery, the large mound of earth beside the grave told me it was plenty deep. After the final benediction, I thanked those who helped in our time of sorrow. I didn't forget the gravediggers—Ed Hayes, in particular. I also managed to tell Reverend Rector that his prayer was touching.

I was the last one to leave the cemetery. Before I left, I stood over Dad's grave and said, "Dad, before I go back to Michigan, I'll come and tell you goodbye, and together we can sing 'Where We'll Never Grow Old' and 'The Uncloudy Day.' But I can't sing now for fear of crying."

Even though I never shed a tear during my father's funeral, even after seventy years, when Dad's favorite songs are sung at Rudement Church, my feelings of respect and pleasant memories cause my tears to flow freely.

...

Now, at ninety-one, the uncloudy sunset of my life is approaching. I don't fear death, but I'm not trying to hasten it on. I think of the song with the line: "Everybody wants to go to Heaven, but nobody wants to die." But when the time comes, I'll be ready. My resting place is already chosen, beside my beloved wife, Evelyn, in the Wallace Family Cemetery at the foot of Womble Mountain. I know we will be reunited, over in the Glory Land, after some fine minister preaches my last funeral.

* * *

Rural Justice

Justices of the peace have a long history in Illinois. Even before Illinois became a state in 1818, when it was still part of the Northwest Territory, justices of the peace were appointed by the territorial governor. Justices of the peace had only limited jurisdiction — in civil cases where the amount involved was less than one hundred dollars and in criminal cases (mainly misdemeanors) where the maximum fine was no more than one hundred dollars (although these amounts increased over time). As court reform took place in Illinois and courts were consolidated, the office of justice of the peace was abolished in 1962, with an effective date in 1964.

Of course, I didn't know any of this when I was young. The first time I really paid attention to the fact that someone was a justice of the peace was when my fifth-grade teacher, John B. Owens, became one.

Mr. Owens was probably in his early sixties when I was in fifth grade, and it may have been his last year of teaching. I later learned that after Mr. Owens had signed a

contract to teach at the school, it had come to the attention of the school directors that Mr. Owens had epilepsy.
The directors had wanted to make the contract null and
void, but Mr. Owens had made it clear to them that a
contract was a contract, and they had backed down.

Mr. Owens was a high-strung, God-fearing man. He
kept his disease under control with medication and his
students under control with fear.

I had no trouble knowing when to speak and when to
be silent. I didn't fear Mr. Owens—I seemed to know how
to relate to and please him. We had an understanding that
we liked each other.

The girls didn't give him any cause to be harsh with
them. But the boys got backhanded or worse—for minor
things that sometimes amused him and other times got
under his skin.

After finishing his teaching at Sadler School, Mr.
Owens ran for and was elected justice of the peace in
the Harrisburg Township of Saline County. I think by that
time, being justice of the peace suited him more than
teaching school. Several years later, I used his services
as justice of the peace, but I'll come back to that a little
later in my story.

In the meantime, when I was fourteen years old, I happened to learn that my grandfather had been a justice of
the peace. I had ridden a mare down to Jim Shelby's farm,
which bordered the Grand Pierre Creek in Pope County,
to breed her to his remarkable jack [male donkey] to
produce an outstanding mule. [Mr. Shelby, who owned the
jack, was the grandfather of Ed Cannon, a star basketball
player from Harrisburg in the sixties.]

When I told Mr. Shelby I was a Wallace, he asked me
if I'd ever heard of Jonathan Wallace. I told him that he
was my grandfather.

Mr. Shelby asked, "Did you know your grandpa was a justice of the peace?"

Shaking my head, I replied, "No, he died twenty-seven years before I was born."

Mr. Shelby declared, "Yep, he sure was a justice of the peace. Fifty years ago tomorrow, he married my wife and me."

Curious, I asked, "What else do you know about Jonathan Wallace?"

Mr. Shelby laughed and said, "If I were to tell you all I know about your grandpa, you would be getting home after dark. When we take care of the business at hand, if you like, I'll tell you a thing or two about a couple of the cases your grandpa heard as justice of the peace."

I replied eagerly, "I'd be happy for you to tell me all about him. About all my dad ever told me about his father were things related to the Civil War, in which my grandpa was a cavalryman."

After we "took care of business," Mr. Shelby sat on a bale of hay in the hallway of his barn and motioned for me to sit on another bale, facing him. Thoughtfully, he said, "There were two cases I'll never forget. I don't know which of them to tell."

I immediately responded, "I know how to handle that. Tell me both."

Shaking his head, Mr. Shelby replied, "I'll only have time to tell you one before my wife rings the dinner bell. When she does, she will expect us to get on in there. She knows you are out here."

A little disappointed, I said, "Then tell me the one you like better."

I remember clearly the case Mr. Shelby described. It went as follows:

"Your grandpa, among other things, ran a sawmill and

a blacksmith shop. He had hired me, part time, to help him with his blacksmith work. That is the reason I know as much as I do about your grandpa.

"He did his justice-of-the-peace business in the evenings after supper—just now and then. I really admired the way he handled a sexual assault case that involved one of your grandpa's friends, 'John,' and a good neighbor friend, 'Elijah,' and his twenty-five-year-old daughter, 'Sarah.' [All names changed]

"The complaint was made by Elijah on behalf of Sarah, who was also there when the complaint was made. Your grandpa told them he would give John a summons to appear two weeks from Thursday at 7:00 p.m., and if he failed to appear, your grandpa would have a constable arrest him and bring him in. However, he had no doubt that John would appear."

I interrupted, "Why did he put off the case for two weeks? Why didn't he just dive in and get it over with?"

Mr. Shelby explained, "Your grandpa thought it would give John time to think of the seriousness of his behavior, and Elijah and Sarah a chance for their anger to cool down."

I asked curiously, "And how did that work out?"

Mr. Shelby replied: "I think it worked well. Your grandpa told me that they all three showed up on time, all civil like. Your grandpa had a 3-foot x 5-foot homemade table in the room he used as a courtroom. On this table, he always had a pad of paper, pen and ink, a Bible, and an old, tattered law book. On this particular occasion, your grandpa said he had also set out a pint of his wife Jane's homemade tonic (peach brandy—about 60 proof), and four dram glasses.

"I will tell you the story just like your grandpa told it to me:

I shook hands with each of them and asked them to be seated in three chairs that I had placed in a semicircle in front of the table. I sat in a chair behind the table. I suggested that we visit a bit before I called the court to order.

I asked John how his herd of hogs was doing. John took pleasure in telling me that his hogs were doing well and would be ready for butchering by Christmas. John went on to say that he salt cured and hickory smoked some of the hams and shoulders and ground some of the choice meat into sausage, which his mother seasoned and canned in quart glass jars. When the jars were opened several weeks later, John said the meat would taste like fresh sausage.

At that point, I said, "Tell me no more. You are making me hungry. Maybe we should sample Jane's tonic." I poured each of us a dram of brandy, and we all drained our glasses.

Then I asked Elijah his secret for growing the best watermelons for miles around. Elijah proudly gave me a step-by-step accounting of the process.

Sarah sat almost motionless with her hands in her lap. Her facial expression was more anxious than sad. Her appearance would make most men take a second look. She seemed alert and intelligent. Her big, brown eyes zeroed in on whoever was speaking. Anyone looking at her would have felt kindly toward her.

I cleared my throat, tapped on the table three times with my Barlow knife, and said, "This court is now in session. I have read the complaint and listened to it verbally as given by Sarah and her father. John, the complaint against you is that you forced yourself on Sarah in a manner that was unlawful, unethical, inexcusable, and sinful."

I then turned to Sarah and Elijah and asked, "Did I state the complaint correctly?"

They both answered, "Yes, sir, you did."

I then looked at John and said, "Before I ask you how you plead, I want to ask you a few questions. I'm a firm believer that perfect knowledge is needed for perfect justice."

Somewhat meekly, John said, "I'll answer your questions to the best of my ability."

I said, "Here's my first question—how long have you and Sarah been friends?"

John replied quickly, "All our lives—twenty-five years."

I followed up. "Here's my second question—do you regret that that friendship has ended?"

John answered, with barely controlled emotion, "Yes, I do."

Taking a clue from the way he had answered my second question, I said, a little more softly, "Third question—how long have you had feelings for Sarah?"

John shifted around in his chair and finally replied, "Since I was about eighteen." I could see him blushing slightly.

Then I looked at Elijah and asked, "What has been your impression of John through the years?"

Elijah replied, with only a slight pause, "He has been courteous and respectful toward me."

I then turned to John and asked, "John, how do you wish to plead? Take your time and ponder your answer."

Without hesitation, John replied, "Guilty as accused, but I ask to be given the opportunity to explain what caused me to do what I did."

I said, "Permission granted. Please continue."

John responded, "This lovely lady, Sarah, is a talented singer. In the course of an evening, she might sing a line or two of a dozen songs. I enjoyed her singing very much. The last time we were out together, after we had had an extended time of being 'cozy,' she suddenly sang a line or two of a song she had either heard or made up. It went as follows: 'Country boy, country boy, country boy—if you don't want my peaches, don't shake my peach tree.' I couldn't help feeling she was trying to tell me something, which had a bearing on how I acted." He finished up earnestly, "It's no excuse, but it might be considered a reason."

I replied, "That's all very interesting, but it does fall short of justification. Sarah, what is your response or reaction?"

Sarah quickly said, "'I think John read far too much into the lines of that song. As an excuse, it is a rather lame one. Frankly, I'd rather have him say he's sorry."

At that point, John got to his feet, stepped to Sarah, and started to get on his knees. Sarah got to her feet and said, "John, you don't have to get on your knees. Just stand up, look me in the eyes, and say you're sorry."

The next thing I knew, Sarah and John were in each other's arms and laughing and crying at the same time. Elijah had tears streaming down his face. I had to take out my handkerchief and blow my nose, which I excused by saying "hay fever."

At the same time, John and Elijah asked, "Mr. Justice of the Peace, what do we owe you?"

To John, I replied, "The next time you are passing by, bring me a quart of that sausage." To Elijah, I said, "Elijah, you can bring me a middle-size watermelon

*out of your next year's crop." And to Sarah, I felt
obliged to add, "Sarah, from now on, ponder what
songs you sing to John. Court adjourned."*

I had followed Mr. Shelby's story intently. When it came
to an end, I thanked Mr. Shelby for telling me about the
case and eagerly asked him to tell me about the other
case he had mentioned, which he said had involved a man
shooting his neighbor's dog. Before Mr. Shelby could get
started, however, the dinner bell rang. I was disappointed,
because I wanted to know all the particulars.

Mr. Shelby said, "Let's go to dinner. I'll tell you that
'dog-gone' story after dinner."

I thanked Mr. Shelby for the invitation to dinner but
reluctantly declined, saying, "I'd better be on my way."

[I always meant to get back down to Pope County and
visit with Mr. Shelby so that I could hear his other story
about my grandpa's cases. But I never did, and I regret it
to this day. With his story-telling ability, Mr. Shelby really
kept me spellbound with the details he could remember
of Grandpa's case.]

As the mare carried me home that day, I had plenty
to think about. That "justice gene" that started with my
grandpa must have been passed down in the Wallace
blood, because Jonathan Wallace's son — my Uncle
Lew — also had been elected as justice of the peace in
Mountain Township. I had only recently learned that
a few years earlier, he had handled a case that a man
brought against two of his neighbors for stealing some of
his chickens. I don't remember the details of the trial now,
but I knew that the two men were found guilty and went
to jail for a few days. However, they were released when
it was learned that the man making the charges was "off
in the head." I was probably a little off in the head when

I thought to myself that, someday, I'd like to be a justice of the peace and continue the family tradition.

Only a few days after meeting Jim Shelby, I was at Uncle Lew's home, about 300 yards from ours. Uncle Lew and I were talking in his wood yard when a man and a woman drove up in a Pontiac coupe. They got out and stated, "We want to get married."

Uncle Lew asked, "Do you have a marriage license?" They produced one.

Getting immediately down to business, Uncle Lew said solemnly, "Will you please join hands."

Uncle Lew said a few words and asked them something I didn't quite catch. They both said "I do" at the same time.

Uncle Lew then declared, "I now pronounce you husband and wife."

The man asked Uncle Lew, "What do I owe you?"

Uncle Lew said, "Two dollars."

I witnessed the marriage. We all shook hands, and the couple went on their way rejoicing.

I thought to myself, "When I get to be a justice of the peace, I'll marry people just like Uncle Lew did—short and sweet."

...

As I have related in other stories, I spent time working in Michigan and then serving in the Navy in World War II. On returning, I bought a remarkable suit to impress my girlfriend, Evelyn Green, who lived in East Prairie, Missouri.

Before seeing Evelyn, I took the suit to one of the cleaners in Harrisburg. Sadly, I never saw the suit again. It was either lost or badly damaged in the cleaning process. Different stories were told as to what happened to it. I was asked to be patient and was promised that they would do right by me.

When my patience ran out, I went to my friend, Justice of the Peace John Owens. Like a lawyer, Mr. Owens was angry that the cleaners would treat me that way. He said, "I'll sue the pants off the cleaners and get you paid for the value of your lost suit."

I won't go into all of the details of the process. In the end, however, Mr. Owens got me only about half of what I had paid for the suit. I made him happy by leading him to believe that I was well pleased.

Throughout the course of the case, I had been in to see Mr. Owens a few times, and we had had some good visits. I told him I was thinking of running for justice of the peace in Mountain Township, just to see what he would say.

He encouraged me to run. At the same time, he suggested that I send in an application to the state to become a notary public. I took his advice and ran for justice of the peace. With the help of the good people on Eagle Creek, on the other side of Womble Mountain, as well as those on my side, I was elected. [I also became a notary public and have been one now for more than sixty years.]

When I next saw Mr. Owens, he congratulated me on getting elected justice of the peace. He blessed me with a big, old law book with small print. I felt sure that it weighed twenty pounds. It may have been handed down to Moses with the Ten Commandments. I couldn't make heads or tails of it. However, he also gave me a typed, good-sounding form to use in marrying couples. It was useful in performing my first wedding.

My first request to perform a wedding came up sudden-like. I was still single, so I was living with Mom and a younger sister and brother. Upon learning about the upcoming wedding, Mom became pleasantly excited. She wanted it to be a big deal, although neither of us personally knew the couple. She sent my brother and sister out to pass the word around to neighbors and relatives that there would be a wedding at the house at seven o'clock that evening.

Among those invited were my Uncle Courty Wallace, who was around sixty years of age and the youngest of a family of fourteen children, and his nephew Gene Affolder (my cousin), about thirty years of age. Both of them were great jokers and pranksters. Neither one was a churchgoer, but both strongly believed that the *other* person should at all times be sober, honest, and truthful, and walk the straight and narrow way.

Gene was born and raised in Southeast Missouri, but for the past several years, he had worked in Michigan. Gene came to Southern Illinois as often as he could get away to visit his relatives who lived near Womble Mountain. When he came down, he spent the lion's share of his time with Uncle Courty because they were both outstanding checker players.

To make their checker games more interesting, they had a tall bottle of — let's say — something stronger than water. The winner of a checker game would get a snort out of the bottle, and the loser would get a big whiff. They loved the game and were about equally skilled. By the time they got their invitations to the wedding, they had played most of the afternoon and into the evening and were feeling pretty good.

The bride and groom arrived at 7:00 p.m., and to everyone's surprise, Uncle Courty and Gene came in on their heels. I played the part of an informal family host and said, "These two gentlemen are my Uncle Courty and my cousin Gene. Reeling only slightly, they shook hands with the bride and groom.

Gene said, "Uncle Courty, we better sit over here in the corner by Aunt Verba [my mother]. She can make us behave if anyone can." [That was pretty funny to me, since at 6'4" and 6'2" respectively, Uncle Courty and Gene towered over my much-shorter mother.]

Mom realized that they had probably played a few more games of checkers than they should have. She put her index finger to her lips. Gene did likewise, while nodding his head, to let her know he understood.

Shortly thereafter, in a loud whisper, Gene asked Uncle Courty, "Do you think the bride is pregnant?"

Uncle Courty replied, "She may not be as pregnant as she seems—she may just be full of good old butter beans."

Mom gave each of them a stern look and again put her finger to her lips. They both looked subdued and nodded that they understood.

I had just barely heard their joking remarks. I raised my voice louder than I ordinarily would in the hope that their remarks would not be heard by others.

After lining up the bride and groom so they could best be seen by all, I began the ceremony. Among other remarks, I stated: "Marriage is honorable. In fact, Jesus placed his approval on marriage by attending the marriage at Cana, where he turned the water into wine."

At this point, Gene whispered loudly to Uncle Courty, "Yummy, yummy, yummy—if we had been there, we could have got a snootful and not had to play checkers!"

Once again, Mom put her finger to her lips and shook her head a bit more vigorously. That seemed to quieten them down for the rest of the ceremony.

The bride and groom said their vows. I pronounced them husband and wife and offered a prayer. When I said "Amen," Uncle Courty and Gene surprised and pleased me by saying simultaneously, "Amen," in clear, reverent voices.

I felt pretty sure that the groom would ask me, "What do I owe you?" I recalled seeing a minister marry a very poor, young couple. At the end of the ceremony, the groom asked the preacher what he owed him. The preacher replied, "Just whatever you think she is worth to you." That answer really put the poor groom on the spot. I had decided then and there that whenever I married a couple, there would be no charge — it would be my wedding gift to the couple.

With a happy smile on his face, the groom asked, "What do I owe you?"

I replied, "This is my first wedding. There is no charge. It is a wedding gift. If it doesn't hold, come back and I'll do it over."

Seeing the humor in my statement, he chuckled and said, "It will hold. We are very much in love." The newlyweds received our well wishes for their happiness and left smiling.

In a short time, all the guests were gone, leaving Mom and me sitting facing each other, while trying to relax and unwind. After a few seconds, we smiled at each other.

Mom was first to speak. She said, "I want to congratulate you on the way you conducted the wedding under what were less than ideal conditions. I hope you're not disappointed that I invited Courty and Gene. Since neither one attends church, I thought they might hear something that would cause them to think. I prayed throughout the ceremony that they would sober up. When they said 'Amen' along with you at the conclusion of your prayer, I thought it sounded sober and sincere."

I replied, "Mom, you probably did more to make my first wedding a success than I did. Thank you."

I didn't approve of the behavior of Uncle Courty and Gene at my first wedding. But we remembered it better than any wedding after that and have had a good many laughs concerning it. In fact, it is a wedding that lives on.

...

In the fall of 1946, I was teaching my first year in the one-room school at Rudement, across the road from a general store operated by Frank Hamp, who was a fine man and a good friend. From time to time, Frank would come across the road to the school to bring me a telephone message.

One day, Frank came into the schoolhouse just after the students had left to go home. I could tell he was upset, verging on being angry. He became angrier as he stated why he had come to see me. He said "I have put up with more than I can stand. I want to bring suit against Buck Turner. A man can just take so much."

Now, Buck Turner was another staunch friend of mine. Our friendship went back to his grandpa, George Turner, who was a blacksmith. Buck had a very friendly, fun-loving daughter in the seventh grade there at Rudement. Buck had also done some very reasonable plumbing work for me.

My first thoughts were "Goody, goody, goody—this may be a dead ringer for one of Grandpa Wallace's famous cases, maybe even better. I'll get all the details firsthand from both parties."

That feeling of elation lasted only seconds when I quickly thought it through and realized that Buck Turner was as good a friend as Frank. My concern was how on earth I could rule on this case and please both of them. I might make one happy and an enemy out of the other, or I might wind up losing both friendships. I probably looked as sad as Frank looked angry.

However, one word flashed through my mind, and that word was "jurisdiction." It gave me a more pleasant expression immediately. I said, "Frank, tell me no more.

My jurisdiction is Mountain Township. You and Buck both live in Independence Township. I won't be able to help you. The best I can do is wish you well."

I never learned how that deal turned out. I was thankful that I continued to be good friends with both of them.

...

As justice of the peace, I was a member of the township board, made up of the township supervisor, the justice of the peace, the trustee, and the road commissioner. We met once a month and discussed matters that concerned the township. Some meetings were long, and some were short. We were paid ten dollars for attending these meetings, which were necessary and often interesting.

My opinion of the office of justice of the peace is that it outlived its usefulness by several years. The office perhaps served well in its day, in times when travel to the county seat for a hearing at the courthouse was much more difficult. However, a big weakness was that many who were elected to the office were poorly qualified to perform properly. It probably took too long to eliminate that weakness by eliminating the office. I stayed with it until its end in 1964.

...

Time passed, and there was to be no end to Wallaces performing weddings. My son, Ray Jonathan, while still quite young and without asking for the wisdom and advice of his father, told me that he had received a license to marry people. He said a copy of the license was recorded in the county clerk's offices in Harrisburg and also in Springfield.

I said, "Ray, sonny boy, you shouldn't have up and done a thing like that without first talking it over with me."

His reply was quick and snappy: "I knew you would have advised against it. But I think if my great-grandfather Jonathan Wallace, my great-uncle Lew, and you could marry people, I should be able to perform weddings, too."

What could I say to that, except, "Congratulations, Reverend. May I be the first to wish you well. Now, where do you plan to perform your weddings?"

Ray responded unconcernedly, "Oh, just here and there and somewhere else—wherever the couple would like to be." He assured me, "Don't worry—same as it was with Great-grandpa Wallace, it will only be a sideline. I'll probably mostly be marrying my friends."

I thought to myself, "Yes, and this is the boy who has no enemies." Since that now long-ago conversation, Ray has married more than 250 couples—here and there and somewhere else.

...

In writing this story, I was thinking more about that "justice gene." For whatever reason, my grandfather, my uncle, and I were led, in turn, to seek and hold the office of justice of the peace. Ray works in a correctional center for youth in Southern Illinois, and my daughter, LeAnn, works for the state court system in North Carolina. I remember when they were young, they would "hold court" with the lid from the piano bench over the arms of an easy chair, surrounded by all their stuffed animals, which held various roles within the courtroom. So maybe there's something to that "justice gene" after all.

* * *

Michigan Memories

In the spring of 1940, having finished high school but with no employment in sight, I started hewing mining ties on our woodlot that ran partway up Womble Mountain. Early that summer, I jumped at an opportunity to accept employment as a carpenter's helper and work with two top-notch carpenters—Claude Barger and Lon Applin—who had contracts to build two houses in Rosiclare, Illinois.

For the first two days, my job was to fetch, carry, and hold. But when the carpenters saw I could measure a piece of lumber, saw a line, and drive a nail, they very generously shared their tools and knowledge and made me feel like one of them. They were good instructors. I was anxious to learn.

That job ended on my twentieth birthday, August 31, 1940. When I got home that day, I was shocked to see the smoldering remains of our home, which had just burned. Evidently, a spark from the cookstove's chimney had landed on the tinder-dry shingles, and the house had burned down quickly.

The family set up living quarters in an abandoned store building on the Wallace property, some 300 yards away. My father's health was such that the responsibility of rebuilding was up to me.

We traded cattle to Ruey Robinson, a sawmill man at Hickstown, for enough oak lumber to frame in a good-sized house over a full basement. We had to put a mortgage on the farm to buy other needed materials.

Luckily, the three months of September, October, and November of 1940 were ideal months for building. My previous experience with carpentry in Rosiclare made it possible for me to do much of the labor and oversee the rest.

We moved into the basement while the rest of the house was being completed. On November 29, the new house was finished. As if it had been holding out just for us, the weather took a sudden change for the worse. On the morning of November 30, at the break of day, I said goodbye to my family to go seek work in Michigan to repay the mortgage.

During that time, with the world at war, many young people from Southern Illinois and elsewhere also headed to Michigan to work in defense plants to support the war effort. Compared to Southern Illinois, where jobs were few and far between, it was seen as the land of opportunity. I remember that Thurman Simpson, who went to Sadler School when I did, hopped a freight train and went to Ypsilanti, Michigan, where he got a job in a foundry. He helped a number of other young men from Sadler get a job there where he worked. However, I headed to Pontiac, and as things turned out, I'm glad I did.

In Pontiac, I rented an upstairs, one-room efficiency apartment in an old house owned by a sour-faced old lady in her eighties. She appeared suspicious of me and kept a revolver nearby. I had to pass through her living room to reach the stairway to my room. I walked as meekly as a lamb without looking to my right or my left.

In a day or two, I got a job at a bakery—working nights for thirty-five cents per hour. That job took care of my needs until I was employed at Jig Bushing, a defense plant.

I went to the plant to seek employment. It had two entrances. I went to the wrong one—a huge double-door entrance. The doors were open for ventilation. Much like a cowboy in a Wild West show, I stood in the doorway and looked the shop over. Many men were working at different machines.

At some distance, I saw a solemn-looking, well-dressed, slightly balding man standing in a strategic position to see everything. He observed me for a few moments and then came to me and asked, "May I help you?"

I said, "Yes, I'm Kestner Wallace. I'm looking for work."

Showing no emotion, he replied, "I'm Fred Mondon. Employees here call me Mr. Mondon. I'm shop superintendent. The hiring is done by Mr. Brownie when I see fit to send someone to him."

I responded, with what I hoped was an encouraging grin, "How about sending me to him?"

Mr. Mondon said thoughtfully, "We need an external grinder, but you appear to be of draft age. About the time we got you broke in on that job, you would be called up."

Ignoring his stated concern, I said, "Mr. Mondon, with your permission, I would like to speak with Mr. Brownie. In a weak moment, he might hire me. I would make you a good hand."

Mr. Mondon took a deep breath and said, "Follow me." He took me to a spacious, caged-in office where Mr. Brownie sat. Mondon said, "I think this young fellow would make us a good hand if you can keep him out of the draft."

Mr. Brownie said, "Have a seat, young man. I'll tell you about this shop. It is a nonunion shop. I want to keep it that way. Would you have any trouble with that?"

I replied quickly, "No, sir."

Mr. Brownie went on: "I own 51 percent of this shop. I run it my way. I'm also on the draft board. If you work out okay, I can get you three 6-month deferments." After chatting with me a bit and apparently deciding I had passed the test, Mr. Brownie declared, "You can come in at 3:00 p.m. tomorrow and work until midnight, six days per week."

I thanked Mr. Brownie. On the way out, I waved to Mr. Mondon and called out, "I'll see you at 3:00 p.m. tomorrow. Thank you!"

About 2:30 p.m. the next day, I entered the shop through the correct entrance. Mr. Mondon saw me and came over to me. He said, "Follow me and I'll show you your machine and introduce you to Woody, who will be working on the machine beside you and coaching you. He is the best and has been with us for years. I'll fill out a work card for you and punch you in at 3:00 p.m. and put your card in the rack. You can punch yourself out at midnight. I'll have a girl come by tomorrow and get the information we need: your name, date of birth, address, and social security number." That said, Mondon left.

Woody and I gazed at each other. He was first to speak. "I'll give you two weeks to quit or get fired."

A bit ruffled, I retorted, "Woody, you don't know how badly I need this job. You don't have much confidence in either your ability to teach or my ability to learn. Which is it?"

Woody replied quickly, "Oh, excuse me. No offense intended. I was speaking based on the luck we have had with keeping a man on that machine."

I spoke with certainty: "Woody, if you can operate that machine, I can operate this one—after you show me how."

Woody immediately changed my name from "Wallace" to "Wally." He gave me a small grin and said, "Wally, I think we'll get along fine. I'll start you out on rough grinding. When you master that, I'll teach you how to do tedious grinding."

I replied thankfully, "You do that, Woody, and I'll be forever grateful to you."

Everything seemed to fall into place. My apartment was only four blocks from work, and a Mom-and-Pop grocery store was within easy walking distance. The old landlady began to give me a half smile, and the revolver was no longer in view. It was at this one-room apartment that I learned to cook.

One clear, cool Saturday morning made me think of perfect weather for a Southern Illinois hog killing. My mind should have been on homemade sausage and tenderloin, but strange as it might seem, I got a craving for pork brains and scrambled eggs. So I went to the corner store. I walked in and was met by a bright-eyed, black-haired boy about ten years old. He very politely asked, "May I help you, sir?"

Without intending the effect, I gruffly asked, "Do you have any brains?"

This boy excitedly and nervously asked, "What?"

My week at the shop may have been getting to me a bit. I replied impatiently, "Brains, brains, you got any brains?"

This poor little boy said, "Just a minute. I'll get my dad."

He was soon back with a very solemn-looking man. He asked, "What seems to be the trouble?"

I answered in a much calmer tone: "No trouble—no trouble at all. I just wondered if you had any pork brains."

With a relieved smile, the man said, "Yes, how much do you need?"

I wanted only a half pound, but since I had unintentionally traumatized the boy, I said, "A pound and a dozen eggs."

On the way back to the apartment, I decided to ask the old lady—I have forgotten her name—if she could use a half pound of pork brains. I told her I had bought a pound and needed only half of it.

When asked, she replied, "I haven't eaten scrambled eggs and brains since I was a kid. I loved them then, and I probably would now."

As I divided the brains, she asked me if I had eggs; she said she had plenty. I told her I did. From then on, we were almost like kinfolks.

...

One night at the plant, during our meal break, a fellow worker asked me if I would be interested in a good 1936 V-8 Ford. He said he had bought a later-model Ford and would sell his older one. I asked him what he wanted for it. He said, "You appear to be a likeable fellow. I'll let you have it for one hundred twenty-five dollars."

I said, "I won't buy it sight unseen, but I'm definitely interested." The next day, after looking it over, I bought it.

Over the next few weeks, I drove around and saw all parts of Pontiac. I saw the good, the bad, and the ugly. Far out on East Boulevard, a church caught my eye. It was large — when compared with Southern Illinois country churches — but not at all gaudy. I decided to attend there. By this time, I had bought some Sunday clothes. The following Sunday morning, I dressed appropriately and showed up at this church at 9:00 a.m., knowing that Sunday school started at 9:30 a.m.

A man, his wife, and two sons were already there. They were all alert and well dressed. The man came to me, smiling, with his hand extended and said, "We are the Marlowe family. I'm the Sunday school superintendent. Everyone calls my wife and me Mom and Pop Marlowe." At this point, Mrs. Marlowe shook hands with me, too. Mr. Marlowe went on to say, "These are our two sons, Melvin and Carl." They nodded at me.

I told the Marlowe family that I was Kestner Wallace and was from a farm in Southern Illinois. I mentioned that I had been in Michigan only a few weeks and that this was my first time to attend church in Michigan.

Mr. Marlowe said, "We are farmers and are involved in other activities around Clarkston." [I learned that Clarkston was less than twenty miles northwest of Pontiac.]

Melvin, the older of the Marlowe brothers, told me that I would be in class with him and Carl, and since it was a large class, it was held in the back quarter of the church auditorium. Classrooms were available for the others.

By half past nine, around a hundred people were in attendance, including many children. Pop Marlowe stepped up to the podium. By standing motionless and gazing at the group for a few seconds, he brought the chattering group to order.

He said, "Thank you. We'll start the service this morning with a prayer. First I want to introduce to you a prospective member of our church. He comes to us from Southern Illinois. Will Kestner Wallace please stand?"

I stood and received a welcoming applause. Then Pop Marlowe prayed. Following the prayer, there was a song, and then the group went to the respective classes.

Twenty or more young people were in the class that Melvin, Carl, and I were in, with ages from eighteen to the early twenties. They were friendly, light-hearted, and giddy. The teacher's name was Troy. He was a friendly, soft-spoken person.

Troy welcomed me to the class. I quickly realized that his voice lacked the forcefulness needed to get and keep the attention of the class. The class appeared to be happy to be in Sunday school but, as a whole, had limited concern about the Bible.

I took a Sunday school book with me to my room and decided that, on the following Sunday, I'd try to help Troy with a comment or a question. The idea worked. Others commented and asked questions, also.

However, about three Sundays later, Troy told the class that the following Sunday would be his last to teach, because he wasn't cut out to be a teacher. He said he would report to Pop Marlowe and the pastor and ask them to select another teacher for the class. Despite the class members' insistence that they liked him as a teacher, he assured them that his mind was made up.

Someone suggested that I teach the class. Others agreed. I told the class that I liked Troy's plan to have the Sunday school superintendent and the church pastor make the selection.

Sunday evening, after the evening service, the pastor and Pop Marlowe asked me if I would fill in teaching the class while they carefully made a good choice for a teacher. I replied, "For a Sunday or two."

The time came for me to stand before the young people's Sunday school class. I told the class: "I am more of a preacher than a teacher. When I was around thirteen years old, my two brothers, some cousins, some neighbor boys, and I cut some trees and made a log structure. At first we called it our clubhouse, but not knowing how to conduct a club, we decided to call it a church. Since it was next to an apple orchard, we called it Red Apple.

"We had all attended church and knew from A to Z how to conduct church. Girls didn't help in the building of the church, but they took a big part in the services. Nearly everyone was gifted in singing except me. We had some pray-ers, some shouters, some guitar-pickers, and some clappers.

"I knew a good many Bible verses by memory and could quote them with vim and vigor, so I was named the preacher. Oftentimes, our services started serious and sincere and then progressed from the sublime to the ridiculous. Now if my teaching sounds a little like preaching, you'll know why. I feel honored and humbled to be asked to teach a Sunday or two until a teacher is chosen.

"I have grown up a great deal since I was thirteen. I'm still young in years but have many miles on me. I'm ready to teach. Are you ready to ask questions and comment?"

I got a resounding "Yes."

I said, "Amen—let's get started."

That class went well, as did the next one. It won't surprise you to learn that, shortly thereafter, I was given the teacher's position for the young people's class.

I became well known and well liked among the church folks. The church was small enough that I came to know most of them. A Mr. Spires and his wife had seven children at that time and another on the way. They believed the large family was in keeping with God's will. Some thought otherwise.

Mr. Spires had a low-paying job as a stockman at a Sears store in Pontiac. The family was the poorest of the church. The children—mostly boys—all wore hand-me-down clothes. One little boy, Jerry, who was about eight or nine years old, came to church one Sunday wearing a suit too large for him. The coat sleeves came almost to the end of his fingers. The trousers were equally large, and he wasn't wearing a belt. He was at church early and took it upon himself to hand out songbooks. He was having a difficult time holding the books under one arm and handing them out with the other, all while trying to hold up his pants.

The Bible says, "All things work together for good. . . ."

Here is an example: That morning, as I was putting on my go-to-church shoes, I pulled too hard on my shoelace and broke off about six inches of it. I readjusted the shoelace and all was well. I slipped the piece of string in my pocket.

When Jerry came to me with books under his arm and one in his hand, while trying to hold up his trousers, I said, "Jerry, let me help you. Lay your books down, take off your coat, and let me fix your trousers." I had him turn his back to me. I took two of his belt loops, which were about eight inches apart, drew them together, and then tied them with the broken-off shoelace.

The trousers looked good in front. Jerry exclaimed, "Ooooh, that feels good." He patted me on the back and said earnestly, "You're a good man." He made my day.

The church pastor was a friendly man and a good preacher. He announced one Sunday that some minor repairs needed to be made around the church, and if any of the men had any extra time, he would appreciate the help.

I joined him a couple of times. We did more talking than working. By spending time together, we knew each other much better thereafter. He seemed to like what I told him about my past. He told me about his daughter, Lucille, who was two years older than I. With a sideways glance at me, the preacher remarked casually, "I'd give anything I own if she would become interested in some fine, young man."

The two of us were quiet for a while. Then the pastor said, "Brother Wallace, I have been thinking." I thought to myself in the silence that followed: "Brother Pastor, I've been thinking, too." Then he continued, "I was wondering if you sing. I thought you might come over to the parsonage in your spare time and practice on a song with my daughter and then sing a special at church sometime. What do you think?"

Sensing his real intent, I thought fast. "Well, I'll tell you what happened when I was in the woods cutting some firewood and started to sing. The birds didn't only stop their singing — they knocked off a bunch of leaves getting away from there, and the squirrels started barking in the distance. I fear if I got up before your congregation, the ones who couldn't make it out the door would go out the windows."

The pastor gave me a reserved smile and commented, "Then maybe that wasn't too good an idea."

I was relieved that he didn't press the matter. I already had a girlfriend in Michigan (but that's another story).

...

At my job at Jig Bushing, I had learned what was expected of me in grinding bushings and felt good about my performance. Even though the job was stressful, I was happy that things were going well.

My job was to grind pieces of steel of different sizes and lengths, from 1/4 inch to 3/4 inch in diameter and 1/8 inch to 2 inches in length, to a specified size. When the pieces of steel reached my machine, they would have been casehardened in hot oil, with a hole of different sizes bored in each. My job was to further process the pieces of steel to specified sizes and shapes. Most would be gauged with a very sensitive micrometer to a tolerance of .003 inches. Some were to be ground to zero tolerance and checked by a specialist with a shadow gauge. The bushing would be pronounced okay or scrapped. I was never told what use was made of the bushings. I knew they were part of the war effort — perhaps for airplanes.

As always, Mr. Mondon kept a close eye on everything at the plant. One day, I looked up from my work and saw him coming toward me. Standing close by my side, he said confidentially, "I want you to do something for me. I have my reasons. [I later learned that Mondon actually had a doctorate in psychology.] See that kid over there? He is spending a lot of time goofing around. I plan to go over and tell him I'll be gone for a while, and you'll be his boss while I'm gone. If you see him goofing around, away from his workstation, you walk over to him and give him hell. What do you think?"

I replied truthfully, "Frankly, I don't like it. But I'll do it."

Mr. Mondon gave a brief nod of approval and said, "Good."

I watched Mr. Mondon. He went over to this barely eighteen-year-old boy, put one arm on his shoulder, and pointed to me with the other hand. He said a few words to the boy and was gone.

I watched to see whether Mr. Mondon left the plant. He didn't. I saw him almost hidden behind an idle machine in the far corner of the plant. He had a pair of field glasses to his eyes.

I kept an eye on this boy. It wasn't long until I saw him away from his workstation. He was just moseying around, goofing off.

I went over to him and turned my back to Mr. Mondon so he couldn't read my lips. I put my hand on this boy's shoulder and shook it slightly. I said somewhat gruffly, "Don't look now, but Mr. Mondon is watching. He told me if I saw you goofing around away from your workstation to come over and give you hell. I'm not going to give you hell, but I'm going to give you some good advice. This is it: If you don't stay at your workstation and do your assigned job, you'll be fired tonight. You won't have a job tomorrow. Do you have any questions?"

Looking suitably chagrined, the boy stammered, "No."

I patted him on the back and said, "Good luck."

I went back to my machine with mixed feelings. I felt bad about the harsh way I had talked but told myself that I may have saved the boy's job. Mr. Mondon did leave the plant and was gone for about two hours. When he returned, he went to this boy, who was working away. He patted him on the back and stuck up two thumbs at me.

The plant had a table that would seat eight to ten workmen for lunch. One fellow who came in at three o'clock and ate along with me and others was a little "touched in the head." However, he still knew his job well and tended to his own business.

One evening, this limited fellow complained of having a sore finger. A workman asked to see his finger. It wasn't bad at all. However, the workman said, "I must go get some first aid, so you won't get blood poisoning and die."

He came back with a big supply of white tape and began to wrap the finger. He wrapped and wrapped and wrapped, against this poor fellow's protests that it was being overdone. When this prankster stopped wrapping, the fellow had a knot on his finger the size of a golf ball.

We all went back to our work. This fellow with the wrapped finger was having a terrible time doing his job. Mr. Mondon came around. He stopped and looked on in amazement. He exclaimed, "What in the hell is wrong with your finger?" From my workstation, I could see that it was beyond the ability of this fellow to recount what had happened.

I went to Mr. Mondon and explained that one of the fellows at the lunch table had wrapped the poor guy's sore finger just for fun, despite the guy's protests. Anticipating Mondon's next question, I said, "Don't ask me who. I'm not a stool pigeon."

Mr. Mondon nodded that he understood and sent the fellow to the office to have the secretary take the tape off and put on a Band-Aid. And that was the end of that.

Along about that time, one morning when I was early to church, I overheard Mom Marlowe and another church member talking. The lady was probably in her fifties. Her husband had died a few years before from a heart attack. She had employment and was getting along okay most of the time.

However, today she was telling Mom Marlowe about her latest challenge. She said, "I heat with a coal furnace. It keeps the house warm, but I have a big problem. I don't have a poker to stir the fire and make it burn well. I have tried to buy one at all the hardware stores and places that sell furnaces. I have found none. I have gone through a number of old broomsticks that I've begged from friends, but they don't hold up very well."

Mom Marlowe said soothingly, "I'll pray that you will locate a poker right soon."

This lady laughed and said, "With the war going on and all, the Lord won't pay much mind to my needing a poker."

Mom Marlowe smiled and replied, "The Lord sometimes responds in strange ways."

I spoke up and said, "I hope you ladies don't mind, but I overheard your conversation. Where I work, there is an abundance of steel rods used in making bushings. It just might be possible for me to come up with a rod of steel and shape it into a poker."

Mom Marlowe said, "Sometimes the Good Lord answers a prayer before it is asked. Kestner, I believe you and the Lord can pull it off."

Jokingly, I replied, "If I can't come up with a poker, I'll round you up a few broomsticks as a Christmas present."

The steel used in the plant was sixteen feet in length, ranging from a quarter inch to four inches in diameter. It was trucked in and put in bins on the east side of the plant.

Many steps or operations were taken before a bushing got over to my side of the shop to finish.

I had a talk with the fellow in charge of the steel on its arrival. I explained the need of this worthy widow.

Without hesitation, he said, "I'll take care of it. It is about time for me to do a good deed."

I explained that the poker should be made out of one-inch steel, with an overall length of about five feet. One end of the poker needed to have a shepherd's hook, and the other end had to be cut at a sharp angle and bent to form a little hook to move clinkers around.

This agreeable fellow said, "I get the picture. I'll get to it in a day or two. I'll bring it over to you when Mondon is out."

Three days later, about 9:00 p.m., this fellow brought over a masterpiece of a poker. He was all smiles and proud of his work. I said enthusiastically, "Good job! How can I repay you?"

He shook his head and said, "Just tell me what the lady says when you give it to her."

My next problem was how to get that poker past the big, good-natured Irish doorkeeper, who was fussy about who or what went in or out of the plant. He believed in doing his job. However, he was also full of jokes and funny stories and had a new one for the fellows as they left the shop every night.

I leaned the poker against the wall behind me and hung my jacket over it. A shop clown sort of a fellow, Tony, whom everyone liked, roamed around a little while Mr. Mondon was out, just before time to go home. I told him about my problem of getting the poker out past the watchman.

Tony said, "Don't worry. I'll take it out for you and put it in your car."

I asked dubiously, "How are you going to get past the watchman?"

Tony said unconcernedly, "I'll slip the poker down the leg of my overalls into my shoe and put the hook over my shoulder under my shirt. I'll tell that watchman I put in the worst night of my life—that I've worked so hard I'm walking stiff-legged, and there's no time for a story or joke tonight."

Tony got the poker in place and went stiff-legged toward the door. I followed close on his heels. After hearing him relate his rehearsed story to the watchman and head on out the door, I quickly said to the watchman, "I'm tired, too, but not too tired to listen to a good joke. But I may be too tired to laugh."

[I wasn't lying about being tired. My shift was ten hours on my feet, except for a thirty-minute lunch break.]

While the watchman was telling me the joke, which was actually very funny, I made up my mind that I wouldn't laugh. When he finished, I really wanted to laugh. Instead—mean old me—I asked, "What happened then?"

Without missing a beat, he said: "I don't know. I had a mule to shave, and I had to go get some soap." Despite my resolve, I burst out laughing at his quick comeback, which had nothing whatsoever to do with the joke.

The lady at church was really happy to get that poker. She gave me a little box of homemade brownies to give to my friend who had made it.

[Now I don't wish to imply that the poker deal was entirely honorable. It was stealing, after all. My mother had made sure that I knew that commandment: Thou shall not steal. However, since it was for another, and not for myself, I excused it at the time.]

...

Mom and I exchanged letters each week. She kept me informed concerning the happenings around Womble Mountain, Rudement, and Herod in Southern Illinois.

In one of her letters, Mom told me that a Reverend Krost, who had been a friend of her parents, was coming to Detroit to pray for a woman. Then in his eighties, he claimed to have the gift of healing. Mom had asked him to pay me a visit. He'd promised to do so. It was arranged that I would meet him on a certain Saturday at the bus station in Pontiac. He was going to spend the night with me, and then I would take him to Detroit on Sunday.

Reverend Krost got to Pontiac early on the appointed Saturday. He had traveled all night and hadn't slept. He had eaten breakfast at a rest stop and wanted to go to bed and get some sleep.

I introduced him to the landlady and told her that he would be spending the night with me. I slipped some money into her hand. She appeared pleased. I told Reverend Krost that when he woke up, we would go to a restaurant and eat a good meal. He surprised me by suggesting that I fix a simple, home-cooked meal instead. (I assume he felt that would be more economical for both him and me.) He then lay down and was asleep immediately.

I quickly took stock of my food supply. I had lettuce for a salad, potatoes, green beans, plenty of milk, and bread. I hurried to the store and got two huge pork chops. When I got back, Reverend Krost was still sleeping away. I put the green beans, seasoned with thick-sliced bacon, on to cook. I started cooking some potatoes for mashed potatoes. Then I breaded those pork chops and began frying them slowly in a big skillet.

As Reverend Krost began to stir and show signs of awakening, I nervously checked the food. Even though my cooking had certainly improved while I was in Pontiac,

I didn't yet feel confident when cooking for others. However, the pork chops were tender. The potatoes were ready for mashing. I put the pork chops on dinner plates and made gravy in the remaining fat. All had gone well so far. I put an extra generous amount of flour in the grease — more than enough, actually. I stirred it smooth and added some milk.

Reverend Krost began to move about. I told him that by the time he got up and refreshed himself, dinner would be served. Unfortunately, my mind was off the gravy for too long. When I checked it, it was as thick as lumpy mashed potatoes.

I put the contents of the skillet in a bowl and turned my attention to the potatoes. They were just right for mashing. Do you think I mashed them? No, I didn't. I added a generous amount of milk and some salt, pepper, and butter in the pot with the potatoes and blended the contents to the consistency of thin gravy. I put this potato mixture in a serving dish. I then took up the green beans and poured two glass of cold milk.

Reverend Krost and I seated ourselves at the table. His eyes were sparkling as they focused on the pork chops. I requested that he ask a blessing on the food. At that moment, a ray of sunlight beamed through the window. This part of the prayer I remember: "Lord, we thank you for the light of the sun, without which there would be no life on the earth. We thank you that the God we serve is greater than the sun."

I passed Reverend Krost the green beans. While he was spooning out some, I put a blob of the thick gravy on my plate and quickly covered it with the thin mashed potatoes, thus showing him how they were to be eaten. He did likewise, following the old saying: "When in Rome, do as the Romans do."

Reverend Krost ate with an amused look on his face. He said, "A man never gets too old to learn." He bragged on how the bacon made the green beans taste. He went so far as to say, "You know how to make pork chops tender and the food taste delicious."

I thought, "You know how to make a learning cook feel good."

Breakfast the next morning was a regular meal—fruit, bacon and eggs, jelly rolls, and coffee. We made it to church a little before 9:30 a.m. I introduced Reverend Krost to Pop Marlowe, who graciously took charge of him. After the preliminaries, he took Reverend Krost off with him to the men and women's class. Reverend Krost must have made a hit in class. He may have even taught it.

When church was over, Mom and Pop Marlowe came to me and said they wanted Reverend Krost and me to come to their home for Sunday dinner. They assured us it was mostly ready. Since they seemed truly sincere, I consented. Mom Marlowe whispered to me, "I want him to pray for me—I'm not well."

We enjoyed a good dinner, and then Reverend Krost prayed for Mom Marlowe. She told me months later that she hadn't had a sick day since he had prayed for her.

After leaving the Marlowe's, we went to my room, got Reverend Krost's suitcase, and took off for Detroit. I was driving close to the speed limit, when a car sped past, abruptly cut in front of us, and moved on briskly. On the back of the car was a sign in bold letters: "If you can read this." Then in much smaller letters were more words that I couldn't read. I guessed it was, "You have 20-20 vision," but I wanted to be sure. I stepped on the gas and got closer and closer—almost dangerously close. When I got close enough to read the words, my face probably turned red. It said, "You are too damn close." I immediately decreased speed. Neither Reverend Krost nor I said anything, but when I glanced over, he had an amused look on his face that lasted for the longest time. I was happy to deliver him safely and return to Pontiac.

...

My deferment lasted the full eighteen months that Mr. Brownie and Mr. Mondon had promised while I worked at Jig Bushing. I continued to teach the young people's class and to spend time with friends from the church. Once in a while, when I didn't have to work on a Saturday, I went to the Marlowe's and worked for my dinner and wonderful fellowship.

My last trip to the Marlowe's was shortly before I went into the service. Mom Marlowe said, "Kestner, you have worked with or for everyone except me. Today I want you to work for me. I have one hundred young pullets [young hens about the size of quails] that are roosting on the ground in the new chicken house, which is against the nature of chickens. The material and the tools are there handy. The menfolk have just been too busy to build a roost."

I said, "Mom Marlowe, the work is as good as done." Everything fell into place. At noon, the job was complete. The next day, a Sunday, Mom Marlowe came to me at church and said it was a thrill the night before to see those young pullets up on the new roost. Many months later, while on Saipan in the South Pacific, I got a letter from Mom Marlowe. Among the church news, she said, "My young hens are laying now. Every time I look at that roost you built for them, I pray for your safety." That lifted my spirits.

After the eighteen months of deferment, Mr. Brownie and Mr. Mondon came to me and said that they were sorry, but they couldn't do any more for me. They assured me that when the war was over, a good job would be waiting for me. I expressed my appreciation for all they had done for me. I had a strong feeling that I'd never work there again.

I went to the military processing center to learn my assignment and get my orders. Despite my saying repeatedly, when asked by the line of officers at the intake table, that I wanted to be in the Army, I was assigned to the Navy. When I asked why, I was told that they needed more men in the South Pacific.

I sold my car and prepared to depart Pontiac for boot camp. I bought an old trunk and shipped my belongings home to my mom, except for one suit and a long, warm, black wool overcoat.

On my last Sunday before I left, the entire church and my Sunday school class wished me well in the most sincere way possible. I was to leave at 6:00 a.m. the following day to go by bus to Great Lakes Naval Base near Chicago.

That night, I sat in an easy chair and propped my feet up to rest and think. Everything seemed to be taken care of. I had said my goodbyes to everyone and tied up all loose ends. While sitting there, I dropped off to sleep. When I awoke, it was time for me to refresh myself, eat a light breakfast, and go to the bus station.

I had already told my landlady goodbye and assured her that I would slip out and not disturb her that morning. However, when I came down the stairs, she was standing there to tell me goodbye. I stuck out my hand to shake hands with her. She slapped my hand and said, "I don't want a handshake—I want a hug." We embraced in a warm, heartfelt hug.

I put on my overcoat and took off to the bus station. I got to the station a little before 6:00 a.m. Twenty-five or thirty young men were waiting to get on the bus when it arrived. I stood a few feet from the group. From the corner of my eye, I saw someone approaching. I felt an arm around my shoulder. I turned my head and looked into the face of Brother Spires, the father of now eight children, including little aforementioned Jerry.

He said, "Brother Kestner, I came to see you off." It was a cold morning. He was wearing a light suit. With his arm around my shoulder, I felt him shiver from the cold.

Remembering his large family and all that it took to clothe them, I felt a wave of sympathy for him. I took off that warm overcoat and said, "Brother Spires, try this on for size." It fit him perfectly. I said, "It is yours."

Brother Spires protested, "I can't take your coat!"

I said, "Yes, you can. Uncle Sam has a blue coat waiting for me."

Then his comment was much like that of his son, Jerry: "Thank you. It feels good. You are a good man."

Brother Spires walked with me to the bus. I was the last one to get on. I found an empty seat about the center of the bus. I relaxed with a determination to keep my chin up, be positive, and see the bright side of things.

As I said goodbye to Pontiac, I recalled how good Pontiac had been to me—employment that lifted the mortgage on the farm and friends that I would never forget. The list of good things went on and on.

As the motion of the bus was beginning to lull me to sleep, I thought to myself: "Southern Illinois, Womble Mountain, and Home Sweet Home—I'm coming home to you by way of the South Pacific." I drifted off while treasuring these Michigan memories of a community that nurtured a young man far from home.

* * *

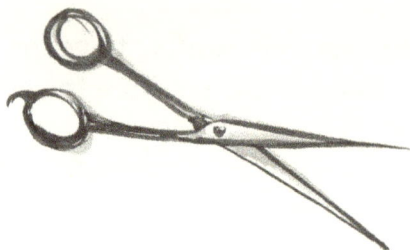

The Hidden Scars of War

What I'm about to write is directly or indirectly related to World War II. My ability to cut hair was a thread that ran through my time in the service. I wasn't a barber, nor did I aspire to become one. My hair cutting came about out of necessity.

My dad was a man of many talents—a farmer must possess many skills to be a good one. However, cutting hair wasn't one of his talents. He was past fifty years of age when he started his family of six children—four boys, of which I was the oldest, and two girls. He cut all of our hair except for that of my youngest brother, who was ten years my junior.

Around the age of eleven or twelve, after some horrible haircuts only slightly better than the bowl-on-the-head variety, I asked my dad if I could take over the job of cutting hair. He gladly turned the chore over to me.

Did hair cutting come natural for me? No, but my work was better than my dad's. For extra practice, I barbered often and could see some improvement each time.

The only time I strayed from my best work was the time I decided to give my seven-year-old, red-headed brother a set of sideburns. In order to do that, I cut his hair to near the top of his crown. I left a streak of hair on each

286

side as far down as the hair grew to look like sideburns. After we had our laughs for two or three days, I removed them and promised not to do that again.

Our farm was one hundred acres of poor, hilly, and rocky land in southeastern Saline County in Southern Illinois. Therefore, in 1940, at the age of twenty, I did as many other young men did: I went to Michigan to work to assist the family.

In another story, I have told of my landing a job at Jig Bushing, so I'll not repeat that here. I was also fortunate to find a welcoming church—one that was friendly and well blessed with poor to moderately well-to-do people. It wasn't long before I was given the job of teaching the young people's Sunday school class, which was made up of around twenty people, with two or three married couples in the group.

The first Sunday that I taught, a young woman attended the class for the first time. She was good looking, with brownish-blond hair and blue eyes. She had a continuous trace of a smile on her face. She never took her eyes off me. I noticed she had a ring on her left hand. I wondered if it might be an engagement ring.

When church was over, I told her that I was pleased to have her in the class. She replied that she enjoyed my teaching. I asked her if she lived nearby, and she replied that she lived close enough to walk. I asked if I could give her a lift home. She accepted my offer. I learned that she was from Kentucky and was working as a beautician in Pontiac. She was buying the house in which she lived and planned to make Michigan her home.

I wasn't brave enough to ask for her phone number when I got her home, but I asked if I could use her phone to make a quick call. After a moment, I announced, "A busy line." In the process, I got her phone number from the label on her phone. That afternoon, I called and asked if I could pick her up for church that night. She consented. For the next year and a half, we attended church and Sunday school together. After three or four Sundays, she removed the engagement ring given to her by her fiancé, Jim, who was in the Army.

I suggested that she put it back on, explaining that I might be drafted any time and not make it back. Then she could tell Jim that she had worn his ring while he was gone. It wasn't long until the church folks thought that we were engaged.

My eighteen-month deferment came to an end. I got my call to come to Detroit to be sworn in. The evening before I left, I made my last call to see Maureen. We sat on her couch in each other's arms, with rivers of tears flowing from our eyes. However, we were both thankful that we had had a long courtship and that we had conducted ourselves in a Christian manner throughout.

We dried our tears. She asked if I would spend my boot leave with her, but I told her that I'd be spending it with my mother; I hadn't been home since my dad had died, two years earlier.

We said our final goodbyes. On the way back to my boardinghouse, my tears returned. I knew within myself that an era had ended, and things would never be the same.

The next day, I was sworn into the Navy in Detroit and bussed to the Great Lakes Naval Base north of Chicago for five weeks of boot training. From boot camp, a company of around 150 of us was sent to Fort Pierce, Florida, for amphibious training. We got instructions in operating a small landing craft—a fifty-foot long LCM [Landing Craft, Mechanized]—which was designed to land troops and vehicles during an amphibious attack. A great deal of our training was conducted at night.

Servicemen looked forward to getting mail. I got very little. Maureen told me that she didn't like to write, but she would make up for rarely writing by thinking of me and praying for me often. I believed that she did.

In Florida, I got out my barber tools—a pair of hand clippers, a comb, and a pair of scissors. These tools, and knowing how to use them, soon made me well known and gave me a feeling of importance.

After three months of rigorous training at Fort Pierce, 150 of us were transported by troop train to Shoemaker, California. At the Shoemaker base, while waiting to be sent to serve in the South Pacific, I applied for a job at the officers' barbershop. I soon learned that I was out of my class. Everything was fancy—white uniforms, electric clippers, and all kinds of bottles and things that I didn't recognize or know how to use.

A customer with a questioning look on his face got in my chair. I tried to turn on my personality, what little I had. I asked him how he wanted his hair cut. With no sign of friendliness, he spit out, "None off the top—sides only." Now, I was under the impression that a head consisted of the two sides and the back. I was pleased with the way I made the sides look, so I shaved around his ears, dusted him off with some powder, and indicated he was ready to go. He took on a sour-pickle expression and said, "You never touched the back!"

I said, "Please excuse the oversight," and I put the cloth back on and took care of the back side, too. The barber working next to me gave me some pointers, and soon I was more at ease.

The trip from Shoemaker to Hawaii took ten days on a slow troop transport. I was seasick all the way.

The day after we landed, I started cutting hair again. As we "island hopped," I cut hair every chance I got.

I found it to be a good tonic for the let-down feeling that can seep into one's bones. I was referred to as Wally the Barber. When there was a shift about of the servicemen, and some were transferred to other divisions, someone would call out, "We still have Wally the Barber with us."

It wasn't until we got settled down on Saipan and assigned to the harbormaster that my spare time became a mixed bag of pleasure and sadness. I spent the entire year of 1945 on Saipan. I allowed my barber customers to ask questions and cry on my shoulder as needed. Some of these boys, having gotten their parents' consent, had joined the Navy as young as seventeen.

I asked one eighteen-year-old about his ambition in life. He said that he wanted to write a book, a bestseller, and wanted to know if I could tell him how to do it, or at least suggest how to get started.

I asked, "What writing have you done?"

He replied, "None."

"Do you write your mother?"

"No, I can't think of anything to say."

I gave him an assignment. "Write long letters to your mother — tell her what a beautiful view it is from here in the hills at sunset looking down at the ships anchored a ways off shore. Tell about the hot days and the not-too-bad nights. Tell her about the food. Don't make it worse than what it is. Don't forget to tell her about your barber. I will expect a report when I see you again."

It wasn't long until he was back for another haircut. He reported that he'd written his mother a long, long letter — he just had had one problem. He said, "I didn't know how to end it."

I had to ask, "How did you end it?"

He replied, "I wrote, 'I hear guns. I have to go.'"

I told him to keep on writing.

One time there was a lull in demand for haircuts. Haircut inspection was lax for a while. I asked myself, "How am I going to turn this around?"

I went to a base barbershop where Japanese from the stockade were hired by the Navy to give free haircuts. They could cut hair, but their hearts weren't in it. But for a small tip, one could get a pretty good haircut.

I had a full head of wavy hair. I went in and gave one of the Japanese a quarter, showed him about a half-inch on the tip of my finger, and rubbed my hand all over my head. He cut my hair short, with a gap or two that I knew I could take out later.

I went back to the barracks and came stomping in to appear to be angry. Several pairs of eyes were upon me. I took off my sun helmet, slammed it on the deck, and made out like I was trying to stomp it. I wailed out, "I cut everyone's hair the way they want it cut and look what I get at the camp barbershop!" It wasn't long until I was back in business — big time!

I only charged twenty-five cents for a haircut, but my hobby was made worthwhile by some paying me fifty cents or a dollar. I had one customer who looked to be about twenty-five years old, with a very conservative, business-like appearance. He wanted a haircut every five to seven days. He liked to ask me questions, but mostly he liked the way I listened when he talked. He reminded me each time I cut his hair that he and his father were in the real estate business together in New York, and that they cleared more than $100,000 per year. One time he commented, "Isn't it ironic that we make that kind of money, and here I am, sitting on a homemade bench, getting a twenty-five cent haircut?"

I knew from past experience that this braggart would give me no tip. However, I stifled my true feelings and replied mildly, "Yep, that is something you can write home about."

It was with a great deal of pleasure that I cut the hair of a kindly officer who came ashore from a ship at sea. He appeared to be well past eighty years of age. He walked slowly but stood tall and was keen of eye and mind.

I asked, "Sir, how do you want your hair cut?"

His slow, pondered reply was touching. "Young man, with scissors only, cut it like you think would be becoming of a seafaring man." I feared he was a lonely widower who had no one to go home to.

I cut the hair of one fellow who was just out of the brig. The last haircut he had had was horrible. He explained that while he was at Shoemaker, California, waiting to be shipped to the South Pacific, he had asked for a leave to go home because his wife was having a baby very soon. His request was denied. He went AWOL. He returned as soon as all appeared to be okay. He never complained about his brig time—he said he would have felt bad if he had done otherwise.

I was deeply touched the next day to learn that he had been killed when the jeep he was driving was ambushed in the hills. I wrote his widow and explained to her that I had cut his hair the day before his death and that he had spoken kindly concerning her.

No matter where I was stationed and had set up my barbershop, I continually listened to both married and single sailors who had received "Dear John" letters. Just listening to them was probably of more help than anything I could have said.

One young man told me that he and his girlfriend had the most wonderful courtship that could be imagined, and with great anticipation, they looked forward to getting married as soon as he got home. I told him that was fine.

However, he went on to say, "Yesterday, I got a 'Dear John' letter, telling me that she had given the engagement ring I had given her to my mother, because she was in love with someone else." He commented that he no longer wanted to live, because of the heaviness of heart and a feeling in his stomach that was worse than seasickness.

He asked, "What would you say in answer to a letter like that?"

I stalled for time by saying, "It is hard for me to concentrate on giving you a good haircut and a good answer to your question at the same time." I paused from my hair cutting and put my finger up to my nose as if I were thinking.

Telling his sad story seemed to have brought him some relief. Before I could say anything, he said, "I'll write her and tell her to go to hell. There are more fish in the ocean than have ever been caught."

I said, "You may have answered your own question." I went on to say, "You could write her that the sad news in her letter had caused you to lose your appetite and sleep. But then add, 'If our love for one another is less solid than the Rock of Gibraltar, it is better for us to know it now rather than later.'"

"Wally, I like that better than telling her to go to hell. Thank you for your advice."

This poor guy offered me two dollars for the haircut as he said, "One is for the haircut and the other for listening and for your advice."

Refusing to take his money, I said, "If what I have said has helped you, that is pay enough."

About that time I got a card from Maureen. It gave me mixed emotions. I had thought that that case was long closed.

A verse on the card read:

Time brings many changes
But never to us two.
Your kind likable ways
And the liking I have for you.

That card, after many months, gave me something to think about. The war had ended, and I was still alive.

Once in a while, I got a letter from someone in my former Sunday school class. In one of those letters, I was informed that Lucille Johnson, the pastor's daughter, had received a "Dear Jane" letter from the boyfriend to whom she was engaged. He was stationed in Germany, and the letter informed her that he had married a German girl. I really didn't give it much thought. Things like that were happening all over—another example of the hidden scars of war.

Along about that time, I wrote a long Mother's Day poem. I sent my mom a copy and also sent copies to a few other motherly women whom I respected and admired. As far as poems go, it was very mediocre. I sent a copy to Pastor Johnson's wife. However, I fear the Johnsons read more into the poem than was intended.

I got a letter from Lucille letting me know that Maureen's old boyfriend had returned from the Army, and they were married. She hoped I wouldn't be too unhappy over the news and assured me that plenty of young women would be glad to take her place in my life.

I can't say that I was surprised at the news of Maureen's marriage. It was exactly what I suspected would happen, but the news gave me a feeling that I can't explain.

I remained on Saipan a few months after the war was over while loose ends were being tied up and transportation to the States was being arranged. The slow voyage home gave me time to think things over.

I cut my last two heads of hair in California before traveling to the Great Lakes Naval Base. Many of my haircut encounters were interesting, but now after many years, most of them seem to run together. However, these two I remember well.

Looking for someone to start on, I went to a barbershop where there was a long waiting line extending outside the shop. I went to the end of the line and said, "It appears that you two will have a long wait." I told them that I cut hair and if they would like, I could save them some time. These two rugged guys must have been Marines around thirty years of age.

One of the two eyed me keenly and asked, "Can you cut hair?"

I assured them that I could and had my tools in my hands to prove it.

One looked at the other and asked, "Pal, what do you think?"

The "Pal" wanted more assurance. He asked, "Can you really cut hair?"

I again assured them that I could.

He then took a deep breath and said, "I'm going to take a chance, and if you don't know how to cut hair, you better know how to shag ass!"

Those were my two best haircuts — wonder why?

I got discharged at the Great Lakes Naval Base and went immediately by bus to Pontiac to visit my married brother, Victor, who was home after spending many months in the Army in Europe. I was anxious to pick up the good used car that I had had him buy for me. In addition, seeing Maureen and her husband, Jim, at church wasn't far from my mind.

The next day being Sunday, I went to church. My anticipation of the first sight of Maureen was giving me the most unusual feeling. I was hoping for definite assurance that she was happy.

I was seated where I could see her when she came in. Several new faces were in the group. They welcomed me as a stranger in their midst. I was warmly greeted by those who knew me. Reverend Johnson and Lucille almost went overboard in expressing their happiness to see me.

Near the time for the service to start, Maureen and Jim came in. He guided her to three pews beyond me. For a split second, her eyes and mine locked. She had not changed. There was a sparkle in her eyes and a trace of a smile on her face that said, "Welcome back."

I made a quick assessment of Jim. I was disappointed that he wasn't more of a Prince Charming. He appeared tall, lank, and lean in his brown suit. His brown, unruly hair didn't do anything for him. His face was expressionless. I felt pretty sure that that match was made somewhere, but not in Heaven. I immediately asked forgiveness for judging.

I sat through the service in a haze, feeling more out of control and less at ease than when I was on Saipan.

The service ended, and different people grouped around me. Maureen and Jim left with only a brief smile from her. The opportunity to meet Jim and for a short visit with them had passed.

Reverend Johnson wondered if he, his wife, their daughter Lucille, and I could go out and eat together. I thanked him and told him that my brother and his wife were expecting me for dinner.

He went on to say, "We hope to see a lot more of you."

I thanked him. He was fearful that I didn't understand and added, "If you and the girl can make a go of it, that will be fine, also."

That was too much too soon. Still, I smiled and said, "Thank you."

Hoping for better luck, I went back to church Sunday night. I got there near church time. Reverend Johnson hurried to me and said, "We are trying to get a quartet together. We need a fourth person. There will be my brother Jim, you, Lucille, and me, with Jim's wife at the piano."

I protested, "I can't sing and probably don't even know the song you have in mind."

"Oh, yes, you know the song. It is, 'There's a New Name Written, and It's Mine, Oh, Yes, It's Mine!' All you will have to do is stand up there and hold the book with Lucille, and we'll sing loud enough to make up for your not singing very loud."

I'll never know why, but I nodded that I would give it a try. I got up there and wished I could fall through the floor. I wished the song were being sung as a trio and that I were back in a pew listening. There sat Maureen with a near smile on her face and Jim registering nothing.

If pianos have a pedal that can be pressed down to make them louder, the pianist must have held this one down all the time. The two Johnson brothers were trying to jar the portals of Heaven; I could barely hear Lucille. I worked my mouth some and probably looked like a mule eating sawbriars. I was glad when Reverend Johnson, in an expression of enthusiasm, put both hands high in the air. I felt that took attention off me. I was unable to calm myself for the rest of the service.

Again Maureen and Jim left the church without our getting to talk to each other.

On Monday morning, I was about to leave for Southern Illinois to see my mom. I decided to call Maureen before I left. I picked up the phone, and her number popped into my mind. I dialed it and, to my surprise, heard Maureen's pleasant, musical voice.

She said, "Kestner, when the phone rang, I knew it

was you. I knew you wouldn't leave Michigan without talking to me—for old time's sake, if for no other reason."

"Yes, I'll be leaving within the hour. I just wanted to call and wish you happiness. You are happy, aren't you?"

"I can't say yes. I can't say no. I'll have to say so-so."

"I hope very much for you that life will grow sweeter day by day. I've been told that the first hundred years of married life are the worst."

"Kestner, I'm sorry I didn't write to you more often. I can think of so many things I would have liked to have said. I'm sorry that Lucille had to jump ahead of me in telling you I was married. I would have told you in my own way."

"Maureen, suppose we allow ourselves no regrets of the past and be thankful for the prospects of a wonderful future."

"I'll feel bad if I tell you what I'm thinking; I'll feel bad if I don't."

"Well, in that case, you'd just as well go ahead and tell me."

"It is on my heart to tell you, if you are interested in me, it is still not too late. I know Jim. If you start entering the picture, he will take off. Tell me frankly what you think and put my heart to ease."

"Maureen, there are two things wrong with what you have suggested. First, it wouldn't be right, and second, your plan is a set-up to get me shot—and maybe you, too. You know Jim. I know him, too. He wouldn't take kindly at all—'no way, no how'—to someone showing interest in you."

Maureen didn't seem at all crushed by my reply. In fact, she seemed a little relieved. She responded, "Okay, Kestner—now that that has been laid to rest in no uncertain terms, allow me to make a wish known. It is none of my business, but please don't become interested in Lucille

Johnson. She is a wonderful girl, and I wish her no ill will, but she is not the one for you."

"You can set your mind at ease. I agree. She is not for me. Now, Maureen, a suggestion for you—at your earliest convenience, make Jim the type of dinner you made for me the last evening we were together before I left for the service. You had country-fried chicken, biscuits, and gravy—the works—and peach cobbler. If that doesn't put a smile on his face, nothing will. I know you would like to see him smile more."

"Kestner, thanks a million for calling. I really needed this talk with you to smooth out the road ahead for Jim and me. Now . . . I heard on the grapevine that you have a good friend in Southeast Missouri in whom you are very much interested. My wish for you is that that friendship will bud, blossom, and bear fruit."

"Thank you for wishing me well. I have the faith of a mustard seed that all will go well for you and for me. Bye, Maureen."

"Bye, Kestner . . . sweetheart."

Starting the long drive to Harrisburg, Illinois, I began to feel free, free, free, as if it were the first day of the rest of my life. I had a firm feeling that an unseen eye had watched over me, and a powerful hand had guided me. My heart went out to my comrades less fortunate. I breathed a silent prayer for them. Then my thoughts shifted, and I felt the pull of Southeast Missouri.

* * *

[Note: I courted that Southeast Missouri gal, the lovely Evelyn Green from East Prairie, and married her in 1950. We were blissfully married for fifty-six years, until her death in September 2006.]

Trains, War, and Memories

I was one of 150 young, newly recruited Navy men who were given five weeks of intensive amphibious training at the Great Lakes Naval Base north of Chicago during World War II. We were to be sent to the South Pacific. Three months of training were crowded into five weeks. Everything was hurry, hurry, hurry. We were trained in marching, boxing, wrestling, swimming, and hand-to-hand combat.

The group was asked for volunteers to become sharpshooters. Their desired number came up short, so I was drafted to try out. Each person trying out had his own target, set out about 150 yards, so the bullets would go out into Lake Michigan. The men taking part lay on their stomachs about six feet apart.

At a given signal, we were to rapidly fire a certain number of shots or rounds. New targets were put up, and the ordeal was repeated three or four times. At least two of the three or four times, a seagull flew over while we were firing. I got a bead on one and brought it down—well, either I or some other wayward soul. I wasn't chosen to be a sharpshooter. However, I got my first and only reprimand for that stunt.

Worse than the reprimand was a partial hearing loss in both ears. The shooters on either side of me were too close. I wasn't given earplugs. No pain was involved, but from that day since, I have been unable to hear a watch tick. Lip reading is a big help, but a downside of lip reading is that I make some people uncomfortable by watching them too closely. On other occasions, when not wanting to stare and only half hearing as a result, I might seem as if I am showing a lack of concern.

At the end of five weeks, we were loaded on a first-class train, complete with Pullman cars with berths and a dining car, to be transported to Fort Pierce, Florida, for training in operation of landing craft. On the train, porters even fixed our beds at night, which was a real luxury after the previous five weeks. We were very relieved to be finished with boot camp. We believed that the quicker we could get gone, the better.

After we were on the train, we were told that the base at Fort Pierce wouldn't be ready to receive us for four days. So a slow train ride was set accordingly. I got a seat by a window, with a goal of not missing anything along the way. However, after leaving the Chicago area, the window shades were closed for a day or two for security reasons. That deprived me of the pleasure of sightseeing.

I amused myself by letting my imagination run wild. I thought perhaps we were passing the farm in Kentucky where my Michigan girlfriend had lived her teen years. I wondered about the well-being of her father and mother and the other members of her large family.

From what she had told me, we had had a similar background. She, too, had gone to a one-room school. I marveled at how well she had adapted to city life in Pontiac, Michigan. She didn't seem at all "country," but in no way was she ashamed of her roots. She told me of working barefoot in the garden—she said that her family's money crop was an acre of tobacco. Her job was to pick off the big, green tobacco worms. I told her that we planted a half acre of potatoes and that my job was to debug the potatoes.

I daydreamed of taking her to visit her folks when the war was over and sampling a meal she had bragged about—cornbread, cabbage, mashed potatoes, fried chicken and gravy, green beans seasoned with smoked side meat, sliced tomatoes, and cucumbers. Deep within, something told me it would never happen, but to me, dreaming about it beat playing cards. It didn't cost me anything.

I asked myself what I'd do on returning when the war was over. I had no desire to go back to my job at Jig Bushing. Recalling Dad's sister—my dear Aunt Florence—gave me an idea. She loved people old and young. Cheering up people and "matchmaking" was one of her missions in life. However, she never married. She loved children and had twelve nieces and nephews who lived near her, just across a field. She would go out of her way to make each of us feel special.

For example, when I was six years old, I had a pet chicken. Mr. Rooster was healthy, greedy, and retarded. He wouldn't eat cracked corn with the other little chickens. He had to eat whole grain corn with the big chickens.

One time he ate too much. The corn swelled, and he got "tight craw," which is often fatal for young chickens.

In tears, I took Mr. Rooster up through the field to receive comfort from Aunt Florence. Dad had already pronounced the death sentence on him. Aunt Florence was sitting and fanning herself on her shady porch. Seeing my tears, she cried, "Son, whatever is the matter?" In a choked-up voice, I managed to tell her.

She took Mr. Rooster from me and entered into my sorrow. She put him up to her cheek and talked baby talk to him. Then she said, "We can't let Mr. Rooster die. Son, you hold Mr. Rooster, and I'll go in the house and get some things we need."

Soon she was back with a sharp paring knife, a small needle, some silk thread, a small hairpin, and some iodine. She had me continue to hold Mr. Rooster. By feeling, she isolated a grain of corn in the craw, cut a little slit the length of the grain of corn, and with the hair pin, fished out most of the corn, one grain at a time. Then she closed the cut with three or four stitches and applied some iodine. When finished, she said, "Son, I'll have to keep Mr. Rooster overnight to keep an eye on him." In the morning, Mr. Rooster was as good as new.

Thinking back on that story, I felt a surge of admiration and inspiration. "Yep," I said, "someday I'll be a surgeon."

By the third day on the train, the shades were open during the daylight hours. I began to study the towns and villages we passed. I observed the open country, farm by farm and mile by mile. It was too early in the season for crops to be up, but by certain telltale signs, I could figure out what crops were grown in the area. Tobacco barns spoke of tobacco crops. Corn and cotton fields were easy to recognize by the residue in the fields from last year's crop.

As the train rolled on, I observed the varying amount of pride held for land and property. Many houses and barns cried out for paint, while others were pristine showplaces.

In Georgia, I saw mile after mile of tall, slender pine trees being harvested. Some older, thicker pine trees were also in the mix. In my mind, I put the trees to three different uses. Some went to paper mills; some were sawed into lumber; others were peeled, treated, and made into telephone and light poles.

I recalled, while in or near Atlanta, that Sherman's march from Atlanta to the sea had played an important part in ending the Civil War. General Sherman had chosen 80,000 seasoned soldiers for this 300-mile march.

My grandfather, Jonathan Wallace (hereinafter, "Grandpa"), was one of the 5,000 soldiers in the cavalry on this march. Some thirty years later, he told my father about the march and put an interesting face on it—he almost made it sound like a "grand old war." He nearly caused Dad to feel the same way. My limited knowledge of the war is enough to tell me that it was the saddest event in the history of the United States. Most people today have no real understanding of the number of soldiers killed or maimed during the war.

Grandpa was in a sort of a mop-up group that traveled close behind the main army. A sergeant by the name of Clark led the men. He was a large, rough-spoken man who didn't leave anyone guessing as to who was in charge. Still, his men held him in high regard and would have gone to the ends of the earth with him. Grandpa admired him for the gentle respect he showed his horse, which he called Buddy Boy. Grandpa knew that Sarge Clark would be kind to women and children.

Grandpa portrayed the men as a happy-go-lucky bunch. They made up songs as they went along. All the verses ended, "As we go marching through Georg-ee."

One was: "We heard the turkeys gobble when they heard the joyful sound, as we go marching through Georg-ee." Another one went like this: "We saw the sweet potatoes as they leaped up from the ground, when they heard the joyful sound, as we go marching through Georg-ee."

One day, Sarge's group came across a small house, which was only slightly better than a shack. Three women and a small boy, all poorly clad and undernourished-looking, stood in front of the house. A small hog that they had already scalded, scraped clean, gutted, and washed was hanging temptingly from a low branch of a tree. The women were getting ready to take the hog down and cut it up.

A couple of birds—or jerks (your choice)—sprang from their saddles and hoped the others would join them as they began to sing, "We will eat roast pig tonight, as we go marching through Georg-ee!"

Sarge Clark bellowed out, "You dumb jackasses—get back on your horses before I get off and bump your heads together!"

The group began to sing, "Sarge is going to kick some ass, as we go marching though Georg-ee!" A big cheer went up for Sarge Clark. The women and the boy joined in.

Sarge addressed the two soldiers. "I hope there will be no hard feelings between us. We'll run across a wild hog up ahead in a thicket. It won't taste as good as the ladies' hog. But we'll sleep better tonight with a clear conscience for not having taken theirs."

The horse that Grandpa had brought from home gave out on the march and was set free. The group helped Grandpa rope a young, wild mule, which he rode until he acquired a fine, young horse. He rode that horse for the rest of the war and then back home to Pope County, Illinois.

Reliving that run across Georgia from Atlanta to Savannah through Grandpa's eyes, as well as other worse accounts of the war, tired me out. So I slept as much as I could the rest of the way to Fort Pierce. [I'll not repeat here what I have already written about what took place in Fort Pierce. You can read it in my book, *A Dollar the Hard Way*.]

...

Are you up to taking another train ride with me? This ride was also by first-class Pullman cars traveling the southern route from Fort Pierce, Florida, to the Camp Shoemaker Navy base in California—the training and distribution center from which we would ship out to the South Pacific. Early on I got the impression that there was an urgency to get where we were going. The fireman must have been busy shoveling coal because it was full steam ahead.

Again, I watched from the window. A great deal of what I saw was "more of the same"—mile after mile of wasteland. My heart went out to the early settlers who had made this journey by covered wagon. I recall seeing a rider in the distance, his horse moving at a gallop. I took him to be a Native American. I wondered where he was going and why.

Another time, I saw a bright yellow bobcat about thirty feet from the tracks. He was lying unafraid, sunning on a large rock.

I liked taking a nap on the train. The clickety-clack of the steel wheels on the steel tracks could lull me to sleep much the same as the sound of rain on a tin roof or on the tents in which we slept in Fort Pierce.

I marveled at how much better off I was, while riding in luxury, than my cousin from Dudley, Missouri. He, for the thrill of it, had hoboed to Oregon by riding in boxcars. He said that when the train whistled, the lonesome hobos would squall, and it would cause cold chills to go all through him.

One evening around nine o'clock, the train stopped seemingly in the middle of nowhere. A fellow took it upon himself to find out why. He reported that the mountains were just ahead, and the train had stopped to hook on another engine. The one in front would pull and the one behind would push.

We were asked to remain seated. An officer tapped me on the shoulder and asked me to stand. He handed me a holstered .45 on a belt and a billy club. He told me to stand guard just outside the passenger car and not let anyone on or off.

I had stood guard only a few minutes when a tall, rugged man approached and started to get on the car. I informed him not to do so. He stopped and glared at me, then let out a stream of vile curse words. I unsnapped the strap that held the .45. He cursed some more and disappeared into the darkness. I hadn't known whether he was drunk, drugged, or crazy, but I was glad my bluff had worked. I hadn't planned to shoot him. In fact, I doubted whether the .45 was loaded.

Overall, this trip was interesting but rather uneventful. Most of us were pleased to see California for the first time.

...

I'll not burden you with what happened in the South Pacific and on Saipan. After the war was finally over, my trip back from Saipan to California was on a troop transport ship that traveled only about seven knots per hour. So I had plenty of time to plan my future. Inspired by my mother, two sisters, three uncles, and five aunts, all of whom were teachers, I decided that I would become a teacher, too.

The ship finally reached California. When our ship neared San Francisco, a boat loaded with cheerleaders came out into the harbor. The cheerleaders, shaking their pom-poms, cheered wildly to welcome us home. I am sure that they had been paid. Whoever had done it had meant well, and I appreciated the gesture, but the cheerleaders' carrying on did nothing for me.

In San Francisco, while we were waiting for transportation to Chicago, a psychiatrist gave a large group of servicemen a lecture on getting back into society. The speaker told us that, even though we didn't realize it, we had changed, and it would be easy for us to fly off the handle and do things that were out of character. He asked us to be aware. He said that we all probably had short fuses that could explode without any warning.

He went on and on. I listened to his talk and thought it was good for those who needed it, but I didn't think it applied to me. I had never been in a fight or had any trouble. However, I did get both eyes blackened by two of the best buddies a person could have. While drunk, they got into a fight. I got between them to stop the fight and caught blows from both of them. The next day, I got sincere apologies from each of my friends. The lesson I learned was, "If two drunks are hellbent to fight, get out of the way and let them."

Traveling the northern route, we were sent on our way to Chicago in January 1946 on dilapidated, bitterly cold coaches without heat, a dining car, or sleeping compartments. Hot, nourishing meals were arranged for us at stops along the way.

We rode one person per seat, with one facing the front and the other facing the back. The person across from me was a shy, black Navy man named Ben. We hadn't met before. He shivered from the cold, and his teeth chattered. At times his face broke out with perspiration, as though he had a fever.

As night came on, I asked him if he had a blanket in his sea bag. He said that he did. I pointed out that the backs of our seats were loose, and we could place them in the space between the seats and form a bed for ourselves. He could put his feet toward my head, and I could put my feet toward his head. We could sleep in our clothes and cover up with our blankets. He thought it was a good idea. We got a good night's sleep.

The next morning, as we were rubbing the sleep out of our eyes, a gruff railroad man came along. With his back to me, he addressed Ben with these words: "What in the hell do you think you are doing, taking your seat apart like that? I should bounce you out on the floor and put you off the train at the next stop!"

That was when I overreacted. I sprang to my feet and laid a heavy hand on his shoulder while clamping down at the same time. He must have seen the devil in my eyes, judging from the wild look on his face. I felt a shiver go through him. I said with exaggerated emotion: "This man, Ben, has been overseas fighting for you and our country. He is a sick man. Fixing this bed was my idea. If you lay a hand on Ben, I'll clean your clock and mop the deck with the seat of your pants. Do I make myself clear?"

He nodded his head, and I removed my hand. He turned to Ben and said, "Sir, I didn't know you were sick. Please excuse me."

My hot flash passed as suddenly as it had come on. I asked myself, "What came over me? I've never acted this way before." I felt as remorseful as I had felt angry a minute before. I said to the railroad man: "Forgive me for losing my cool. This past year on Saipan was stressful."

Tears appeared in both of our eyes. We shook hands, and he went on his way. Although I was proud of myself for defending Ben, I spent the day feeling remorseful for my unbecoming behavior. I vowed never again to be violent with anyone.

As we made our stops to eat while going across the country, the greetings we received were far different from those of the cheerleaders. They felt genuine and filled with warmth and love. Old and young gathered around, shook our hands, patted our backs, and said: "We are glad you are back. Thank you for fighting for our country!"

I'll never forget a tiny girl in her grandmother's arms, who said with a twinkling smile, "Happy back, happy back." All of those sincere expressions of appreciation made me happier than I had been for many months.

On reaching home, after an absence of five and a half years, Womble Mountain and our humble home nearby were the loveliest sights I had seen in a long time. I have lived at the foot of Womble Mountain ever since.

*   *   *

My Beloved and Our Guiding Hand

D o you believe in a Guiding Hand?
More people have been led by and
benefited from a guiding hand than they realize
or have given thanks for.

Many events that enhance our lives, we chalk up to chance, and they very well could be. However, I believe it would be better to be thankful for a number of happenstances than to fail to express appreciation for an honest-to-goodness case of being led by a guiding hand.

I believe that a guiding hand led me to my beloved Evelyn and guided our paths through fifty-six years of marriage. Because of incidents that I'll relate, how could I not believe?

If not for a guiding hand, Evelyn and I would never have met. She was from East Prairie, Missouri, and I lived in Harrisburg, Illinois. However, during World War II, we both ended up in Pontiac, Michigan, where we worked in different defense plants.

In 1943, right before I was drafted into the Navy and sent to the South Pacific, Evelyn and I happened to meet at the home of her Uncle George and Aunt Mertie Green, whom I had met years before in Dudley, Missouri. They were friends and neighbors of my Aunt Rosa Affolder. The Greens had invited me to Sunday dinner, and Evelyn dropped in to say hello while I was there. Her aunt and uncle insisted that she stay for dinner.

Now I had had girlfriends in the past, but this was my first and only case of "love at first sight." Evelyn was a real beauty, with black shoulder-length hair, ruby-red lips, and a body that curved in all the right places. I watched and admired her throughout dinner. Her easy conversation and sense of humor told me that she had a pleasing personality, to match her beauty.

Evelyn's aunt saw the gleam in my eye. In casual conversation, she managed to get Evelyn to confirm that her address was 84 Oliver Street, which I carefully engraved in my mind.

Although I was smitten, Uncle Sam required my presence in the Navy, so I made no attempt to get in touch with Evelyn before I left a few weeks later. I was soon caught up in the whirlwind of basic training before being sent to Saipan in the South Pacific.

Being in the Navy without a real girlfriend brought on spells of loneliness from time to time. I was often jealous of the mail that other sailors would receive. I had only my daydreams of what might be.

My daughter, LeAnn, recently discovered among my papers a poem I had written in 1945, while I was stationed on Saipan. It is an accurate reflection of my feelings at the time, so I'll reproduce it here.

How It Came to Be
Around the first of October
In the year of forty-four,
I chose you for my dream girl
And in my dreams I often soar.
Soar from the dullness of my surroundings
To a lady that is fair
And gaze with awe and admiration
At the beauty of her hair.

On this particular evening
Of which I'm about to tell,
I found myself so lonely —
I recall it quite well.
My tent was still in darkness
Though it was past the twilight hour;
Sudden flashes of lightning
Foretold of a coming shower.
I lay on my cot in quietness
And recalled the events of the day;
No one was there to disturb me
For each sailor had gone his way.
I remembered the lad that morning
Who, as I cut his hair,
Inquired of my home state with interest
And asked if I had a wife back there.
In reply I told him
That my state was Illinois;
To go back would make me happy—
Indeed it would be a joy.
In attempting to change the subject,
I asked him if he liked the sea.
He said, "Just a minute —
You have not answered me.
I want to know if you are married
And how it came to be,
And if your answer is yes,
I have questions, one, two, three."
"No, my lad, I'm single,
Single as I can be,
Just one of those things,
You see, you see, you see."
"Well, we have more in common,
Lovers both are we,

My girlfriend is a singer
And loves no one but me."
As I lay on my cot that evening,
I thought of the lad and the girl he said he'd won,
Then I thought of myself,
How different—a girlfriend, I had none.
I realized it more fully
Than I ever had before,
Had I been brought up differently,
I probably would have swore.
Then I thought quite likely
There was some girl that I knew
Who also might be lonely—
Why not with letters pursue?
That thought involved a question—
A huge one to me;
I spent some time a pondering
Who that person might be.
In my mind I made a list
Of all the girls I could recall—
It included the good and friendly
Also the large and small.
Each of them had qualities
To be admired by one and all,
But the list was not perfect
For one name I failed to recall.

Then came the marking off of their names;
It seemed almost like a sin
The way I struck off some of the fair ones
With an imaginary pen.
When my marking off was completed,
My trouble had brought me naught;
It caused me to think still more seriously—

What is wrong with me, I thought.
Is there none among my acquaintances
I can love and not mere pretend?
For to say, to love each other,
Is more than I can comprehend.
My mood was at its lowest ebb,
I had reached the end of my rope.
I can assure you, my listeners,
I had just about lost hope.
Then to myself
I breathed a prayer,
My soul became as light as air—
I was delivered from despair.
There appeared to me a girl so fair,
With teeth so white and lovely hair,
I thought to myself, a girl so rare!
She is the answer to my prayer.
She hesitated not nor lingered,
In a moment she was gone;
Because of the one smile that she gave me,
In my mind she lingers on.
I knew her name and address
And that was almost all,
So with a pen and pad of paper,
I began to get on the ball.
What will be the outcome?
We will have to wait and see;
For those that might be curious,
This is how it came to be.

So I wrote Evelyn that fateful letter and waited anxiously for a reply. Evelyn answered, but it took months for her letter to catch up with me in the South Pacific. We then exchanged a few heartfelt letters during my remaining time in the Navy. Due to the distance and the disrupted mail service during the war, the time between letters was unbearably long.

I treasured each of her letters. In fact, I still have all of them. To show you why it was so easy to fall in love with Evelyn, I am including one paragraph from one of her letters:

> *I have here the most bee-u-tiful rosebud, and was just thinking if I were a little fairy, I could just open up each petal and in the center I would find you. Well, I can dream, can't I? They're singing, "I'll Buy That Dream," and it's quite suitable right now, for I'm dreaming like mad. (ha!) Wouldn't time drag and be dull if we had no imagination at all? Then too, it doesn't pay to let it run away with us, for we might wake up and sometimes be disappointed. But Honey, what I was thinking, I know there wouldn't be any disappointment.*

Through our letters, we had a strong feeling that we were in love. Each of us had qualities admired by the other. However, Evelyn had one picture of me in her mind, while the reality was somewhat different. The war had changed me in several ways.

The day we met in 1943, I was looking pretty good. I had just come from church in suit and tie, shoes shined, and all. I was clean-shaven and had a full head of wavy, reddish-brown hair. When I returned in 1946, I had a butch Navy haircut and a mustache. I also had a bad case of war nerves.

I was anxious to go visit Evelyn in East Prairie. However, our first meeting didn't go too well, although she was happy to see me again. Over time, I found out that she didn't like my haircut or my mustache or my out-of-style, blunt-toed, black Navy shoes. My personality wasn't quite as she had remembered. And the 1937 Terraplane I was driving—the only one I could find after the war, when cars were scarce—had definitely seen better days and was an embarrassment to her. So, all in all, I was a bit of a disappointment to her.

At that time, we were both twenty-six years old and had a desire to be married. But we each thought that the drawing force was too weak for us to take that step. However, at the same time, the feeling for each other was too strong to throw in the towel and give up.

I know now that a guiding hand can hold back or speed up progress. Although it was an agonizing time for me, I see that our waiting was just the thing we needed to do, rather than making a rash decision, which we might live to regret.

So what did we do? We marked time for the next four years. The distance that separated Evelyn and me—from Harrisburg to East Prairie—was only one hundred miles. I could easily drive it in less than three hours. But the lack of agreement and direction regarding our relationship put us miles and miles apart.

I didn't go often to East Prairie to see Evelyn, although I was never denied a request to visit. I was always treated royally by Evelyn, her grandfather (the mayor of the town), and her grandmother, whom she called Big Mom. She had been raised by her grandparents.

My visits were few because I got involved in teaching in a one-room school, taking college courses, building a house to rent, and dealing in used cars. I hoped we could keep our romance alive by corresponding between visits. However, that didn't work out too well. Evelyn's penmanship was beautiful. She expressed herself well. But I would almost pass out waiting for a reply to my letters. I got a feeling—out of sight, out of mind.

While those four years were civil and involved a fair degree of happiness, it was a period lacking in harmony. In the language of a sailor, "We sailed the seas of dry land." We went through a period when we had neither a north star nor a compass to guide us. A meeting of the minds was a concept we couldn't grasp.

The time came when our romance was hanging by a thread. But before that thread gave way, the guiding hand intervened. It seemed to me that each of us had an awakening at the same time; however, I can speak only for myself. I came to the shocking realization that if I let Evelyn slip through my fingers, I would regret it for the rest of my life. I began to act in the way I had known all along that I should.

I proposed marriage to Evelyn. To my delight, she accepted.

I realized that one reason I had dragged my feet about marriage was a fear I had, dating back to when I was a little boy. We had a neighbor lady around thirty years of age who married a mild-mannered man about her age. He had a big team of black mules, a large farm wagon, and a Model T Ford. This woman started henpecking that poor man from day one. She took over driving that Model T. Her husband would sit beside her like a little boy. When they took his mules and wagon to a slope coal mine five miles away to lay in their winter's coal, she would drive the mules while sitting high and wild-eyed on the spring seat of the wagon, with her husband sitting slumped over dispiritedly beside her. Even as I boy, I knew I never wanted to be like that husband.

I feared I would upset the apple cart, but before Evelyn and I were married, I felt I needed to discuss this issue with her. I related the above story to Evelyn, and then I said that if and when we got married, I expected to be the head of the house.

I'll never forget her reply, which pleased me very much: "I'm old-fashioned enough. I'll have no trouble with that."

We were married on August 22, 1950. It was one of the happiest days of my life. I firmly believe that a guiding hand had kept our romance from falling apart and brought us to that day.

I always felt as if I was the head of the house, but Evelyn got me to do just about whatever she wanted by combining a charming smile with a sweet tone for any request she made of me: "Would you mind doing" this or that or "I'd be happy if you would do" thus and so. I did what she wanted me to do and enjoyed doing it. Evelyn's guiding hand helped enlighten me as to how married couples should behave.

Evelyn started out by leaving no doubt in my mind of her love for me. She loved and respected my mother as if she were her own. She joyfully changed the house I had built before we were married into a happy home. Her motto concerning the home was "Cleanliness is next to godliness."

Believe me, I could knock myself out telling you how wonderful Evelyn was for the fifty-six years of our marriage. She kept a clean house, cooked delicious meals, and gradually and skillfully civilized me by removing some of the rough edges. I can say without any doubt that Evelyn made me a better man. I felt blessed and honored that she was my wife.

Evelyn had dozens of smiles daily for me—on arising each morning, on my leaving, if only to go outside for lawn and garden work, and on my returning home, when the smiles were the biggest.

Evelyn had a wonderful sense of humor. She loved to play jokes on others and giggled uncontrollably when someone played a joke on her.

Before we were married, Evelyn worked in a five-and-dime variety store in East Prairie along with her best friend, Evelyn Sanders. When I went to East Prairie to see Evelyn, I spent some time in the store where the two worked. It was easy to see the love and respect they had for each other.

The two Evelyns sought out ways to razz each other in a good-natured, fun manner. This is an example:

Evelyn Sanders told me that during the '37 flood, much of the area around East Prairie was covered with water. However, the train track was high enough that the trains continued to run. The engineer stopped the train daily across the street from the store to take on corn, wheat, beans, and cotton. Each day, the engineer would take that opportunity to use the restroom in the back of the variety store.

Evelyn Sanders told me that one day, when the flood waters were at their highest, this engineer was returning from the restroom when *my* Evelyn stopped him to ask a question. She thought everyone would be interested, so she called out loudly, "Sir, did you pass much water this morning?"

Evelyn Sanders said she and the other clerks barely muffled their laughter until the engineer was out the door. Then they laughed until they cried. My Evelyn was embarrassed at first and then laughed along with the others. She laughingly repeated the story in later years, and it became a family legend.

Having a sense of humor is key to making a marriage work. I am so grateful for Evelyn's. It wasn't in her nature to fuss at me, even if she had a good reason to do so.

Instead, her sense of humor smoothed the way. Here's an example:

One evening, after a long day's work and a late supper, I relaxed in my easy chair. I slipped off my work shoes, and Evelyn sweetly brought me a pair of house shoes and placed them at my feet. However, I didn't ever put them on and later went to the bedroom in my sock feet.

The next morning, before I got up, I was trying to decide whether I'd work in the garden or go fishing. I had different shoes for fishing and for working in the garden, so I took both pairs to my chair, intending to decide later.

Evelyn always made our bed, brushed her hair, and put on a little makeup before coming through the living room on the way to the kitchen. She always looked like a movie star to me. On this particular day, she stopped in front of me and looked at the four pairs of shoes and at me.

She would have been in step with many wives, and rightly so, to have said, "Get up from there this minute and put those shoes where they belong." What do you think Evelyn said? She said, "Honey, do you want me to get your Sunday shoes and put them with these shoes?" Then she smiled and went on in to the kitchen to fix breakfast.

I put all of the shoes back where they belonged, with happiness in my heart for having such a loving, caring wife. I'm sure that other men have wives with Evelyn's qualities. I hope they realize that their wives are more precious than silver and gold and rubies and diamonds.

Evelyn Sanders passed up no opportunity to tell me what a wonderful, tender-hearted person my Evelyn was. Among the many stories, she told me how Evelyn would go across the street from the variety store and buy a quart of milk to feed a hungry stray cat.

I saw that same compassion for animals many times over the years of our marriage. We always had one or more dogs that absolutely adored her, as she did them. Evelyn fed the birds, squirrels, deer, and even the catfish in our pond. At one of her schools, she would even feed a little mouse crumbs from her lunch. Fish, fowl, or mammal—she cared for them all.

One Sunday afternoon, Evelyn and I loaded our twelve-foot aluminum boat into our pickup and headed for the Ohio River, where we put out a short trotline baited with dough balls to attract fish, particularly catfish. We trolled around for about an hour and then took up the line. On one of the hooks, we had a beautiful, blue channel catfish—perhaps a five-pounder. I was thrilled; I knew it would be good eating.

Evelyn immediately said, "Isn't it a beauty? It is so full of life and wanting to live. Suppose we give it a dough ball and let it go?" (That phrase had been coined by her on a previous fishing trip after we caught a particularly nice fish.)

I didn't have the heart to spoil a pleasant afternoon for Evelyn. So we let that blue cat go. However, still today in our family, we use the quote as a humorous solution to various problems pertaining to people or animals: "Give them a dough ball and let them go."

One time, when a varmint was helping itself to our sweet-corn patch, I set a live trap to catch the offender. Evelyn went with me to check the cage trap. There sat a big raccoon, as stately as if it owned the garden. I had Evelyn's little Ruger Bearcat .22 pistol in my pocket. She asked, "What are you going to do with the raccoon?" I replied, "I ought to shoot it and feed it to the buzzards."

When I saw the sad look on Evelyn's face, I said, "But I guess I'll give it a dough ball and let it go." I rejoiced at Evelyn's smile of approval. I loaded the cage into my truck, took the raccoon to the top of Eagle Mountain, and released it.

With her gentle, loving nature, Evelyn made quite an impression when she lived in East Prairie (as she did wherever she was). Fifty years after we were married, her sister June wrote the following to LeAnn:

> *Your mother has always been a beautiful, wonderful girl. She was always so good to the kids when she worked at the dime store — a lot of the boys would go in the store just to look at her. People still remember Evelyn when she worked at the dime store. That is because she was so beautiful they couldn't forget her, and she was always so sweet and nice to everyone, just like she is today. She is one special sister that I love very much.*

Evelyn's sweet, loving personality endeared her to all who knew her, whether her family, her co-workers, her friends, or her students.

Before we started our family in 1955, Evelyn joined me in attending night classes and summer school while we pursued a teaching certificate for her and a bachelor's degree for me. Besides doing her own lessons, she found time to type my term papers. As we continued our education, she also typed my master's degree thesis for Dr. Bock, who had the reputation of being the most difficult professor to please on a research thesis. How Evelyn could do all she did and keep smiling, I'll never know. Our schooling together was far from being drudgery — it was a pleasure. Evelyn received her bachelor's degree the same day that I got my master's degree.

That wonderful guiding hand didn't stop its magic with our marriage. By guiding Evelyn into the teaching profession, it shifted into overdrive, enhancing the lives of many others and making Saline County a better place.

I had been teaching in a one-room school in Rudement for five years when the three-man board of education at Pankeyville's two-room school invited Evelyn and me to teach their school. Evelyn was to teach grades one through four, and I, grades five through eight, while also serving as principal.

That was when Evelyn blossomed into a one-of-a-kind teacher. She loved the children of both rooms as if they were her own children. She administered kindness and first aid to all and received love and affection from not only the children in her room but also mine—and the parents as well.

Evelyn went from teaching first through fourth grades at Pankeyville to teaching first grade in the Harrisburg school system, first at McKinley and then at West Side—thirty years in all. At the beginning, she had well over thirty students. Later the class size was much smaller.

The exchange of teacher-student love and friendship that sprang up between Evelyn and her students was nothing short of amazing. The students knew they were loved and accepted. They knew they would receive a smiling greeting on their arrival, and those who needed it got a hug of encouragement at the end of the school day. Evelyn hugged and held the children even when it was not commonplace in the schools at that time. She seemed to know when a child needed a little extra love.

Her schoolchildren never forgot her. Through the years and even after we retired, her former students would come up to her on the street or in a restaurant to say hello and to tell her that she was their favorite teacher ever. She always remembered them and gave them a motherly hug.

Her love was transformative for many of her students.

One child wrote many years later, while in college, of her experience in first grade, after a particularly traumatic kindergarten year in another school, with a harsh teacher who had criticized her for frequent daydreaming. Her mother was kind enough to send the following to Evelyn:

> *Thankfully, I soon realized that Mrs. Wallace was nothing like my previous teacher. . . . I was so starved for one glance of approval or one shred of positive reinforcement that I promptly fell in love with her. Mrs. Wallace did not stop at merely praising my ingenuity. Instead, she started exploring the kaleidoscopic dreamscape of each of her students. Each afternoon, she gave a student an opportunity to share either a topic of interest or an imaginary adventure. She never told any of us our dreams were grandiose or impossible. Instead, we were told to believe in our dreams, to explore the uncharted depths of our imagination, and to define both our world and ourselves as we saw fit. Our daily revelations became the basis for spelling lessons, reading, math, and writing. The imaginary world permeated every remote corner of our first-grade curriculum and the whole class connected with the material on a personal level. Mrs. Wallace both healed my heart and restored my innate curiosity. No day was ever complete without a hug and an encouraging word from my new idol. In her eyes, I was capable of anything, and my grades reflected her support. . . . Her care fostered a new sense of self-worth and confidence in me—things for which I shall always be grateful.*

Evelyn also worked on establishing rapport with her students' parents. For parent-teacher conferences, she would bring in fresh flowers, along with her coffeepot and pretty cups to serve coffee to the parents. Her consideration for them and her obvious love of the children led the parents to also love and admire her. Second-generation students would say words such as these to Evelyn: "Mommy wanted me to get you for a teacher because you are so loving." Many times, I waited patiently to pick her up after school, while she hugged one more child or talked to one more parent. Parents would often come in to tell her about their troubles. She always had time for all of them.

As much as Evelyn loved her students, she also loved her fellow teachers. She was quick to recognize admirable qualities in other first-grade teachers in the Harrisburg school system and was grateful to them for their willingness to help her get off to a good start in becoming an outstanding first grade teacher.

About the same time that Evelyn became a first grade teacher in the Harrisburg school system, I became superintendent and principal of the newly formed Independence School, which was composed of thirteen former one-room school districts. I served thirty years as the only principal of Independence School.

Evelyn had made me aware of the importance of the first grade to a student's subsequent success in school. Whenever I was hiring a new first-grade teacher, I strived to find one with the fine qualities of Evelyn and the good first-grade teachers of the Harrisburg school system.

Evelyn's teacher friends all loved to play jokes on each other, and Evelyn evidently gave as good as she got. For example, her fellow first-grade teacher, Paula Talley, told me about one of the times that Evelyn had played a prank on her.

Evelyn got to school early, because I dropped her off each day before heading back to Independence. Paula said that, that day, she happened to come to school early, too. As Paula came around the corner into her room, there Evelyn stood, by Paula's bulletin board, systematically turning all her decorations upside down and restapling them. When Evelyn heard steps, she turned around, saw Paula, turned back around, and continued her stapling. Then, as if suddenly realizing that she had been caught, she threw her hands over her mouth with a "you-caught-me" look. Then they both doubled over in laughter. Paula said that she liked to play tricks on Evelyn just to see her laugh.

Evelyn definitely loved the camaraderie she shared with the teachers. When we finally retired in 1987, it is hard to say whom she missed more—her students or the teachers. Throughout retirement, she still thought about what they might be doing at school that day.

As much as Evelyn excelled as a teacher, she exceeded all usual standards as a mother and grandmother. She lavished love and kindness on our two children and all of our grandchildren.

In 1955, we had a daughter, LeAnn, and seventeen months later, along came Brother Ray. Never for a moment could either of them doubt how much they were loved. Evelyn doted on them and me, ensuring that we were always well-dressed, well-fed, and cared for. She stayed home with the children for five years before resuming teaching. Then, after taking care of all of us each day, she would often stay up until after midnight, grading papers and getting ready for school the next day. But she never complained about the long hours—she loved what she was doing, and it showed.

One time, while viewing the calendar, LeAnn remarked to Evelyn, "There's Mother's Day and there's Father's Day—why is there no Children's Day?" Evelyn responded,

"Every day is Children's Day." And that is how she lived — as if each day was our children's and, then later, our grandchildren's special day.

She had even more time, since she was retired, to dote on our grandchildren. One of them, Caitlin, spent a lot of her pre-school years with us, since both Ray and his wife, Lisa, worked each day. Caitlin has turned out to be quite a writer herself. I am going to quote just a bit of the many sweet things she has written about her grandmother:

My grandma made such a big difference in my life and I still think about her all the time. The impact that she made on my life is hard to describe. I owe many of my morals and values and a lot of my personality to her. She practically raised me. I learned homemaking from her. I cooked with her, cleaned with her, and helped her organize her pantry and deep freeze. I played school with her. She taught me to read and write and draw. She encouraged me to be creative and paint and draw and sculpt with play dough.

We played games outside and worked in the yard and garden. I spent my childhood at her house. I was there all the time. I remember sitting on her counter and eating cornmeal out of the jar she kept it in at the top of the cabinet. She only got it out to use to fry fish my grandpa had caught. I remember stirring the sugar into the tea in its pretty, curvy pitcher. I remember making mashed potatoes and making gravy in the grease from meat with flour and milk. I remember pounding meat and making hummingbird food.

I remember sitting at the dining room table and drawing swirly designs and coloring them in with her. I remember the birds that lived under her porch. I remember her drawing on my back with her finger and trying to guess what she'd drawn. I remember playing "I spy" and dressing up in her jewelry and scarves. I remember this little box that she had that I would find something from her room to put in it and make her guess what was in it. Then she would hide something and I would guess.

I remember sitting outside in the swing and watching the cars that would come by on the highway. We would get points for every car that passed. I always got the cars and vans and gave her the trucks and SUVs. We would give Papaw the semis although he was never outside with us. I always won. There were always more cars. Sometimes I would lie in the hammock in her yard, while she sat on the swing.

Drawing and painting are still some of my favorite things. I still love to cook, and mashed potatoes are one of my favorite foods. I still love being outside and lying in the hammock.

Evelyn was so loving and generous that all of our grandchildren loved to come visit. The thought of getting to visit with her sent waves of happiness throughout their being.

One day I went down to see my son Ray's garden, to compare his with mine. It took only a minute. I was about to leave when our youngest granddaughter, six-year-old Jillian, ran up and asked "Papaw, can I go up and see Mom-maw?"

I hesitated for a moment, wondering whether it would be a good time for Evelyn to entertain her. I'll never forget what I saw as Jillian and I looked into each other's eyes. Like I'd never before seen in anyone else's eyes, Jillian's eyes literally sparkled.

I replied, "Sure, Jillian, you may go. But first go get permission from your mother." Jillian scurried into her house and soon came back, beaming. We drove up to our house.

Evelyn, as always, was delighted to see one of her grandchildren. She exclaimed, "Jillian, you are here just in time to go with me to the barn and feed the kittens!"

...

The late Will Rogers once said, "I never saw a man I didn't like." I'm a lot like Will Rogers. I never saw a woman I didn't like.

However, love is a different matter. I will always place Evelyn and the memory of her at the top of my list. Why? Because I loved her with all of my heart and will always love the memory of her. She became mine by divine design—I shall always believe that.

I don't believe it was a happenstance that Evelyn became my beloved wife, an outstanding grade-school teacher, a devoted friend, and a wonderful mother and grandmother, to name just a few of her roles. I believe a guiding hand brought it about. Evelyn was a godsend sent to all of us.

I will always be grateful to that guiding hand, which allowed us to have fifty-six happy years together. Even though I now live alone, I'll never be lonely because of the rich and happy past that Evelyn and I experienced together. I trust that the blessings of memory and recall will be with me the rest of my days. I truly believe that the guiding hand responsible for bringing me this far will lead me on.

* * *

Blessed Beyond Measure

It took many moons for me to realize that one day I would become an educator in Saline County in Southern Illinois. My first eight years of schooling took place in a one-room school where a different teacher each year taught all eight grades. With my feelings toward schooling after those first eight years, the idea of being a teacher was not even a distant thought.

Nothing was inherently wrong with the one-room schoolhouse system. Rather, it was some of my father's idiosyncrasies that contributed to my seeming lack of aptitude for my lessons.

My dad was in his late sixties before I reached my teens. He didn't claim to be a preacher, doctor, lawyer, mechanic, or carpenter. However, he knew more than the average man concerning all of the above. He quietly went about his profession of farming and animal husbandry.

Dad wasn't afraid of man or beast. However, he was deathly afraid of storms—wind, lightning, and thunder. Night or day, at the threat of a storm, he would take off to our underground combination storm, fruit, and vegetable cellar. It was cool and damp and could very likely be a habitat for snakes. Dad didn't like to go to the cellar alone, so he took me with him. Those dashes for the storm cellar often deprived me of a night's sleep, which affected my performance at school the next day.

When I was nine and ten years old, Dad often kept me out of school to help build or repair a fence for our herd of sheep. The old rail fence, which enclosed sixty acres of fields and a wood lot, was capped with strands of barbed wire and required frequent attention.

I'm sure that my company meant more to Dad than did my labor. He required my presence whenever we were performing a certain operation on male lambs, and again at shearing time. My help and company were apparently also essential in the fall to help with corn shocking. I wasn't strong enough to handle a regular corn knife, so I used a large butcher knife for cutting the stalks of corn before we bound them together upright into little teepees about six feet wide at the base.

During my years at the one-room Sadler School, my attendance was no more than half time, and my interest in school was no better. However, Mom was very determined that I go to high school. Dad's health failed, which forced us to sell our sheep and reduce our cattle to one milk cow. We were still farmers but on a smaller scale.

High school, in the mid-1930s, was a huge change for me—going from a school with only five or six students per class to a school of more than a thousand total students, with thirty students per class. My biggest handicap was that of being poorly prepared for high school. For example, I remember what a surprise it was to learn that every word was assigned a part of speech—noun, pronoun, verb, etc.—based on its function in the sentence or phrase.

For two summers in my mid-teens, when school was out, I worked on a farm near Ypsilanti, Michigan, for an ambitious, well-to-do farmer named Fred Parsons. He ran cattle, harvested wheat and hay, and owned a ten-acre apple orchard. All of the time I had spent helping Dad instead of going to school had made me a good farmhand. I worked hard, had plenty to eat, and got a wide range of eye-opening experiences while in Michigan. However, after being gone from home for two months, it was grand to be back. The family made a fuss over me. My dog, Tige, hadn't forgotten me and was glad to see me.

A neighbor, Don (not his real name), who was about three years older than I, owned an old jalopy. Soon after I returned from my summer farmhand job, Don asked me to go fishing with him. Now, I hadn't fished much in my earlier years. When I was a youngster, my father thought that it was more important for me to chop weeds out of the corn and to cut the winter's heating and cooking wood. My fishing up to that point had consisted of putting an open safety pin on a string and tossing it into the creek behind our house. So when Don presented me with the opportunity, I jumped at the chance.

We fished in a little creek near Herod. Even with my limited experience, it didn't look too promising to me. We caught ten or twelve catfish—just barely pan-size. But we were happy to be fishing and had a good time.

Spring Valley Church had services the second Saturday evening each month. Don asked me to go with him that evening, and I was pleased to go. Before a number of people in front of the church, Don proclaimed, "Kestner and I went fishing today. We caught the biggest stringer of forktail catfish you ever saw, didn't we, Kestner?"

I wasn't happy lying about our fishing catch, but I didn't want to walk home, either. So I swallowed hard and replied, "We shore did." Little did I know, this would be my last fishing trip and last opportunity to brag about my catch (whether justified or not) for many years to come.

That summer soon came to an end, and it was back to high school again. It was with much difficulty and the benefit of now-perfect attendance that I gradually learned what I should have learned in grade school and managed a passing grade in all of my classes. In my senior year, I even made the honor roll one time. My high school days and two summers working for Mr. Parsons had changed my attitude toward school from a lack of interest to a thirst for learning.

After high school, I took correspondence courses from two different colleges while working in a defense plant in Pontiac, Michigan, before being drafted into the Navy in 1943. When the war was over, I attended the University of Saipan while waiting for transportation home. When all of my credits were evaluated, the Saline County Superintendent of Schools issued a teacher's certificate to me. In the fall of 1946, I began teaching all eight grades in the one-room school at Rudement.

My friend, Don, hadn't had to go to war because of his involvement in large-scale farming. So he gladly filled me in on things I'd missed out on during the time I had been in Michigan and in the Navy. He had been married a few years, and he bragged on his wife being a good housekeeper and a marvelous cook. I could see that she was good looking. Don didn't say, but I soon observed that she had him on a short leash. Don, his wife (whom we'll call "Mary"), and his son (whom we'll call "Bobby") had settled in Pankeyville.

One time Don asked me to go coon hunting with him. He said, "While the dog hunts, we can do a lot of talking." So one dark, coon-hunting night, we were in an area of tall timber. Both of us sat and leaned against a tree, our faces dimly illuminated by a carbide light. I was pleased to see how happy and at ease Don seemed.

He commented, "I pulled a slick one on Mary. I sneaked my boots and coveralls out and put them in the trunk of the car. I left my dog, carbide light, and rifle down at Pop's. I told Mary I planned to visit with Mom and Pop until bedtime." I laughed with him, but I realized that Mary had him buffaloed.

After a long wait, Don's dog, King, let out a loud bawl about 300 yards to the east of us. He had jumped something and was pushing it hard in a counter-clockwise direction while barking with every jump. The chase stayed 300 yards away from us as King and his prey passed to the north of us. I thought that if old King was after a coon, it would take to a tree at any time. However, the chase continued. Finally, when King was due west of us, he barked, "Treed," which was a different kind of bark.

Don and I hurried to King. He sat under a large tree, which would have made three saw logs to the first limb. King continued to bark until Don said, as he petted him, "Now, now, King, good dog. You did your job." Then King stopped barking and looked pleased with himself.

The tree was so tall that neither my flashlight nor Don's carbide light would do more than shine a pair of big, yellow eyes. We couldn't determine what we had treed.

Don said, "I'll shoot it between the eyes, and we can see what it is."

I commented, "We should give that a little thought first."

Don seemed surprised and asked, "Why so?"

I replied, "That might be someone's pet tomcat on a night out."

Don argued, "No, that's not a cat—its eyes are too far apart—maybe it's a huge bobcat."

To delay the shooting, I said, "The Department of Conservation has released some huge Mississippi coons to upgrade our coon population. Should this be one of them, we ought to let it do its thing."

We were enjoying our debate, and it would have gone on longer had that varmint not decided to come down that tree on the side away from us. From previous observations, I had learned that cats generally back down trees. However, the sound we heard was that of something running down the tree headfirst, while making an alarming amount of noise. From a height of about ten feet, it leaped to the ground and took off through the woods. King had stood with his bristles up at the sound of the animal coming down the tree. Don ordered, "No, no, stay." Obediently, King didn't make chase, although every muscle trembled with the effort he made to stay still.

With a sudden return to reality, Don exclaimed, "Do you know what?"

"No—what?"

"It is Mom and Pop's bedtime. We need to hightail it out of here." Thus ended my first and only coon hunt with Don. But Don was to play a further role in my life later on.

...

I married my one and only, lovely Evelyn Green from East Prairie, Missouri, in 1950 and settled on Wallace land in rural Saline County. Not too long after we were married, Bill Butterworth and Mike Gibbs started razzing me. They said, "We are sorry that since you are married, you won't be able to go on an all-night bank-pole fishing trip with us Friday night."

Not wanting a repetition of Don's situation, I quickly protested. "My being married doesn't have anything to do with my going fishing with you."

Arrangements were made. Since Evelyn was a town girl, I thought that she might be afraid to spend a night in the country alone. I asked her if it would be all right for me to go on an all-night fishing trip with a couple of friends, providing that I got my mother to spend the night with her. Her answer surprised and pleased me. She said, "If you want to spend a night fishing with your buddies, I won't be afraid to stay by myself. Old Rover (our big collie) will protect me."

Bill, Mike, and I had a successful night of fishing. We didn't have to lie about our catch. But that was my only all-night fishing trip. I much preferred being home with Evelyn. However, I was happy to know that I could go if I wanted to.

...

One Saturday, I took three of my Rudement School students fishing. They were Billy Duncan, Lyndell Osman, and Jimmy Williams. Evelyn packed us a picnic lunch.

We went to a creek known as the Three Mile Creek. I had been there twice before. Back then, there was no road to it. One had to drive as far as possible and then brave a growth of horseweeds and a thin scattering of cane.

I warned the boys that we needed to stay close together and move forward very, very slowly while keeping a close lookout for snakes. I told them I hadn't seen a snake either time I had been there, but I had been told that cottonmouth snakes lived in the area. So, as far as possible, we proceeded shoulder to shoulder.

Then, all of a sudden, we all saw a coiled-up snake about ten feet in front of us. Its head was sticking up about six inches from the center of the coil, which was about sixteen inches in diameter. There was no doubt in any of our minds what kind of snake it was, even though none of us had ever seen one before. The snake lay there displaying a wide-open, cotton-white mouth.

Before we had left on the fishing trip, the three boys and I had done some rifle practice. Lyndell had proven to be the best shot with a rifle. He was standing on my right. I cautiously handed him a cocked, six-shot revolver loaded with hollow-point bullets — the kind that explode on impact. Privately, I thought that he would miss, and then I would display my marksmanship. I didn't take into consideration that Lyndell might wound the snake, and if it didn't bite us, it might scare us to death.

Lyndell took the pistol and appeared to remember the instruction at rifle practice. He took a fine bead down the sights of the revolver and slowly squeezed the trigger. The bullet hit about a half an inch below the head, and when the hollow point exploded, it took off the snake's head. We all breathed a sigh of relief.

For some strange reason, the desire to fish had left us. Since the small river town, Rosiclare, wasn't far away, we decided to go there and eat our lunch in the park. The snake excitement hadn't affected our appetites. The boys interacted with some other young people and enjoyed the playground equipment. They expressed their appreciation to me for the outing and eagerly related the experience to the students at school on Monday.

One day after school, near the end of my fifth year at Rudement School, I was alone sitting at my desk and running through my mind the events of the day. To my surprise, Don walked in and sat down. Almost immediately he asked, "How long have you been teaching here?"

I told him, five years. With what sounded like the intent

to give good advice, he said, "It is time for you to have a change of scenery and come to Pankeyville to teach our school—both you and your wife. I understand Evelyn has a teacher's certificate. Our two women teachers are going elsewhere. We want a man to be principal and teach the four upper grades. Evelyn can teach the four lower grades."

He continued, "I'm the clerk of the Board of Education. I know, for a fact, that you and your wife can have the school for the asking. Floyd Johnson and Dan Beal are the other two board members. Suppose you come to my house about dark tomorrow evening, and we'll discuss strategy for approaching Dan and Floyd."

I called at Don's home. Mary and Bobby stayed in an adjoining room with the door ajar, although I believed that they were listening. Don and I talked about bygone days. After some time, Don got around to asking, "Kestner, do you ever whip a kid?"

I told him that I had whipped a few but afterwards regretted doing so. Then he wanted to know how I made the kids mind. I told him that I appealed to the children's better side; if that didn't work, I'd give them reason to believe that I might land on them.

"That sounds good. Can you give me an example how that works?"

I drew a blank. I couldn't think of a good example. The incident I related to Don caused him to laugh and almost cost Evelyn and me the opportunity to teach at Pankeyville School for the next five years.

I said, "Don, in the seventh-grade spelling class, I was pronouncing words for the students to write. A good student we'll call 'Mike' was sitting next to the wall. He appointed himself to be watchdog to see if anyone copied. He sat on his leg to make himself taller, so he could see everyone. I didn't feel I needed his help. I saw all I wanted to see and sometimes more. So I said, 'Mike, turn around and sit down.'

"He twisted an inch to the right and an inch to the left and remained the same. I made a bugle-like roll out of the soft-cover spelling book in my hand. I drew back and, making sure not to touch him, I struck the wall just inches above his head with a mighty blow that sounded like a gunshot. I very quietly asked, 'Didn't you hear me say to turn around and sit down?'"

That amused Don, as I knew it would. But I afterwards concluded that the eavesdroppers, Mary and Bobby, didn't think it was funny.

Don saw me out and insisted that I come back another time and tell him more. He said he looked forward to having Evelyn and me teach at their school.

A day or two later, I got a call from Don. He told me that I'd better hold on to my job at Rudement School because something had come up that would stand in the way of our getting Pankeyville School.

Fortunately, I was personally acquainted with Floyd Johnson. He hauled passengers to and from Pontiac, Michigan. On at least two occasions, I had ridden with him. Dan Beal was an electrician; he had done some work for me on some of my rental houses. I called on both Floyd and Dan and believed their word, along with a handshake, was as good as a contract. It held for five years, until I was hired to be superintendent and principal of Independence Consolidated School, and Evelyn was given a teaching position in the Harrisburg school system.

There at Pankeyville, Evelyn had around twenty students in grades one through four. I had about the same number in grades five through eight. Evelyn loved her

students as though they were her own children. She was
like a mother to all the students, in both rooms.

One of my students, Denver Long, was courteous
and mannerly toward me. However, he fell short of being
fully accepted by the majority of the students. I got the
attention of the entire room and asked why Denver was
sometimes shunned, chosen last, and too often blamed
for things.

Denver volunteered, "Last year I didn't behave very
well. I got paddled often and kept in at recess. I got the
feeling the teacher didn't like me. I was snitched on for
the things I did and some things I didn't do. Many of the
students felt I was worse than I really was."

I said, "Tell me no more. I have the picture. I know your
last year's teacher. Please remember her for her love for
learning and her ability to teach well." Then to the class, I
said, "I hope you will see Denver as I see him—as one who
wants to do the right thing and treat others as he would
like to be treated." Denver didn't say "Amen," but I could
tell he was agreeing with me.

I went on to say, "I plan to keep an eye on how you treat
Denver and how he responds to your good treatment."
I'm happy to report that all went well thereafter with no
need for further comment on the subject.

In the course of time, I observed that another of my
students, Darrell Mattingly, was a clock watcher. From
five to ten minutes before dismissal time in the afternoon,
he would drop all pretense of learning. I had a little talk
with him and told him that he was shortchanging himself
in getting an education. I suggested that he improve his
spelling and penmanship at the same time. I pointed out
that he could write his name and spelling words over
and over while trying to do better each time. I assured
him that an attractive signature would impress people

throughout his life that he was an educated person. He said that he would try.

With the consent and blessings of the parents, Evelyn and I took most of our students home with us to spend the night — four at a time. Evelyn made a point of finding out in advance what they would most enjoy for an evening meal. Usually it was hot dogs, hamburgers, potato chips, and the like.

One evening, we had four from my room: Darrell Mattingly, Roger Lane, Denver Long, and Jimmy Johnson. I don't remember what Evelyn fixed for dinner. It must have been good, however, because I remember Darrell pushing back from the table with a big smile and saying, "I do believe this was the best meal I ever ate."

It was planned in advance that we would do some rifle shooting, take in a show at a theater in Rosiclare, and then go to a haunted house. The haunted house, a one-room log house with a lean-to kitchen built on, was the abandoned former home of Billy Boston, his wife, and their daughter, Mertie. All three of them were mentally disadvantaged and were unable to read or write. However, much good could be said about them, including that they weren't afraid of work. Billy had had a small team of mules. He had raised enough corn to feed a cow and some chickens and to fatten two hogs. They had raised a big garden and had canned, dried, and preserved food for winter.

All three of them were well blessed with the ability to hallucinate about things small and great. One time, when I was in my mid-teens, I rode my mule over to see how they were getting along. Billy told me that, while he was chopping wood that morning, President Roosevelt had come by and talked to him for about an hour. Mrs. Boston said, "I took him out a piece of apple pie." Mertie chimed in, "I took him a glass of cold milk. He smiled at me and said sometime he would bring his wife and spend the day with us."

In the late forties or very early fifties, Mrs. Boston died. It took Billy and Mertie two days to determine that she wasn't just sleeping. When Billy died, a year or so later, Mertie told neighbors who came to check on them that he was dead during the day, but at night he would get up and check on things and chop some wood. Neighbors notified the proper authorities, who saw to it that Billy was laid to rest by his wife and that Mertie was placed in a home.

Next of kin took what they wanted, but for the most part, things were left as they were. Even the door was left ajar. Night hunters would go in the log house and leave with a weird feeling that the place was haunted. Some of the stories were frightening and convincing.

I told the boys all of the above. They still wanted to go to the haunted house. Evelyn was also excited about going.

As we drove along the north-south road east of Womble Mountain, something white floated across the road ahead of us. It was about ten feet long, four feet wide, and four feet above the road. We all saw it and wondered what it was. To add to the excitement of the evening, I pretended to be frightened. The stage was set for what followed.

The little old lane that ran from the main road to the haunted house was too rough to drive a car over. So we faced the dark night by the light of a lantern and a flashlight. Evelyn carried the flashlight and held fast to my arm; I carried the lantern. The boys stayed close to Evelyn and me.

When we reached the house, we found the door wide open. Since Evelyn and I were carrying the lights, we went in first. The boys pressed in close behind us. I quoted President Roosevelt: "The only thing we have to fear is fear itself." Then I made my voice as weird as I could and added, ". . . and the ghost of Billy Boston." We all turned around a time or two in order not to miss anything then took a peek into the kitchen.

We observed a homemade ladder nailed to a wall. The ladder led to a three-foot square hole in the ceiling. As we all gazed upward, the most ungodly, blood-curdling noise came from the loft. It sounded like two buck deer locking antlers. Evelyn was clinging to my arm and trembling with fright. The boys were shouting, "Let's get out of here!"

We all did just that. Everyone was convinced that the house was really haunted. (I regret that I don't have a recording of their telling about the experience at school the next day.)

...

Evelyn and I agreed that at play time, I would supervise outside and she, inside. That worked well. There was almost no trouble inside or out.

There was a tall boy (whom we'll call Eddie) in the fourth grade along with Don's son, Bobby. Eddie was polite, friendly, and well-spoken. However, he was so frail that at times he wobbled when he walked. He tried hard to be a part of everything. He admired Bobby and strived to be his friend.

Bobby was a husky boy and big for his age. He never caused me any trouble, but he never looked me in the eye or warmed up to me. I observed that he was sometimes rude to Eddie. One time, he had a light rope around Eddie's neck and was leading him around, saying, "Come on, my little donkey." Thinking that this was a good time to intervene, I walked up to them and said, "Bobby, you shouldn't treat Eddie that way."

Bobby replied, "I'm not hurting him. He doesn't mind. Do you, Eddie?"

Eddie said, "No, I don't mind." I said no more.

A few days later, Don was at school before any students arrived. He greeted me in a friendly manner but had a serious look on his face. He said, "I have a little matter I'd like to take up with you. It concerns Bobby and Eddie. Bobby came home from school yesterday with a skinned forehead, nose, and chin. He said Eddie did it, and that was about all I could get out of him. Mary thought I should have you look into the matter and handle it the way you feel best. We are not suggesting that you paddle Eddie. I'm sure if you feel that Eddie needs a little dressing down, you'll do it. We would rather you didn't mention to Eddie's dad and mom that I had this talk with you. We are neighbors and good friends, and they are good people."

I said reassuringly, "Don, I'll look into the matter the first thing this morning."

Don replied, "I knew I could depend on you."

When Bobby got to school, I asked, "Bobby, what happened to you?"

Bobby, his wounds highlighted with Mercurochrome, replied huffily, "Eddie can tell you. I would like to know why he did what he did. I thought he was my friend."

I told Bobby that I was glad he hadn't been injured any worse and hoped he and Eddie could continue to be friends. Bobby frowned at that statement.

Bobby sat in his seat, which was across the aisle from Eddie's. I sat in a folding chair in the aisle, a few feet from the two seats, while we waited for Eddie to come.

Looking somewhat pale, Eddie came in with his usual reel and wobble. I said, "Good morning, Eddie."

In a soft but clear voice, he replied, "Good morning, Mr. Wallace."

I asked, "How are you, Eddie?"

He answered dully, "Not very good."

"What seems to be your trouble?"

"I didn't sleep very well last night."

"Why didn't you sleep well?"

"I was afraid I was in trouble with you."

"Did you do something you shouldn't have done?"

"I did what I thought I had to do. I hope you don't ask me to say I'm sorry I did it."

"Eddie, you may or may not be in trouble. It depends on what you did and why you did it. Bobby has told me nothing. He asked me to have you tell me. So will you tell me from start to finish what happened?"

Again Eddie addressed me: "Mr. Wallace, you know I'm not very strong like Bobby. I'm no match for him. I think you know he hasn't treated me very nice at times. I never complained, but I didn't like it. Yesterday after the last recess, I felt I had had all I could take. So I put my head down on my desk and thought about what to do." (He showed me how he had wrapped his arms around his head and thought.)

"When school dismissed, I left the schoolhouse and ran out to the road ditch. The water was about ten inches deep, with mud and gravel across the bottom. I got very close to the water by putting one knee on one side and the other knee on the other side of the ditch. Then I put one elbow on one side and the other on the opposite side. My nose was almost touching the water. I cupped my hands around my eyes so I could see better and stared down at the bottom of the ditch.

"Bobby was standing over me within seconds. He asked, 'Eddie, what are you looking at?' I didn't say anything. He asked again, more loudly, 'Eddie, what are you looking at?' I still didn't answer. Bobby grabbed me by the shoulder and demanded, 'Get up, Eddie, so I can see.'

"I got up without saying a word. I just pointed down at the spot where I had been doing my viewing. Bobby got down in the exact position I had been in, with his butt in the air. I grabbed him by the seat of his pants and stood him on his head. Then I took off running for home."

Shame on me, but that struck me as being funny. I knew that I couldn't laugh, so I buried my face in my handkerchief, faked a sneeze and a cough, and rubbed my eyes. I finally managed to say, "Excuse me. The hay fever is bad at this time of year."

With myself under control, I continued, "I get the picture—not too good of a picture. I need a minute or two to think about the proper way to handle this." I knew the suspense would be some punishment. Then, too, I needed to give a little thought as to what message I wanted Bobby to take home to his parents. Then I thought, "Who in his right mind would paddle poor little Eddie?"

After a minute or two, I asked, "Eddie, do you realize the seriousness of your actions? You could have done great injury to Bobby. You could have caused him to suck water into his lungs and drown. You could have caused injury to his eyes or broken his neck or worse. I feel that kind of behavior calls for strong action."

Bobby had a pleased look on his face. Eddie must have taken a deep breath and been holding it. When he let it out, it came out with a whoosh, similar to the sound a mother deer makes to warn her young of danger.

Eddie exclaimed, "I knew it would happen sooner or later!"

I said, "Eddie, when I was in school, I did something as bad as you did. My good teacher gave me a second chance. If you will promise me that you won't do anything like that again, I'll let you off this time."

I almost laughed at Bobby's comment: "Don't worry. He won't do *that* again."

...

Several decades have passed since those days at Rudement and Pankeyville. Independence School District was formed in 1958 and educated thirty years' worth of children, before the school was closed in 1987. Evelyn and I retired in 1987 and enjoyed nineteen more years together. During these years of retirement, I have been able to fish any time my bones told me that the fish would bite.

Darrell Mattingly eventually became owner and successful operator of the Garden Patch Restaurant in Pankeyville. Once while I was dining there, Darrell asked me, "Do you remember suggesting that I write my name over and over to improve my penmanship?"

I told him I did.

He then replied, "I'm proud of the way I write my name. I think of you each time I do so."

About three months ago, I attended the funeral of a friend at the Reed Funeral Chapel in Harrisburg. Before the service began, I stood for a few seconds with the spouse of the deceased. I brushed a tear from my eye as I started toward the back of the chapel to find a seat. About halfway back, a tall, well-dressed man with a neat mustache and graying hair stood and reached past two people to shake my hand. He realized that I didn't recognize him. He said, "Denver Long—you were the best teacher I ever had."

I said, "Thank you, Denver." I managed to get seated before the computer of my mind took me back to the little scene that concerned Denver at Pankeyville School. Tears filled my eyes.

...

Now at eighty-eight, after forty-one years of teaching and twenty-two years of retirement, I sit here at my kitchen table and recall a few of the many blessings I've enjoyed in those sixty-three years. All of them are too numerous to mention.

I recall the last day of school at Independence School at the end of May 1987. The students came to school on that date to get their grade cards and say their final goodbyes to the school. With the school's closing, the fifty-five-square-mile area that had made up the Independence School District was becoming part of the Harrisburg school system.

At 10:30 a.m., an automatic bell rang to dismiss the children. The teachers had said their goodbyes and best wishes to me and were going out the side doors as the students stormed out the front entrance. I just barely got one of the double doors fastened back and was holding the other as the students rushed out, forgetting they were to walk—just being children.

The students were on their buses before it dawned on them that they hadn't told me goodbye. So the next scene was one that blessed my heart. With dozens of heads and arms sticking out of the bus windows, the students shouted, "Bye, Mr. Wallace. We love you. You are a good principal."

I went into the office and sat in a chair fit for a king. The good parents of the PTA had bought it for me. My heart was full of love. My eyes were full of tears. The past forty-one years flashed before my eyes. I realized then, and I realize even more now, that I have been blessed beyond measure.

* * *

Politics of Years Ago

I guess politics is in my blood. In 1948, when I was twenty-eight, I decided to run for the office of justice of the peace in Mountain Township in Saline County. My grandfather, Jonathan Wallace, and my uncle, General Lew Wallace (whose looks reminded me of Abraham Lincoln), had been justices of the peace, so I decided to keep up the tradition.

Since I had begun teaching at Rudement's one-room school a couple of years earlier and was busy with other activities, I hoped to enjoy the ease of running unopposed. However, it didn't work out that way.

Not long after I announced my candidacy, a friend of mine also announced that he was running, but on the opposing ticket. Had he announced before I did, I wouldn't have come out against him for fear it would affect our night fishing and coon hunting together. But I decided that if my opponent wanted a race, I'd give him a good friendly one—just for the fun of it.

About that time, a number of men stopped wearing hats unless the weather was cold. I was one of them. But I decided that if I wanted to look important and respectful

350

to the women from Mountain Township, I'd need to get myself a good-looking hat to tip when I happened to see any of them in town on Saturdays.

Shortly thereafter, I was dining at a restaurant in Harrisburg. At the table next to me sat a man and a woman. The man was wearing a fancy Stetson. I commented to him that I admired his hat. The man replied, "I am a minister of the gospel. My wife doesn't like my hat. She says it makes me look too haughty. If it fits you, I'll sell it to you."

Shaking my head, I replied, "I can't afford a hat that expensive."

Then he asked, "Will you give me a dollar for it?"

I was surprised at the low price. Knowing I would feel guilty if I paid only a dollar for the hat, I answered, "Since you are a minister, I'll even give you two dollars for it." When I left the restaurant, I was wearing a perfectly fitting Stetson hat. I was well pleased with my bargain.

Time was getting away from me. I was behind in letting the good people of Mountain Township know that I was a candidate. Early one Saturday morning three weeks before the election, I decided to call on some of the folks north and east of Somerset. To my disappointment, few people were at home.

Among those I found at home was an old-timer who lived alone. He appeared gruff and grumpy. I said cheerily, "Good morning, sir. How are you?"

He replied irritably, "I'm not worth a darn. If the arthritis don't get me, the lumbago will. What do you want? I bet you want money."

"No, I'm not after money. Guess again."

He then said, "With shined shoes, necktie, and a twenty-dollar hat, you must be a preacher. If you are, you can't save me. I'm not even lost. More than that, nobody cares for me, and I don't care for nobody."

"Mister, you sound like an unhappy man. I hope all of your tomorrows will be better."

"That's right pretty talk, but you ain't told me what you want."

"You're right. I haven't. I was so carried away with your unhappy state of affairs, I just about forgot why I stopped by. I came to ask you to vote for me for justice of the peace. Do you vote?"

"Sometimes I do, and sometimes I don't. Most of the time I do."

Suddenly, the old man's face brightened up as he said slyly, "If you'll do something for me, I'll do something for you."

By that time, I began to think that I was wasting my time. I replied, "Mister, I'll make you this promise: if I'm elected justice of the peace, whether or not you vote for me, I'll see that you get justice if you come before me." As I made my exit, I said earnestly, "I hope you are feeling better when I see you next."

Since I like people, I don't regret the time I spent with this man. After all these years, I still remember him well.

It was still early Saturday morning. I decided that the majority of these country folks had probably gone to Harrisburg to do their Saturday shopping, so I decided to beat it to town and start tipping my hat. I figured I'd be pretty good at it because, for practice, I had tipped my hat to our old red rooster and the pet goat of my youngest brother, Gaylord.

When I got to town, I decided that I wouldn't mention to the ladies that I was a candidate. I thought the word would get around, and my friendliness would get the job done. I hoped that the women would have a good influence on the men in the family.

I have no way of knowing how many votes I gained by my hat-tipping. For fear I was making a fool of myself, I only tried it that one Saturday.

I was courting my future wife, Evelyn, at that time. She had been reared by her grandparents, Mr. and Mrs. Ray Fulkerson. Mr. Fulkerson was mayor of East Prairie, Missouri, and he felt the importance of his office. Mr. Fulkerson and I got along well. We both loved to trade, trying to get the best of the other. Mrs. Fulkerson commented that Mr. Fulkerson would rather trade than eat.

The next Saturday, when I was visiting Evelyn in East Prairie, I had Mr. Fulkerson try on my hat. We both agreed that the Stetson looked better on him than it did on me. So I traded it to him for an almost-new Case pocketknife.

Now, I'll tell you a result of my friendly hat-tipping. The next week, I got five invitations—to birthday parties, wedding showers, and a baby shower. I ended up attending all except the baby shower. I asked my sister Hazel to go to it in my place and take a present and a card that read "From Hazel and Kestner Wallace."

When Hazel returned from the shower, I asked, "Hazel, did you do me any good tonight?"

She answered, "You be the judge. When our nice present was held up and it was announced from 'Hazel and Kestner Wallace,' one of the ladies called out, 'Hazel, is your brother Kestner running for justice of the peace?'

"I said yes. This lady then asked, 'Do you think he will get elected?'

"I answered honestly: 'I don't know—I hope he does. He really is a good, honest fellow. But instead of election-eering Saturday, he left early and went to East Prairie, Missouri, to see his girlfriend. He took his hat and some trading stuff with him to trade with Evelyn's granddad and his cronies while he waited for Evelyn to get off work at the variety store. He came back with a pocketknife, a beat-up .38 pistol, and no hat. He had fun. But that won't get him elected justice of the peace.'

"This gal wasn't ready to let the subject drop. She up and asked, 'How can this group help your brother get elected?'

"I thought for a moment and then said, 'There isn't much you can do. However, I suppose you could use your influence on his behalf and ask others to vote for him.'"

I had a big smile on my face when Hazel stopped talking. I declared, "Hazel, you did me more good than I'd have done if I'd stayed in Mountain Township and electioneered." Encouraged by Hazel's success, I attended the other parties and hoped that I did some good, as well.

Election Day drew near. I began to have mixed emotions. I feared that I'd feel bad however the election went. It would make me feel a little sad to lose the election. That might keep me from ever running for anything else. On the other hand, if I were to win, I worried that my opponent friend—who was a little thin-skinned—would be standoffish and refuse to go hunting and fishing with me. There wasn't much I could do about that, so I decided to let things run their course.

Rudement School, where I taught, was in Independence Township, which adjoined Mountain Township. Therefore, my students didn't know that I was a candidate for justice of the peace in Mountain Township. With thirty students scattered throughout eight grades, I almost forgot that I was a candidate while I was at school.

On Election Day, at the close of the school day, my mind turned to voting. I hurried home and picked up Hazel, my mother, and an older couple whom we had lined up to ride with us to the polling place at Somerset.

We were traveling on the rough gravel road from Route 34 to Somerset. Road conditions caused cars to move along slowly. At a particularly rough, narrow spot, my opponent and I were almost stopped side by side, going in opposite directions. I threw up my hand in a friendly gesture. I observed his jaw tighten, and he looked straight ahead without waving back.

My gang and I went in and voted. We learned that, for some reason, the voting turnout was particularly large. I took my passengers home and later went to the polling place to observe the vote count, which was permitted. I saw that my opponent had had the same thought.

At first, my name and my opponent's name were called about equally. I thought to myself that it was turning out to be a close race. I was sitting where I could observe my opponent's face. Each time that my name was called, his jaw tightened a little. Now and then, my name was called twice to his once.

Then the vote count began to change clearly in my favor. I knew that my Uncle Sherman had put in a good word for me on the Eagle Creek side of the mountain, so I figured it was the Eagle Creek vote that was putting me over the top. To myself, I predicted victory. I quietly slipped from the voting house and went home. I had no desire to gloat over my winning.

Through the years, my interest in politics never waned. I was a candidate and was elected for other minor Saline County positions, such as precinct committeeman and representative committeeman.

One time, with a write-in vote, I was placed in nomination to run against the well-known and well-liked C. R. Gardner for superintendent of schools in Saline County. I knew, and Mr. Gardner knew, that there wasn't a chance of my defeating him. At the same time, I recognized that he would prefer the comfort of running unopposed. My party had put my name in nomination mostly to round out the ticket and also possibly to bring out other votes that would benefit the ticket.

I went to Mr. Gardner and said, "Mr. Gardner, I know you are trembling in your boots about my opposing you, aren't you?"

His answer was slightly sharp: "Not really."

I laughed and replied, "That is the answer I expected. However, you and I know that sometimes strange things happen. Probably if you had your druthers, you would just as soon run unopposed." I went on without giving him a chance to comment. "I'm here with a proposition concerning my request that my name be dropped from the ballot. I have it all written out here." I indicated the paper in my hand and continued. "In it, I thank those who nominated me as a candidate with a write-in vote in the primary. I state a number of reasons why I'm requesting that my name be withdrawn from the ticket. Mr. Gardner, all I'm asking for is a little publicity for my withdrawal. I know if I were to take this letter to the *Daily Register* and ask them to publish it for me, they would throw it into the waste can. But with your prestige, they will publish it for you."

I paused, gave him a little grin, and added, "However, without a public withdrawal, I'll stay in the race. I took debating and public speaking in high school. I'll go to all the meetings, talk up a storm, and have the time of my life."

I handed him the paper and said, "Read it over and tell me what you wish to do."

With a serious look on his face, Mr. Gardner read what I had written. I was the one shaking in my boots. I knew that Mr. Gardner was aware of my All-Grade Supervisory Certificate—a requirement for county superintendents of schools — because it had come from Springfield through his office. However, I also knew that I wasn't well known throughout other parts of Saline County. Mr. Gardner was well known and well liked in Eldorado, Harrisburg, Galatia, and Carrier Mills.

As I waited and Mr. Gardner read, I could almost hear what I feared his reply would be: "I don't want to have anything to do with this letter. I welcome a race with you."

My fear turned to gladness when Mr. Gardner finished the letter and stuck out his hand to shake mine. He said, "I'll take this letter to the *Daily Register* within the hour. It will probably be in tomorrow's paper."

At that moment, our everlasting friendship was established. Mr. Gardner and his good assistant, John Murphy, seemed to go the extra mile to be helpful to me concerning the running of Independence School, where I was the principal by that time. I was happy to have Mr. Gardner's grandchildren as students at Independence School. On seeing them, I would think pleasantly of their grandfather. Years later, when Mr. Gardner happened to see my son, Ray, he would always kindly inquire about me.

The years passed, and I continued to be reelected as precinct committeeman in Mountain Township. In 1987, when I retired as an educator after forty-one years in the school system, I decided it would be a good time to retire as precinct committeeman, too. At the age of sixty-seven, after holding the office for many years, I had become weary of the responsibilities.

Ray evidently has politics in his blood, too. When I retired, he ran for precinct committeeman of Mountain Township and has held the office ever since.

Often, late at night, Ray and I discuss the politics of Mountain Township, Saline County, the state of Illinois, and the nation. We are fairly loyal to our own political party but also hold the other party in high regard. We both look forward to the day when the two parties will work together for the well-being of our wonderful country. While I still love to listen to all the political jawboning on TV, I am content to pass the torch to the next generation and beyond.

*   *   *

Granddaddy and Pony Boy

C upid worked fast in my case. During World War II, Evelyn Green and I worked in different defense plants in Pontiac, Michigan. In the spring of 1943, we met and talked for less than an hour at her aunt's house. Her black shoulder-length hair, ruby-red lips, and attention-getting body made a lasting impression on me. Through the intervention of Evelyn's aunt, who evidently saw the gleam in my eye, I learned her address—84 Oliver Street—and engraved it forever in my mind.

Soon thereafter, Evelyn and I left Pontiac on different missions. Uncle Sam wanted me in the U.S. Navy. I learned later that Evelyn was called back to East Prairie, Missouri, to care for her ailing grandmother, who, along with her grandfather, had raised her from a very young baby.

After a few months in the Navy, I got an East Prairie address for Evelyn, and we corresponded sporadically until I was discharged from the Navy in 1946. On coming home, I went to East Prairie and became acquainted with Evelyn's grandparents. They took an immediate liking to me. I felt as if I had I lost a good friend when Evelyn's grandmother died a few weeks later.

Evelyn's grandfather, Ray Fulkerson, who was long-time mayor of East Prairie, after some period of time married an outstanding woman, Willie. I was amazed how well suited they were for each other. They both made me feel welcome when I went to see Evelyn.

Evelyn and I were married in 1950. In the years before our marriage as well as after, Ray and I did some big trading on a small scale. Ray loved to trade. He would buy, sell, or trade anything from pocketknives and watches to cars, houses, and building lots. Trading between the two of us was mostly focused on cheap guns. At that time, a person could buy a used gun for ten dollars, sell it for fifteen dollars, and be proud of himself.

I recall one time when I was sitting at the "old-timer's" table across the street from Falkoff's Department Store, where Evelyn worked. Several older men liked to sit, talk, and play checkers under a big shade tree there. I didn't know any of them, and they didn't know me. Mr. Fulkerson came walking up. One of the guys commented softly to the others, "Here comes the skinflint mayor." The one who said that was the first one to say, "Hi, Ray, old pal."

Ray didn't say anything but reached into his pocket, pulled out a knife, and handed it to the guy. In turn, that guy handed him a knife. Both did some serious knife inspecting. They checked the number of blades and the condition of the back spring. They took notice of a certain snapping sound in closing. Finally, the other fellow said to Ray, "I'll give you my knife for yours."

Ray jumped as if he had been touched with a charged cattle prod as he said, "I wouldn't think of trading even . . . but I would trade for a quarter."

The fellow replied, "Ray, you are the hardest fellow I ever traded with, but I'm going to take you up on your offer." Both seemed pleased.

Evelyn told of a man who asked her granddaddy how he would trade houses. In less time than it sometimes took to trade knives, Ray told him that he would trade for $5,000. The man took him up on the offer. Ray spent the $5,000 improving the house he'd traded for. In the end, everyone was happy.

I was never the trader that Ray was, but I picked up a few pointers. He would take me around to some old-time gun traders each time we visited. I'd bring home two or three guns that I could sell for a few more dollars than I'd given for them.

One time, after visiting Ray and Willie with Evelyn and our children, I had two .38 pistols and a sawed-off shotgun under my seat. I got stopped by two policemen just outside of Charleston, Missouri, and wondered if I was being checked to see whether I had any illegal guns in my possession. I was relieved to be informed that a robbery had taken place and that they were checking to see if I had any hitchhikers. I told them that I had two outlaws in the backseat, but they were under seven years of age. They used their flashlights, saw that I was telling the truth, and waved me on.

Ray was a strong Democrat. I found him wrong about some things. But he wasn't wrong about believing that Evelyn and our children, LeAnn and Ray, were the "finest people on the top side of the earth," as he liked to say.

I have always regretted that I didn't ask him for Evelyn's hand in marriage, because it would have done him so much good to get to lecture me about how I would have to treat her. I thought a lecture to that effect was something that I didn't need, since we were already in our late twenties.

However, that failure on my part didn't affect our friendship. He took pride in introducing me as his son-in-law, and he loved being "Granddaddy." He was thrilled that our son was named Ray after him. He was just as proud of LeAnn and bought her a cowboy outfit that included a cowboy hat, belt, holster, and two real-looking pistols. She liked being a cowboy more than her brother Ray did.

Granddaddy promised LeAnn and Ray that he would be on the lookout for a pony for them. Along about that time, the grocery store owner near Granddaddy's home set up a drawing for a pony. People could put their name in a box each time they came into the store and bought something. Granddaddy saw that as a way of getting his grandchildren a pony without it costing him anything. Willie told me that he was embarrassing her by going to the store so often and buying only one small item. He especially liked to stand around in front of stores just off Main Street, puffing on cigars that he'd bought one at a time.

Granddaddy called and told us when the drawing was to be—7:00 p.m. on a certain day at the neighborhood grocery store—and that he hoped we could come down for the drawing. Evelyn wasn't free to go, so she and Ray stayed at home. LeAnn, who was about seven, and I headed to East Prairie. She was very excited about the prospects of getting a pony. I secretly hoped that we wouldn't get one. In my younger days, I had gotten my fill of horses and mules. Still, I tried to act excited.

At 7:00 p.m., Granddaddy, LeAnn, and I were standing in the store, which was packed with people. The store owner shook the big box of names, gave the slips a vigorous stirring, and called on a little girl to pick out a name. She did so and handed it to him. He looked at the name for the longest time with what I thought was a disappointed look on his face. Then he announced: "Ray Fulkerson." LeAnn and Granddaddy were happy beyond words. After she caught her breath from screaming and jumping up and down, LeAnn immediately said, "We're naming him 'Pony Boy.'"

We had promised Ray that we would call him just after the drawing to let him know if Granddaddy's name had been called. Evelyn later told me that Ray was watching the clock and at exactly 7:00 p.m., he said, as though he had had a vision, "Granddaddy just won a pony." Within minutes, we were calling to let him know for sure.

We led Pony Boy over to Granddaddy's. I could tell that Willie was about as excited as I was. But she played her part well.

Granddaddy and I pondered how we could best get Pony Boy to Illinois. I commented that if my car were a four-door instead of a two-door, we could haul Pony Boy in the back of the car.

Granddaddy liked the idea and said that his car had headroom and four doors; we could take Pony Boy in his car. We put the backseat cushion in the trunk and opened the doors on both sides. We walked Pony Boy around the car a time or two, then walked him into the car and quickly closed the doors on both sides — just like clockwork. Having gotten that four- or five hundred-pound, all-muscle, buckskin-looking pony loaded made us proud of ourselves.

We said goodbye to Willie and told her that we would see her sometime the next day. We thought we would be a first—transporting a pony in a passenger car.

All went well down Main Street. Just as we reached the outer edge of East Prairie, however, Pony Boy became restless. He decided that he was facing the wrong direction and proceeded to turn around. In the process of doing so, he pushed his rump into the back of the driver's seat, forcing me painfully into the steering wheel.

I quickly pulled the car onto the shoulder. We were fully convinced that we weren't going to make it to Illinois with that pony in the car.

About that time, a city police officer stopped and asked if were having trouble. Fortunately, Pony Boy was quiet at that moment. I put on a big smile and said, "Thank you for asking. Everything is under control." He drove off. I never knew whether the officer saw the pony or recognized the mayor in the car.

We got Pony Boy out of the car, and Granddaddy walked him back to his house. We called Evelyn and Ray to let them know that we had decided to spend the night with Granddaddy and Willie and would bring the pony home in a U-Haul the next day, getting there in time for dinner.

Granddaddy wasn't willing to share the blame in the unwise attempt to transport a contrary, undisciplined pony in a car. He commented, "Anyone who would try such a thing wasn't too smart under the hat." That was just a passing thought that ran through his mind, and he had to put it in words. That little incident had no lasting effect on a most wonderful friendship. In fact, as time passed, it became downright funny, and we laughed many times over our backseat pony.

* * *

Don't Rob Another Man's Castle

I started fishing in the early 1950s and continue to this day. Did I set any records for size or number? No, but I caught plenty for the table and some to give away — provided that I cleaned them first.

My wonderful wife, Evelyn, liked fish and was an expert at frying them. Even more delightful, she didn't mind my fishing often. It was also fine with her if I gave the catch away before I got home.

At first I felt guilty going so often when there were always things that needed to be done. It didn't take her long to catch on to when I wanted to go fishing. I'd walk around like a caged lion until she would say, "Why don't you and Cletus go fishing?"

I'd say, "That's the best idea I've heard today." By and by, she would just ask, "Are you and Cletus going fishing today? I thought I would ask and save you some shoe leather."

When I went fishing alone, I didn't take a lunch. I just came home when I got hungry. When Cletus went with me, Evelyn fixed us a lunch in a little cooler: two drinks — a Coke and a Mountain Dew — a couple of cans of Vienna Sausages, a banana each, and perhaps some cookies.

One day, I called Cletus. His phone was busy. I supposed his wife was on the phone. I loaded my fishing equipment, bait, and cooler of food into the trunk of my fishing car and went to Cletus's home. When I got there, no one was home. I took off alone, which I didn't mind.

As I crossed the upper end of Pope County into Hardin County, I pondered whether to fish Big Creek just north of Elizabethtown or Three Mile Creek just south of Rosiclare. When I got to what used to be called the Humm's Wye, I decided to fish the mouth of Lusk Creek at Golconda.

On reaching Golconda, I turned left and went through town and up onto the levy. On the river side of the levy, I followed a little road that led to the mouth of Lusk Creek. Within a few yards of the creek was a shelter, complete with picnic tables.

A suntanned, pleasant-faced man of medium build, with blue eyes and salt-and-pepper hair, sat at one of the tables. I guessed him to be in his late sixties or early seventies. He appeared to be solemn, but friendly. Near the shelter was a sturdy bicycle with a two-wheeled trailer attached. It was well-laden with a camping outfit. The man had a neat, burned-down fire going.

He and I spoke. I got the feeling that we might have something in common—if nothing else, perhaps a love for nature and water.

I commented that the fire couldn't be for heat. The sun was taking care of that. "Where are the fish?"

He answered: "I love fish, but I'm not a fisherman. I built the fire to warm some pork and beans. My food supply is temporarily down to only pork and beans. I'm burned out on them, so I wait until I'm hungry, heat them over a campfire, and eat them hot. But that will change today or tomorrow. I hope to get my Social

Security check by General Delivery at the post office."

I stepped out of character for a moment and bragged on my fishing ability. The truth of the matter is that sometimes I catch fish and sometimes I don't. However, I egotistically claimed, "We will have fish cooking on that fire in nothing flat."

He replied, "Sounds good to me. I can already hear my gut growling."

"Since fish don't bite until they are ready, let's eat a little snack I have in a cooler in the trunk of my car. My wife fixed a lunch for my fishing buddy and me. He wasn't home, so you can be my buddy." I stuck out my hand and said, "My name is Kestner."

My new buddy clasped my hand as he exclaimed, "That's music to my ears. I'm Jake."

We cleaned up everything I had brought for lunch. It did my heart good to see Jake eat. When we were about finished, Jake said, "If you had asked me, I would have said grace before we ate. I'm not all that religious, but I'm really grateful to you and God for a good meal."

"You are more than welcome. It tasted better to me having someone to eat it with."

"I'm fortunate your buddy wasn't at home."

"Can you clean fish?"

"You bet I can. I have a sharp knife—that is more than half the battle."

"What kind of fish do you like?"

"When you haven't had fish in a long time, any kind tastes good."

"I've fished here different times and have caught different kinds of fish. I've also fished here and caught nothing—not even a nibble."

"Is that what is called 'well-digger's luck'—a wet butt and an empty gut?"

"Yep, you got that right, even if you are not a fisherman."

Jake asked if I had any children. I told him that I had two grown children — a daughter, LeAnn, and a son, Ray. Before going on to tell him more about them, I asked him to give me a thumbnail sketch of his life.

He replied, "I made a mess of my life forty-five years ago, and I will regret that the rest of my life. I don't wish to talk about it."

I quickly assured him, "Your choice. Don't tell me anything that will make you uncomfortable."

After thinking deeply for a few moments, Jake offered, "If you will tell me one incident in your life that you will never forget, I'll do the same."

Put on the spot, I couldn't come up with anything about myself that seemed appropriate. Instead, I said, "Jake, I've had few experiences worth writing home about. If I may, I'll tell you a story another fellow told me about an incident that alarmed him and made him feel that it was a warning from God. This happened long ago and was told only to me."

With a little grin, Jake stated knowingly, "What you are doing, Kestner, is taking the Fifth Amendment to keep from telling on yourself. But go ahead and tell his story."

"This fellow told me he was in love with a fair lady that lived in another state. The love affair was one-sided. His feelings for her were far greater than her love for him. He almost went overboard expressing his feelings for her. He let her know that life without her would be meaningless — a horrible existence. He told her that his heart ached when he realized her love for him, when weighed in the balance, was found wanting. He complimented her to high heavens for the fact that she was pleasant and courteous to the point that he couldn't throw in the towel and call it quits. He went on to tell her that he didn't think he would live long without her.

"This friend told me she listened to his lament while scarcely breathing. He began to hope he was making progress.

"This took place late at night in his car in the driveway of her home, before he left for home. Silence prevailed for a long time. When she finally replied, she put a dagger in his heart. In a soft voice just above a whisper she said, 'As you go home, when you are on top of the bridge that crosses the river, stop the car and get out.' At that point, she went silent for the longest time—long enough for him to think she was intending to say something like 'toss in a coin and make a wish.' That was not what she said. She said, 'And jump off the bridge.'

"He said there was no goodnight kiss. In silence, he made his departure. While her final words were ringing in his ears, it dawned on him that she didn't love him. As the old saying goes, 'His skull must have been six ax handles thick.'

"Now the man really wasn't as dumb as I've made it sound. He admitted to me that in his heart of hearts he knew and had known all along she didn't love him, and he was almost ready to throw in the towel when she suggested that he jump off the bridge.

"As he drove swiftly along that moonlit night around midnight, he began to ponder what he should do next. A former girlfriend crossed his mind. He had reason to believe she would leave her husband for him. The thought lifted his spirits some. He thought this ungrateful girl he had just left could jump off the bridge herself.

"That being settled, this troubled man decided to listen to some music on the car radio. He was topping a moonlit hill and knew the reception would be good. With the turn of the radio knob, a pleasant voice sang out, 'Don't rob another man's castle.' That caused cold chills to go over my friend.

"He said, 'I snapped off the radio and drove on home, fully believing I had received a message from God through the radio.' My friend didn't know—and I didn't tell him any differently—that what he had heard was the title of a poem written by Jenny Lou Carson and made famous by Eddy Arnold in 1949. And that's the end of the story."

Jake exclaimed, "Heavenly days! There is no way I can top that story."

Shaking my head, I said, "Jake, you don't have to top it. Your story is just what it is."

Jake replied, "I'm going to streamline my story, so you can catch me a mess of fish. This is it in a nutshell.

"I met, fell in love, and married the sweetest girl I ever saw. We lived together happily for more than two years when new neighbors, a man and wife, moved within a mile of us. This man was large, pleasant, and inclined toward being happy-go-lucky, if you can envision that.

"This man's young wife was one-of-a-kind. She could say more with her eyes and mouth without saying a word than any other woman I'd ever seen. The movement of her eyes, mouth, and body behind her husband's back caused cold chills to run all over me. She didn't have me fooled. I knew her type. My ego told me she needed a hot-blooded he-man like me to bring her down a notch or two. What a fool I was.

"She got me word that her husband would be gone a certain time in case I wanted to drop in for a chat. In the middle of our chat, her husband popped in. He was entirely a different man than I had seen before. He didn't say a word but went to a dresser, took out a small caliber pistol, and shot me in the gut. The pain and the thought of dying caused me to faint.

"When I came to my senses, this man was kneeling over me, saying, 'I didn't mean to kill you. I just meant to scare the hell out of you. This gun is easy on the trigger and went off before I intended for it to. I meant to shoot you in the foot.'

"The man took me to a hospital in Memphis, Tennessee. On the way, we agreed that my getting shot was an accident.

"The gunshot wasn't as bad as it might have been. The bullet went through me without striking any bones or causing much internal bleeding. I was told I might have to spend a week or ten days in the hospital. I was one lucky bird. Soon I'd be back with my good wife nursing me back to health.

"Well, I was wrong about getting nursed back to health by my wife. That other wayward wife or beguiling gal or whatever you want to call her wasted no time in telling her best girlfriend the whole story. Of course it was too good for her girlfriend to keep to herself. When the word reached my wife, she packed my clothes, threw them out along with me, and filed for a divorce. And that's my story in a nutshell."

I never took my eyes off Jake as he told his story. He had a faraway look in his eyes. His story touched a tender spot in my heart. I thought that it was only by the grace of God that more men hadn't made the same mistake. I said, "Jake, I'm always a man of few words, but your story leaves me speechless. Thank you for sharing something so personal with me."

I was ready to fish and hoped that I would catch a big one for my new friend. I could see that Jake was glad that I was finally ready to fish.

Jake sat under the shelter. I took my extension pole with a hook and a line for catching blue gill and crappie. The line was rather strong. I baited the hook and adjusted the float to fish about three feet deep. When I dropped the line in the water, the float didn't stop when it hit the water. It continued to sink.

I thought the sinker must have been too heavy for the float. I was wrong. A fish had nabbed the bait almost as soon as it had hit the water. I set the hook and soon realized that I had a big one on the line. It felt like trying to lead an unruly dog with a twine string.

I allowed the fish to pull the pole until it almost touched the water. I managed to get the fish turned toward me and called for Jake to get the five-foot bamboo stick that I had seen on the picnic table and to come give me a hand.

He hurried down with the stick and kidded, "Did you hook one you'll have to knock in the head before you can land it?"

I replied, "You'll see why I need the stick."

I handed the fishing pole to Jake and asked him to keep the same amount of pull or pressure on it. I used the stick like a staff in my left hand to balance me, and following the line with my right hand, waded in slowly toward the fish.

As I neared my fish, it slowly submerged. I was hip deep in the water as I reached underwater for the fish. Finally, with my cheek only inches from the water, I felt the hook in the tough rim of something's mouth. Was it a catfish, a gar, a carp, or a turtle? I didn't know. But, cautiously, I was going to find out. When I ran my hand past the head and felt scales, I knew that it wasn't a turtle or a catfish. My fingers reached the pulsing of the fish's gills. That was when I nailed it and told Jake that he could ease off because I had it. I backed out of the water while keeping my balance with the stick.

With the fish on the bank, I was happy. Jake was over-joyed. He'd already planned to eat a filet off each side of the fish that day, then cram the rest in a glass jar and preserve it with salt and vinegar for the next day. The fact that the fish was a carp didn't bother him at all. Jake said he would filet it while I caught some fish to take home. I told him that living through two stories and landing that fish had me all tuckered out. I further told him that I had forgotten some of my fishing trips, but this was one I'd never forget.

I drip-dried for a few minutes before going back to my car. I had left my billfold in the trunk just in case I got wet. I decided to give Jake some money. On looking in the billfold, I saw I had no ones. In my imagination, I heard Evelyn say, "Give the poor man a ten." Being less generous than Evelyn, I gave him a five.

He took the five and said, with emotion, "I don't know how to thank you, Kestner."

Touched with his gratitude, I replied, "Don't thank me—thank the Man above."

As I prepared to leave, I had a feeling that I had known Jake for more than just a short time. Perhaps he felt the same way. With questioning eyes, we gazed at each other. He may have been reading me like a book. At best, I could only wonder about the forty-five years since his wife had kicked him out. Had he gone to school? He appeared to be educated. How had he earned his Social Security?

Just before I left, Jake and I shook hands. I said, "Jake, I really have enjoyed the time we've spent together today. I hope all will go well with you day by day."

Jake replied, "Kestner, blessings on you. I'm going to mention you in the book I am writing."

Maybe I should have just thanked him, but I couldn't let him have the last word. I said, "And I'll mention *you* in a short story sometime."

* * *

Don't Rob Another Man's Castle
They say a man's home is his castle
He's like a king on a throne
It may be a shack down alongside the track
But everything in it's his own.
So don't think of taking his loved one
It's written Thou shall not steal
Don't rob another man's castle
No matter how lonesome you feel.
Don't rob another man's castle
Don't take his treasures away
Strange as it seems when you steal a man's dreams
You'll never know then how you'll pay.
So don't rob a man of his loved one
You'll break his heart don't you see
I robbed another man's castle
Now someone just stole her from me . . .

Don't Rob Another Man's Castle
By JENNY LOU CARSON
© 1948 (Renewed) UNICHAPPELL MUSIC INC. (BMI)
All Rights Reserved
Used by Permission from ALFRED MUSIC

Oklahoma Bill

A little more than a year after the death of my darling wife, Evelyn, I, at age eighty-seven, was in the kitchen of my home, about twelve miles south of Harrisburg, Illinois. It was nearly noon, and I was finishing up cooking a pot of vegetable soup I had started much earlier.

Evelyn had convinced me that I needed a large variety of fruits and vegetables in my diet to stay healthy. So about once a week, I make a pot of soup. A little of everything available goes into my vegetable beef soup, so it never is the same twice. Whatever is handy in the refrigerator or cupboard looks like a good candidate to me.

All at once, there was a loud, greatly exaggerated knock at the kitchen door. To myself, I exclaimed, "What in the world!" and went over and opened the door. There stood a man who looked like Senator Fred Thompson, who was a candidate for president in '08. He appeared to be a size smaller and several years younger. His mannerisms were pleasant, and his first comment was, "Something smells mighty good."

I told him that onions make poor cooking smell good. Then I jokingly said, "If you're a hobo, I'll fix you up with a bowl of it."

He laughed and said, "I'm in your driveway with a tire almost flat. Would you happen to have a jack I could use to put on my spare?"

375

I told him that if he would pull ahead to a little building I pointed to, he could use a floor jack and an air compressor in case his spare needed more air.

He answered, "You are more than a hobo feeder. You are a rescuer of a man ready to get home."

He introduced himself as Bill Boatright. I told him that I was Kestner Wallace.

Bill made short work of the tire change as I looked on. His skill impressed me. When he was finished, he asked if he could have a damp paper towel to clean his hands. Instead, I asked him to come in, wash his hands, and get another smell of my soup—perhaps even try a sample of it. I wanted a second opinion as to how good it was.

I told Bill that my son, Ray, stopped by each day on the way home from work, and the best I could get out of him concerning my cooking was, "It smells good."

Bill and I enjoyed a meal of soup and cornbread. He made me feel good by asking for seconds. He enjoyed talking as much as eating. Luckily, I have always been a better listener than talker.

With a little coaxing, I got him to tell me some of his life's story. I learned that *his* wife, also, had died a little more than a year before. Among other things, he told me that he had retired when he was fifty-five years old. He said that he had an income from investments and got two checks each month. He stated that he wasn't wealthy but didn't lack for spending money.

From things he mentioned, I surmised he had had a religious upbringing, so I asked, "Bill, just how religious are you?"

Bill replied, "Before I answer, please allow me to ask you, 'How religious are you?'"

I had to admit—that was a harder question to answer than I thought it would be when I had asked it. I slowly replied, "Well, I go to church, pray, and try to tell the truth. I should have said grace before we ate. So you see, I have room for improvement."

Bill replied, "It appears to me we are like two peas in a pod. If we were two pigs in a poke and shaken up, it would be anyone's guess which one would come out first."

I said, "It is too bad we weren't neighbors growing up."

With a broad smile, Bill said, "We might have been like two sheep-eating dogs."

I protested, "No, no, no, Bill, not that bad. You might have been elected sheriff—and I, dogcatcher."

Bill replied, "With this kind of talk, we surely could have entered a contest as to which one of us could tell the bigger lie."

I said, "Bill, you would win that. I'm like George Washington. I can't tell a lie."

Bill was quick in his retort: "I have you beat. I can, but I won't."

Tiring of our banter, I said, "Suppose we cut the clatter, and you tell me what you have been doing since you retired."

"Kestner, I'm on my way back to Oklahoma. I have reservations at a hotel in Marion tonight and plan to drive nonstop to Oklahoma City tomorrow. The story I'm about to tell you is like the lyrics to a song, 'For I have a sad story to tell you, it's a story that's never been told.' You will be the *first* to hear this story from beginning to end."

"Bill, I feel honored to be first. However, I don't have to be first. I'm that much like George Washington."

Bill pounced quickly: "Kestner, don't you remember your history? George Washington was first in war, first in peace, and first in the hearts of his countrymen."

He had fallen for my trap. "Yes, Bill, and he married a widow."

"Ha, ha, Kestner, you led me into that."

After we went into the living room and made ourselves comfortable, I said, "Now, Bill, tell me a story never before told."

Bill took on a look of both pleasure and sadness. He seemed anxious to tell his story. It was as follows:

"I was born and raised in rural Oklahoma. I met the woman who was later to become my wife—Dollie Bell—in Oklahoma City. She told me she was a coal miner's daughter and had lived her teen years in the hills of Kentucky and West Virginia. She was twenty years old at the time. I was twenty-three.

"I was lonely and praying for a soul mate but doing nothing about getting one. When I saw her, I knew she was the answer to my prayer. Her petite body and beautiful brown eyes and hair made her everything I had hoped and prayed for. She was very much to my liking in every way. Had I been an assistant of the Almighty, I wouldn't have changed a thing about her. She seemed like an angel to me. In fact, that was my pet name for her."

"Bill, I take it you fell hard for her from the jump start. Did she fall equally hard for you?"

"Yes, our feelings of instant love and kindness were mutual."

"Did you get married soon after meeting?"

"No, we decided to wait until we were sure our love wasn't like a desert rose that blooms and soon fades away. We also wanted to get the go-ahead from our Heavenly Father. However, we did get married before our next birthdays. We both felt our marriage was made in Heaven."

"Where did you live after you were married?"

"We bought a house just beyond the city limits of Oklahoma City, in a semi-rural area that suited us well."

"What did you like about that area?"

"It was an up-and-coming neighborhood with a lot of young couples about our age. It was where Dollie Bell and I started our happy life together—where she thrilled me by telling me she was happy I was her husband. The fact that Joe and Mollie Driskell were our next-door neighbors was an added blessing.

"Joe and I were close friends, but Mollie and Dollie Bell were like sisters. Since Joe and I did well in our separate lines of business, our wives didn't work outside the home. They had time for a number of worthy charitable causes and kept us engaged in a swirling social life. They were wonderful wives, as well as our best friends."

At this point, Bill choked up for just a second. I was afraid that he was about to end his story. I wanted very much for him to continue, so I remained silent and gave him my most expectant look.

Finally, with a heavy sigh, he continued. "The years zipped by. One fine spring day last year, Joe had to go to Tulsa on business. Mollie and Dollie Bell decided to go along to shop while he was in his meetings. When the three of them were driving into Tulsa, a light at a railroad crossing malfunctioned. Joe's car was struck by a freight train. Joe and Dollie Bell were killed. Mollie wasn't hurt seriously."

Bill was quiet again. To break the silence, I said, "Bill, I can sympathize with you. My wife died unexpectedly. It seems that the more sudden the loss, the greater the shock."

Nodding, Bill continued. "Mollie loved Joe dearly, but she held up better over her loss than I did. I'm truly ashamed of how poorly I took Dollie Bell's death. I almost went off my rocker. For most of the next year, I stayed to myself. I was mainly a recluse—grumpy and unfriendly with people who tried to cheer me up. Even acts of kindness from Mollie didn't help. I cried myself to sleep at night and longed for my sweet Dollie Bell.

"After a year of feeling sorry for myself, I decided that in order to save my sanity, I needed to get out of there for a change of scenery. From that moment on, I began to feel as if there was some glimmer of hope that I could go on. As I pondered where to go, the mining country of Kentucky and West Virginia came to mind. Since Dollie Bell was from that area, a part of me held on to the thought that I might find another Dollie Bell—a look-alike or a woman just like she was. I knew the possibility was unlikely, but the idea appealed to me."

Again, Bill fell silent. When he continued, he said, "I told Mollie I planned to be gone to Kentucky and West Virginia for a period of time to look for another Dollie Bell. I asked her if she would look after my place and feed my cat and dog while I was gone. Her answer was, 'Bill, I would do that and more for you.' The look on Mollie's face said, 'I'm sorry that you are going, but I wish you well.'

"With a rush of gratitude, I replied, 'You're an angel, Mollie—thanks.'

"I didn't go directly to Kentucky. In order to get back in the mainstream of society, I spent a few days in that magnificent area around Gatlinburg, Tennessee. As I gazed at the smoky shades of blue in the Great Smoky Mountain range, I marveled at the artistic ability of the Creator. It made me think of the song, 'How Great Thou Art.' The time I spent there was good for my soul, mind, and body."

"Bill, that really is a lovely area around there. . . . Now, you've made me anxious to know—once you left there, did you have any luck in your search for a wife?"

"Well, I'll have to say 'yes' and 'no,' for now. I will tell you that I met some fine down-to-earth people. A gal here and there made my heart beat a little faster now and then, but none was just like my Dollie Bell."

"What methods did you use in your search?"

"I went to many restaurants and slowly ate whatever my body called for—sometimes a full meal, sometimes just a burger or even pie and coffee. I liked the people and was treated well, but saw none that really turned me on."

"Bill, wasn't there even one lady who got your attention?"

"I had a close call with one who was in Kentucky. Since you asked for it, here it goes. . . ."

One day, around one o'clock in the afternoon, I pulled into a little town and saw an attractive, good-size restaurant with an attention-getting sign out front that said, "Ding Dong Bell—Come and Dine." I went in.

A woman who appeared to be in her mid-forties approached. She had a pleasant voice and a sweet smile and reminded me of Dollie Bell. As she handed me a menu, she said, "Good afternoon. My name is Mary. Welcome to Ding Dong Bell. I'll clean this table and take your order in a jiffy."

As she cleaned the table, I took notice how she was alike and different from Dollie Bell. Based on first impressions, although she was taller than Dollie Bell, the resemblance was remarkable.

Mary asked, "Sir, are you ready to order?"

"Yes, Mary," I replied, "And you can call me Bill."

Mary quipped, "Now we're truckin'. We're on a first-name basis after knowing each other for less than a minute."

I told her, "They don't call me 'Speedy' for nothing. I'll have today's special."

With a smile, Mary said, "Speedy Bill, you made a good choice."

I decided to make haste more slowly. I looked at her often — only when she wasn't looking. However, her two co-workers caught on. I learned later that Mary was the owner.

When I went to Ding Dong Bell the following day about the same time, the set-up was much the same. The three waitresses were fairly busy, but not too busy to send messages by sleight of hand and head motions that "that guy" was back. It appeared that Mary was pre-assigned to me. She came to the table with a bounce in her step, a sparkle in her eye, and music in her voice.

She said, "Hi, Bill. Today's special is different from yesterday's and is very good. I haven't eaten yet. With your permission, I'll eat with you. We can learn more about each other."

I eagerly replied, "Mary, please eat with me. Nothing would please me better."

Mary sat down and signaled for us to be served the special. Mary then said, "Bill, I want you to tell me what has brought you from Oklahoma to Kentucky." In response to my look of surprise, she said, "I saw you have Oklahoma plates on your car. Tomorrow, if you are back and are interested, I'll tell you about myself. My two sidekicks are trying to convince me you are interested in me to some extent."

"Mary, I'll take you up on that offer. My being in Kentucky is part of a get-well therapy I have assigned to myself. I'm making rapid progress in becoming myself again."

Mary never took her eyes off me as I gave her a thumbnail sketch of my past, as I have told you. From time to time, we shed tears together. When I finished, Mary said, "Bill, I commend you for holding Dollie

Bell in such high esteem and for whipping your long siege of depression." I thought that was a very sweet thing to say.

The next day, I went in as before and sat at the same table for two. I noticed, in the far corner of the dining area, a sulky-looking man. I thought to myself that he must have been born on the shady side of a sour apple tree and weaned on a sour pickle. When he realized I was looking at him, he appeared to take on the appearance of an attack dog. I just didn't look at him any more.

Very promptly, Jeanette, one of Mary's helpers, came and sat at my table. She quickly said, "I'm a sit-in for Mary. Hope you aren't too disappointed. She extends her regrets."

Although puzzled, I calmly replied, "I'm sure she has her reasons."

Barely containing her excitement, Jeanette exclaimed, although in a low voice, "You bet she does! Don't look now, but that man sitting over in the corner is her husband. He is half drunk and mean as hell. He doesn't drink often and is mostly a good guy. But when he gets a snootful of moonshine, he is like a volcano ready to erupt. Mary is sending you today's special 'to go,' along with her regards. She fears for your safety."

Trying to lighten up the situation a little, I told Jeanette, "You tell Mary I'm not one to run from trouble, and I'm not much of a card player, but I know when to hold and when to fold. I'm not much of a stand-up-and-fighter. I'm more of a cutter-and-a-shooter. I'm going to cut out that door and shoot across town. Please extend my appreciation to Mary for being a good listener and for giving me the warning."

Jeanette grinned and said, "Just don't go out and cut your throat and shoot yourself in the foot."

It was my time to grin. I placed a ten on the table, gave the two at the kitchen door a little salute, picked up my container of food, and walked to the door like a tall, brave Indian. Miles out of town, I opened my lunch container. I found on top of the food a napkin and a folded note that read, "Lunch is on me. Best of luck, Mary." Inside the note was a ten-dollar bill. I left Kentucky for West Virginia with a warm heart and a full belly.

It was strange though—although this chance meeting with Mary had sparked an interest in my heart that I feared had forever been extinguished, I had the feeling that I had learned an important lesson, too. It was as if I now knew with a certainty that the woman I was seeking for my new Dollie Bell need not—and indeed would not—look like Dollie Bell. I pondered this new knowledge as I drove on to West Virginia.

"Bill, you should write a book. Surely there are more Kentucky stories to tell, not to mention anything that happened in West Virginia!"

"Thank you, Kestner, but I like talking better than writing. I'll tell you a little of what happened in West Virginia, and then I'll be on my way."

Well over in West Virginia, I entered a small town around the area that Dollie Bell grew up. I began to look for lodging—perhaps a room to rent. By chance, I saw an attractive home with a neatly printed sign in the window that said: "Room to Rent or Room and Board."

My knock at the door was answered by a kind-looking, gray-haired couple who appeared to be in their mid-seventies. After exchanging greetings, I said, "I'm Bill Boatright, and I'm interested in your room to rent, and perhaps room and board."

They each extended a friendly smile. The woman said, "We are the Parsons. Our neighbors call us Mom and Pop. Please come in. Just this morning, without really knowing why, we decided to put that sign in the window. We hoped to break the day-to-day monotony and perhaps help a person in need at the same time."

I asked, "What would room and board cost me for one week?"

Mrs. Parsons looked at Mr. Parsons. He replied, "We aren't money hungry. We're new at this—just whatever is right—maybe twenty-five dollars a day. If money is close with you, less will be fine, if it is okay with Mom." Mrs. Parsons beamed at her husband and answered, "Sounds good to me."

Touched by their generosity, I quickly replied, "Mr. Parsons, money is no problem. Your warmth and friendliness are what's important to me. I will double your asking price and pay you in advance."

Reluctantly, they agreed. Mr. Parsons said, "Well, if you insist. But please call us Mom and Pop."

I interjected, "Bill, that was a fast deal."

"That is for sure. For me, Mom and Pop Parsons were far more than temporary landlords or even short-term friends. They proved to be angels from the Most High."

"What do mean by that?"

In answer, Bill continued on with his story:

Until age fourteen, I lived in a foster home that gave me everything a growing boy needs except love and understanding. As unlikely as it seems, Mom and Pop

Parsons gave me that and more in just those few short days of my stay there. As I sketched the stories of my life, from boyhood to the present, they felt the pain of my woes and misfortunes and glowed with pleasure at my good fortunes. Our fellowship and friendship were boundless. Their responses were as nuggets of gold to me. The food they served was plain but plentiful and prepared to perfection. The days went by quickly. I scouted around some each day, but I felt drawn to spend most of my time with Mom and Pop.

On Sunday, I asked them where I might go for an evening church service. They suggested that I attend a little white church that was about ten miles out of town. They knew the church and the pastor there and thought I would enjoy the service. They said that they would wait up for me so I could give them a report afterwards.

When I got out to this church, I observed that the lawn was neatly trimmed, a brick parsonage was nearby, and a dozen or more cars were in the parking area. Circling the church to park, I could see it had a beautiful stained-glass angel at one end. Glowing brightly from the lights inside, it seemed to reach out to me.

I went into the church as the song service was about to begin. The song service was impressive—no choir—everyone sang old-time favorites. Some put life in the service by clapping their hands. I picked up a hymnal so that I could sing along. As I opened the book, a small card with an angel printed at the top dropped out and onto the floor. I picked it up and read the words printed there. What I saw on that card made me bow my head right then and there in prayer.

As you can imagine, I was dying to ask Bill what was on the card, but he continued on with his story without a pause. Not wanting to interrupt, I stifled my question with some difficulty and kept on listening.

The song service concluded after a few more rousing songs. The pastor, who I learned was Reverend Frank Johnson, stood up and approached the pulpit. Appearing to be in his mid-forties, he was tall and slender with brown, wavy hair. His voice was clear and pleasant—one that demanded attention.

After requests for prayer, Reverend Johnson asked us to stand. His prayer was forceful, sincere, and lengthy. From time to time, I took a little peek to see how people were responding and realized that different ones were sizing me up. They were wondering who I was and why I was there. One woman with strawberry-blond hair was looking at me each time I looked her way. Even from where I sat, I could tell her eyes were a brilliant blue.

Following the prayer, Reverend Johnson announced, "I have a treat for you. My wife's sister, Grace, has consented to lead the service tonight in my stead. She is well versed in the Bible. I'm looking forward to hearing what she has to say. However, before I turn the service over to her, I would like to welcome our guest and have him tell us who he is and whatever he wants to tell about himself."

I stood and said, "I'm Bill Boatright. I'm from Oklahoma. This is my first time east of the Mississippi River. I'm enjoying the beauty of your state as I travel around. And now, I'll sit down, for I, too, am looking forward to hearing Grace's message."

Reverend Johnson said, "Welcome, Brother Bill. We are glad to have you in our service."

Immediately, the woman who had been eyeing me stood up and said, "My dear Brother Frank, with shame and regret, I feel led to report that the inspiration I had this morning when I promised to speak tonight has left me. Therefore, I wish to be excused."

Reverend Johnson didn't seem to be excited at Grace's announcement. He said, "I've always found that when one door closes, the Lord opens another. Perhaps Brother Boatright could bless us with his testimony and whatever else the Lord might put on his heart to say."

At that point, I had to comment, "Bill, that had to come as a shock to you. How did that request grab you?"

"I'm sure that I blinked my eyes a few times like a frog in a hailstorm and wished I had more time to think what to say!"

"Did you lead the service?"

Nodding, Bill continued:

I was too egotistical to turn down a chance to sound off. I walked to the podium and stated: "This is an honor I don't deserve." Then I added, "The Lord sure does work in mysterious ways."

I went on to say, "I came in here to get a little closer to the Lord—perhaps by having you good folks pray for me. However, the excellent song service made me renew my commitment to the Lord. Now in the words of the Psalmist David, 'My cup runneth over.'

"I'm going to talk to you a few minutes on a story that Jesus told—one that you and I have heard many times from way back. You know the story, so I won't

read it or tell it in its entirety. It is the parable of the Prodigal Son.

"Jesus is a great storyteller. He got my attention in this story on the first sentence when he said, 'A certain man had two sons.' We immediately wonder — what about these two sons? The younger son wanted his share of the inheritance immediately, if not sooner. Are we not or have we not been like the Prodigal Son, wanting things on our timeline rather than on the Lord's?

"On getting his share of the inheritance, the younger son went into a far country and wasted it on riotous living, and then he came to want and almost starved. Finally, he came to himself and decided to return to his father. (I really stressed 'he came to himself.') We need to take inventory often — in other words, come to ourselves lest we get too far removed from the straight and narrow way. We don't do the parable justice if we fail to point out that the gracious way the father received his son is typical of how the Heavenly Father receives us when we come or return to him after straying away."

I was amazed at how the group hung on to every word as though they were hearing it for the first time. Grace leaned slightly forward, smiled, nodded approval, and at times, appeared to be in deep thought. After I finished and sat down, Reverend Johnson complimented me on my talk. He made other closing remarks and dismissed the service.

After the benediction, people shook my hand and said they hoped I would come back and worship with them. Last of all, Grace came to me and took my hand in both of hers. She said, "Your message was like manna from Heaven. It was food to my soul. It made me think. It brought up questions I would like to discuss with you." She would have said more, but Reverend Johnson stepped up, started talking, and Grace just disappeared. Reverend Johnson said, "Brother Bill, my wife, Helen, and I would like for you to come over to the parsonage next door for some blueberry muffins and coffee. She is making the coffee now."

I replied, "With pleasure, I accept your invitation." I left my car parked by the church and walked with Reverend Johnson to the parsonage.

When we stepped inside the door, I was surprised to be greeted by Grace. She was there visiting her sister and Reverend Johnson. Reverend Johnson suggested that she go into the kitchen and help Helen with the coffee and muffins, but she replied, "Helen doesn't need any help. I have a question to ask Brother Bill."

"Kestner, I have to say that while I waited for her question, I felt strangely nervous. How do you think you would have felt?"

"I think I would have just hoped I had a good answer."

"I wasn't really sure all that I was feeling at the time. Time seemed to slow as I waited."

"So what was Grace's question?"

In answer, Bill continued:

With a sort of coy smile, Grace asked, "Do you think a person can love two people at the same time?"

Caught off guard, and not sure where she was coming from, I evasively replied, "Yes, I do. I love everybody."

Grace retorted, "You know what I mean! Do you think I, for example, could love my husband and someone else at the same time —*you know, love at first sight sort of thing?"*

All sorts of warning bells went off in my head. I answered cautiously, "Grace, that has never been a problem of mine. My love for my late wife was deep and sincere. She has been gone now for more than a year. I've spent many lonely days. So I'll have to say that I've never had a problem of loving anyone else other than my Dollie Bell. I've prayed to the Good Lord above for an angel like her."

My feeble answer to her question must have touched a tender spot in her heart. There was a tear in her eye as she drew really close to me and whispered, "I could be all that and more."

All of a sudden, time seemed to slow to a crawl as several things happened all at once. With one part of my mind, I could still comprehend what was taking place there in the room: Grace was on the verge of embracing me, and I felt myself recoiling at the thought. At the same moment, there was a loud knock on the door. But the greater part of my mind was not there in the room with Grace but was still hearing those words: "Be all that and more." No, it had been "Do all that and more," and it had been Mollie, sweet Mollie, who had said that to me . . . Mollie — who was back in Oklahoma City, waiting to welcome me home. . . .

This flash of awareness passed in an instant, and then I was drawn back abruptly into the room as the door knocker didn't wait for his knock to be answered. In bolted a tall, well-built man in his early fifties. In his nice dress suit, he would have been good looking had he not taken on an angry look at what he saw.

He stood motionless as he viewed his wife, starry-eyed, standing too close to me. He struggled to ward off an outburst of anger. The silence was deafening. When he spoke, he said, "Excuse me if I have interrupted what was about to happen." His words were dripping with sarcasm.

Grace said, "Carl, honey, this is Bill. He preached for us this evening. I didn't get to tell him at church how I was touched by his message."

With a sneer, Carl replied, "That is explanation enough for now. We will further discuss how much you were touched when we get home tonight."

I was much relieved at this point when Helen and Reverend Johnson came in with the coffee and muffins. Reverend Johnson and Carl shook hands in a friendly manner, and we all began to sip our coffee.

Reverend Johnson did much to put me at ease by explaining to Carl: "Bill was touring the state and by chance stopped to attend our evening service at church. I invited him to preach, and he did."

Carl remarked, "I'm sorry I didn't get back from my trip a little sooner." He might have been thinking, "I could have jerked a knot in Grace's tail before she almost made a fool of herself."

After I thought an appropriate amount of time had passed, I thanked Helen for the refreshments and stated that I needed to be going. Reverend Johnson and Carl stepped forward and shook hands with me. I nodded a farewell to the women and left.

When I got back and gave Mom and Pop a brief sketch of what had taken place that evening, they went through a series of emotions. In the end, though, they were pleased and murmured, "Another prayer answered."

Then they wanted to know more about Mollie. I told them that Mollie was a wonderful friend and neighbor. Letting me know that Mollie had been on their minds and in their prayers, Mom Parsons asked, "Bill, why don't you pray for her, and then call and tell her how wonderful she is?"

Resistant, I said, "Mom, she already knows that I think that."

Mom replied, "Yes, but women love to be told."

But I didn't make the call. After I went to bed that evening, sleep evaded me. I decided that I would pray for Mollie, as Mom had suggested. When I finally fell asleep, I had a very vivid vision — or dream — in which it was revealed to me that Mollie was the one to take Dollie Bell's place in my life.

When I awoke the next morning and remembered the dream, joy flooded my soul. A calm, happy certainty about Mollie settled over me, as well as wonderment that I had not been able to figure that out before I had traveled so many miles.

At the breakfast table, I told Mom and Pop what had happened. They smiled, raised their arms, and with tears in their eyes said, "Praise the Lord!"

Some people see angels. Mom and Pop were as near angels as I ever expect to see. I finished up my breakfast, gave both of them a big hug, and then made haste to head to Oklahoma.

"And now I'm on my way to Mollie."

I had to admit that I was impressed. I exclaimed, "Bill, now that definitely is a story for the books!"

Nodding, Bill said, "Yes, Kestner — sad, but with a good ending. However, I bet if I would give you a chance, you could match it."

I had to tell him. "Well, I have written a story or two in my time. In fact, I have a book of short stories: *A Dollar the Hard Way.* I want to give you a copy for a wedding present."

I picked up one of my books nearby and wrote in it: *To Bill and Mollie, Best wishes, Kestner Wallace.*

Bill sprang to his feet and thanked me for the book. He slipped something into my shirt pocket, shook my hand, and left.

As he drove out of my driveway, I reached into my pocket and pulled out a little card. With a jolt, I realized that it must have been the angel card that had fallen out of the church hymnal. The card simply said:

> *All those who wander*
> *Searching for love*
> *Need only seek*
> *His help from above.*

* * *

Nina —
Ledford, Eagle Creek, and Beyond

In the many short stories I have written, a number of them have featured men — men who were not only poor and educationally deprived to some degree but also blessed with the ability to meet life's challenges and cope. Even though some of them had done time in prison, I looked beyond the error of the way in which they had fouled up and saw threads of gold in the fiber of their character, which caused me to reach my hand to them in friendship. Far too many people allow the ten percent of the bad in the underprivileged and downcast to make them blind to the ninety percent of the good in the individual.

At the risk of sounding as if I'm bragging and blowing my own horn, I believe that I have had a little part, along with other good people, in helping these people think of things Above. We expect to see them on the Golden Shore.

Now, I would like to change from featuring men to singing the praises of a woman — not my mother or my late darling wife, Evelyn, for it would take books to do justice by them — but a close neighbor and friend, Nina Modglin. Never in the many years that I've known Nina have I ever heard an unkind word spoken against her. A compliment often stated is "She is the sweetest person I've ever known."

The following is just one small example of that sweetness. Before writing this story, Nina and I knew each other only as neighbors who are more than a quarter-mile apart know each other—we were always friendly, but I didn't know a lot of details about her life. I would drop by occasionally to say hello since Nina and I each live alone.

Nina takes great pride in operating her riding mower and does a masterful job keeping her no-less-than-three acres of lawn mowed. When I complained that the rainy season was causing me to have to mow my equally large lawn every week, Nina said, "I'll come down with my mower and help you with your mowing." (She made this offer even as she was still recovering from a broken wrist, which had happened when she had slipped and fallen as she was out feeding the birds after one of our late ice storms.) Although I was quite touched by the offer, I assured her that I could manage. She then said that if I got sick or needed help, she would lend me a hand. Again, I was impressed and appreciative but assured her that my son and granddaughters, who live nearby, would look after me. In return for her sweet offer, I told Nina that if she ever had a feeling that someone was pilfering around, I would be happy to come frighten away any potential offender.

I feel inadequate to put Nina in her proper place in the sun, but I don't want to be like the person testifying in church who exclaimed, "If I had ten thousand tongues with which to praise Him, I could not enough my Blessed Lord adore." Someone asked, "What are you doing with the one you have?"

Even though I'd known Nina in a casual roundabout way since the 1940s, taught her grandchildren, and admired her interest and cooperation with the school, I came to the sudden realization that I didn't know enough about her to write a story.

To better prepare myself, I called at Nina's home. As I drove up the long, curving driveway and through the entrance, which was marked by wheels from an old-time corn planter, the first things that struck me were the immaculate landscaping on Nina's land (which I was later to learn was a five-acre plot) and the carefully placed statuettes that tastefully decorated the lawn. As I walked toward Nina's door, I was impressed by her beautiful view of Womble Mountain.

I knocked on Nina's door. Nina very graciously invited me in and expressed her pleasure that I'd dropped by. As I entered Nina's home, I could tell that she kept her house as neat and pristine as she kept her yard. It felt very warm and welcoming. The rows of books on her shelves indicated a passion for reading. On my way into the living room through the dining room, the cabinet of beautifully displayed glassware and the shelves of other collectibles spoke to her love of things of fragile beauty.

After exchanging a few pleasantries, I stated my reason for calling. With amusement and some disbelief, she said, "You have chosen a pretty poor person to write about. I can't imagine anyone wanting to read about me."

I countered, "Your life's experiences may be enough different from most others that people will likely find them interesting. If it is all right with you, I'll ask you a few questions."

Nina shrugged and while smiling, said, "It is okay with me. Ask whatever you wish."

Relieved that she had agreed, I jumped right in with my first question. "When and where were you born?"

Without hesitation, Nina answered, "November 22, 1924, in Ledford, Illinois."

Surprised, I said, "I thought you were born on Eagle Creek."

Shaking her head, she replied, "I liked Ledford, but I liked Eagle Creek better, so I led people to believe that I was born there."

"Where did you go to school?"

"For eight years, I went to West Ledford—I had two different teachers. In grades one through four, I had Elmo Williams. He was a good teacher. I liked him very much."

I commented, "Nina, it might surprise you to know that Elmo Williams taught his first year at Sadler School, when I was a student in the fourth grade. I liked him, too. He actually boarded with us."

Nina went on to say, "I had a woman teacher in grades five through eight. I liked her, too, but I don't remember her name just now."

"Did you go to high school?"

"Yes, I went one year to Harrisburg High School."

Curious, I asked, "Did you quit school?"

Shaking her head, she said, "My high school ended, but my learning continued. I'll explain. We lived in a rented house in Ledford—the middle house in a row of three close together. One night, all three of them burned."

In an attempt to get her to comment further, I said, "Probably one caught on fire and caused the others to burn."

She hesitated, then nodded and said, "Maybe."

Not wanting to press her further, I asked, "How did you wind up on Eagle Creek?"

"A man from Eagle Creek heard of our loss and sent my dad word that he would sell him a tract of land for next to nothing, and that his neighbor had several acres of fine white oak timber and would give him enough logs to build a log house. He made mention of a 'log rolling.' With Dad and some of his relations and the bighearted men of Eagle Creek, the house went up fast."

"Where did you live while the log house was being built?"

"In an old abandoned post office building in Ledford."

"I never knew there was a post office in Ledford."

"Yes, there was. . . . Now back to your question — did I quit high school? I had an opportunity to stay with an elderly couple and work for my room and board while going to high school. My dad wouldn't hear of it. That was a big disappointment in my life."

"So that was the end of your formal education?"

"No, not exactly. I went to Colbert School on Eagle Creek with my brothers and sister. I took the eighth grade again after doing well in my one year at high school. My teacher was Wallace Baldwin. He lived in Pope County, south of Herod. He rode a horse when it was too bad to get over the road in his car. He was the best teacher I ever had, and I treated him the worst."

Curious, I asked, "In what way did you treat him badly?"

"The Eagle Creek boys respected Mr. Baldwin, but they were all boys and had a mean streak in them. I tried to impress them that I was tough, also, in a sneaky sort of way."

Wanting more details, I asked, "Nina, what was the worst thing you did at Colbert?"

Nina hesitated and looked down. I got the feeling that she wasn't intending to tell me anything, probably thinking I had been a model student at school. So I said, "I was no angel in school. I should have been skinned alive for some of the things I did."

Glad to have the spotlight off her, Nina replied, "How about giving me an example?"

I launched into my story. "One time I took two fire-crackers and a yard of twine string. I glued the string to the fuse of one of the firecrackers. Then I broke the other firecracker open, took the powder out, and spread it very, very thinly on the string extension fuse. After the last recess, I was the last one to go in the schoolhouse. As I went in, I lit the fuse and hung it on the outside doorknob.

"About ten minutes later, I had forgotten about the firecracker and was standing up in a geography class, telling about my assigned topic. That firecracker exploded and made the teacher think it was dynamite. It startled me, along with the teacher. I dropped my geography book. The teacher was as pale as death. I quickly recovered and asked her if she would like for me and my buddy, Quay, to check things out. She nodded. We took our time goofing around and then returned and reported we saw nothing out of the ordinary."

That incident amused Nina and caused her to tell me the worst thing that she had done at Colbert School. She went into detail—it was hilarious. We laughed as we hadn't laughed in years. Our laughing did us more good than any tonic we could have taken. Her joke had been on her teacher, Wallace Baldwin. Even though Nina admired him, she'd wanted to impress the mean boys at school, so she let them in on what she had done. She said the Code of the Hills had kept them from snitching on her.

Nina said that her sister took much delight in telling her mother any bad thing Nina said or did. That day, on the way home from school, her sister ran ahead and told her mother. Nina's mother was waiting for her and gave her a good switching.

When Nina finished her story, she said, "I told you this in confidence. Give me your word you won't tell it."

I replied, "Nina, we had a Code of the Hills on our side of the mountain, also. It still holds today. What you told me in confidence will remain that way."

[My dear readers, I'm sorry to disappoint you by not telling you Nina's story. I hope you will understand.]

Nina said earnestly, "I felt ashamed of myself when I later realized that Mr. Baldwin knew I was the guilty one and didn't make a big deal out of it. I turned over a new leaf and tried to be a model student the last half of the year. My getting converted at Bethel Baptist Church and, afterwards, baptized helped a great deal."

Thinking of an often-quoted saying, I asked Nina, "Do you believe that 'all things work together for good . . .'?"

She replied, "Yes, I surely do."

. . .

Later, as I went over Nina's funny incident in my mind, I asked myself, "What was really so funny about her story that gave us such a bang?" I came to the conclusion that, after all her hard times — some of which I've mentioned and some, not — we just needed a good laugh.

I recalled another time when I had had a similar laugh. An elderly bachelor, a buddy of mine, and I went coon hunting. The three of us very much hoped we would get two or three coons and have the pelts to sell and the carcasses to barbecue. The dog hunted hard but treed no coons. After about three hours of walking, we, somewhat discouraged, sat down to rest and wait for the dog to tree. We got to talking about wild game good to eat: deer, rabbit, squirrel, duck, and quail.

Our bachelor friend said, "I'm going to surprise your pants off by telling you how to cook an eel so it is good to eat."

I commented, "They may be good to eat — some people say so — but they look too much like a snake to suit me."

He went on with his story. "They are so slick you have to nail them to a tree to skin and remove the insides. You take the eel down from the tree, wash it clean, rub it with corn meal, season it with salt and pepper, and nail it to a board about thirty inches long and six inches wide, and sharpened on one end so it can be stuck in the ground upright next to a bonfire."

This old gentleman went on and on with the cooking procedure. He definitely had our attention. He finally said, "Then take the eel off the board, throw it away, and eat the board."

The surprise ending caused us to burst out laughing. We laughed until we were gasping for breath, and then we laughed some more—the type of laughter that lifts your spirits, which is the same sort of laughter that Nina and I shared after her story. I highly recommend it.

…

Just to set the record straight, for those who think of Podunk and Eagle Creek in the same breath, I'm set and ready to jump down their throats. I know the people of Eagle Creek as well as any non–Eagle Creeker and have found them to be friendly, truthful, honest, and hard-working. In fact, before I was born, my dad's older sister, Sarah, married Sherman Raymer, an Eagle Creeker through and through.

In the mid-thirties, I rode a mule along the mountain range in the southeast corner of Saline County to Sherman and Sarah's home, southeast of Horseshoe. I got there at noon.

Aunt Sarah was a good cook. The table was set with food that one would have to see to appreciate, including a beautiful, steaming ham. I still remember Uncle Sherman coming in for dinner with his shirt wet with perspiration. After greeting me warmly, he admired the good dinner and said, "I feel so unworthy."

Aunt Sarah exclaimed, "Oh, Sherman, you are more worthy than you feel!"

Seventy-five years later, I still remember the tender, smoked ham. The memory makes my mouth water.

Years later, I learned that Uncle Sherman was a Democrat, as most people on Eagle Creek are. He knew that I was a Republican. I told him I was a candidate for justice of the peace in Mountain Township. I didn't ask him to vote for me, but he said, "Kestner, you worry about the vote on your side of the mountain, and I'll take care of the vote over here." It was the Eagle Creek vote that put me over the top.

You might ask, "What does that have to do with Nina Modglin?" The answer is "Nothing," but it is one of many examples of the goodness of the people of Eagle Creek. And Nina is proud to consider herself an Eagle Creeker.

...

Returning another day to continue the interview, I started out on a fresh line of questioning. "Nina, did you have many boyfriends in the various schools you attended?"

With a pleasant look on her face, void of any trace of feeling sorry for herself, she answered, "No, I didn't have any. I was ugly, tall, and skinny, with straight hair. The boys at school didn't give me a second look."

"How did that make you feel?"

"Since we were poor, the thing most important to me was that we had a roof over our heads and food on the table."

Hoping to give Nina a chance to speak well of her father, I asked, in a leading style, "Did your father later on have a good job—perhaps foreman at one of the slope mines on Eagle Creek?"

Unwilling to sugarcoat anything, she answered with a grin, "He was water boy on the WPA [Work Projects Administration]."

"When did life begin to seem good on Eagle Creek?"

"Almost from the jump start. Dad raised a big garden. We grew much of our food. Dad spent his WPA money wisely. He bought a horse, a cow, a sow, and some chickens. Mom raised some baby chickens. We ate the roosters as fryers and saved the pullets for egg production. The cow furnished us plenty of milk and butter. The sow had eight pigs that were big enough to butcher the following winter."

With an amused look on her face and a little sparkle in her eye, Nina asked, "Kestner, did you own a goat when you were young?"

I knew that she had a story to tell about a goat. I answered, "No, we had sheep but no goats. However, when LeAnn and Ray were quite young, I got each of them a half-grown, long-eared, long-legged nanny goat. They named them Flip and Flop. I was amazed at the pleasure the goats brought them. The goats would play hide and seek with each other. They also liked to race LeAnn and Ray around the house and seemed to enjoy the fact they could outrun them.

"Flip and Flop almost caused my sister Mabel to have a heart attack. She and her husband drove up, on their way home with a brand new Ford Galaxy 500. Before the car was completely stopped, Flip and Flop bounded up on the trunk of the car and then conquered the top, where they pranced around a bit, acting like kings of the mountain. Then, slipping and sliding, they leaped from the top to the hood to the ground and chased each other around the house." Although it wasn't funny at the time, since Mabel was about to burst a blood vessel, recalling the incident amused me. Nina and I laughed together.

I urged, "Nina, tell me about your goat."

Nina responded, "Our goat was a billy goat. He was a pain in the neck all of the time we had him. He belonged to all five of us children."

I asked, "How did you get the goat?"

Nina replied, "We picked blackberries and sold them and bought an old, worn-out bicycle. We traded the bicycle for the goat. He was too mean for my sisters and me. My brothers teased him and made him meaner. My dad hated him but still tolerated him. Dad threatened to kill him when he ate the legs out of Dad's long-john underwear when they were on the clothesline, drying. But it was the last straw when that goat got up on Dad's Model T Ford and ate holes in the top. It rained on us on the way to church. . . . I never knew what happened to that goat."

I thought it unlikely that the goat had wandered off to a neighbor's house. But it did give me a thought for my next question. "How were your neighbors there on Eagle Creek?"

"Our neighbors were the best people this side of Heaven. We were always helping and sharing with each other. The boys and men, who were thought of by many as being mean, had hearts of gold. They had an extra-special measure of respect for women and older men."

"Did Kenneth [her late husband] go to school at Colbert when you went there?"

"No, he left school to join the CCC [Civilian Conservation Corps] camp. My first date with Kenneth was when I was fifteen. We got married at Cape Girardeau [Missouri] when I was sixteen.

"We bought a house and a few acres and fared much the same as other people did. Work for Kenneth was scarce. He had to go to Hammond, Indiana, to work on construction. He made good money, and we got out of debt. He became able to make a living on Eagle Creek. We were happy and wanted to spend our life there."

She now lived just over a quarter of a mile up the road from me and not on Eagle Creek. I asked, "Why did you leave?"

"Strip mining was taking place all around us. There was a layer of rock over the coal. The mining company would remove the dirt down to the rock with a bulldozer. Then they would drill holes in the rock with jackhammers and set off numerous sticks of dynamite at once. As they got closer to our house, the blasts would rattle the dishes and windows. When the rocks began to fall on our house, we decided to move.

"Kenneth learned of this three-acre plot, just up and over the hill north of where you live. The owner didn't want to sell it, but Kenneth kept after him and finally bought it. This plot had a shed-like building on it that we managed to live in while a new house was being built."

"How did you finance the new house?"

"Kenneth had saved a little money. He borrowed the rest from the bank. He got a job working for the county and paid off the bank. I worked at the general store and post office at Herod and carried the mail on one of the mail runs, which helped make ends meet."

Looking around, I asked, "Who did you get to build this house? They did a good job."

"We got Matthew Roberts, a Baptist preacher, and his son-in-law, Annis Smith. They never took a break. They would hardly stop long enough to get a drink of water. They paid no attention to Kenneth's telling them to take a break now and then."

Nina was surprised when I told her that I knew and

respected Reverend Roberts. She eagerly asked me to tell her what I knew about him. I told her that I had heard him preach several times. He liked to preach on the parables. He also told of the change that his conversion had made in his life. He said that when he was a young man, he was so timid that if he was walking down a country road and was about to meet a man, he would cross over a fence to keep from speaking.

Nina asked, "Kestner, do you remember any of the parables he preached on?"

Thinking back nearly seventy years ago, I replied, "Yes, the Prodigal Son, the Ten Virgins, the Lost Sheep, and others. He did well in putting his point across."

"Did he ever do any work for you?"

"Yes, in the fall of 1940, he and Annis framed up a house for me. His skill and perfection impressed me. Being amazed at his skill in cutting a set of rafters, I asked, 'Mr. Roberts, who taught you to be such a good carpenter?'

"In his slow, clear, impressive voice, he said, 'No one. It is just a God-given talent.'"

...

"Nina, you are too much like my late wife, Evelyn, to say anything bad about your dear husband, Kenneth. So as we wind down this interview, what good things do you want to say about him? First, before you start and before I forget, I'll give you an example of what impressed me about Kenneth.

"One Saturday, I asked Kenneth to break and disk my garden. He sounded sincerely sorry as he said he had to work, but he insisted I take his tractor, plow, and disc and do it myself. I didn't take him up on his offer. But I was impressed by his bigheartedness. He made me ashamed I hadn't been a better neighbor to him."

Nodding, Nina replied, "That was just like Kenneth. He had a heart of gold. He loved me and his children. His daughters thought there was no one like him. After all these years, we still miss him."

"Nina, that speaks well of Kenneth, as well as you and your daughters. The sting of death has touched my life, also. I hope a quote by Job in the Bible will be of comfort to you as it has been to me. It is as follows: 'The Lord gave, and the Lord hath taken away; blessed be the name of the Lord.'"

"Kestner, that is a good quote. My standby is 'The Lord is my shepherd; I shall not want.'"

She continued on. "I like the way you say things in your stories. I have read a number of them."

"Thank you for telling me, Nina. I'm impressed by all of the complimentary things I have heard other people say concerning you. You are praised and admired by all who know you. You are kind and considerate to everyone, as you are to me.

"Your daughter Brenda confirmed what I already knew —you were and are a wonderful mother. Brenda said that you played games with them when they were children and went swimming and fishing with them. You insisted that they be honest and truthful and that they treat others as they wanted to be treated, thus instilling values for a lifetime.

"I have heard how you read mail for some non-readers on your mail route and even wrote short letters. You delivered groceries and feed for some who didn't have a car. To me, that fulfills the scripture: 'Inasmuch as ye have done it unto one of the least of these my brethren, ye have done it unto me.'"

Very modestly, Nina replied, "Thank you, Kestner, for your kind words."

"Nina, if I were to ask you to put the final touch to this story, what would you say?"

"Well, Kestner, I would say I'm humbled and almost speechless at you considering me as the subject for a story. This is something I will remember always. Life is a bit lonesome at times.

"Your questioning has brought back precious memories—more valuable than silver and gold. My parents were poor, but what they lacked in worldly goods, they made up in love. I have no enemies. My friends are of more value to me than diamonds and pearls. The friendship expressed to me on my mail route was as refreshing as May flowers. For example, my heart used to leap with joy as I passed your home going to Herod to carry the mail and your beautiful wife, working in her flowers, would give me a friendly wave. My dear children treat me like a queen. I have to say, all in all, life has been good."

...

The Rime of the Ancient Mariner ends with this line, "A sadder and a wiser man, He rose the morrow morn." I certainly don't plan to rise a sadder man tomorrow, but I expect to rise a wiser man who has a pleasant awareness of a good friendship. Nina and I feel a kinship through some similar experiences we had while coming through the Great Depression and hard times, and yet we have maintained a good attitude toward God and man. I will always be grateful to her for allowing me to visit with her for the sake of a story, with the unexpected outcome being an enduring friendship. I would say to her, in the words of the late Reverend Matthew Roberts, "Blessings on you."

* * *

Lest I Forget

Today, April 27, 2008, I returned from church at Rudement. Instead of stopping at my home just two miles south, I went to the next driveway, which led to the Wallace Family Cemetery, where Evelyn, my dear wife of fifty-six years, is buried, in close view of Womble Mountain. This is a Sunday ritual I have carried on for the past twenty months.

I disagree with a long-time good friend of Evelyn's from East Prairie. Now ninety-two years old, her name is also Evelyn. When I told her that I visit Evelyn's grave each Sunday after church, she praised me and commented that Evelyn knows all about my visits. For me to agree would have been wishful thinking. Still I appreciated her desire to cheer me up. I would be happy to know that Evelyn is aware of my visits, but I have to console myself with the knowledge that her precious soul never died and is in paradise.

I don't consider my frequent trips to the cemetery to be strange. For me it is the right thing to do, "lest I forget, lest I forget." Lest I forget what? Lest I forget that God smiled on me in helping me recover from the scars of war and in bringing me through a long and sometimes uncertain romance. He drew Evelyn and me together with strong chords of love.

Those chords of love made it possible for the twain of us to become one—enabled Evelyn to leave friends and family in lovely East Prairie, Missouri, and cast her lot with an ordinary, ex-Navy, country school teacher who loved her at first sight.

...

At the edge of the gravesite, I sit in a padded lawn chair that my son, Ray, placed here for my comfort. I talk to Evelyn without moving my lips or making a sound. Today, I tell her that it is a pleasant sunshiny day. The Easter flowers have faded, but all around, the dogwood are in bloom. Old timers say the catfish will bite when the dogwood blooms. The redbuds are in bloom, also. The greenery of the trees is coming on full speed, and the mountain view is breathtaking.

I tell her of the morning church service and of my sitting at the end of the pew where she and I sat. It appears to me that out of sympathy for me, Sam DeNeal sits next to me. He isn't too well but isn't nearly as much out of it as I am. When Reverend Jason Farmer says, "Let us *all* stand for prayer," most of the time I sit—not that I couldn't stand, but I feel better sitting. Sam sits with me, much like the friends of the boy who lost his hair due to chemo treatments. These friends shaved their heads in sympathy for him.

I tell Evelyn that Reverend Farmer's sermon was especially thought-provoking. A small part of it was his quoting Second Chronicles, Chapter 7, verse 14, elaborating on it, and weaving it into his message. I believe, as I think Brother Jason does, that this verse has the potential of changing the United States for the better, if followed.

I whisper to her, "Evelyn, sweet Evelyn, the best part of church our last year, aside from good singing led by Gerald DeNeal and inspirational preaching by Reverend Farmer, was having you reach over and grasp my hand so that we, unnoticeable to others, held hands. That stays with me like the song I wrote for you about 'The Smile Across the Room.' To me, there was a vast difference in your taking my hand than my taking your hand. The handholding was the same either way, but the thrill on my part was greater. I knew the handholding was pleasing to you and not just tolerated.

"Evelyn, baby doll, I truly felt I was a pretty good husband, but I realize now I could have been many times better. A second chance to do better would be a great blessing. I'm happy I took pleasure in walking you to the car and opening and closing the car door for you, even though doing so was somewhat out of style. I was happy to drive you wherever you wanted to go. However, I made a garden four times larger than we needed instead of taking an interest in planting roses and flower beds that would have been more pleasing to you.

"Even though you stated many times you were thankful for our home, I could have provided you with a home you liked better. You never considered me to be lazy, but I fell miserably short of stepping up and doing my share of the housework when you were a full-time teacher with more students than you should have had. All I can do about that now is hang my head and cry. For many years, I never cried. Now crying comes easy. I feel better when I shed a few tears.

"Precious one, I was truthful with you with the exception of telling you before going fishing that I'd be back in time for dinner at noon, and then not getting back until two o'clock and finding you patiently waiting to eat with me. I never got badly criticized, but I feel much worse about it now than I did then.

"I cleaned the fish after we ate. You froze them and later brought them out and fried them to perfection.

"Sweet baby doll, thank you for not discussing my faults and shortcomings with others. Your so doing might have put me at a disadvantage if I were to decide to run for President.

"I'm beginning to realize why you asked me not to remarry if you were to die first. You didn't want others to know *what a mean man you married.*"

[To my readers, I'll explain the origin of that statement. When our son, Ray, was five years old, I got him a pair of beautiful beagle pups. They were his dogs, but I planned to rabbit hunt with them. Ray would excite them and make them chase each other and bark as if they were running a rabbit.

The pups weren't allowed in the garden. One day, I set out two long rows of tomato plants. Ray was training his pups just outside the unfenced garden. He had the pups beside themselves with excitement. One chased the other pup through the garden, down a tomato row, while taking out about every third plant. At the end of the row, the pups switched, and the one being chased became the chaser. They came back down the other tomato row and did the same amount of damage.

That raised my hackles against the pups. I picked up a handful of dried dirt about like shelled corn, and once their eyes were turned from me, scolded them and let them have it with the dirt. They took off out of the garden, while howling and carrying on as if they had been shot.

Ray immediately put his disgust with me on display. He proceeded to give me a harsh scolding. I told him to get out of the garden or I'd give him a little of what I gave the pups. When I reached for a handful of lumpy dirt, he took off. I gave him an underhanded sprinkling. He sounded off the same way the pups had. All the way to the house, he called out "Mommy, Mommy, Mommy!" and almost tore down the screen door as he stormed inside.

I straightened up the tomato plants the best I could and went in for dinner. When Ray wasn't around, I asked, "Evelyn, what did Ray say when he came in?"

With amused laughter, she answered, "Mommy, Mommy, Mommy, you don't know what a mean man you married!"]

...

Evelyn's personality and loving nature brought out the best in me. Maybe I wasn't too bad, but she made me so much better.

After getting married in 1950 and finishing our bachelor degrees, Evelyn and I decided that we should bless our home with a couple of children. LeAnn was born October 7, 1955; Ray, March 2, 1957.

LeAnn and Ray both took after their mother as far as smarts go. LeAnn's knowledge and understanding at seventeen months of age was remarkable. I didn't give her keen mind and alertness much notice. I just thought that all kids were like that.

Evelyn and I made a grave mistake by not telling LeAnn that we were going to bring her a playmate. We didn't know whether the newcomer would be a boy or a girl.

We went to the hospital and then brought Ray home. We knew it wouldn't do for LeAnn to ride in the front seat of our two-door car with Evelyn, Ray, and me, so we put her in the backseat. She wasn't happy. It showed in her eyes, face, and every fiber of her being. She behaved like a wildcat. She tried to climb over the seat. We explained to her that the baby was "Baby Ray." Then we began to stress "Brother Ray." She quickly picked up on "Brother Ray" and announced, "I don't like Brother Ray."

As time went on, progress was slow and slight. LeAnn had been easily weaned from the bottle when under one year of age. But upon Ray's appearance, she had to have a bottle again. She was also well blessed with flashes of temper. She could lovingly pat Ray's hand and repeat over and over, "Brother Ray, Brother Ray," and then up and bite him.

Once when Ray was quite young and helpless, LeAnn was rocking happily in her little rocking chair. She sweetly asked, "Mommy, can I rock Brother Ray?" Evelyn thought that LeAnn had had a change of heart and carefully placed Ray in LeAnn's arms. Evelyn was happy that at last LeAnn was beginning to love Brother Ray. LeAnn caressed Ray very tenderly and rocked him gently for about a half a minute and then gleefully shoved him onto the floor.

By the time LeAnn was around five years old, some improvement had been made. The jealousy seemed to be in the normal range.

At that time, partly to enrich the children's lives, we had a small number of different farm animals—a cow, two goats, chickens, ducks, and three hogs. One time when LeAnn and I were observing the hogs, a devious streak in me caused me to want to have a little fun, while checking to see whether LeAnn really loved Brother Ray.

One of the hogs was more of a pet than the others. I told LeAnn that that one was Brother Pig. I would rub it and pet it and say, "Good old Brother Pig." I asked LeAnn if she wanted to rub Brother Pig. She did. Then I asked, "LeAnn, who do you like better, Brother Pig or Brother Ray?" She didn't answer immediately. I kept scratching Brother Pig's back. Then she up and answered, "Brother Pig."

Do you think we let LeAnn live that down? No, never. Recently, more than forty-five years later, on one of LeAnn's trips from her home in Raleigh, North Carolina, to visit me, Ray picked her up at the airport in Paducah, Kentucky. He took her out to eat before bringing her on to stay with me.

Upon their arrival, shame on me, I had to ask, "Who do you like better—Brother Pig or Brother Ray?" She didn't have to think. With a big, hearty laugh, she said, "Brother Pig."

Now, here is an example of LeAnn's and Ray's behavior that made me happy when they were in their early teens. I had bought each of them a .410 gauge shotgun. I took them and our two young beagle dogs rabbit hunting on a hillside near the Battle Ford Bridge area. I told them where to stand, about fifty yards apart. I informed them that I would get the dogs to jump a rabbit [flush it from the underbrush] and most likely run it their way. Just about as soon as Ray and LeAnn got situated, the dogs jumped a rabbit. The dogs were in puppy dog heaven. They made beagle dog music. My day was made as the dogs took off in the direction where LeAnn and Ray were standing.

In a very short time, I heard a gunshot. I wondered if I actually had heard two shots so close together that it sounded like one. I watched LeAnn and Ray walk to the same spot. The next thing I saw was the two kids shaking hands. Ray held up the rabbit for me to see.

Unlike the way I was with my fishing, they had a rabbit and were ready to go home and show it to Mommy. (Or maybe they were hungry for what Evelyn was fixing for dinner.)

On the way home, I asked LeAnn and Ray why they were shaking hands. They said it was because they had agreed to say they had both shot the rabbit. I was pleased they had come to this agreement rather than to blows.

...

Now, at eighty-seven, I am moving a good way down the western slope of my life. I find happiness on the road I'm traveling. Much of this happiness is derived from looking at the many pleasant sights in my rearview mirror. My wonderful children and precious memories of my angel of a wife will sustain me now and always.

* * *

Unforgettable Red

My dear late wife, Evelyn, was an animal lover through and through. She encouraged flocks of birds to take up residence, with the numerous bird feeders that she devotedly kept filled. The squirrels always had ears of corn stuck on a special squirrel feeder. The deer felt free to help themselves to the birdseed and a little block of salt that Evelyn set out just for them. She even carried fish-food pellets out to our small pond to feed the supposedly wild catfish that lived there.

And we always had dogs, beginning from when we were first married. Having one or more dogs was deemed essential. One rare time, when our dog had just died and we'd not yet gotten a replacement, I mused that perhaps we did not need another dog. My daughter, LeAnn, loves to recall what Evelyn said: "If we don't get another dog, then you better start thinking about a divorce." Of course, I didn't take her too seriously, but we did acquire another dog without delay.

In the early years, I managed to impose my wishes to keep all pets outside. Over the years, though, I was worn down by the pleading of the kids and Evelyn's obvious desire to have a lapdog. Then followed a series of dogs that came into the house but slept outside. By the time we retired, however, Molly, Evelyn's little toy poodle-Shih Tzu mix, had become a permanent fixture in the house.

No doubt, Molly loved both of us. When I was out in the yard or the garden, she would happily be with me and run and chase anything that moved. Once inside the house, though, she preferred Evelyn's lap to anyone else's. She was as loving and devoted as any dog could possibly be. After fifteen wonderful years together, we sadly said goodbye to Molly and buried her in the yard, near Evelyn's rose garden. Evelyn bought a special stone with Molly's name on it, which we placed over her grave.

Our son, Ray, a firm believer in "Life's no good without a dog," brought Evelyn a puppy the next day. Ginger was a miniature pinscher with an attitude. She definitely did not learn the rule: "Don't bite the hand that feeds you." She loved sleeping on Evelyn's lap but quickly expressed her displeasure at the prospect of being moved, by nipping whatever she could reach. Anytime Evelyn sat down, Ginger was in her lap. Since Evelyn frequently needed to be moving around, Ginger also learned that sitting in "Daddy's" lap was a good thing, too. She would snuggle into the crook of my left arm or get up on my shoulder while I sat in the recliner. Somehow she knew that she shouldn't try to nip at *me*.

Over the years, she did mellow some. When Evelyn died, Ginger was lost and confused but comforted herself by sitting in my lap even more than before. I have to admit, she was a comfort to me, too. When I otherwise would have been inclined just to sit in my recliner and do nothing, she gave me numerous reasons to get up, either to feed her or to take her outside. She was a lot of company, and we shared many meals and snacks together.

Sadly, Ginger came to an untimely end under the wheels of a car in my driveway in the spring of 2009. Ray was all cocked and primed to find me another dog, but I had to repeatedly tell him that I did not want another one. I appreciated the company, but the strain of getting up at all hours—regardless of the weather—was wearing on me, and I was sure that I was too old to start all over again with a puppy. Eventually, Ray became convinced that I was serious.

Life went on, and I was doing pretty well, even if I did feel somewhat lonesome at times. As I told LeAnn, I was "keeping soul and body together." I cooked my own food, did my own shopping, and kept my lawn mowed.

Mowing the lawn that summer was particularly frustrating, however, due to the excessive amount of rain we had. Even when it didn't rain for a day or two, the dew would keep the grass too wet to mow until the afternoon. Then the sun would make the temperature ninety degrees or above.

I took care of the excessive heat by soaking a hand towel in cold water, wringing it out, and placing it around my neck and shoulders. On one particular day, I had already eaten my lunch. To keep from losing time, I put a can of Vienna Sausage in my pocket and a gallon jug of water under a tree at the edge of the lawn—just in case I needed to be refreshed.

As I mounted my 42-inch riding mower, I felt happy and thankful that I was still able to do so. After an hour of mowing, I pulled up under the shade tree to get a drink of water from the jug. I slipped off the mower into a lawn chair under the tree.

I had no more than gotten seated when I heard a loud

blast from the horn of an eighteen-wheeler on the highway. I thought to myself—a deer. But it turned out to be a medium-size, reddish-brown dog, walking on the shoulder of the road. The truck driver had just wanted to make sure that the dog didn't get in his pathway.

Even from that distance, I could tell the dog was a sturdy, well-built "mutt" that was probably lost but still seemed to know his way around. However, the way he carried himself, he appeared to be tired and probably hungry.

The dog came on up the hill to my driveway. He made his way to me as if he belonged there. He stopped about ten feet from me as though waiting for an invitation to come closer. I gave him that invitation by holding out my hand. The dog moved forward until I could pat him on the head. He accepted my gesture with a friendly—but tired—wag of his tail.

I poured some water from the jug into a pan that happened to be lying nearby. The dog drank heartily. He then tried to show his appreciation by sidling up close to me, so that I could pet him on his side. It was then that I realized he had been missing some meals. Still, he was an attractive dog.

Being tired and weak, the dog slumped down at my feet. I took the can of Vienna Sausage from my pocket and pulled the tab to remove the top. Immediately, the dog's sense of smell identified "food." He got to his feet and eyed me as though he were a birddog pointing a quail. I pulled out a sausage with my fingers. The dog lost his pointing pose and wagged not only his tail but also the back half of his body.

I wasn't at all hungry, but I wanted to study his reaction. I slowly put the sausage to my mouth and took a little nip off the end. The dog intently followed my every move. Feeling that I was being cruel, I offered the sausage to him. He surprised me by taking the food from my hand in the gentlest way. I repeated this procedure, with the dog drawing closer and closer, until the entire can of sausages was gone. Then I went into the house and got him a meal of leftovers from my noonday meal.

I decided to call the dog Red. Despite what I had told Ray earlier, I was fast becoming fond of Red. He further increased my respect for him when the mail carrier came in fast and made an abrupt stop at my box at the end of the driveway. Red moved closer to me and burst forth with a loud, protective bark that amazed me. I thought to myself, "Red, for not being a gambler, you sure are playing your cards right."

I went to the carport, got a little cast-off throw rug, and put it on the ground near my chair. Red seemed to know it was for him to lie on. He lay down for a nap, and I went on with my mowing.

As I mowed, I wondered what had separated Red from his owner. I liked him and was willing to give him a home, but I had no desire to deprive a rightful owner of his or her pet. However, days passed, and Red and I began to feel as if we belonged to each other. He slept on his throw rug in the carport and reported on anything unusual taking place, especially at night.

Things seemed to be going almost too well, but that changed suddenly one afternoon. A well-dressed woman, perhaps around thirty — whom I would have considered to be attractive under a different set of circumstances — banged on the door as I was watching TV. She was hysterical. She demanded to know my name and address and stated that she planned to have me arrested for allowing my dog to run loose. She asked if I knew there was a leash law for dogs in Illinois.

I asked her to calm down and tell me about her problem. With a frantic, hate-filled expression on her face and her arms flailing about in the air, she exclaimed, "I'll tell you what the problem is. Your damn mutt dog has just killed my darling, pedigreed Manx show cat, Prince Tom."

With surprise and disbelief, I asked, "Killed your cat?"

With a sneer, she retorted, "Yes, are you hard of hearing? I just said your damn dog killed my cat."

Maintaining my calm in the face of her anger, I replied, "Lady, I'm sorry about the loss of your cat. But may I ask what your cat was doing on my property?"

Taken aback only for a moment, she protested, "I was hardly on your property. I just pulled into your driveway a short way."

Somewhat reluctantly, it seemed, she decided to give me more details. "I was returning to Chicago from a cat show in Florida, and I decided to take the back roads once I reached Illinois, so that I could enjoy the beauty of Southern Illinois. I crossed the Ohio River on a ferry at Cave-in-Rock. With Prince Tom on a leash, he and I stood at the railing of the ferry as we crossed the river. We had to wait mid-river for a long coal barge to pass, and the wake of the barge rocked the ferry.

"When we got back in the car on the Illinois side, Prince Tom was acting like he didn't feel well. I had his carrier on my front seat so that I could keep an eye on him as I drove. By the time we reached this stretch of road, he was acting as if he was going to throw up. I pulled into your driveway, so that I could get him out of the car to give him some fresh air. I barely had the leash on him when Prince Tom and your mutt saw each other at the same time. Prince Tom jerked loose from me, dashed a few steps toward your dog, while hissing and arching his back, afraid of nothing.

"Your mutt came dashing up, bristles up and teeth bared, which made him look more like a demon than the mutt that he is. He jumped on my darling Tom, shook the life out of him, and dropped him only when I managed to give him a good kick." She suddenly burst into tears.

Taking advantage of the temporary lull in her attack, I said, "Ma'am, I'll be happy to give you directions to my vet clinic in Harrisburg, so that someone can check out your cat. Shall I help you get him in your car?"

Despite my good intentions, that suggestion fired her up again. She replied hotly, "Why in the world would I need a vet? Prince Tom is dead! I picked up his limp body and put him in his carrier just before I came up to your door. There's no point in going to the vet," she finished disgustedly.

Willing myself to remain conciliatory, I stated, "It may take several words and a few minutes to get this matter settled short of a major lawsuit. I'm Kestner Wallace. What is your name?"

Almost unwillingly, she said, "You can call me Jane."

"Okay, Jane, please come in and have a seat." Jane hesitated, and then followed me into the house, with Red trailing behind. Once inside, Red sat upright on his haunches, as if I had given him a command to sit.

When we were all seated, I commented, "Jane, it is my understanding that the leash law doesn't apply to the country. In the country, as opposed to in town, dogs have more freedom. However, that doesn't give them a right to kill cats."

Her huffiness returned quickly, and in an icy tone, she replied, "You bet your a** it doesn't. A dog that does should be sentenced to a lifetime in a cage and then executed!"

I replied, "Jane, you wouldn't give a poor dog a second chance?"

"No, no second chance," she retorted angrily. "Furthermore, I plan to demand full compensation for the loss of Prince Tom."

Curious, I asked, "What amount do you have in mind?"

As Jane and I talked, Red looked at whoever was speaking. When I talked, he held his head high. When Jane talked, he lowered his head and looked at his feet.

In response to my question, Jane protested, "It would be an insult for me to put a price on Prince Tom. I paid five hundred dollars for him as a kitten nearly four years ago."

Shocked, I replied, "That sounds excessive for a cat!"

Jane replied haughtily, "We are not talking about just a cat. We are talking about Prince Tom, a champion Manx."

I didn't know a Manx from a housecat, so that meant nothing to me. I rebutted, "Yes, but five hundred dollars for a kitten! I didn't pay that much for a top-notch team of mules and a span of well-matched bay horses."

Rolling her eyes, Jane said, "Yes, Mr. Wallace, but that was *way* back when, and this is now."

I decided to drop my bombshell. "Well, Jane, I hope the real owner of this dog, Red, is pretty well off, so he can reimburse you."

Disbelieving, Jane cried, "What! Isn't Red your dog?"

I replied, "The answer to your question is yes and no."

Impatiently, Jane said, "Leave off the double talk. Either he's yours, or he isn't. Which is it?"

I explained, "Red wobbled up my driveway less than a month ago. He was worn out and hungry. I fed him and talked kindly to him, and he didn't leave. I'm inclined to believe his real owner is feeling his loss deeply. I'm fighting not to become too attached to him in case I learn who the real owner is."

Jane complained, "Mr. Wallace, it seems that you are trying to wiggle yourself out of taking any responsibility for the loss of my cat. What would you suggest that I do?"

With my tongue in my cheek, I suggested, "Well, you could hire a detective to see if he can locate Red's owner and go from there."

She didn't take me seriously on that suggestion and was somewhat disgusted at the ridiculousness of it. Ending the conversation, she got to her feet and insisted that I go out and see how mangled her precious cat was. Red stood as if to go also. I put my hand out and down and said, "Stay." Red flattened himself on the floor and didn't move a muscle.

We walked out to where her car was parked at the end of my driveway. On the way out there, Jane said begrudgingly, "I'll have to admit that Red minds well. After I kicked him and scolded him, he did stop mauling Prince Tom."

I replied, "I have had trouble believing all along that Red would kill any cat. Maybe Prince Tom has a possum gene." Seeing her blank look, I explained, "You may or may not know that an opossum, in time of danger, will pretend to be dead when it is not."

Totally unconvinced, Jane said, "Prince Tom was carrying on as if he were being killed and then suddenly lay perfectly still. If he wasn't dead, then he sure had me fooled."

We reached the car, and Jane opened the door so that we could look into the cat carrier. We bent down a bit to look more closely at Prince Tom's body. To Jane's total surprise and my great relief, we observed that Prince Tom's eyes were open and his cat motor was running—which I took as a good sign that all was well.

Joyfully, Jane exclaimed, "My darling Prince Tom." At the sound of Jane's voice, Prince Tom got to his feet, stretched leisurely, then circled around the carrier's interior, which gave me an opportunity to see his whole body. At first I thought he had lost his tail in the fight, but I quickly deduced that having no tail was one of the Manx's characteristics. From all appearances, Prince Tom seemed to be just fine.

With a happy expression and a touch of embarrassment, Jane said, "Mr. Wallace, I owe you an apology. I lost my cool and overreacted. I've been a bit on edge ever since I left Chicago for the cat show. My husband and I had a big fight just before I left, so I was probably taking some of my anger out on you."

I was tempted to give her some marital advice but then thought I better leave well enough alone. Instead, I replied, "Don't worry about it. 'All's well that ends well.' You and Prince Tom have a safe trip." With a wave of her hand and a big smile, Jane and her dear Prince Tom were off to Chicago.

I went back into the house. Red was still lying flat on the floor. I said, "Red, we are entitled to a treat." He immediately stood and started wagging his tail. I got him a can of Vienna Sausage from the cupboard and me a Dilly Bar from the freezer, and we went out under the shade tree to eat.

As we ate, I decided that if Red was going to be my dog, I would take him to the vet to have him checked out. During the examination, to my surprise, the vet found a microchip under Red's skin, which contained the name and phone number of Red's owner. (I didn't even know such a thing existed.) That information gave me very mixed emotions. I had prayed that I would find Red's owner but, at the same time, had hoped that I wouldn't.

I knew what I had to do. When I rang the number, a pleasant voice answered, "Hello, this is John."

I responded, "I'm Kestner Wallace, south of Harrisburg. Do you have a dog missing?"

I heard a gasp on the line, followed by, "Yes, Mr. Wallace—praise the Lord, I sure do. Is Red all right?"

Shocked by the coincidence, I asked, "Is 'Red' his name? That is the name I gave him, also."

John briefly told me Red's story. "Red was a castaway. I got him at a garbage dump when he was about four weeks old. He is three years old now. I named him Red because of his color. My wife and I have no children, so Red became the child we couldn't have."

Feeling my hopes slipping away, I decided to at least ask, "Now that you haven't had him for more than a month and have learned there is life after Red, would you be interested in selling him to me? I would give you a high dollar for him and provide him a good home."

John quickly replied, "The answer is 'No—a thousand times no.' Give me directions to your home, and I'll pick up Red and pay you well for his keep."

I gave him directions and assured him that I'd accept nothing for Red's keep. I told John that since I lived alone, Red's company had more than paid for his keep.

John said, "From where I live near St. Louis, I can be there and pick up Red in about three hours."

Reluctant to let Red go that soon, I countered, "How about making it around ten o'clock tomorrow morning? As corny as it sounds, I would like to fix Red and me a steak dinner and enjoy one last night together."

John agreed. "I will be happy to go along with your wishes. Ten o'clock tomorrow morning it will be."

That evening, Red and I had our steak dinner. Breaking my cardinal rule, I allowed Red to sleep next to my bed that night on a soft rug, which I had placed on the floor for him.

About 9:15 a.m. the next day, Red and I were seated

under the large maple tree—I in a lawn chair and Red on his rug by my side. Not even the birds gliding through the air or the leaves whispering in the breeze could lift my spirits, although I tried—for Red's sake—not to be sad.

Red was first to detect a car slowing to turn into the driveway. He would have sounded off had I not placed my hand on his head and said, "No, no."

The car stopped on the circle drive around the tree. A tall, good-looking, middle-aged man stepped out of the car and took two or three steps toward me. Red took a step or two toward him. He seemed puzzled. He looked at John and then at me. John, unable to control his emotions, uttered the one word, "Red."

Red went beside himself with joy. He rushed to John, and whining with elation, he spanked John's leg with his tail.

John bent down and gave Red a big hug, then rubbed him all over as Red danced around in excitement. I stood as John stepped forward to shake my hand. "It is a pleasure to meet you, Mr. Wallace." I then suggested that we sit while he told me how he and Red had gotten separated.

John explained that he, his wife, and Red had been vacationing in and around the Great Smoky Mountains and were on their way home. They had planned to see the Garden of the Gods in Southern Illinois. In the middle of the afternoon, they stopped at the Dairy Bar in Golconda for a meal.

John continued, "As we had many times before on days when it was not too hot, we left Red in the car with all of the windows rolled down. We would always bring him a treat afterwards, which we told him was a reward for guarding the car.

"After thirty minutes or more, we finished our meal and headed back to the car with a scrap of meat for Red.

However, Red was nowhere to be seen. I theorized that he had noticed a cat passing by — he loves to chase cats — and bolted through the window. We drove numerous times all over the small town and made frequent stops at the Dairy Bar. We got a room and spent the night in Golconda so that we could search more the next morning. When we could find no trace of him, we decided someone must have taken a liking to him and claimed him for his own.

"We finally gave up and went on home. Every day, we hoped and prayed that we would get him back. You know the rest of the story, except the way he spent the days from his disappearance in Golconda until he arrived at your house."

I responded, "That would make an interesting story. You will have to reprimand Red for not keeping a diary."

Grinning and shaking his head, John said. "I'm too happy to have him back to give him even a cross look."

We both knew the time of departure had arrived. We stood, and John reached out to shake my hand. When he saw a tear in my eye, he embraced me instead. In response to another offer from John, I again insisted that I wanted no money for taking care of Red.

Convinced that I meant what I said, John turned to open the car door on the passenger's side and then stood back, as I had done for Evelyn many times. Red jumped into the car and sat upright, facing forward. John closed the door, got in on the driver's side, and lowered the window on Red's side. Red stuck his head out as far as he could, as if saying farewell. I gave him a little salute. John drove down the driveway and turned onto the highway. I gazed at the car until I could see Red no more.

I returned to my chair under the tree and sat motionless for a while, staring into space. Then I tried to shake myself out of feeling sorry for myself by rejoicing in the knowledge that Red would be loved and cared for when I had ceased the walk of man. That did make me feel somewhat better.

As I sat there, my thoughts drifted off. The prospects of "ceasing the walk of man" made me think back to a standing-room-only funeral that I had attended at a country church close to the Eagle Creek area when I was eleven or twelve years old. Standing near me, in the double-door entrance, was a man with a week-old beard. He was dressed in overalls and a blue work shirt, damp with perspiration. In his left hand, he held a beat-up felt hat; in his right hand, he held a red bandana, which he used now and then to remove tears and perspiration from his face.

At the close of the service, this man said, "That sermon makes me believe more than ever that there is a 'hereafter.'" Then, slightly altering 1 Corinthians 15:19, he said, "In fact, if in this life only I have hope, I would be of all men most miserable."

Many pet lovers believe strongly that there is a "hereafter" for their beloved pets. Far be it from me to deprive anyone of the pleasure of believing as they do. I'll keep my personal opinions on the subject to myself. But, who knows, perhaps Molly and Ginger are frolicking with Evelyn now in Heaven, as will Prince Tom and Red with their owners in the (I hope) distant future. Regardless of our pets' ultimate destination, it is my sincere belief that we should follow the Golden Rule as much with our pets as with people and treat them as we would like to be treated.

Red had definitely softened up this old heart and lessened my resolve to have no more pets. Perhaps there will be another dog . . . but, Ray, don't bring one home yet!

* * *

Ghostly Saints

George was driving his Model T Ford on the way to the country store when he decided to stop at Uncle Charlie's to check the car engine. This was something he did often, whether or not anything was wrong. Usually after one of these stops, he would take off with a lot of zip to prove that he had fixed whatever had been wrong.

George was in his late teens or early twenties. He was honest, likeable, and trustworthy. He was impressively handsome, which really doesn't have any bearing on this story. With only a slight idea of the duties of a lawyer or a detective, he said from time to time that he planned to become one or the other.

Uncle Charlie and his wife, Mollie, were very spry for being in their early seventies. They were always friendly with George. He felt comfortable around them even though others—not a few—thought that, behind their smiles and soft-spoken voices, they were strange people. Not all people referred to Charlie as "Uncle" Charlie, but inasmuch as he liked the ring of it—and Charlie continually referred to himself that way—it just came natural for George to call him Uncle Charlie, as well.

George picked up several bits of gossip hinting that Uncle Charlie and Mollie practiced witchcraft and were devil worshippers. However, when George could get no proof beyond hearsay, he tried to dismiss the whole matter from his mind. Still, the seed had been planted.

When George stopped in front of Uncle Charlie's house to put some air in one of the tires with a hand pump or replace a spark plug wire that he had intentionally removed back down the road, he told himself that he was getting a jump start practicing his future profession of being a detective.

George was much impressed by the fact that Uncle Charlie and Mollie volunteered to do the grass cutting and the sweeping at the community country church, which had a nearby cemetery. They seldom attended church services, although they seemed at ease when they did. The two insisted that their work was a small contribution for the privilege of living in such a fine community.

Uncle Charlie and Mollie lived about a mile south of the church. George observed that, very oddly, Uncle Charlie and Mollie did their church sweeping and cleaning after dark and often late at night. Uncle Charlie, for some reason, always parked his Model T pickup rather close to the cemetery, even though it seemed that the other side or front of the church would have been better places. George thought that perhaps Uncle Charlie was trying to prove to himself that cemeteries late at night were not to be feared.

On this particular fall morning, George had just gotten the hood up and was fiddling around with the distributor when Uncle Charlie walked up and called out a pleasant "Good morning." George quickly completed the engine adjustment and entered into small talk with Uncle Charlie.

Just before George drove off, Uncle Charlie asked him if he could help butcher a couple of hogs the following morning. He said that his brother had helped him for years, but he had died since the last hog killing. George noticed that an uncomfortable look—rather than one of sorrow—flashed over Uncle Charlie's face. However, his smile quickly returned. Charlie said that he would gladly pay George and give him some fresh meat, to boot.

George fleetingly wondered about Uncle Charlie's masked emotion, but dismissed it and replied, "Uncle Charlie, I'll help you if you will promise me you won't offer me any money. My service to you will be as your service to the church—an act of neighborliness."

Uncle Charlie smiled and replied, "George, I'll be forever grateful to you. I'll see you in the morning." George smiled and waved a friendly goodbye to Uncle Charlie.

He arrived early the next day. Uncle Charlie and Mollie already had all the preparations made. The fire heap was going. They had set a wooden barrel at a forty-five degree angle, with one end sitting in a hole in the ground. They had put hot rocks from the fire heap into the water in the barrel, which had brought the water temperature to a degree suitable for scalding.

George had brought his rifle along in case Uncle Charlie wanted him to shoot the hogs. Uncle Charlie turned down his offer, saying "Mollie and I have always taken turns killing and sticking the hogs."

George then said that, as long as it didn't make any difference, he wouldn't even watch the killing, since he was a little chicken-hearted. Uncle Charlie and Mollie seemed pleased to have that part of the operation left completely to themselves—so pleased that George became curious and decided to watch through a crack in the adjoining stall.

He saw Uncle Charlie hand Mollie the rifle once they were inside the stall where the two 250-pound hogs were. In turn, she handed him a sharp-pointed butcher's knife. She gave Charlie a gleeful smile. The same instant that the rifle butt touched her shoulder, she pulled the trigger. The hog dropped without a sound. She winked at Uncle

Charlie and laughed excitedly. Uncle Charlie struck the jugular vein with the same ease with which Mollie had hit her mark. He winked and smiled at her as he withdrew the knife and the blood gushed forth. Mollie grabbed the dipper that she'd had at the ready and quickly caught some of the blood. She drank then passed the dipper to Uncle Charlie, who drained the remainder.

In the past, George had seen shooting and sticking performed at a high degree of perfection, but the operation had never before given him such a strange feeling. He was shocked at the pleasure the couple seemed to have derived from the precision of their performance and the drinking of the blood.

George hesitantly rejoined Uncle Charlie and Mollie. Together they dragged the hog to the scalding barrel. The water must have been the correct temperature. In other words, they "got a good scald." They soon had the hog scraped clean of hair, hung up, and gutted.

Feeling weak-kneed, George went back to his "peeking crack," where he had a ringside view for the next go-round. This time, on entering the stall, Uncle Charlie handed Mollie the butcher knife; she handed him a four-pound sledgehammer. With the speed of a lion trainer, he wheeled and struck the remaining hog in the head, killing it with one blow. George again saw Uncle Charlie wink with delight. By the time that George fully comprehended what had happened, Mollie was already displaying expressions of glee over her perfect job of sticking. Again, George was shocked and surprised. He wondered, with all their skill and ability, why they needed him. He supposed that it would have been difficult for them to have done the dragging, scalding, and hanging without his assistance.

Uncle Charlie and Mollie thanked George most sincerely for his help and gave him a large pan containing

liver, ribs, and tenderloin. He expressed his great appreciation for the meat. The thoughts of his family having some
fresh meat caused him to suppress the strange feelings
the whole experience had given him.

He stopped a couple of days later at Uncle Charlie's
to return the meat pan. Both Uncle Charlie and Mollie
seemed really pleased to see him. George told them that
he couldn't stay long; he needed to go to the store for
his family.

After a short visit, Uncle Charlie and Mollie walked
with him partway to the car. They asked if he would stop
at the church on his way back from the store and get
their broom. They said that they had left it in the broom
closet when they had done their recent cleaning. George
assured them that he would gladly do so.

It didn't take George long to get the things on his family's shopping list and make his way to the church. He
hurried inside and flung open the broom closet door.

There on the floor—slumped over on his side—was
a medium-sized man with black hair, streaked with gray.
He was wearing glasses and bore a striking resemblance
to Uncle Charlie.

George was startled, to say the least. When his eyes
became adjusted to the dim light, he realized that the
man was dead. George was rendered motionless and
speechless.

When he recovered from the initial shock, he reached
out with a weak and trembling hand and picked up the
broom. He closed the door and was about to leave the
church when he told himself that he had to be unmis-
takably sure that the man was dead. So he reluctantly
opened the door and placed an unsteady hand on the
man's wrist. That left no doubt in his mind. The body
was cold and stiff.

George went to the car, but he didn't leave immediately. He couldn't decide whether to return to the store and report his finding or go tell Uncle Charlie and Mollie.

Then the bright idea occurred to him that this would be a good chance for him to play detective. He took the broom and placed it on the porch at Uncle Charlie's. George was about to leave when Mollie gave him what sounded like a pleading invitation to come inside and tell them the store news.

George felt surprisingly calm. He told them that only four or five people were around the store, and that they weren't talking very much. As a result, he hadn't learned a thing. He went on to say that he didn't have to go into the church to get the broom because it was just outside the door.

Uncle Charlie and Mollie both had their eyes riveted on George as he delivered this last bit of news. They exchanged concerned glances then quickly returned to their natural selves again. After a few more general comments, George went on home.

He told no one of the dead man. He suspected that Uncle Charlie and Mollie knew of his find and hoped that he would report it, leaving them uninvolved. On the other hand, had he reported back to them first, they might have offered their help in getting rid of the body, thus removing George from any suspicion. George reminded himself that he would have to be careful and not let his imagination run away with him.

George could not get the dead man off his mind. About the time most people would be going to bed, he positioned himself on a knoll in the field in front of the church. It was a rather dark night. He had been there at least two hours when he heard a vehicle approaching from the south. It had no lights on and was just creeping along. From where George was stationed, he was unable to tell whether the car was a pickup or a touring car. All he could tell was that it pulled up close to the front of the church and, after five minutes or less, left, returning in the direction from which it had come.

George felt sure that the person or persons in the car had removed the dead man from the church. He wasn't about to go down there and find out. However, he did feel relieved. When he finally pillowed his head, he didn't have any trouble going to sleep. He did check the next morning and found that the body was gone.

As George thought of the dead man over the next few days, he decided that he would be contented if he knew, for his own satisfaction, what had happened to him. He concluded that he didn't want to try to pin anything on anybody.

This is how George set his mind at ease. It wasn't proof that would have satisfied anyone else. It came about this way. He had been fishing for catfish after a big rain, around the last of April, some six weeks following the discovery and disappearance of the dead man. On impulse, he stopped at the church cemetery on the way home.

Three people had been buried there in the past year. Two of the graves were fairly close to the entrance of the cemetery, and the other was at the far corner.

George took a straight, strong, sharp-pointed cane pole and easily forced it into the soft dirt of the two nearest graves. In both cases, about three or more feet down, he could tell the cane was striking the wooden box that held the casket.

Then he went over to the third grave. He pushed the cane down into the center of the grave. A little more than two feet down, he struck a spongy object. He continued his prodding until he outlined what he thought was a human being buried on top of the wooden box in the grave. George carefully covered all of his prodding holes and went on home, feeling that he had solved his first mystery. But the surprise of his life was yet to come.

Soon after his visit to the cemetery, George went to Kentucky to help his grandfather with his spring planting. When he returned about a month later, he learned that Uncle Charlie had died, followed by Mollie, a week later. He was told that the funerals were well attended. The minister had said many good things concerning their lives and had referred to them as "saints."

They were buried in the center of the church cemetery. The church folks contributed enough money to provide the largest tombstone in the cemetery for them. They also pitched in and did a good job mowing the grass, trimming the trees, and generally cleaning up the cemetery.

George regretted that he had lost two friends and that he had missed their funerals. He vowed to himself that he would go to their graves and pay them his respects, but he kept putting it off from day to day until he forgot about it altogether.

That fall, George bought a young coon dog that was only partly trained. One night, he decided to take him out for a little pre-season training. As he had done many times before, he parked in a little lane not far from the church and walked into the big woods to the northeast. George was happy that there was a full moon; he didn't need to carry a light. However, he realized that coon hunting would have been better on a dark night.

After about three hours of top-notch trailing and two good "up-the-tree" experiences for the young coon dog, George decided it was time to return home. His return to the car was a little off course. Before he realized it, he had walked from the wooded area straight into the church cemetery.

By the light of the full moon, the first thing to grab his attention was the large tombstone in the center of the graveyard. A little tremor went up George's spine, but he found comfort in the fact that his dog, Bowser, was next to him. George thought to himself that it would be a good time to stand by the graves of Uncle Charlie and Mollie and show his respect with a moment of silent prayer.

A deep growl from Bowser as he hugged closely to George's leg caused George to bring his meditation to an abrupt end. When George opened his eyes, he beheld the dead man who had been in the church, Uncle Charlie, and Mollie, all standing no more than ten feet from him. Uncle Charlie had his right arm around the shoulders of the man and his left arm around Mollie's waist. Seeing the man next to Uncle Charlie, George was again struck by their resemblance.

At first he was too scared to move, for he remembered the whispered stories about Uncle Charlie and Mollie. When he got enough strength to speak, he said in the most authoritative voice he could manage, "In the name of God, rest in peace!"

With that said, he made an abrupt about-face and walked for some thirty feet before daring to stop. Bowser tried to wrap himself around George's legs and never ceased trembling. Attempting to get rid of the eerie feeling that had overcome him, George repeatedly said to himself, "I'll not look back. I'm not afraid of anything living or dead." However, he made himself turn around to see what was taking place.

Uncle Charlie and Mollie stood by their tombstone. In the twinkle of an eye, they dropped into their graves, while the man from the church walked slowly to the far corner of the cemetery, where he, too, disappeared.

Many years have passed since George had his ghostly encounter. Despite his making occasional visits to the cemetery over the years, George never again saw any of the three. Now George also lies at rest in the same neglected country cemetery. Perhaps George's detective work continues — underground, of course.

* * *

Self Defense

On the first day of June 2009, I was sitting in the shade of my carport while admiring the beauty of the newly mowed lawn and noting the various shades of green in the large expanse stretching southward. A gentle breeze carried the pleasant aroma of the wild roses and honeysuckle bordering the wet-weather creek just beyond the lawn. From where I sat, Womble Mountain was less than a half a mile to the east.

The morning sky was a lovely blue. It was pleasantly warm, but not hot—just the type of day that made a person glad to be alive. All that kept the day from being perfect was the fact that my sweet wife, Evelyn, was in the Wallace Family Cemetery, near the foot of Womble Mountain, instead of in the empty chair by my side. At times, the more than two-and-a-half years she had been gone seemed like an eternity. At other times, I still expected her to walk out of the house and take a seat beside me—as if no time had passed at all and nothing had changed. To ward off being too cast down and feeling sorry for myself, I focused my meditation on thanking the Good Lord for the fifty-six years that Evelyn and I had had together.

While I was lost in thought, a fancy car pulled up and stopped no more than ten feet from me. I had time only to get to my feet when an attractive, stylishly dressed woman stepped out of her car. She looked to be about five feet seven inches tall, with brown hair and eyes and a light tan complexion. She asked, "Are you Ray Wallace, the gun dealer?"

I answered, "No, I'm Kestner Wallace, Ray's father."

"Is Ray also a minister?"

"Ray's full-time job is a counselor/supervisor at the Youth Center in Harrisburg—a prison. However, he is a licensed minister and performs weddings when called upon. But buying, selling, and trading guns is a hobby that he loves very much. Does that sound like the fellow you are looking for?"

"Yes, however, I'm also interested in you, since you are Kestner Wallace."

Puzzled, I said, "Maybe you should tell me who you are and what I can do for you."

A little embarrassed, she said hastily, "Excuse me for not introducing myself." She held out her hand to shake mine. "I'm Doris Jean. I'm a sister to Bob, who bought a very special revolver from Ray last November." She paused, then said, "I'm afraid my story is sort of long and drawn out."

Indicating one of the lawn chairs, I said, "In that case, have a seat."

Thanking me, she settled into a chair. She gazed out over the lawn and remarked, "I can see why you are sitting here. The scenery is so lovely. Yesterday, I visited the Garden of the Gods and was impressed and awestruck by the beauty there, too. At the risk of giving you the impression that I'm more religious than I am, I'm going to say, 'There has to be a God in Heaven.'"

"That was beautifully said. If I were a singer, I'd sing you a verse of 'How Great Thou Art.'"

As I looked at Doris Jean and waited for her to respond, I thought, "Despite her looks, style, and class, it doesn't seem to have gone to her head." But I wondered why in the world she was here and interested in finding both Ray and me.

Doris Jean looked at me, seemingly lost in thought. Finally she said, "I know you better than you know me. Allow me to explain. . . . I'm Bob's twin sister. He came to Southern Illinois to deer hunt in Pope County last deer season. He returned happier than I'd ever seen him. He said that he had had a grand time—he'd shot an eight-point buck the first day and given it to an Indiana hunter who was downcast because he was sure he wouldn't get a deer and would lose a hundred-dollar bet. Bob also attended the Deer Festival at Golconda and raved about the barbecue he had eaten.

"However, what had really turned him on was the fact that he saw Ray Wallace's gun sale ad in the Golconda paper. He looked up Ray. He said that they hit it off well from the very start. After five minutes, they were talking and laughing as if they had known each other for years. Bob was pleased that Ray's guns were of high quality and reasonably priced. The thing that made Bob's day, however, was the fact that Ray had a very special kind of revolver—one that Bob had been looking for for years. It was like the one owned by my late husband, Earl. Earl, Bob, and I all had loved the gun and named it Self Defense.

"Bob bought the gun like Self Defense. It was the last of its kind that Ray had. Bob got carried away and also bought four or five other short guns to resell to friends as a favor. Guns sell much higher up our way.

"Ray told Bob that that was the biggest sale he had ever made to one person in the twenty-five years he had been in business, and for that reason, he wanted to give him a present—a book, *A Dollar the Hard Way*, written by his father. Bob read the book and then gave it to me for a birthday present. I have read it twice. That is why I can say that I know you better than you know me."

Pleased as I was to hear that she had liked my book well enough to read it twice, I was more curious about the rest of her story. I said, "Well, you make me want to know more about you, Earl, Bob, and Self Defense."

Doris Jean obviously had another agenda. "Before going into that, I want to let you know that Ray told Bob that you have a gun like Self Defense, too. It's the one that Ray gave you for Christmas last year."

I knew immediately which gun Doris Jean was talking about. Ray had told me that he had gotten the pair of guns from a wealthy, retired New York banker whose hobby was gun collecting, buying them from private collectors or at estate sales. When the banker had acquired the two revolvers, he learned that they were made by a former watchmaker somewhere in Europe. The brand was an odd name I can never remember.

Seeing my look of comprehension about what gun she was referring to, she warned me with a raised eyebrow and a smile, "Don't be surprised if I try to buy it from you."

I returned her smile. Knowing no sale would be made unless I wanted it to be made, I said, "I'll keep that in mind. Now, tell me about you."

She thought for a moment then launched into her story. "If I were to write an autobiography, it would very much involve two marvelous men in my life. The first was Charles. I was eighteen, and he was twenty-one. We were engaged. We loved each other with every fiber of our beings. Two weeks before we were to be married, Charles was killed on a construction job. I died along with him . . . or at least I wished I had. I almost lost my mind.

"Outwardly, I had to pull myself together—enough to earn a living. I held a job as a receptionist at a large hotel near Chicago. Just below the surface, however, I was lonely and broken-hearted.

"Earl was an older man who stayed occasionally at the hotel over the next five years. I thought his face brightened a bit when he saw me. I really wasn't sure, but I tried to look more pleasant anyway. I noticed that Earl began to dress and groom much better and was more pleasing to the eye.

"Over time, I thought I detected a change in his feelings for me. I knew it wasn't my imagination the day he walked up to my desk, handed me a single, long-stem rose, and said, 'A lovely rose for a lovely lady.' I thanked him and smiled as kindly as I knew how.

"A few months later, he asked if I would have dinner with him. I accepted. That dinner lasted for hours. He had a sad story to tell me. He mentioned two business partners. They had been like brothers to him since junior high. He was evasive as to their line of business but said that it was very lucrative.

"Earl told me that he had been married for several years and had mostly considered his marriage to be sound—until his wife and one of his partners came to him and asked if they could have a little talk. They told him they were and had been in love for a long time and had been carrying on a secret love affair. Earl said that he had had a deep-down feeling that something was wrong with their marriage, but he couldn't ever put his finger on what it was. He wished they had told him sooner. He and his wife divorced, but the business partnership continued."

I had to express my surprise that the partnership could continue after that revelation. Doris Jean responded, with obvious feeling, "The partnership was a lot more solid than their marriage ever was. He was too good for her.

His guardian angel delivered him from her so that I could have him."

With a knowing smile, I said, "I assume you and Earl got married and had a good life together soon thereafter?"

Doris Jean shook her head no. "It didn't happen all of a sudden. But after that dinner together, I had deeper feelings for him and thought he felt the same way.

"Some time thereafter, the transmission went out on my ten-year-old Buick. I took it to the Buick garage and dealership to get it replaced. I was furnished a car to drive while the replacement was being made.

"In a day or two, Earl told me that he had just checked and learned my car was fixed. He said he would go with me to get it. When we got there, the first thing we saw was a new maroon Buick with a ribbon on it and a sign that said, 'Happy Birthday, Doris Jean.' The kind, loving look on Earl's face and the Buick caused my love for him to go up like a hot air balloon.

"Not many days passed until Earl asked me to marry him. I told him that I would be happy to be his wife. He wanted to take me immediately to pick out an engagement ring. It wasn't easy to convince him that I didn't want a large, gaudy stone. It isn't in my nature to show off." Seeing my quick glance over at her car, she added, "However, I do like to drive a nice car and wear clothes that are in style."

Feeling fairly confident in my predictive powers, I said, "Allow me to tell you what happened next. You got married, and Earl requested that you not work outside the home."

Looking a bit surprised, Doris Jean asked, "How did you know?"

I confessed, "I didn't know. I just guessed."

Doris Jean confirmed my intuition. "Earl wanted me to run our home and supervise a housekeeper."

I commented, "Your life story sounds a lot like a fairy tale."

Nodding, Doris Jean continued, "The several years I had with Earl were happy years indeed. If he had a dark side, I never saw it. Earl was a law school graduate but got too busy to take the bar exam. His knowledge of the law and his connections with people in high places helped him keep his partners just barely inside the law a good part of the time. His partners appreciated the part he played in making what they did profitable."

I remarked, "I can see, Doris Jean, there was much about Earl's life that you didn't know."

With no defensiveness, she replied, "That was the way he wanted it. I was happy to comply with his wishes."

Trying to steer the story back around to the gun, I said, "I'd like for you to explain to me what made Self Defense so special."

"Earl bought the gun for a high dollar and claimed it for his very own. But his partners contended inasmuch as he had paid for it out of the petty cash fund of the business, it really belonged to all of them. They had a friendly ongoing discussion as to the real owner. Each of the three carried it concealed on occasion, but Earl kept it most of the time. My brother, Bob, felt that Earl would one day give him Self Defense. I, as Earl's wife, was just as sure it would be mine."

Still wanting to know more, I replied, "That's all very interesting. But that still doesn't explain what made it so special."

Doris Jean thought for just a moment. With a hard-to-decipher look on her face, she said, "It was special because of the way it felt in a person's hand. It was neither too heavy nor too light. It had perfect balance. The sights seemed to line up with the target automatically.

The bounce, when fired, was less than that of other guns. Its color didn't draw attention to itself. Any gun owner would have loved to have owned it."

I decided to focus more on the name of the gun. "Doris Jean, all of you called the gun Self Defense. Can you tell me why?"

Doris Jean responded readily, "Strangely, each of the three partners used it to defend themselves against at least two people who were about to take their lives. I don't know the particulars about the two partners' incidents, but Earl told me what happened in his. He was sitting at his desk in their office. Self Defense was in the center drawer. Two rough, criminal types of men rushed in with pistols drawn and said, with vulgarity, 'We are going to blow you full of holes.' Earl said he heard two shots and then saw the two thugs lying on the floor. A smoking gun was in his hand. Earl gave the magic of Self Defense credit for his life being saved. I personally believe God spared his life so that he could make peace with his maker."

Curious, I asked, "Doris Jean, to keep me from wondering any longer, please tell me who ended up with that remarkable gun."

She replied, with a teasing, warning tone in her voice, "My telling you to set your mind at ease will just keep you sitting in that chair a lot longer."

I urged her on, "You talk—I'll listen. That and sitting in a chair are the two things that I do best."

With a little "you-asked-for-it" look, she continued. "Both Bob's wife and Earl were diagnosed with a rare type of cancer within a short time of each other. Bob's wife died within three months. Earl's cancer seemed to go into remission. His doctor advised him to retire and stay free of stress.

"Earl and I insisted that Bob come and live with us in our large home. Since he didn't enjoy living alone, he gladly moved in with us. We were a happy threesome."

I inquired, "Did Earl go on working?"

"Earl told his partners that he was giving them two-week's notice that he was retiring. They were regretful but understood. They promised to take inventory and deliver to him his share of the business. Earl had taught them a lot, and they felt they could carry on by being careful."

I interjected, "I hope his partners were fair with Earl."

"They were fairer with him than I gave them credit for at the time. Earl put in his two weeks and left everything in good shape.

"Two weeks passed after he left without any communication among them. At nine o'clock one evening, Bob, Earl, and I were watching TV. Bob answered a loud knock at the door. Two stern, hard-looking men stepped inside without being invited. I could tell that Bob had seen them before but didn't hold them in high esteem. Earl's greeting was pleasant. He introduced them to me. They improved my feeling toward them by commenting, 'It's a real pleasure at last to meet the wonderful lady who took a man as rough around the edges as we are and made a gentleman out of him.' I smiled in acknowledgement of the introduction and said, 'I'm happy that you, along with me, recognize what a marvelous man Earl is.'

"One of them responded, 'We do for a fact. You had a good influence on Earl. In turn, he made a positive influence on us. We have decided to operate within the law.'

"We were all surprised when Earl said, 'Praise the Lord!' That encouraged me to think he had made things right with the Lord.

"The partners addressed Earl: 'In addition to the heretofore settlement, there is some additional money in this pouch. It is our way of thanking you again.'

"With some effort, Earl got to his feet, embraced them, and said, 'Thank you.'"

Anxious to steer the story back to the gun, I had to ask, "Doris Jean, what happened to Self Defense?"

Doris Jean replied, "That was the disappointing part of the partners' visit. At some point, they said, 'By the way, we want to pick up Self Defense.' That was when I overreacted. I flared up and said, 'Self Defense is not going to leave this house.'

"A hush fell over the room and a surprised look came over the faces of all four of the men, so then I added, 'unless Earl says so.' I studied the faces of Bob and Earl. Each of them looked at me seriously and shook their heads so slightly I barely detected it. I took it to mean, 'Pull in your horns and be quiet.'

"With some difficulty, I calmed myself down and waited to see what Earl would say.

"Earl addressed me, 'Baby doll, get Self Defense and give it to them.' Swallowing my pride, that is exactly what I did. They thanked me and took their leave."

I said, "You seemed mighty anxious to keep Self Defense." When I saw that Doris Jean didn't feel a need to respond to that comment, I dropped the subject and asked, "How long did Earl live in retirement?"

With what I interpreted as a fleeting look of relief, followed by sadness, Doris Jean replied, "He lived only a year. It was a happy year, though. Earl was an easy patient to care for. Along with our housekeeper, Bob and I took care of him. He was cheerful and free from pain."

I inquired, "Did Earl's death hurt you as much as Charles's had?"

Thoughtfully, she answered, "No—I loved Earl no less than I had loved Charles, but I was older and was better able to cope with the loss."

I commented, "You are doing a good job of handling life's difficulties. I see a rosy road ahead for you."

Doris Jean used her teasing, warning voice again (although the warning portion was a little stronger this time): "Mr. Wallace, there is a side of me you haven't seen. If you refuse to sell me your Self Defense, I'm going to throw a conniption fit."

With a chuckle, I replied, "I can hardly wait to see that."

Doris Jean smiled and said, "If you are willing to sell, I'll give you a good price, or I'll trade you a new Remington Wingmaster 20-gauge shotgun."

Surprised, I asked, "You have the shotgun with you?"

She announced proudly, "Yes, in the trunk of my car. I bought it new in the box from a man in Cave-in-Rock. An elderly uncle had left it to him."

I told Doris Jean that if she would get her 20 gauge out so that I could see it, I'd bring out my pistol so she could do likewise. I brought out a bath towel to lay the guns on and a box of tissue to remove fingerprints. Doris Jean's face lit up when she saw my Self Defense. I knew it was what she was looking for.

I liked the 20 gauge equally well, but I held a poker face. I picked up the gun. It was of medium weight. The stock and forearm were made of beautiful walnut with a fancy finish. I put the shotgun to my shoulder. The drop [the amount of bend in the stock] was perfect. I laid the gun down on the towel without comment.

Doris Jean asked, "What do you think?"

Nonchalantly, I said, "I think it is a 20-gauge shotgun" —using an old trader's trick of not showing too much excitement about the other person's merchandise.

Crestfallen, she replied slowly, "In other words, you are saying you are not interested in trading."

Shaking my head, I said, "No, I'm not really saying that. I like to trade. But I've been trading since I was a little boy attending a one-room school, and my instincts tell me that there is more to the story than you are telling me. I still don't really understand why you are so eager to have another gun like Self Defense, especially when your brother already has one. I've listened to everything you have told me about why the original Self Defense was important to you, but honestly, these reasons hardly seem worth a drive the length of Illinois and back to get another gun like it." Fixing her with my most convincing "you-should-tell-me-everything" look, I said, "Are you sure there isn't any other reason you want the gun?"

Doris Jean was unnerved at the question and hesitated to answer. It was clear to me she did not have a trader gene. After a long pause, she finally said, "Yes, but to me, this reason is of lesser importance. . . . I hope you believe me."

I waited in silence for her to continue. After shifting about nervously, Doris Jean finally told the rest of the story: "One day, while cleaning Self Defense, Earl noticed six tiny gold dots on the butt of the gun. At first he thought they were to add to the gun's uniqueness. But when he looked at the dots with a magnifying glass, he saw they were tiny screws. Having no screwdriver small enough, he took the revolver to his jeweler, who removed the six screws. Behind the butt plate was a small cavity, which held a diamond about four times the size of the one I'm wearing." She held up her finger to show me a ring with a sparkling diamond that I estimated to be more than a carat.

I thought, now this is certainly much more interesting. I asked, "What did Earl do with the diamond?"

"He had the jeweler mount it in a white gold ring and gave it to me for our fifth anniversary. It fits me perfectly, but I don't wear it very much because I'm attached to this one."

I picked up my revolver. Sure enough, there were six small screws and a butt plate on the butt of the gun. Doris Jean's eyes met mine. In hers were a mixture of guilt, despair, hope, and calculation. I was still trying to sort out exactly how I was feeling about her attempting to buy the gun without telling me there might be a diamond in it.

To assist in my sorting, I asked, "I would like to know whether there was a diamond in the revolver Bob got from Ray. Was there or was there not?"

Doris Jean, appearing to speak truthfully, said, "I truly don't know. Bob said that he wonders but really doesn't want to know. He just likes to daydream that there is. And when . . . er . . . *if* I become the owner of your Self Defense, I'll do the same. It's just a little bit of twin rivalry that makes me want my own."

At that point, my mind went into overdrive. Trading was in my blood. My grandfather was a part-time black-smith. He loved the statement: "Strike while the iron is hot." Despite everything, I liked this gal. I didn't want to cheat her, but I sure didn't want her to cheat me. Without the diamond in the picture, I figured it would be an even trade between the revolver and the shotgun. But on the strength of the fact there might be a diamond enclosed, I should ask for some difference. The question was — how much?

Doris Jean interrupted my thoughts: "I see you are in deep thought. Tell me what you are thinking."

Being quite forthright with her, I said, "Doris Jean, I have a dilemma. One part of me wants to keep the revolver, and one part of me wants you to have it. I also know there may or may not be a diamond behind that butt plate. So, if I decide to let you have my gun, I will obviously have to have some cash to go with the shotgun."

While Doris Jean's eyes lit up with hope, she still tried to play the part of the gun trader: "So tell me how many dollars and how many cents you will have to have to part with your Self Defense."

I came to a decision. "I'll give you Self Defense for your shotgun and one thousand dollars."

Doris Jean's face glowed with happiness. Losing all pretense of cool, gun-trading demeanor, she exclaimed, "I could hug your neck! I came down from home with fifteen hundred dollars in cash to buy your Self Defense. I paid five hundred dollars for the shotgun. So you see how everything is working out perfectly."

As I accepted the cash, I commented, "Ray will be pleasantly surprised when I give it to him."

She picked up her newly acquired Self Defense. Together we walked to her car, where she placed the revolver in the trunk. She gave me a quick hug of thanks.

I opened the car door for her, as I had done for Evelyn hundreds of times. She started up her car, and with a quick wave, she was gone. And I saw her (to borrow from Edgar Allan Poe's "The Raven") "nevermore."

* * *

My Guardian Angel

On this thirty-first day of July, 2011, I'm ninety years and eleven months old. Those years and months have broken the speed limit zipping by. At this stage of life, I have a lot less inclination to get things done and a lot more inclination to think and meditate, which I do admirably well while holding down my comfortable recliner.

On this particular day, I have been thinking over the colorful patchwork of experiences and events—both good and bad—that have pieced together to form my life. Although every life has some trials and some hard times, I have to say that when viewed as a whole, my life has had far more good than bad.

In my mind's eye, I relive some experiences that had the potential to be bad—sometimes dangerously bad—but that miraculously turned out all right. In pondering these events, I have come to the conclusion that I must have had a guardian angel at my side. Let me relate a few stories, and you see if you don't agree. I would say that my guardian angel has had a job of it throughout my life.

...

When I was around fourteen years old, I was careless around a wild, shiny black, three-year-old mule. I thought I was out of reach of his heels. I was almost, but not quite. The mule kicked at me with both feet. His hind legs and heels were stretched out parallel with the ground about five feet high. One foot missed my right eyebrow by inches. His other foot caught me at the inside of my right eyebrow. Had I been an inch closer, I would have been gone these many years. In other words, I came within an inch of being killed—literally. The wound should have been sewed up, but it swelled shut and healed on its own. I bear the scar to this day as proof that mules kick and that guardian angels exist.

...

My first two years of high school, I hitchhiked the twelve miles to and from school. For the last two years, when two of my brothers also needed a ride to school, I brought our eighteen-year-old Model T Ford out of storage. I was able to get it refurbished and running again with some money that I had earned at a summer job in Michigan. The Model T furnished transportation for me, my two brothers—Byrum and Victor—and five other small students. Crowded? Yes. But we had lots of fun.

One morning I was cutting across from Route 34 on what was then called the Number 9 crossing. There was a stop sign where we crossed Route 45. It was winter. Our vision wasn't the best because of the side curtains [detachable celluloid windows]. One student said, "It is okay from this direction." Another said, "And it is okay from this direction." I was about to move forward when

I decided that I'd better look for myself. Just then a car whizzed past. It would have wiped us out had I not looked. The trouble was that both students were reporting from the same side. Our guardian angel was surely on duty that day.

...

At age twenty, I found it necessary to leave my beloved Southern Illinois, as many other young men in the area did to find work. So I went to Pontiac, Michigan.

Many factories or plants were union and paid well. But for some reason, I accepted employment at Jig Bushing, a nonunion plant that didn't pay as well. However, I believe that my guardian angel placed me there; the management there had ties with the draft board and was able to get me deferred from the draft for eighteen months. That extra time gave me a chance to earn enough money to remove a small mortgage on the farm.

After I had worked at Jig Bushing for about six months, my brother Byrum turned eighteen and came to Michigan to find work. He got a job at Jig Bushing, also. Another Harrisburg fellow—Little Man Ragan—worked the second shift along with us. Little Man drove a 12-cylinder Lincoln Zephyr. He bragged that his Lincoln's cruising speed was eighty miles per hour.

One day Little Man suggested, "After we complete our shift on Friday, suppose we take my Lincoln and head off for Harrisburg for the weekend." Byrum and I readily agreed.

We left Pontiac around one o'clock Saturday morning. That Lincoln was really a smooth ride. Little Man held it at eighty miles per hour much of the time. I rode in the front while Byrum slept in the backseat. Traffic was light. We just seemed to float along.

Somewhere in Indiana, Byrum roused from sleep and asked, "Little Man, where are we?" Little Man didn't say anything.

I said, "Byrum, lie back down and go back to sleep. You wouldn't know if he told you."

The three of us visited relatives and friends until Sunday evening, and then we started back to Pontiac. We hadn't gone far before Little Man asked, "Byrum, on the way down, do you remember asking, 'Where are we?'"

Puzzled by his question, Byrum answered, "Yes, I remember."

Little Man said, "That question probably saved our lives. When you asked me that, I was sound asleep. We were going eighty-five miles per hour."

I was a bit sleepy, but Little Man's confession woke me up. I decided to stay awake and see to it that Little Man didn't go back to sleep. However, despite my best efforts, I grew sleepy and began to slur out questions like a drunken man. I asked, "Do you like to catfish?" "What kind of bait do you use?" "Have you fished at night with trot lines and bank poles?"

After a few questions, Little Man laughed and said, "I took a long nap this afternoon. You won't have to ask me any more questions. I'm going to stay awake." I didn't sleep, but I didn't ask any more silly questions. I felt sure that my guardian angel had been riding with us on that trip to Southern Illinois and would be with us on the way back.

...

One time, while I was still in Michigan, my cousin Gene Affolder, his wife, Louise, and I had an extended weekend off from work in Pontiac and went to Southern Illinois in Gene's car.

Before we started back to Michigan, a fellow about twenty-five years old, by the name of Shadowens, "Shad" for short, offered to help Gene with the driving if Gene would give him a free ride to Pontiac. Gene felt sorry for him and said he would.

We took off with Gene and Louise in the backseat, with Louise's dog, Pedro, in her lap. I was in the front passenger seat, and Shad was behind the wheel. He was a good driver, and all was going well.

Just beyond Toledo, Ohio, we were traveling about sixty miles per hour on a two-lane road. Suddenly, an oncoming car crossed about three feet over the center line, thus forcing Shad to put two wheels onto the shoulder, which was lower than the pavement. Once we were past the other car, Shad overcorrected. The car went out of control and rolled over twice in the middle of the road. Somehow I managed to turn off the key before the second roll. The car landed, right side up, on the shoulder of the road.

The windshield was broken out. The top was caved in about a foot, and the doors wouldn't open. Both sides were badly damaged. We checked to see if anyone was hurt. Miraculously, no one was—no cuts, scratches, or bruises. Gene and I were as calm as if it were an everyday happening. However, Shad and Louise were unnerved and beside themselves. Pedro never made a sound, but he had wet Louise's dress, which added to her stress.

Gene wondered if his newly wrecked car was drivable. Shad said, "I'm too shaky to drive."

Gene then turned to me and asked, "Kestner, will you drive? I'll need to try to keep Louise calm." Shad climbed over me from the driver's seat. I slipped under the wheel.

Amazingly, the car started, and I pulled onto the road. The front wheels shimmied some at twenty miles per hour, but the shimmying stopped if I drove a little faster. So, I drove on to Pontiac at twenty-five miles per hour without further mishap.

Would you say our guardian angel was watching over us?

...

In 1946, after my safe return from serving three years in the Navy in World War II, I began my first eight-month term of teaching. At the end of the school year, I had four months during the summer to work at something else. I accepted a job on the night shift at the P.M.T. Fluorspar Mine in Hardin County. Another fellow and I were working on the hundred-foot level, extending a tunnel on a vein of spar — a process called "driving a drift." We were using a jackhammer to drill another set of twenty-seven holes to use to shoot down more spar. Unbeknownst to us, the day shift had failed to install support timbers overhead for our protection. At midnight, we went on top to eat our "lunch." When we returned about an hour later, forty tons or so of spar and rock had fallen right where we were working. That event, as well as two other close calls, definitely kept my guardian angel busy during my time in the mines.

The $1.25 per hour that I was paid for my spar-mining experience wasn't my only benefit. Of far greater importance to me was the empathy that was instilled in me for the many miners who were crippled or killed in the mines in the years following.

...

Once upon a time, many years ago, before my dear wife, Evelyn, made me feel sorry for poor little wild animals, I liked to cross the road and a wet-weather creek in the woods across from our house and shoot a mess of fat, young squirrels.

One day I crossed the creek and went to a pignut grove where squirrels were cutting [feeding on] nuts. The area was also a habitat for rattlesnakes and copperheads. I wasn't afraid of snakes but was very, very cautious any place where they tended to live. I proceeded with great care and moved along as silently as possible. I'd search the ground eight to ten feet ahead of me, and then I'd look up and try to see or hear a squirrel. Once, I realized that I'd taken a few steps without looking down. My right foot was raised to take another step when I glanced down. My guardian angel must have warned me. There, where I'd been about to put my foot, was the biggest copperhead I'd ever seen—and I'd seen some big ones. It was coiled and ready to strike. I pivoted on my left toes and brought my right foot down as far from where I was standing as I could. Then I shot that snake's head off and trembled all over. That put an end to that day's hunt.

...

The most outstanding accomplishment of my lifetime was meeting and marrying Evelyn, my sweet wife for fifty-six years. No better wife and mother of our two children ever lived. She was an angel on earth. She taught first grade for thirty years. To relate all the kindnesses she extended to me and others would make a large book. However, I will tell the following incident:

About six years ago, I got up from my easy chair in the living room and was passing through the archway into the kitchen when a darkened dizziness came over me. I may have allowed my knees to buckle, thus easing myself to the floor without bumps or bruises. While lying on the floor, I faintly heard, as if from far away,

Evelyn's pleading cry, "Daddy, Daddy, please don't leave me. Please, Lord, don't let him die." These words may have saved my life. My angel on earth and my guardian angel were a powerful pair.

Evelyn called our son, Ray, and an ambulance. I was later told that, after being put in the ambulance, they worked on me for about thirty minutes before leaving the driveway. Once, for a few seconds during the twelve-mile run to the hospital, I realized that I was alive and on the way to the hospital.

In the emergency room, I came to myself. Evelyn, Ray, and the medical staff were around me. I had no aches or pains. In fact, I was in a mischievous mood. I was asked if I knew who I was. I said, "Yes, I am Abraham Lincoln." Then, I was asked, "Where are you?" I answered, "Chicago."

Evelyn saw a certain look in my eye. With a greatly relieved smile, she merely said, "Kestner," much in the same gentle manner she had corrected our son and daughter when they were small. It worked. I quickly changed my story: "I am Kestner Wallace. I'm in the Harrisburg Medical Center. Furthermore, I am ready to go home."

Despite my declared readiness to go home, I was assigned a room. Two days later, it was determined that I needed a pacemaker, which was to be installed in Herrin, Illinois. Ray could have taken me in his car, but my doctor recommended that I be taken in an ambulance.

I asked the driver if it would be okay for my wife and son to follow in a car behind us, as Ray had planned. He said, "No, I'll be driving fast — in and out of traffic — and it won't be safe." I was amazed to discover that he considered this ride to be an emergency. I think he was just enjoying the prospect of speeding to Herrin.

The ambulance left the hospital like a bat out of hell, with the siren blaring continuously all of the way to Herrin.

The ride could have been more pleasurable had it not been so rough. I held on to some straps with both hands to lessen the shock on my back. I could have used a little more help from my guardian angel on that trip. However, once in Herrin, all went well with the procedure. The pacemaker must be a good one. I've had no more fainting spells since then. The pacemaker has kept my heart regulated and gives me no trouble.

...

Can you stand a bonehead fishing story? If so, here goes. Only weeks before my ninetieth birthday, I went alone to my favorite fishing spot—across the John English farm down at Big Creek in Hardin County, just north of Elizabethtown. I was fishing with two extension poles, with one in my hand and the other at my feet as I sat in a folding chair. A bucket for my fish and my container of worms were within easy reach. It was late afternoon. I was in "hog heaven."

Suddenly, bliss changed to chaos. Just as I pulled in a prize-winning bluegill with the pole I was holding, the pole at my feet began to slip toward the creek. I didn't want to lose that pole since Ray had given it to me the previous Christmas. I hurriedly slipped out of my chair onto my stomach to reach for the pole. I scooted as far down the bank as I dared but was unable to grab it.

With great difficulty, I crawfished back up onto level ground, but I was too exhausted to get to my feet. The more I tried, the more tired I became. After repeated efforts, I decided to stop trying and wait for Ray to come looking for me. Fortunately, I had told him where I'd be fishing that afternoon. I knew it would be awhile before he became worried, however, since I normally would have been attending prayer meeting that evening.

I didn't criticize myself for using poor judgment, nor did I feel sorry for myself. I just made myself as comfortable as possible and tried to be thankful that I wasn't in a foxhole with danger all around. The afternoon sun faded to dusk then to dark.

After several hours of waiting, I was one happy "sad sack" when Ray's headlights shined on me. Ray was so relieved at finding me alive and unharmed that he didn't fuss at me for fishing alone. He got me to my feet and put my fishing gear in the trunk of my car. I drove home as happily as if I had caught a bucket of fish.

I was happy and thankful that I hadn't slid head first into the creek. While keeping me from danger, my guardian angel, I suspected, slowed down the rescue process to teach me a valuable lesson: "No more fishing alone."

At home I gladly went to my easy chair and refreshed myself with a Dilly Bar. I then gave thanks for the guardian angel that watches over me.

* * *